It Pays to Get Certified

 **W9-CFG-336**

In a digital world, digital literacy is an essential survival skill. Certification proves you have the knowledge and skill to solve business problems in virtually any business environment. Certifications are highly valued credentials that qualify you for jobs, increased compensation, and promotion.

Security is one of the highest demand job categories – growing in importance as the frequency and severity of security threats continues to be a major concern for organizations around the world.

- **Jobs for security administrators are expected to increase by 18%** -the skill set required for these types of jobs map to CompTIA Security+ certification.

- **Network Security Administrators -** can earn as much as $106,000 per year.

- **CompTIA Security+ is the first step -** in starting your career as a Network Security Administrator or Systems Security Administrator.

- **CompTIA Security+ is regularly used in organizations -** such as Hitachi Information Systems, Trendmicro, the McAfee Elite Partner program, the U.S. State Department, and U.S. government contractors such as EDS, General Dynamics, and Northrop Grumman.

How Certification Helps Your Career

IT is Everywhere	**IT Knowledge and Skills Gets Jobs**	**Retain your Job and Salary**	**Want to Change Jobs**	**Stick Out from the Resume Pile**
IT is ubiquitous, needed by most organizations. Globally, there are over 600,000 IT job openings.	Certifications are essential credentials that qualify you for jobs, increased compensation, and promotion.	Make your expertise stand above the rest. Competence is usually retained during times of change.	Certifications qualify you for new opportunities, whether locked into a current job, see limited advancement, or need to change careers.	Hiring managers can demand the strongest skill set.

Steps to Getting Certified and Staying Certified	
Review Exam Objectives	Review the certification objectives to make sure you know what is covered in the exam. http://www.comptia.org/certifications/testprep/examobjectives.aspx
Practice for the Exam	After you have studied for the certification, take a free assessment and sample test to get an idea what type of questions might be on the exam. http://www.comptia.org/certifications/testprep/practicetests.aspx
Purchase an Exam Voucher	Purchase your exam voucher on the CompTIA Marketplace, which is located at: www.comptiastore.com
Take the Test!	Select a certification exam provider and schedule a time to take your exam. You can find exam providers at the following link: http://www.comptia.org/certifications/testprep/testingcenters.aspx
Stay Certified! **Continuing Education**	Effective January 1, 2011, new CompTIA Security+ certifications are valid for three years from the date of certification. There are a number of ways the certification can be renewed. For more information go to: http://certification.comptia.org/getCertified/steps_to_certification/stayCertified.aspx

How to obtain more information

- **Visit CompTIA online -** www.comptia.org to learn more about getting CompTIA certified.

- **Contact CompTIA -** call 866-835-8020 ext. 5 or email questions@comptia.org

- **Join the IT Pro Community –** http://itpro.comptia.org to join the IT community to get relevant career information.

- **Connect with us :**

CompTIA® Security+® (Exam SY0-301)

Part Number: 085707
Course Edition: 1.1

NOTICES

The logo of the CompTIA Authorized Curriculum Program and the status of this or other training material as Authorized under the CompTIA Authorized Curriculum Program signifies that, in CompTIA's opinion, such training material covers the content of CompTIA's related certification exam. CompTIA has not reviewed or approved the accuracy of the contents of this training material and specifically disclaims any warranties of merchantability or fitness for a particular purpose. CompTIA makes no guarantee concerning the success of persons using any such Authorized or other training material in order to prepare for any CompTIA certification exam. The contents of this training material were created for the CompTIA Security+ exam covering CompTIA certification exam objectives that were current as of 2011.

How to Become CompTIA Certified: This training material can help you prepare for and pass a related CompTIA certification exam or exams. In order to achieve CompTIA certification, you must register for and pass a CompTIA certification exam or exams. In order to become CompTIA certified, you must:

1. Select a certification exam provider. For more information, visit **www.comptia.org/certifications/testprep.aspx**.

2. Register for and schedule a time to take the CompTIA certification exam(s) at a convenient location.

3. Read and sign the Candidate Agreement, which will be presented at the time of the exam(s). The text of the Candidate Agreement can be found at **www.comptia.org/certifications/policies/agreement.aspx**.

HELP US IMPROVE OUR COURSEWARE

Your comments are important to us. Please contact us at Element K Press LLC, 1-800-478-7788, 500 Canal View Boulevard, Rochester, NY 14623, Attention: Product Planning, or through our Web site at **http://support.elementkcourseware.com**.

CompTIA® Security+® (Exam SY0-301)

Lesson 5: Access Control, Authentication, and Account Management

Lesson 6: Managing Certificates

Lesson 7: Compliance and Operational Security

Lesson 8: Risk Management

Lesson 9: Managing Security Incidents

Lesson 10: Business Continuity and Disaster Recovery Planning

Appendix A: Mapping Course Content to the CompTIA® Security+® (Exam SY0-301) Objectives

About This Course

CompTIA® Security+® (Exam SY0-301) is the primary course you will need to take if your job responsibilities include securing network services, devices, and traffic and your organization as a whole including the physical security elements and operational security measures. It is also the main course you will take to prepare for the CompTIA Security+ Certification examination. In this course, you will build on your knowledge and professional experience with security fundamentals, networks, and organizational security as you acquire the specific skills required to implement basic security services on any type of computer network.

This course can benefit you in two ways. If you intend to pass the CompTIA Security+ (Exam SY0-301) Certification examination, this course can be a significant part of your preparation. But certification is not the only key to professional success in the field of computer security. Today's job market demands individuals with demonstrable skills, and the information and activities in this course can help you build your computer security skill set so that you can confidently perform your duties in any security-related professional role.

Course Description

Target Student

This course is targeted toward the information technology (IT) professional who has networking and administrative skills in Windows®-based Transmission Control Protocol/Internet Protocol (TCP/IP) networks and familiarity with other operating systems, such as Mac OS® X, Unix, or Linux, and who wants to further a career in IT by acquiring a foundational knowledge of security topics; prepare for the CompTIA Security+ Certification examination; or use Security+ as the foundation for advanced security certifications or career roles.

Course Prerequisites

Basic Windows skills and a fundamental understanding of computer and networking concepts are required. Students can obtain this level of skill and knowledge by taking the following Element K courses: *Introduction to Networks and the Internet* and any one or more of the following:

- *Introduction to Personal Computers: Using Windows 7*
- *Microsoft® Windows® 7: Level 1*

CompTIA A+ and Network+ certifications, or equivalent knowledge, and six to nine months experience in networking, including experience configuring and managing TCP/IP, are strongly recommended. Students can obtain this level of skill and knowledge by taking any of the following Element K courses:

- *CompTIA® A+® Certification: A Comprehensive Approach for all 2009 Exam Objectives (Windows® 7)*
- *CompTIA® Network+® Certification (2009 Objectives)*

Additional introductory courses or work experience in application development and programming or in network and operating system administration for any software platform or system are helpful but not required.

Course Objectives

In this course, you will implement and monitor security on networks, applications, and operating systems, and respond to security breaches.

You will:

- Identify the fundamental concepts of computer security.
- Identify security threats and vulnerabilities.
- Examine network security.
- Manage application, data, and host security.
- Identify access control and account management security measures.
- Manage certificates.
- Identify compliance and operational security measures.
- Manage risk.
- Manage security incidents.
- Develop a BCP and DRP.

Certification

This course is designed to help you prepare for the following certification.

Certification Path: The CompTIA® Security+® (Exam SY0-301) course is designed to help you prepare for the SY0-301 exam. Attending this course and using this student guide will help you prepare for certification. You should also refer to the exam objectives to see how they map to the course content.

How to Use This Book

As a Learning Guide

This book is divided into lessons and topics, covering a subject or a set of related subjects. In most cases, lessons are arranged in order of increasing proficiency.

The results-oriented topics include the relevant and supporting information you need to master the content. Each topic has various types of activities designed to enable you to practice the guidelines and procedures as well as to solidify your understanding of the informational material presented in the course.

At the back of the book, you will find a glossary of the definitions of the terms and concepts used throughout the course. You will also find an index to assist in locating information within the instructional components of the book.

In the Classroom

This book is intended to enhance and support the in-class experience. Procedures and guidelines are presented in a concise fashion along with activities and discussions. Information is provided for reference and reflection in such a way as to facilitate understanding and practice.

Each lesson may also include a Lesson Lab or various types of simulated activities. You will find the files for the simulated activities along with the other course files on the enclosed CD-ROM. If your course manual did not come with a CD-ROM, please go to **www.elementk.com/courseware-file-downloads** to download the files. If included, these interactive activities enable you to practice your skills in an immersive business environment, or to use hardware and software resources not available in the classroom. The course files that are available on the CD-ROM or by download may also contain sample files, support files, and additional reference materials for use both during and after the course.

As a Teaching Guide

Effective presentation of the information and skills contained in this book requires adequate preparation. As such, as an instructor, you should familiarize yourself with the content of the entire course, including its organization and approaches. You should review each of the student activities and exercises so you can facilitate them in the classroom.

Throughout the book, you may see Instructor Notes that provide suggestions, answers to problems, and supplemental information for you, the instructor. You may also see references to "Additional Instructor Notes" that contain expanded instructional information; these notes appear in a separate section at the back of the book. Microsoft® PowerPoint® slides may be provided on the included course files, which are available on the enclosed CD-ROM or by download from **www.elementk.com/courseware-file-downloads**. If you plan to use the slides, it is recommended to display them during the corresponding content as indicated in the instructor notes in the margin.

The course files may also include assessments for the course, which can be administered diagnostically before the class, or as a review after the course is completed. These exam-type questions can be used to gauge the students' understanding and assimilation of course content.

As a Review Tool

Any method of instruction is only as effective as the time and effort you, the student, are willing to invest in it. In addition, some of the information that you learn in class may not be important to you immediately, but it may become important later. For this reason, we encourage you to spend some time reviewing the content of the course after your time in the classroom.

As a Reference

The organization and layout of this book make it an easy-to-use resource for future reference. Taking advantage of the glossary, index, and table of contents, you can use this book as a first source of definitions, background information, and summaries.

Course Icons

Icon	Description
	A **Caution Note** makes students aware of potential negative consequences of an action, setting, or decision that are not easily known.
	Display Slide provides a prompt to the instructor to display a specific slide. Display Slides are included in the Instructor Guide only.
	An **Instructor Note** is a comment to the instructor regarding delivery, classroom strategy, classroom tools, exceptions, and other special considerations. Instructor Notes are included in the Instructor Guide only.
	Notes Page indicates a page that has been left intentionally blank for students to write on.
	A **Student Note** provides additional information, guidance, or hints about a topic or task.
	A **Version Note** indicates information necessary for a specific version of software.

Course Requirements and Setup

You can find a list of hardware and software requirements to run this class as well as detailed classroom setup procedures in the course files that are available on the CD-ROM that shipped with this book. If your course manual did not come with a CD-ROM, please go to **http://www.elementk.com/courseware-file-downloads** to download the files.

1 Security Fundamentals

Lesson Time: 4 hour(s)

Lesson Objectives:

In this lesson, you will identify the fundamental concepts of computer security.

You will:

- Identify the basic components of the information security cycle.
- Identify information security controls.
- List common authentication methods.
- Identify the fundamental components of cryptography.
- Identify fundamental security policy issues.

Introduction

There are many different tasks, concepts, and skills involved in the pursuit of computer security. But most of these tasks, concepts, and skills share a few fundamental principles. In this lesson, you will identify some of the most basic ideas involved in securing computers and networks.

Just as the construction of a building is started with bricks and mortar, each security implementation starts with a series of fundamental building blocks. No matter what the final result is, you will always start with the same fundamentals. As a security professional, it is your responsibility to understand these fundamental concepts so you can build the appropriate security structure for your organization.

This lesson covers all or part of the following CompTIA® Security+® (Exam SY0-301) certification objectives:

- Topic A:
  - Objective 3.2 Analyze and differentiate among types of attacks

- ■ Objective 3.3 Analyze and differentiate among types of social engineering attacks
- ● Topic B:
  - ■ Objective 1.2 Apply and implement secure network administration principles
  - ■ Objective 1.6 Implement wireless network in a secure manner
  - ■ Objective 2.1 Explain risk related concepts
  - ■ Objective 2.8 Exemplify the concepts of confidentiality, integrity and availability (CIA)
  - ■ Objective 3.2 Analyze and differentiate among types of attacks
  - ■ Objective 5.2 Explain the fundamental concepts and best practices related to authentication, authorization and access control
  - ■ Objective 6.1 Summarize general cryptography concepts
- ● Topic C:
  - ■ Objective 3.2 Analyze and differentiate among types of attacks
  - ■ Objective 5.2 Explain the fundamental concepts and best practices related to authentication, authorization and access control
- ● Topic D:
  - ■ Objective 6.1 Summarize general cryptography concepts
  - ■ Objective 6.2 Use and apply appropriate cryptographic tools and products
- ● Topic E:
  - ■ Objective 1.2 Apply and implement secure network administration principles
  - ■ Objective 2.1 Explain risk related concepts
  - ■ Objective 2.2 Carry out appropriate risk mitigation strategies
  - ■ Objective 3.2 Analyze and differentiate among types of attacks
  - ■ Objective 5.2 Explain the fundamental concepts and best practices related to authentication, authorization and access control

TOPIC A

The Information Security Cycle

This lesson covers fundamentals of computer security. The most fundamental ideas are the ones that spring from the information security cycle that forms the basis of all security systems. In this topic, you will identify the components of the information security cycle that are common to all security systems.

To be successful and credible as a security professional, you should understand security in business starting from the ground up. You should also be able to understand the key security terms and ideas used by other security experts in technical documents and in trade publications. Security implementations are constructed from fundamental building blocks just like a large building is constructed from individual bricks. This topic will help you understand those building blocks so that you can use them as the foundation for your security career.

What Is Information Security?

Information security refers to the protection of available information or information resources from unauthorized access, attacks, thefts, or data damage. It is necessary for a responsible individual or organization to secure their confidential information. Due to the presence of a widely connected business environment, data is now available in a variety of forms such as digital media and print. Therefore, every bit of data that is being utilized, shared, or transmitted must be protected to minimize business risks and other consequences of losing crucial data.

What to Protect

As an information security professional, you need to know what information to secure in an organization and why those assets need protection.

Information Security Asset	Why They Need Protection
Data	This is a general term that relates to the information assets of a person, customer, or organization. In a computer system, the files are the data. You need to protect data from getting corrupt or from being accessed without authorization.
Resources	These are any virtual or physical components of a system that have limited availability. A physical resource can be any device connected directly to a computer system. A virtual resource refers to types of files, memory locations, or network connections.

Collateral Damage

As an information security professional, you are directly responsible for protecting an organization's data and resources. If the security of an organization's data and resources is compromised, it may cause collateral damage to the organization, in the form of compromised reputation, loss of goodwill, reduced investor confidence, loss of customers, and various financial losses. Although you are not directly responsible for customer relations, finances, or the business' reputation, any such collateral business damage that results from a failure of your primary security duties could be considered your indirect responsibility.

Goals of Security

There are three primary goals or functions involved in the practice of information security.

Security Goal	Description
Prevention	Personal information, company information, and information on intellectual property must be protected. If there is a breach in security in any of these departments, then the organization may have to put a lot of effort into recovering losses. Preventing users from gaining unauthorized access to confidential information should be the number one priority of information security professionals.
Detection	Detection is the step that occurs when a user is discovered trying to access unauthorized data or after information has been lost. It can be accomplished by investigating individuals or by scanning the data and networks for any traces left by the intruder in any attack against the system.
Recovery	When there is a disaster or an intrusion by unauthorized users of a system, data is sometimes compromised or damaged. It is in these cases that you need to employ a process to recover vital data present in files or folders from a crashed system or data storage devices. Recovery can also pertain to physical resources.

Vulnerabilities

Definition:

At the most basic level, a *vulnerability* is any condition that leaves a system open to attack. Vulnerabilities can come in a wide variety of forms, including:

- Improperly configured or installed hardware or software.
- Bugs in software or operating systems.
- The misuse of software or communication protocols.
- Poorly designed networks.
- Poor physical security.
- Insecure passwords.
- Design flaws in software or operating systems.
- And, unchecked user input.

Example:

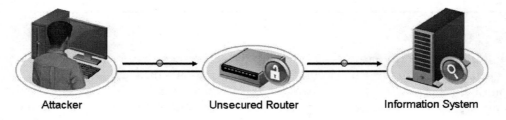

Attacker   Unsecured Router   Information System

Figure 1-1: A vulnerability.

Threats

Definition:

In the realm of computer security, a *threat* is any event or action that could potentially result in the violation of a security requirement, policy, or procedure. Regardless of whether a violation is intentional or unintentional, malicious or not, it is considered a threat. Potential threats to computer and network security include:

● Unintentional or unauthorized access or changes to data.

● The interruption of services.

● The interruption of access to assets.

● Damage to hardware.

● And, unauthorized access or damage to facilities.

Example:

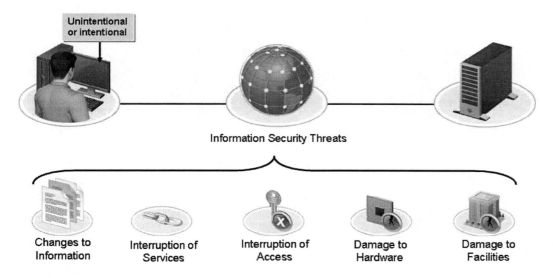

Figure 1-2: Threats.

Attacks

Definition:

In the realm of computer security, an *attack* is a technique that is used to exploit a vulnerability in any application on a computer system without the authorization to do so. Attacks on a computer system and network security include:

● Physical security attacks.

● Network-based attacks including wireless networks.

● Software-based attacks.

● Social engineering attacks.

● And, web application-based attacks.

"Physical security attack," "software attack," and so on are terms used in this course to group threats into general categories for ease of discussion. They are not meant to imply that the security industry makes technical distinctions between these broad groups.

Example:

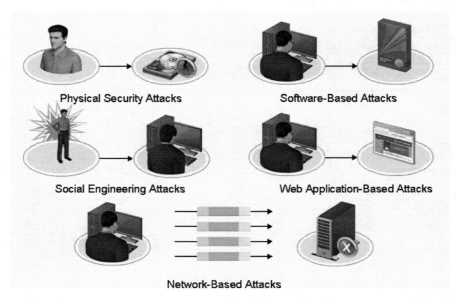

Figure 1-3: Attacks.

Intrusions

Definition:

In the realm of computer security, an *intrusion* occurs when an attacker accesses your computer system without the authorization to do so. An intrusion occurs when the system is vulnerable to attacks and may include:

- Physical intrusions.
- Host-based intrusions.
- And, network-based intrusions.

Example:

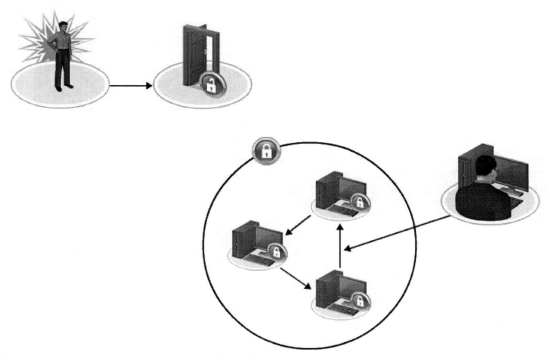

Figure 1-4: Intrusions.

Risk

Definition:

As applied to information systems, *risk* is a concept that indicates exposure to the chance of damage or loss. It signifies the likelihood of a hazard or dangerous threat occurring.

In information technology, risk is often associated with the loss of a system, power, or network, and other physical losses. Risk also affects people, practices, and processes.

Example:

A disgruntled former employee is a threat. The amount of risk this threat represents depends on the likelihood that the employee will access their previous place of business and remove or damage data. It also depends on the extent of harm that could result.

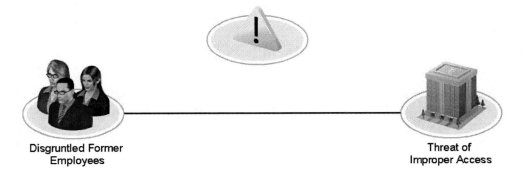

Disgruntled Former
Employees

Threat of
Improper Access

Figure 1-5: Risk in information systems.

Risk Factors

Risk is the determining factor when looking at information systems security. If an organization chooses to ignore risks to operations, it could suffer a catastrophic outage that would limit its ability to survive.

Controls

Definition:

In the realm of computer security, *controls* are the countermeasures that you need to put in place to avoid, mitigate, or counteract security risks due to threats or attacks. In other words, controls are solutions and activities that enable an organization to meet the objectives of an information security strategy. Controls can be safeguards and countermeasures that are logical or physical. Controls are broadly classified as prevention, detection, and correction controls.

Example:

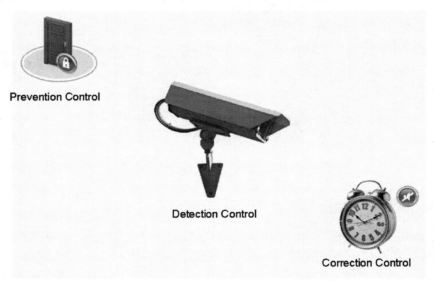

Prevention Control

Detection Control

Correction Control

Figure 1-6: Controls.

Types of Controls

The different types of controls include:

- *Prevention controls:* These help to prevent a threat or attack from exposing a vulnerability in the computer system. For example, a security lock that exists on an access door to a building.
- *Detection controls:* These help to discover if a threat or vulnerability has entered into the computer system. For example, surveillance cameras that record everything that happens in and around a building.
- And, *correction controls:* These help to mitigate the consequences of a threat or attack from adversely affecting the computer system. For example, a silent alarm that goes off when an intrusion occurs in the system that will enable a security officer to handle the incident.

The Security Management Process

Security management objectives can include the process of identifying, implementing, and monitoring security controls.

Security Management Objective	Description
Identification	This involves detecting problems and determining how best to protect a system: • Find out when security breaches occur. • Log details of the breaches, showing information regarding the failed attempts, such as typing a wrong user name or password. • Select the appropriate identification technique, such as a network intrusion detection system (NIDS).
Implementation	This involves installing control mechanisms to prevent problems in a system: • Authenticate users appropriately or control access to data and resources. • Match implementation security controls with the management requirements in any organization. • Install a complex mechanism such as an intrusion detection system (IDS) or an intrusion prevention system (IPS) to prevent any attacks on the system.
Monitoring	This involves detecting and solving any security issues that arise after security controls are implemented: • Run tests on the various controls installed to see if they are working correctly and will remain effective against further attacks on the system. • Analyze important steps that improve the performance of controls. • Document each control failure and determine if a control needs to be upgraded or removed.

ACTIVITY 1-1
Identifying Information Security Building Blocks

Scenario:
In this activity, you will identify the components of the information security cycle.

1. **As an information security officer, what are the information security goals that you need to keep in mind while defining the protection you will need? (Select all that apply.)**
   a) Prevention
   b) Auditing
   c) Recovery
   d) Detection

2. **What are applicable forms of vulnerabilities? (Select all that apply.)**
   a) Improperly configured software
   b) Misuse of communication protocols
   c) Damage to hardware
   d) Lengthy passwords with a mix of characters

3. **Match each fundamental security concept with its corresponding description.**

   ___ Vulnerability   a. Exposure to the chance of damage or loss.

   ___ Threat   b. An event where an attacker has access to your computer system without authorization.

   ___ Risk   c. A countermeasure that you need to put in place to avoid, mitigate, or counteract a security risks due to a threat or attack.

   ___ Control   d. A condition that leaves a system open to attack.

   ___ Intrusion   e. An event or action that could potentially result in the violation of a security requirement.

4. **Match each security description(s) to its security management process.**

   ___ Select the appropriate method to protect systems.   a. Implementation

   ___ Install the selected control mechanism.   b. Identification

   ___ Analyze important steps that improve the performance of controls.   c. Monitoring

5. Detail the differences between a threat, vulnerability, and risk.

TOPIC B
Information Security Controls

You have identified the components of the information security cycle so far. The importance of identifying the components of the information security cycle is to find out how they control computer security. In this topic, you will identify the security controls in more detail and identify how controls are implemented in computer security.

Understanding the basics of the information security cycle is just the start to finding out how these factors control computer security as a whole. You should also be able to understand how you can implement security controls as used by other security experts in this field.

The CIA Triad

Information security seeks to address three specific principles: confidentiality, integrity, and availability. This is called the *CIA triad*. If one of the principles is compromised, the security of the organization is threatened.

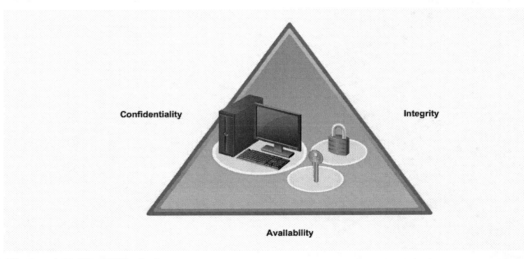

Figure 1-7: *The CIA triad.*

The CIA triad is made up of three principles.

Principle	Description
Confidentiality	This is the fundamental principle of keeping information and communications private and protecting them from unauthorized access.
	Confidential information includes trade secrets, personnel records, health records, tax records, and military secrets.
Integrity	This is the property of keeping organization information accurate, free of errors, and without unauthorized modifications.
	For example, in the 1980s movie *War Games,* actor Matthew Broderick was seen modifying his grades early in the movie. This means that the integrity of his grade information was compromised by unauthorized modification.

Principle	Description
Availability	This is the fundamental principle of ensuring that systems operate continuously and that authorized persons can access the data that they need.
	Information available on a computer system is useless unless the users can get to it. Consider what would happen if the Federal Aviation Administration's air traffic control system failed. Radar images would be captured but not distributed to those who need the information.

Non-repudiation

Non-repudiation is supplemental to the CIA triad. It is the goal of ensuring that the party that sent a transmission or created data remains associated with that data. You should be able to independently verify the identity of a message sender, and the sender should be responsible for the message and its data.

Figure 1-8: Non-repudiation.

Authentication

Definition:

Authentication is the method of uniquely validating a particular entity or individual's credentials. Authentication concentrates on identifying if a particular individual has the right credentials to enter a system or secure site. Authentication credentials should be kept secret to keep unauthorized individuals from gaining access to all confidential information.

Example:

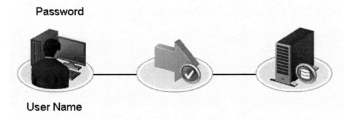

Figure 1-9: Authentication.

Identification

Definition:

In security terms, *identification* is a method that ensures that the entity requesting authentication is the true owner of the credentials. The investment and effort that goes into implementing a method of identification varies depending on the degree of security or protection that is needed in an organization.

When authentication involves providing credentials such as an email address or user name together with a password, identification ascertains whether or not the individual who enters the credentials is also the owner of those assigned, particular credentials.

Example:

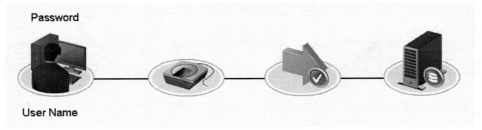

Figure 1-10: Identification.

The Four As

Most security systems rely on four major factors to achieve security goals:

- *Authorization* is the process of determining what rights and privileges a particular entity has.
- *Access control* is the process of determining and assigning privileges to various resources, objects, or data.
- *Accountability* is the process of determining who to hold responsible for a particular activity or event, such as a log on.
- And, *auditing* or *accounting* is the process of tracking and recording system activities and resource access.

Access Control Methods

There are four general mechanisms for managing access control.

Objects — not users or user groups

Access Control Method	Description
Mandatory Access Control (MAC)	When you are trying to access a file that is labeled "Top Secret," it will only open if you are a person with access to view Top-Secret files. In this method, access is controlled by comparing an object's security designation and a user's security clearance. Objects, such as files and other resources, are assigned security labels of varying levels, depending on the object's sensitivity. Users are assigned a security level or clearance, and when they try to access an object, their clearance level must correspond to the object's security level. If there is a match, the user can access the object; if there is no match, the user is denied access. MAC security labels can generally be changed only by a system administrator and not by the object's owner.
Discretionary Access Control (DAC)	When you are trying to access a file that is protected, all you need to do is request the administrator to allow access and then start using the file. In this method, access to each object is controlled on a customized basis, which is based on a user's identity. Objects are configured with an *Access Control List (ACL)* of subjects (users or other entities) who are allowed access to them. An administrator has the discretion to place the user on the list or not, and to configure a particular level of access. Unlike MAC, in a DAC authorization scheme, object owners can generally modify their objects' ACLs.
Role-Based Access Control (RBAC)	When you are trying to access a file labeled "employee database," it comes up as access denied. This is because your role as an employee does not allow access to files in the HR folder. In this method, users are assigned to pre-defined roles, and network objects are configured to allow access only to specific roles. Access is controlled based on a user's assigned role. A user might have more than one role assigned to him at one time, or might switch from one role to another over the course of his employment. An administrator can assign to a role only those privileges users in the role need to complete their work. Often, the roles are dynamically assigned at the time access is requested, based on policies and rules determined by the administrator.
Rule-Based Access Control	A set of firewall restriction rules is a Rule-Based Access Control. This is a non-discretionary technique that is based on a set of operational rules or restrictions. Rule sets are always examined before a subject is given access to objects.

Common Security Practices

Common security practices help implement access controls in ways that provide effective measures for the protection of data and resources. The following is a list of common security practices:

Defense in Depth

- Implicit deny.
- Least privilege.
- Separation of duties.
- Job rotation.
- Mandatory vacation.
- Time of day restrictions.
- And, privilege management.

Implicit Deny

Definition:

The principle of *implicit deny* dictates that everything that is not explicitly allowed is denied. Users and software should only be allowed to access data and perform actions when permissions are specifically granted to them. No other action is allowed.

Example:

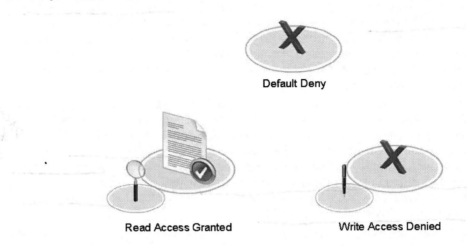

Default Deny

Read Access Granted

Write Access Denied

Figure 1-11: Implicit deny.

Least Privilege

Definition:

The principle of *least privilege* dictates that users and software should only have the minimal level of access that is necessary for them to perform the duties required of them. This level of minimal access includes facilities, computing hardware, software, and information. Where a user or system is given access, that access should still be only at the level required to perform the necessary task.

Example:

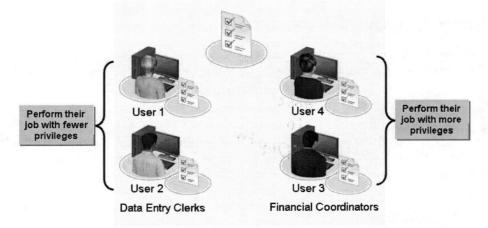

Perform their job with fewer privileges

User 1

User 4

Perform their job with more privileges

User 2

User 3

Data Entry Clerks

Financial Coordinators

Figure 1-12: Least privilege.

Privilege Bracketing

The term *privilege bracketing* is used when privileges are given out only when needed, then revoked as soon as the task is finished or the need has passed.

Separation of Duties

Definition:

Separation of duties states that no one person should have too much power or responsibility. Duties and responsibilities should be divided among individuals to prevent ethical conflicts or abuse of powers. Duties such as authorization and approval, and design and development should not be held by the same individual, because it would be far too easy for that individual to exploit an organization into using only specific software that contains vulnerabilities, or taking on projects that would be beneficial to that individual.

Example:

An example of separation of duties can be found in IT departments where, typically, the roles of backup operator, restore operator, and auditor are assigned to different people.

Figure 1-13: Separation of duties in an IT department.

Job Rotation

Definition:

The idea of *job rotation* is that no one person stays in a vital job role for too long a time period. Rotating individuals into and out of roles, such as the firewall administrator or access control specialist, helps an organization ensure that it is not tied too firmly to any one individual because vital institutional knowledge is spread among trusted employees. Job rotation also helps prevent abuse of power, reduces boredom, and enhances individuals' professional skills.

Example:

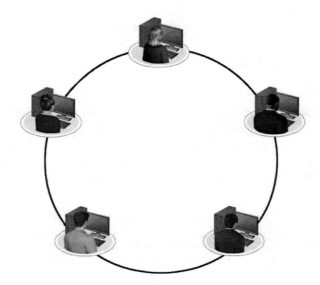

Figure 1-14: Job rotation.

Mandatory Vacation

Mandating employee vacations is a personnel management issue that has security implications. From a security standpoint, *mandatory vacations* provide an opportunity to review employees' activities. The typical mandatory vacation policy requires that employees take at least one vacation a year in a full-week increment so that they are away from work for at least five days in a row. During that time, the corporate audit and security employees have time to investigate and discover any discrepancies in employee activity. When employees understand the security focus of the mandatory vacation policy, the chance of fraudulent activities decreases.

Figure 1-15: Mandatory vacation.

Time of Day Restrictions

Definition:

Time of day restrictions are controls that allow users to access a system for a certain time period, which can be set using a group policy. Time of day restrictions can also be applied to individual systems and to wireless access points.

Example:

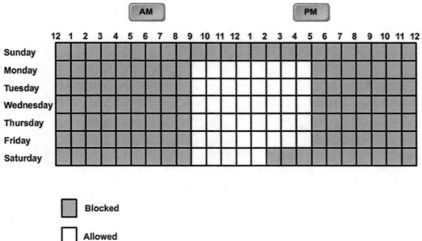

Figure 1-16: Time of day restrictions.

Orphaned Accounts

Orphaned accounts are user accounts that remain active even after the employees have left the organization. Not terminating these accounts may give an attacker access to the system. Large organizations have found that isolating orphaned accounts can be a very difficult task, and so they remain a potential avenue for attackers.

Privilege Management

Definition:

Privilege management is the use of authentication and authorization mechanisms to provide centralized or decentralized administration of user and group access control. Privilege management should include an auditing component to track privilege use and privilege escalation. Privilege management can also offer *single sign-on (SSO)* capabilities by providing users with one-time authentication for browsing resources such as multiple servers or sites.

Example:

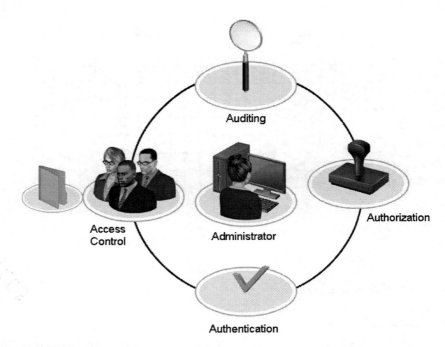

Figure 1-17: Privilege management.

PMI

An implementation of a particular set of privilege management technologies is called a *Privilege Management Infrastructure (PMI)*. The purpose of a PMI is to issue specific permissions and rights to users within the infrastructure. PMI functions in a similar way to Public Key Infrastructure (PKI) in that both have authoritative resources that issue rights or certificates to nodes below them in the infrastructure. Most often, PMI is leveraged alongside PKI because PKI is used to validate signatures for PMI. PMI should follow ITU-T (International Telecommunication Union-Telecommunication Standardization Sector) Recommendation X.509 as the basis for implementation.

ACTIVITY 1-2
Discussing Information Security Controls

Scenario:

In this activity, you will discuss information security controls.

1. **The three most fundamental goals of computer security are: (Select all that apply.)**
   a) Confidentiality
   b) Auditing
   c) Integrity
   d) Privilege management
   e) Availability

2. **A biometric handprint scanner is used as part of a system for granting access to a facility. Once an identity is verified, the system checks and confirms that the user is allowed to leave the lobby and enter the facility, and the electronic door lock is released. This is an example of which of the Four As? (Select all that apply.)**
   a) Authentication
   b) Authorization
   c) Access control
   d) Auditing

3. **Katie's handprint is matched against a record in the system that indicates that she has been assigned clearance to view the contents of secret documents. Later, at her desk, she tries to connect to a folder that is marked Top Secret, and access is denied. This is an example of:**
   a) MAC.
   b) DAC.
   c) RBAC.
   d) Rule-based access control.

4. **At the end of the day, security personnel can view electronic log files that record the identities of everyone who entered and exited the building along with the time of day. This is an example of:**
   a) Authentication.
   b) Authorization.
   c) Access control.
   d) Auditing.

5. **An administrator of a large multinational company has the ability to assign object access rights and track users' resource access from a central administrative console. Users throughout the organization can gain access to any system after providing a single user name and password. This is an example of:**

   a) Auditing.

   b) Security labels.

   c) Privilege management.

   d) Confidentiality.

6. **Match the access control principle to its definition.**

___	Implicit deny	a.	No one person should have too much power or responsibility.
___	Least privilege	b.	Everything that is not explicitly allowed is denied.
___	Separation of duties	c.	Users and software should only have the minimal level of access that is necessary for them to perform the duties required of them.
___	Job rotation	d.	No one person stays in a vital job role for too long a time period.

7. **Match each security control with its description.**

___	Authentication	a.	Validating an individual's credentials.
___	Authorization	b.	Tracking system events.
___	Access control	c.	Determining rights and privileges for an individual.
___	Auditing	d.	Assigning rights and privileges on objects.

TOPIC C
Authentication Methods

In the last topic, you learned that authentication is one of the primary controls in computer security. Although authentication always has the same goal, there are many different approaches to accomplish it. In this topic, you will discuss some of the primary authentication methods used today.

Strong authentication is the first line of defense in the battle to secure network resources. But authentication is not a single process; there are many different methods and mechanisms, some of which can even be combined to form more complex schemes. As a network professional, you will need to familiarize yourself with the major authentication methods in use today so you can implement and support the ones that are appropriate for your environment.

Authentication Factors

Most authentication schemes are based on the use of one or more authentication factors. The factors include:

● Something you know, such as a password.

● Something you have, such as a token or access card.

● And, something you are, including physical characteristics, such as fingerprints or a retina pattern.

User Name/Password Authentication

The combination of a user name and password is one of the most basic and widely used authentication schemes. In this type of authentication, a user's credentials are compared against credentials stored in a database. If the user name and password match the database, the user is authenticated. If not, the user is denied access. This method may not be very secure because the user's credentials are sometimes transmitted through the network in unencrypted text, making the user name and password easily accessible to an attacker.

Figure 1-18: *User name/password authentication.*

Tokens

Definition:

Tokens are physical or virtual objects, such as smart cards, ID badges, or data packets, that store authentication information. Tokens can store personal identification numbers (PINs), information about users, or passwords. Unique token values can be generated by special devices or software in response to a challenge from an authenticating server or by using independent algorithms.

Example:

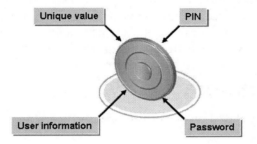

Figure 1-19: Tokens.

Smart Cards

Smart cards are a common example of token-based authentication. A smart card is a plastic card containing an embedded computer chip that can store different types of electronic information. The United States Department of Defense (DOD) has introduced a type of smart card called a Common Access Card (CAC) that is used as identification for all its military personnel, contract personnel, non-DoD government employees, and state employees of the National Guard. The contents of a smart card can be read with a smart card reader.

Biometrics

Definition:

Biometrics are authentication schemes based on individuals' physical characteristics. This can involve a fingerprint scanner, a retinal scanner, a hand geometry scanner, or voice-recognition and facial-recognition software. As biometric authentication becomes less expensive to implement, it is becoming more widely adopted.

Example:

Fingerprint Scanner

Figure 1-20: Biometrics.

Multi-Factor Authentication

Definition:

Multi-factor authentication is any authentication scheme that requires validation of at least two of the possible authentication factors. It can be any combination of who you are, what you have, and what you know.

One-, Two-, and Three-Factor Authentication

An authentication scheme with just one factor can be called a one-factor authentication, while a two- or three-factor authentication scheme can simply be called multi-factor authentication.

Example: A Multi-Factor Implementation

Requiring a physical ID card along with a secret password is an example of multi-factor authentication. A bank ATM card is a common example of this.

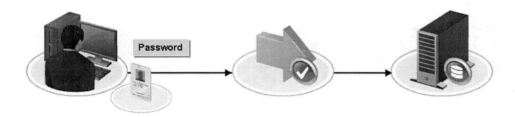

Figure 1-21: Multi-factor authentication.

Mutual Authentication

Definition:

Mutual authentication is a security mechanism that requires that each party in a communication verifies each other's identity. A service or resource verifies the client's credentials, and the client verifies the resource's credentials. Mutual authentication prevents a client from inadvertently submitting confidential information to a non-secure server. Any type or combination of authentication mechanisms can be used.

 Mutual authentication helps in avoiding man-in-the-middle and session hijacking attacks.

Example:

Figure 1-22: Mutual authentication.

ACTIVITY 1-3
Discussing Authentication Methods

Scenario:

In this activity, you will discuss the characteristics of various authentication methods.

1. **Brian works at a bank. To access his laptop, he inserts his employee ID card into a special card reader. This is an example of:**

   a) User name/password authentication.

   b) Biometrics.

   c) Token-based authentication.

   d) Mutual authentication.

2. **To access the server room, Brian places his index finger on a fingerprint reader. This is an example of:**

   a) Password authentication.

   b) Token-based authentication.

   c) Biometric authentication.

   d) Multi-factor authentication.

3. **To withdraw money from an automatic teller machine, Nancy inserts a card and types a four-digit PIN. This incorporates what types of authentication? (Select all that apply.)**

   a) Token-based

   b) Password

   c) Biometrics

   d) Multi-factor

   e) Mutual

4. **What is the best example of token-based authentication?**

   a) It relies on typing a code.

   b) It relies on a card and a PIN.

   c) It relies on a user's physical characteristics.

   d) It relies on a card being inserted into a card reader.

5. **True or False? Mutual authentication protects clients from submitting confidential information to an insecure server.**

___ True

___ False

---

6. **Match each authentication method with its description.**

___	Mutual authentication	a.	A security mechanism where a user's credentials are compared against credentials stored on a database.
___	User name/password authentication	b.	A security mechanism that requires that each party in a communication verify its identity.
___	Biometric authentication	c.	An object that stores authentication information.
___	Token	d.	Authentication based on physical characteristics.

---

7. **How does multi-factor authentication enhance security?**

TOPIC D
Cryptography Fundamentals

Earlier in the lesson, you identified the elements of security as confidentiality, integrity, and availability. Encryption is one of the most versatile security tools you can use to do justice to these elements. In this topic, you will identify fundamental cryptography components, concepts, and tools.

Cryptography is a powerful and complex weapon in the fight to maintain computer security. There are many cryptography systems, and the specifics of each cryptography implementation varies. Nevertheless, there are commonalities among all cryptography systems, which all security professionals should understand. The basic cryptography terms and ideas you will learn in this topic will help you evaluate, understand, and manage any type of cryptographic system you choose to implement.

Cryptography

Definition:

Cryptography is the science of hiding information. The practice of cryptography is thought to be nearly as old as the written word. Current cryptographic science has its roots in mathematics and computer science and relies heavily upon technology. Modern communications and computing use cryptography extensively to protect sensitive information and communications from unauthorized access.

Example:

 The word cryptography has roots in the Greek words kryptós, meaning "hidden," and "gráphein," meaning "to write," translating to "hidden writing."

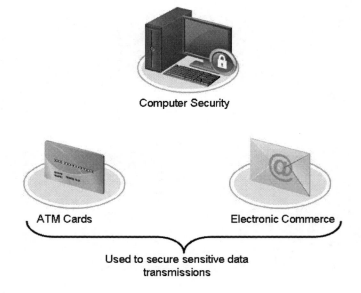

Computer Security

ATM Cards   Electronic Commerce

Used to secure sensitive data
transmissions

Figure 1-23: Cryptography.

Use of Proven Technologies

Any new technology should be rigorously tested before being applied to a live, production network. Particularly with cryptography, the technologies and techniques should have a well-documented history of investigation by industry professionals.

Encryption

Definition:

Encryption is a cryptographic technique that converts data from plain, or *cleartext* form, into coded, or ciphertext form. Only authorized parties with the necessary decryption information can decode and read the data. Encryption can be one-way, which means the encryption is designed to hide only the cleartext and is never decrypted. Encryption can also be two-way, in which the ciphertext can be decrypted back to cleartext and read.

Example:

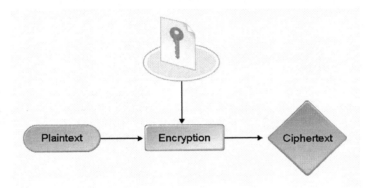

Figure 1-24: *Encryption.*

Quantum Cryptography

Quantum cryptography is an emerging method of data encryption based upon quantum communication and computation. A qubit is a unit of data that is encrypted by entangling data with a photon or electron that has a particular spin cycle which can be read using a polarization filter that controls spin. If a qubit is read with an incorrect polarization filter, then it becomes unreadable and the receiver will know that someone may actually be eavesdropping. For more information, visit **www.csa.com/discoveryguides/crypt/overview.php**

Ciphers

Definition:

A *cipher* is a specific set of actions used to encrypt data. *Plaintext* is the original, un-encoded data. Once the cipher is applied via *enciphering,* the obscured data is known as *ciphertext.* The reverse process of translating ciphertext to cleartext is known as *deciphering.*

Ciphers vs. Codes

Ciphers are differentiated from codes in that codes are meant to translate words or phrases or act like a secret language, whereas ciphers operate on individual letters or bits and scramble the message.

Cryptanalysis

Cryptanalysis is the science of breaking codes and ciphers.

Example:

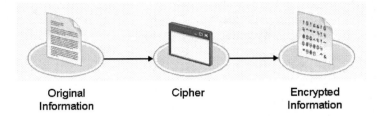

Original   Cipher   Encrypted
Information   Information

Figure 1-25: Ciphers.

Cipher Types

There are two major categories of encryption ciphers: stream and block.

Cipher Type	Description
Stream cipher	A type of encryption that encrypts data one bit at a time. Each plaintext bit is transformed into encrypted ciphertext. These ciphers are relatively fast to execute. The ciphertext is the same size as the original text. This method produces fewer errors than other methods, and when errors occur, they affect only one bit.
Block cipher	This cipher encrypts data one block at a time, often in 64-bit blocks. It is usually more secure, but is also slower, than stream encryption. Some common modes of block cipher encryption are: ● *Electronic Code Block (ECB) encryption* ● *Cipher Block Chaining (CBC) encryption* ● *Propagating or Plaintext Cipher Block Chaining (PCBC) encryption* ● *Cipher Feedback mode (CFB) encryption* ● *Output Feedback mode (OFB) encryption* ● *Counter mode (CTR)*

Encryption and Security Goals

Encryption is used to promote many security goals and techniques. Encryption enables confidentiality by protecting data from unauthorized access. It supports integrity because it is difficult to decipher encrypted data without the secret decrypting cipher. It supports non-repudiation, because only parties that know about the confidential encryption scheme can encrypt or decrypt data. In addition, some form of encryption is employed in most authentication mechanisms to protect passwords. Encryption is used in many access control mechanisms as well.

Forms of Encryption

It is becoming more common to encrypt many forms of communications and data streams, as well as entire hard disks. Some operating systems support whole-disk encryption and there are many commercial and open-source tools available that are capable of encrypting all or part of the data on a disk or drive.

Encryption Algorithms

Definition:

An encryption *algorithm* is the rule, system, or mechanism used to encrypt data. Algorithms can be simple mechanical substitutions, but in electronic cryptography, they are generally complex mathematical functions. The stronger the mathematical function, the more difficult it is to break the encryption.

Example:

Text   Vgzv

Figure 1-26: An encryption algorithm.

Example: A Simple Encryption Algorithm

A letter-substitution cipher, in which each letter of the alphabet is systematically replaced by another letter, is an example of a simple encryption algorithm.

Steganography

Definition:

Steganography is an alternative cipher process that hides information by enclosing it in another file such as a graphic, movie, or sound file. Where encryption "hides" the content of information, but does not attempt to hide the fact that information exists, steganography is an attempt to obscure the fact that information is even present. Steganographic techniques include hiding information in blocks of what appears to be innocuous text, or hiding information within images either by using subtle clues, or by invisibly altering the structure of a digital image by applying an algorithm to change the color of individual pixels within the image.

Example:

Figure 1-27: *Steganography.*

Keys

Definition:

An encryption *key* is a specific piece of information that is used in conjunction with an algorithm to perform encryption and decryption. A different key can be used with the same algorithm to produce different ciphertext. Without the correct key, the receiver cannot decrypt the ciphertext even if the algorithm is known. The longer the key, the stronger the encryption.

Example:

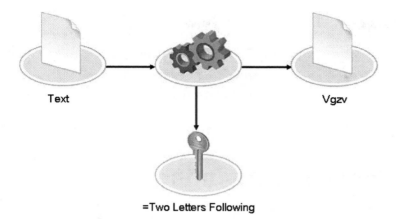

Text   Vgzv

=Two Letters Following

Figure 1-28: *A key.*

One-Time Pad

The one-time pad is an encryption algorithm that was developed under the assumption that if a key was used once, was completely random, and was kept totally secret, then it constituted the perfect method of encryption. However, because the successful use of a one-time pad relies on an absolutely perfect setting to work correctly, one-time pad encryption has very little practical value. It is so named because the earliest encryption involved pads of paper where the various sheets could be destroyed after use.

Example: A Simple Encryption Key

In a simple letter-substitution algorithm, the key might be "replace each letter with the letter that is two letters following it in the alphabet." If the same algorithm were used on the same cleartext but with a different key—for example, "replace each letter with the one three letters before it"—the resulting ciphertext would be different.

Hashing Encryption

Definition:

Hashing encryption is one-way encryption that transforms cleartext into ciphertext that is not intended to be decrypted. The result of the hashing process is called a *hash, hash value,* or *message digest.* The input data can vary in length, whereas the hash length is fixed.

I NTEGRITY

Uses of Hashing

Some of the uses for hashing are:

● Hashing is used in a number of password authentication schemes. Encrypted password data is called a hash of the password.

● A hash value can be embedded in an electronic message to support data integrity and non-repudiation.

● A hash of a file can be used to verify the integrity of that file after transfer.

Example:

Figure 1-29: Hashing encryption.

Hashing Encryption Algorithms

Some common encryption algorithms are used for hashing encryption.

Hashing Algorithm	Description
Message Digest 5 (MD5)	This algorithm produces a 128-bit message digest. It was created by Ronald Rivest and is now in the public domain.
Secure Hash Algorithm (SHA)	This algorithm is modeled after MD5 and is considered the stronger of the two. Common versions of SHA include SHA-160, which produces a 160-bit hash value, while SHA-256, SHA-384, and SHA-512 produce 256-bit, 384-bit, and 512-bit digests, respectively.
NT LAN Manager (NTLM#)	NTLMv1 is an authentication protocol created by Microsoft® for use in its products and released in early versions of Windows® NT. NTLMv2 was introduced in the later versions of Windows NT.
RACE Integrity Primitives Evaluation Message Digest (RIPEMD)	This is a message digest algorithm (cryptographic hash function), which is based along the lines of the design principles used in *MD4*. There are 128, 160, 256, and 320-bit versions called respectively RIPEMD-128, RIPEMD-160, RIPEMD-256, and RIPEMD-320. The 256- and 320-bit versions reduce the chances of generating duplicate initialization vectors (IV) but do little in terms of higher levels of security. RIPEMD-160 was designed by the open academic community and is used less frequently than SHA-1, which may explain why it is less scrutinized than SHA.
Hash-based Message Authentication Code (HMAC)	A method used to verify both the integrity and authenticity of a message by combining cryptographic hash functions, such as MD5, or SHA-1 with a secret key. The resulting calculation is named based on what underlying hash function was used. For example, if SHA-1 is the hash function, then the HMAC algorithm is named HMAC-SHA1.

(handwritten note: Replace by KERBEROS)

LANMAN

LAN Manager (LANMAN) is a legacy authentication protocol used by Windows systems prior to Windows NT. LANMAN creates weak and easily crackable passwords.

RACE

RACE is the acronym for Research and Development in Advanced Communications Technologies. It is a program that was launched in Europe by the Commission of the European Communities in 1988 to introduce integrated broadband communications, which can provide high-speed bandwidth and the services that would follow. RACE managed these services and the critical steps that needed to be taken to apply cryptographic techniques to a high-speed network.

Symmetric Encryption

Definition:

Symmetric encryption is a two-way encryption scheme in which encryption and decryption are both performed by the same key. The key can be configured in software or coded in hardware. The key must be securely transmitted between the two parties prior to encrypted communications. Symmetric encryption is relatively fast, but is vulnerable if the key is lost or compromised. Some of the common names for symmetric encryption are secret-key, shared-key, and private-key encryption.

Example:

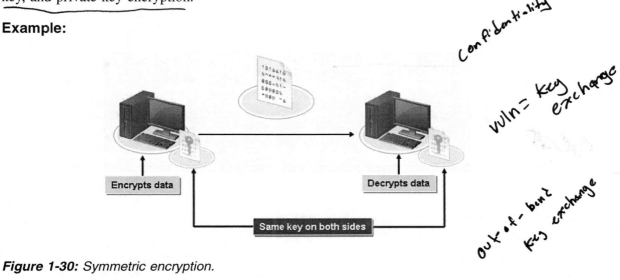

Figure 1-30: *Symmetric encryption.*

Symmetric Encryption Algorithms

Some algorithms are used for symmetric encryption.

Symmetric Algorithm	Description
Data Encryption Standard (DES)	A block-cipher symmetric encryption algorithm that encrypts data in 64-bit blocks using a 56-bit key with 8 bits used for parity. The short key length makes DES a relatively weak algorithm.
Triple DES (3DES)	A symmetric encryption algorithm that encrypts data by processing each block of data three times using a different key each time. It first encrypts plaintext into ciphertext using one key, it then encrypts that ciphertext with another key, and it last encrypts the second ciphertext with yet another key.

Symmetric Algorithm	Description
Advanced Encryption Standard (AES) algorithm	A symmetric 128-, 192-, or 256-bit block cipher developed by Belgian cryptographers Joan Daemen and Vincent Rijmen and adopted by the U.S. government as its encryption standard to replace DES. The AES algorithm is called Rijndael (pronounced "Rhine-dale") after its creators. Rijndael was one of five algorithms considered for adoption in the AES contest conducted by the National Institute of Standards and Technology (NIST) of the United States.
Blowfish	A freely available 64-bit block cipher algorithm that uses a variable key length. It was developed by Bruce Schneier.
Twofish	A symmetric key block cipher, similar to Blowfish, consisting a block size of 128 bits and key sizes up to 256 bits. Although not selected for standardization, it appeared as one of the five finalists in the AES contest. Twofish encryption uses a pre-computed encrypted algorithm. The encrypted algorithm is a key-dependent *S-box* which is a relatively complex key algorithm that when given the key, provides a substitution key in its place. This is referred to as "n" and has the sizes of 128, 192, and 256 bits. One half of "n" is made up of the encryption key and the other half contains a modifier used in the encryption algorithm.
Rivest Cipher (RC) 4, 5, and 6	A series of algorithms developed by Ronald Rivest. All have variable key lengths. RC4 is a stream cipher. RC5 and RC6 are variable-size block ciphers.
Skipjack	A block cipher algorithm designed by the U.S. National Security Agency (NSA) for use in tamper-proof hardware in conjunction with the Clipper Chip.
CAST-128	Named for its developers, Carlisle Adams and Stafford Tavares, it is a symmetric encryption algorithm with a 128-bit key. It was one of the contenders in the AES competition.

Asymmetric Encryption

Definition:

Unlike symmetric encryption, the mainstay of *asymmetric encryption* is using public and private keys. The *private key* is kept secret by one party during two-way encryption. Because the private key is never shared, its security is relatively maintained.

The *public key* is given to anyone. Depending on the application of the encryption, either party may use the encryption key. The other key in the pair is used to decrypt. The private key in a pair can decrypt data encoded with the corresponding public key.

Example:

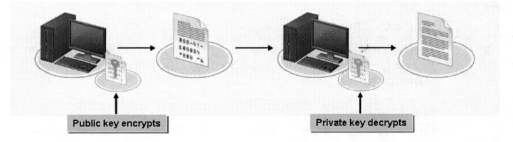

Figure 1-31: Asymmetric encryption.

Key Generation

Key generation is the process of generating a public and private key pair using a specific application.

Asymmetric Encryption Algorithms

Some algorithms are used for asymmetric encryption.

Asymmetric Algorithm	Description
Rivest Shamir Adelman (RSA)	Named for its designers, Ronald Rivest, Adi Shamir, and Len Adelman, RSA was the first successful algorithm for public key encryption. It has a variable key length and block size. It is still widely used and considered highly secure if it employs sufficiently long keys.
Diffie-Hellman	A cryptographic protocol that provides for secure key exchange. Described in 1976, it formed the basis for most public key encryption implementations, including RSA.
Elgamal	A public key encryption algorithm developed by Taher Elgamal. It is based on Diffie-Hellman.
Paillier Cryptosystem	An asymmetric encryption algorithm developed by Pascal Paillier.
Elliptic curve cryptography (ECC)	An asymmetric, public key encryption technique that leverages the algebraic structures of elliptic curves over finite fields. ECC is used with wireless and mobile devices.

Some books on cryptography and computer security that are written for a general audience are:

- The Code Book by Simon Singh
- Cryptography Decrypted by H. X. Me and Doris M. Baker
- Secrets and Lies by Bruce Schneier
- Introduction to Modern Cryptography by Jonathan Katz and Yehuda Lindell

Digital Signatures

A *digital signature* is a message digest that has been encrypted again with a user's private key. Asymmetric encryption algorithms can be used with hashing algorithms to create digital signatures. The sender creates a hashed version of the message text, and then encrypts the hash itself with the sender's private key. The encrypted hash is attached to the message as the digital signature. The sender provides the receiver with the signed message and the corresponding public key. The receiver uses the public key to decrypt the signature to reveal the sender's version of the hash. This proves the sender's identity, because if the public and private keys did not match, the receiver would not be able to decrypt the signature. The receiver then creates a new hash version of the document with the public key and compares the two hash values. If they match, this proves that the data has not been altered.

Digital signatures support message integrity, because if the signature is altered in transit, the receiver's version of the hash will not match the original hash value. They support non-repudiation because the specific encrypted hash value is unique to the sender.

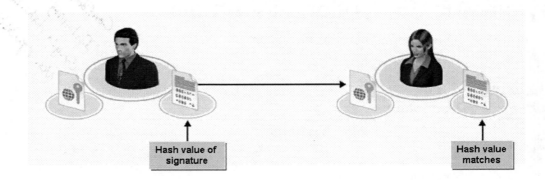

Figure 1-32: *A digital signature.*

Encryption of the Hash

It is important to remember that a digital signature is a hash that is then itself encrypted. Without the second round of encryption, another party could easily:

1. Intercept the file and the hash.

2. Modify the file.

3. Re-create the hash.

4. Send the modified file to the recipient.

ACTIVITY 1-4
Discussing Cryptography

Scenario:

In this activity, you will discuss fundamental cryptography concepts.

1. **Match each symmetric encryption algorithm with the correct description.**

   ___ DES

   ___ 3DES

   ___ AES

   ___ RC 4, 5, and 6

   ___ Twofish

   ___ Blowfish

   a. A symmetric encryption algorithm that encrypts data by processing each block of data three times using a different key each time.

   b. A series of algorithms all containing variable key lengths.

   c. A block-cipher symmetric encryption algorithm that encrypts data in 64-bit blocks using a 56-bit key with 8 bits used for parity.

   d. A freely available 64-bit block cipher algorithm that uses a variable key length.

   e. A symmetric key block cipher that uses a pre-computed encrypted algorithm called an S-box.

   f. A symmetric 128-, 192-, or 256-bit block cipher developed by Belgian cryptographers Joan Daemen and Vincent Rijmen and adopted by the U.S. government as its encryption standard to replace DES.

2. **Which algorithm is a hashing encryption algorithm?**

   a) SHA

   b) AES

   c) RSA

   d) 3DES

3. **Which of the following is a specific set of actions used to encrypt data?**

   a) Steganography

   b) Key

   c) Cipher

   d) Digital signature

4. **Match each asymmetric encryption algorithm with the correct description.**

___ RSA

___ Diffie-Hellman

___ Elgamal

___ Elliptic curve cryptography

a. A cryptographic protocol that provides for secure key exchange and formed the basis for most later public key implementations.

b. A public key encryption algorithm named for its developer that is based on Diffie-Hellman.

c. The first successful algorithm for asymmetric encryption. It has a variable key length and block size and is still widely used.

d. A public key encryption technique that leverages the algebraic structures of elliptic curves over finite fields.

5. **True or False? A digital signature is an application of hashing encryption, because the signature is never transformed back to cleartext.**

___ True

___ False

6. **What are the distinctions between an encryption algorithm and a key?**

7. **What is a potential drawback of symmetric encryption?**

8. **What makes public key encryption potentially so secure?**

9. **Considering that hashing encryption is one-way and the hash is never decrypted, what makes hashing encryption a useful security technique?**

TOPIC E
Security Policy Fundamentals

Throughout this lesson so far, you have looked at successively more complex components of security systems. Once all the components and requirements of a security system are identified, they are typically documented and maintained in security policies. In this topic, you will identify how security policies are constructed to meet the security needs of an organization.

In most organizations, security policies are the documents that have the greatest influence over the actions taken and decisions made by security professionals. A well-constructed security policy is a great weapon in the fight to preserve the safety and integrity of an institution's technical and intellectual assets. As you pursue your career, you will certainly be called upon to read, understand, and conform to security policies, and you might even be charged with designing, implementing, and maintaining them as well. Thus, whatever aspect of the security profession you pursue, the fundamental security policy terms and ideas you learn in this topic will always serve you well.

Security Policies

Definition:

A *security policy* is a formalized statement that defines how security will be implemented within a particular organization. It describes the means the organization will take to protect the confidentiality, availability, and integrity of sensitive data and resources, including the network infrastructure, physical and electronic data, applications, and the physical environment. It often consists of multiple individual policies. All implemented security measures should conform with the stated policy.

Example:

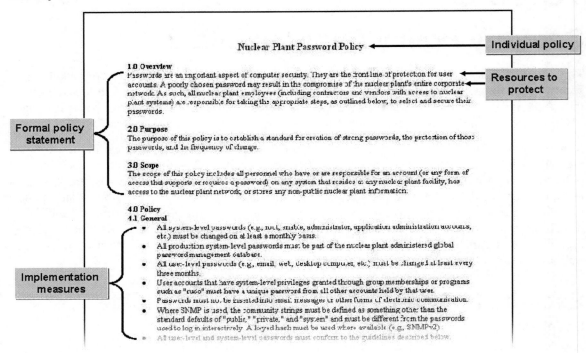

Figure 1-33: *A security policy.*

Example: A Password Security Policy

A nuclear plant has a password policy that is required for all employees. Each employee is responsible for using strong passwords and protecting those passwords accordingly. The password policy contains guidelines for strong passwords to use and weak passwords to avoid.

A Security Policy is Like a Government Policy

A good security policy provides functions similar to a government's foreign policy. The policy is determined by the needs of the organization. Just as a nation needs a foreign policy in part because of real and perceived threats from other countries, organizations also need policies to protect their data and resources. A nation's foreign policy defines what the threats are and how the government will handle those threats. A security policy does the same for an organization; it defines threats to its resources and how those threats will be handled. A policy forms the plan that ties everything together. Without a formal policy, you can only react to threats instead of anticipating them and preparing accordingly.

Windows Security Policies

Windows security policies are configuration settings within the Windows operating systems that control the overall security behavior of the system. They are found in a policy object in the Computer Configuration\Windows Settings\Security Settings node. The policies can be set on a centralized basis, through a Group Policy in Windows Server® systems, or can be set in the individual policy objects on each computer.

Security Policy Components

Each subsection of a security policy typically consists of several standard components.

Policy Component	Description
Policy statement	Outlines the plan for the individual security component.
Standards	Define how to measure the level of adherence to the policy. *rule*
Guidelines	Suggestions, recommendations, or best practices for how to meet the policy standard. *suggestion*
Procedures	Step-by-step instructions that detail how to implement components of the policy. *step-by-step*

Security Policy Issues

Security policies should specify the organization's responsibilities for a number of common security issues.

Security Policy Issue	Description
Acceptable use	A statement of the limits and guidelines that are set for users and others to make use of an organization's physical and intellectual resources. The policy should define what use of organizational assets, such as computers and telecommunications equipment, will be considered acceptable and what will be considered in violation. Acceptable use guidelines must be reasonable and not interfere with employees' fundamental job duties or human rights.
Privacy	The policy should specify to what extent organizational information as well as users' personal information will be kept private, and the consequences of violations of privacy. Users should also understand which of their workplace actions and communications are not considered private.
Separation of duties (or separation of roles)	The policy should define how security privileges and responsibilities are divided among users in different appropriate roles; these users can act as checks and balances to each other as well as back each other up in case of an emergency. The policy should provide guidelines to aid in determining which duties should be separated.
Job rotation	Policies should include guidelines for rotating individuals through mission-critical job roles to prevent over-reliance on a single individual or the potential for abuse.
Mandatory vacation	The policy should determine which job roles require mandatory vacation, setting a minimum time required out of the office and specifying audit procedures for when the employee is out of the office.
Need to know	The policy should specify who should have access to privileged information and on what basis. Employees should only be able to access sensitive information if it is essential for their jobs.
Least privilege	The policy should reinforce that users have only the minimum set of rights, permissions, and privileges that they need to accomplish their jobs, without excessive privileges that can provide them with unauthorized access to systems. Policies should mandate that users and software should be given the lowest level of permissions that will allow them to perform explicitly specified duties.

Security Policy Issue	Description
Implicit deny	Implicit deny should be called out in the policy. Information or action rights that are not explicitly specified should be denied.

Common Security Policy Types

There are several common security policy types that are included in most corporate security policies.

Policy Type	Description
Acceptable use policy (AUP)	Defines the acceptable use of an organization's physical and intellectual resources.
Audit policy	Details the requirements and parameters for risk assessment and audits of the organization's information and resources.
Extranet policy	Sets the requirements for third-party entities that desire access to an organization's networks.
Password policy	Defines standards for creating password complexity. It also defines what an organization considers weak passwords and the guidelines for protecting password safety.
Wireless standards policy	Defines which wireless devices can connect to an organization's network and how to use them in a safe manner that protects the organization's security.

Security Policy Standards Organizations

The SysAdmin, Audit, Networking and Security (SANS) Institute has identified a list of standard policy types and policy templates, ranging from the acceptable encryption policy to the wireless communication policy. To view the complete list of policies from the SANS Institute, see **www.sans.org/resources/policies/**.

There are other organizations, such as the Internet Engineering Task Force (IETF), that provide templates, such as Request for Comments (RFC) 2196 for different security policies. To view RFC 2196, see **www.cse.ohio-state.edu/cgi-bin/rfc/rfc2196.html**.

The International Organization for Standardization (ISO) has published ISO/IEC 27002:2005, which is a standard for information security. To view information on ISO/IEC 27002:2005, see **www.iso.org**.

Security Document Categories

There are several categories of documents that you will need to securely maintain, so they should be addressed in the security policy.

Security Document	Description
System architecture	Physical documentation about the setup and configuration of your network and systems must be stored securely. This is a valuable source of information for potential attackers.
Change documentation	Changes in the configuration of data, systems, and services are often tracked and documented to provide an official record of the correct current configuration. Changes to documents themselves should be internally noted with the current revision number, the revision date, the revision author, and the contents of each revision.
Logs	System logs, especially those generated by the auditing security function, need to be protected from unauthorized access or tampering. Altering audit or activity logs is one approach attackers might take to cover their tracks following a system breach.
Inventories	Equipment and asset inventories provide a valuable source of information for attackers, whether they plan to mount an electronic attack against the system or resort to physical damage or theft. You should maintain accurate inventories and keep those inventories secure.

Change Management

Definition:

Change management is a systematic way of approving and executing change in order to assure maximum security, stability, and availability of information technology services. When an organization changes its hardware, software, infrastructure, or documentation, it risks the introduction of unanticipated consequences. Therefore, it is important for an organization to be able to properly assess risk, to quantify the cost of training, support, maintenance, or implementation, and to properly weigh benefits against the complexity of a proposed change. By maintaining a documented change management procedure, an organization can protect itself from the potential adverse effects of hasty change.

Example:

Jane has identified a new service pack that has been released that fixes numerous security vulnerabilities for the operating system on a server. The server that needs this service pack is running a custom in-house application, and significant downtime is not acceptable. The company policy states that a change management form must be approved for all service packs. The form comes back from the approval process with a qualification that the service pack must be tested on a lab system prior to deployment on the production server. Jane applies the service pack in a lab and discovers that it causes the custom in-house application to fail. The application must be sent back to the software developers for testing before the service pack can be applied in production.

Figure 1-34: *Change management.*

Documentation Handling Measures

Your policy should specify standards and guidelines for the measures you take when handling sensitive documents.

Document Handling Measure	Description
Classification	Many organizations assign classification levels, such as Public, Internal, Confidential, and Restricted, to their official documentation. The classification of a document not only determines who has the right to see or alter the document, but also determines the correct procedure for storing, archiving, and handling the document. The classification system can also serve as the basis for a MAC access scheme implementation. Employees should be notified as to their security level and should understand the procedures for accessing documents at each level. Also, the classification level should be stated clearly within the document itself.
Retention and storage	Your policy should include standards and guidelines for how long different types of documents are retained to meet legal or policy requirements. You should also have a plan for consistent and secure storage, and retrieval of all document types. Storage recommendations take into account the nature of the information, the physical media on which it is stored, and the security measures for the documents.
Disposal and destruction	There should be a plan for disposal or destruction of outdated documents. Some documents can simply be recycled or thrown away. However, confidential information must have an approved destruction method to ensure that the data cannot be retrieved. The destruction method depends upon the sensitivity of the data and the media it is stored on, and can range from shredding and then burning paper documents, to reformatting computer disks multiple times.

ACTIVITY 1-5
Examining a Security Policy

Data Files:

NuclearPlantPasswordPolicy.rtf

Setup:

You have a Windows Server 2008 R2 computer to work with. The computer name is Server##, where ## is a unique number. Log on as Administrator with the password !Pass1234.

The policy document is stored on your workstation at C:\SPlus\NuclearPlantPasswordPolicy.rtf.

Scenario:

As the new security administrator for a nuclear plant, you will be responsible for maintaining and updating the documentation related to security policies, as well as for understanding and enforcing the policies. Before you can be effective in these new duties, you have decided that you need to familiarize yourself with the existing policy documents in the organization.

1. **Open and review the policy file. What type of policy document is this?**

   a) Acceptable use policy

   b) Audit policy

   c) Extranet policy

   d) Password policy

   e) Wireless standards policy

2. **Which standard policy components are included in this policy? (Select all that apply.)**

   a) Policy statement

   b) Standards

   c) Guidelines

   d) Procedures

3. **How often must system-level administrators change their passwords to conform to this policy?**

4. **To conform to this policy, how often must regular system users change their passwords?**

5. According to this policy, what is the minimum character length for a password and how should it be constructed?

_____

6. Why is "password1" not a good choice for a password?

_____

Lesson 1 Follow-up

In this lesson, you identified some of the most basic components, goals, and tools involved in securing computers and networks. The information you learned in this lesson will help you communicate effectively with other security professionals you encounter during your career, as well as help you make informed choices as you select, implement, support, and maintain network security measures.

1. **Which of the basic security concepts in this lesson were familiar to you, and which were new?**

2. **Can you describe some situations in which you have used basic security techniques such as authentication, access control, and encryption, or made use of a security policy?**

2 | Security Threats and Vulnerabilities

Lesson Time: 2 hour(s), 30 minutes

Lesson Objectives:

In this lesson, you will identify security threats and vulnerabilities.

You will:

- Identify social engineering attacks.
- Identify physical threats and vulnerabilities.
- Identify network-based threats.
- Identify wireless threats and vulnerabilities.
- Identify software-based threats.

Introduction

Security is an ongoing process that includes setting up organizational security systems, hardening them, monitoring them, responding to attacks in progress, and deterring attackers. As a security professional, you will be involved in all phases of that process. But, in order for that process to be effective, you need to understand the threats and vulnerabilities you will be protecting your systems against. In this lesson, you will identify the various types of security threats and vulnerabilities that you might encounter.

Unsecured systems can result in compromised data and, ultimately, lost revenue. But you cannot protect your systems from threats you do not understand. Once you understand the types of possible threats and identify individuals who will try to use them against your network, you can take the appropriate steps to protect your systems and keep your resources and revenue safe from potential attacks.

This lesson covers all or part of the following CompTIA® Security+® (Exam SY0-301) certification objectives:

- Topic A:
    - Objective 3.2 Analyze and differentiate among types of attacks
- Topic C:
    - Objective 1.1 Explain the security function and purpose of network devices and technologies

- Objective 1.4 Implement and use common protocols
- Objective 1.5 Identify commonly used default network ports
- Objective 1.6 Implement wireless network in a secure manner
- Objective 3.2 Analyze and differentiate among types of attacks
- Objective 3.5 Analyze and differentiate among types of application attacks
- Topic D:
  - Objective 3.2 Analyze and differentiate among types of attacks
  - Objective 3.4 Analyze and differentiate among types of wireless attacks
- Topic E:
  - Objective 1.5 Identify commonly used default network ports
  - Objective 3.1 Analyze and differentiate among types of malware
  - Objective 3.5 Analyze and differentiate among types of application attacks

TOPIC A
Social Engineering

When you think about attacks against information systems, you might think most about protecting the technological components of those systems. But people—the system users—are as much a part of an information system as the technological components; they have their own vulnerabilities, and they can be the first part of the system to succumb to certain types of attacks. In this topic, you will learn to identify social engineering attacks—threats against the human factors in your technology environment.

For technically oriented people, it can be easy to forget that one of the most important components of information systems is the people using those systems. Computers and technology do not exist in a vacuum; their only benefit comes from the way people use them and interact with them. Attackers know this, and so they know that the people in the system may well be the best target for attack. If you want to protect your infrastructure, systems, and data, you need to be able to recognize this kind of attack when it happens.

Social Engineering Attacks

Definition:

A *social engineering attack* is a type of attack that uses deception and trickery to convince unsuspecting users to provide sensitive data or to violate security guidelines. Social engineering is often a precursor to another type of attack. Because these attacks depend on human factors rather than on technology, their symptoms can be vague and hard to identify. Social engineering attacks can come in a variety of methods: in person, through email, or over the phone.

Example:

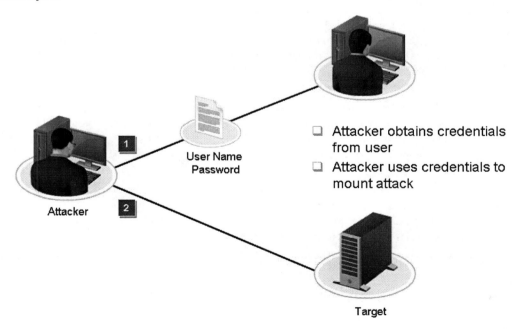

Figure 2-1: A social engineering attack.

Social Engineering Attack Scenarios

These are a few typical social engineering attack scenarios:

- An attacker creates an executable program file (for example, a file with a .vbs or .exe file extension) that prompts a network user for his user name and password. The attacker then emails the executable file to the user with the story that the user must double-click the file and log on to the network again to clear up some logon problems the organization has been experiencing that morning.

- An attacker contacts the help desk pretending to be a remote sales representative who needs assistance setting up his dial-in access. Through a series of phone calls, the attacker obtains the phone number for remote access and the phone number for accessing the organization's private phone and voice-mail system.

- An attacker sends an executable file disguised as an electronic greeting card (e-card) or as a patch for an operating system or a specific application. The unsuspecting user launches the executable, which might install email spamming software or a key-logging program, or turn the computer into a remote "zombie" for the hacker.

Social Engineering Targets

Social engineering typically takes advantage of users who are not technically knowledgeable, but it can also be directed against technical support staff if the attacker pretends to be a user who needs help.

Types of Social Engineering

There are various types of social engineering attacks.

Social Engineering Type	Description
Spoofing	This is a human-based or software-based attack where the goal is to pretend to be someone else for the purpose of identity concealment. Spoofing can occur in Internet Protocol (IP) addresses, network adapter's hardware (Mandatory Access Control [MAC]) addresses, and email. If employed in email, various email message headers are changed to conceal the originator's identity.
Impersonation	This is a human-based attack where an attacker pretends to be someone he is not. A common scenario is when the attacker calls an employee and pretends to be calling from the help desk. The attacker tells the employee he is reprogramming the order-entry database, and he needs the employee's user name and password to make sure it gets entered into the new system.
Hoax	This is an email-based or web-based attack that is intended to trick the user into performing undesired actions, such as deleting important system files in an attempt to remove a virus. It could also be a scam to convince users to give up important information or money for an interesting offer.

Social Engineering Type	Description
Phishing	This is a common type of email-based social engineering attack. In a phishing attack, the attacker sends an email that seems to come from a respected bank or other financial institution. The email claims that the recipient needs to provide an account number, Social Security number, or other private information to the sender in order to "verify an account." Ironically, the phishing attack often claims that the "account verification" is necessary for security reasons. Individuals should never provide personal financial information to someone who requests it, whether through email or over the phone. Legitimate financial institutions never solicit this information from their clients. A similar form of phishing called *pharming* can be done by redirecting a request for a website, typically an e-commerce site, to a similar-looking, but fake, website.
Vishing	This is a human-based attack where the goal is to extract personal, financial, or confidential information from the victim by using services such as the telephone system and IP-based voice messaging services (Voice over Internet Protocol [VoIP]) as the communication medium. This is also called voice phishing.
Whaling	This is a form of phishing that targets individuals who are known to possess a good deal of wealth. It is also known as *spear phishing*. Whaling targets individuals that work in Fortune 500 companies or financial institutions whose salaries are expected to be high.
Spam and spim	Spam is an email-based threat where the user's inbox is flooded with emails which act as vehicles that carry advertising material for products or promotions for get-rich-quick schemes and can sometimes deliver viruses or *malware*. Spam can also be utilized within social networking sites such as Facebook and Twitter. Spim is an IM-based attack similar to spam that is propagated through instant messaging instead of through email.

VoIP

VoIP is a technology that enables you to deliver telephony information over IP networks. The voice information that is sent over the IP network is in digital form in packets, as compared to the implementation on the Public Switched Telephone Network (PSTN) which includes circuit-committed protocols.

Human Factor Vulnerabilities

There are additional vulnerabilities to be aware of that can take advantage of human carelessness or inattention.

BAITING
- Dropping thumbdrives

Vulnerability	Description
Shoulder surfing	An attack where the goal is to look over the shoulder of an individual as he or she enters password information or a PIN. This is very easy to do today with camera-equipped mobile phones.
Dumpster diving	An attack where the goal is to reclaim important information by inspecting the contents of trash containers. This is especially effective in the first few weeks of the year as users discard old calendars with passwords written in them.

Vulnerability	Description
Tailgating	Also known as piggy backing, this is a human-based attack where the attacker will slip in through a secure area following a legitimate employee. The only way to prevent this type of attack is by installing a good access control mechanism and to educate users not to admit unauthorized personnel.

Hackers and Attackers

Definition:

Hackers and *attackers* are related terms for individuals who have the skills to gain access to computer systems through unauthorized or unapproved means. Originally, a *hacker* was a neutral term for a user who excelled at computer programming and computer system administration. "Hacking" into a system was a sign of technical skill and creativity that gradually became associated with illegal or malicious system intrusions. "Attacker" is a term that always represents a malicious system intruder.

 The term *cracker* refers to an individual who breaks encryption codes, defeats software copy protections, or specializes in breaking into systems. The term "cracker" is sometimes used to refer to a hacker or attacker.

Example:

Hacker

Attacker
Always Malicious Intent

Figure 2-2: *A hacker and an attacker.*

White Hats and Black Hats

A *white hat* is a hacker who discovers and exposes security flaws in applications and operating systems so that manufacturers can fix them before they become widespread problems. The white hat often does this on a professional basis, working for a security organization or a system manufacturer. This is sometimes called an "ethical hack."

A *black hat* is a hacker who discovers and exposes security vulnerabilities for financial gain or for some malicious purpose. While the black hats might not break directly into systems the way attackers do, widely publicizing security flaws can potentially cause financial or other damage to an organization.

Some who consider themselves white hats also discover and publicize security problems, but without the organization's knowledge or permission. They consider themselves to be acting for the common good. In this case, the only distinction between a white hat and a black hat is one of intent. There is some debate over whether this kind of unauthorized revelation of security issues really serves the public good or simply provides an avenue of attack.

White hats and black hats get their names from characters in old Western movies: the good guys always wore white hats, while the bad guys wore black hats.

Categories of Attackers

Attackers have many different motivations, and recognizing some of the different types may help you detect and deter attacks.

 There are many ways to categorize attackers, and sometimes there is no firm distinction between one type and another. The important thing to realize is that attacks can come from many sources, and that the motivations and goals for the attacks might be highly subjective, and not necessarily seem reasonable or logical to a rational observer.

Attacker Category	Motivations and Goals
Malicious insiders (employees and contractors)	A *malicious insider threat* is a threat originating from an employee in an organization who performs malicious acts, such as deleting critical information or sharing this critical information with outsiders, which may result in a certain amount of losses to the organization. Internal attackers might be fueled by some kind of resentment against the organization, in which case their goal might be to get revenge by simply causing damage or disrupting systems. Or, they might be motivated by financial gain if they want to obtain and sell confidential information to competitors or third parties.
Electronic activist ("hacktivist")	The *hacktivist* is motivated by a desire to cause social change, and might be trying to get media attention by disrupting services, or promoting a message by replacing the information on public websites. The hacktivist also might want to cause damage to organizations that are deemed socially irresponsible or unworthy.
Data thief	This kind of attacker blatantly steals resources or confidential information for personal or financial gain. They are likely to try to cover their tracks so their attacks are not detected and stopped. Usually in data theft, the attacker exploits unauthorized access or acts in collusion with a disgruntled employee.
Script kiddie	The novice attacker, known as a *script kiddie,* has limited technical knowledge and is motivated by a desire to gain and display technical skills. The script kiddie will use simple means, such as virus code samples or automated attack tools available on the Internet, to mount attacks that might have no specific target or any reasonable goal other than gaining attention or proving technical abilities. These tools are often known as "script kiddie tools" and are often used by security professionals for testing.
Electronic vandal	This attacker simply wants to cause as much damage as possible, without any particular target or goal. The motivation might be for fun, or to gain attention or admiration, or stem from some type of social or personal resentment against a person or institution.
Cyberterrorist	This type of attacker attempts to blackmail companies in exchange for not stealing or damaging their data and websites. The motivation of this type of attacker is usually to cause disruption and chaos.

ACTIVITY 2-1
Identifying Social Engineering Attacks

Scenario:

Your IT department wants to know when they are being attacked and what type of attacks are occurring. As the new security administrator for your organization, you will be responsible for determining which events are true social engineering attacks and which are false alarms. Your organization's upper management is concerned about these false alarms and has tightened security too much in response, and they want to make sure they know the difference between attacks and normal activity. They do not want customers or users to be halted in their tracks when they are performing normal tasks with no malicious intent. They have asked you to analyze a list of recent network interactions and classify them as true social engineering attacks or as false alarms.

1. **Social engineering attempt or false alarm? A supposed customer calls the help desk and states that she cannot connect to the e-commerce website to check her order status. She would also like a user name and password. The user gives a valid customer company name, but is not listed as a contact in the customer database. The user does not know the correct company code or customer ID.**

    ___ Social engineering attempt

    ___ False alarm

2. **Social engineering attempt or false alarm? The VP of sales is in the middle of a presentation to a group of key customers and accidentally logs off. She urgently needs to continue with the presentation, but forgets her password. You recognize her voice on the line, but she is supposed to have her boss make the request according to the company password security policy.**

    ___ Social engineering attempt

    ___ False alarm

3. **Social engineering attempt or false alarm? A new accountant was hired and would like to know if he can have the installation source files for the accounting software package, so that he can install it on his computer himself and start work immediately. Last year, someone internal compromised company accounting records, so distribution of the accounting application is tightly controlled. You have received all the proper documentation for the request from his supervisor and there is an available license for the software. However, general IT policies state that the IT department must perform all software installations and upgrades.**

    ___ Social engineering attempt

    ___ False alarm

4. **Social engineering attempt or false alarm? Christine receives an instant message asking for her account name and password. The person sending the message says that the request is from the IT department, because they need to do a backup of Christine's local hard drive.**

___ Social engineering attempt

___ False alarm

5. **Social engineering attempt or false alarm? Rachel gets an email with an attachment that is named NewVirusDefinitions.vbs. The name in the email is the same as the IT software manager, but the email address is from an account outside the company.**

___ Social engineering attempt

___ False alarm

6. **Social engineering attempt or false alarm? A user calls the help desk stating that he is a phone technician needing the password to configure the phone and voice-mail system.**

___ Social engineering attempt

___ False alarm

7. **Social engineering attempt or false alarm? A vendor team requests access to the building to fix an urgent problem with a piece of equipment. Although the team has no work order and the security guard was not notified of the visit, the team members are wearing shirts and hats from the preferred vendor.**

___ Social engineering attempt

___ False alarm

8. **Social engineering attempt or false alarm? The CEO of the organization needs to get access to market research data immediately. You definitely recognize her voice, but a proper request form has not been filled out to modify the permissions. She states that normally she would fill out the form and should not be an exception, but she urgently needs the data.**

___ Social engineering attempt

___ False alarm

9. **Social engineering attempt or false alarm? A purchasing manager is browsing a list of products on a vendor's website when a window opens claiming that software has detected several thousand files on his computer that are infected with viruses. Instructions in the official-looking window indicate the user should click a link to install software that will remove these infections.**

___ Social engineering attempt

___ False alarm

TOPIC B
Physical Threats and Vulnerabilities

You have seen how social engineering attacks can be very dangerous to an organization. There are many other attack categories that can threaten your organization, starting with the physical components of your network and your organization's overall physical plant. In this topic, you will identify the types of attacks that are directed against the physical resources in your enterprise.

It is important to keep attackers off your network's computers, but it is also important to keep them from stealing, compromising, or destroying the hardware in which you have invested, or attaching unauthorized hardware to your systems or networks. In order to do that, you need to know about the kinds of attacks that can be mounted against the hardware inside those systems, as well as the vulnerabilities of your organization's overall physical plant.

Physical Security

Physical security refers to the implementation and practice of various control mechanisms that are intended to restrict physical access to facilities. In addition, physical security involves increasing or assuring the reliability of certain critical infrastructure elements such as electrical power, data networks, and fire suppression systems. Physical security may be challenged by a wide variety of events or situations, including:

● Facilities intrusions.

● Electrical grid failures.

● Fire.

● Personnel illnesses.

● Or, data network interruptions.

Physical Security Threats and Vulnerabilities

Physical security threats and vulnerabilities can come from many different areas.

Physical Security Threat and Vulnerability	Description
Internal	It is important to always consider what is happening inside an organization, especially when physical security is concerned. For example, disgruntled employees may be a source of physical sabotage of important security-related resources.
External	It is impossible for any organization to fully control external security threats. For example, an external power failure is usually beyond a security specialist's control because most organizations use a local power company as their source of electrical power. However, risks posed by external power failures may be mitigated by implementing devices such as an Uninterruptible Power Supply (UPS) or a generator.

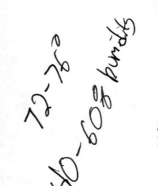

Physical Security Threat and Vulnerability	Description
Natural	Although natural threats are easy to overlook, they can pose a significant threat to the physical security of a facility. Buildings and rooms that contain important computing assets should be protected against likely weather-related problems including tornados, hurricanes, snow storms, and floods.
Man-made	Whether intentional or accidental, people can cause a number of physical threats. For example, a backhoe operator may accidentally dig up fiber optic cables and disable external network access. On the other hand, a disgruntled employee may choose to exact revenge by deliberately cutting fiber optic cables. Man-made threats can be internal or external.

Hardware Attacks

Definition:

A *hardware attack* is an attack that targets a computer's physical components and peripherals, including its hard disk, motherboard, keyboard, network cabling, or smart card reader. One goal of a hardware attack is the destruction of the hardware itself or acquisition of sensitive information through theft or other means. A second goal of a hardware attack is to make important data or devices unavailable through theft or vandalism. This second goal is meant to disrupt a company's business or cause embarrassment due to data loss.

Example:

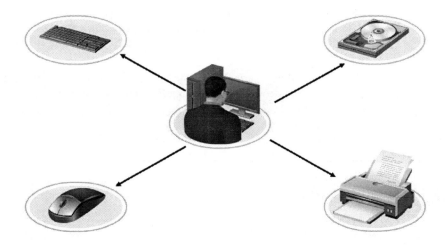

Figure 2-3: Hardware attacks.

Example: Keylogging

One type of hardware attack is a technique known as keylogging, which uses software or hardware to capture each keystroke a user types. Keylogging can capture passwords as well as other sensitive data. There are a wide variety of software keyloggers available on the Internet.

Environmental Threats and Vulnerabilities

Environmental threats pose system security risks and can be addressed with specific mitigation techniques.

Environmental Threat	Effects and Mitigations
Fire	Fire, whether natural or deliberately set, is a serious environmental security threat because it can destroy hardware and therefore the data contained in it. In addition, it is hazardous to people and systems. You need to ensure that key systems are installed in a fire-resistant facility, and that there are high-quality fire detection and suppression systems on site so that the damage due to fire is reduced.
Hurricanes and tornados	Catastrophic weather events such as hurricanes and tornados are major security threats due to the magnitude of the damage they can cause to hardware and data. You need to ensure that your information systems are well contained and that your physical plant is built to appropriate codes and standards so that damage due to severe weather is reduced.
Flood	A flood is another major security threat that can cause as much damage as fire can. You should check the history of an area to see if you are in a flood plain before constructing your physical plant, and follow appropriate building codes as well as purchase flood insurance. When possible, construct the building so that the lowest floor is above flood level; this saves the systems when flooding does occur. Spatial planning together with protective planning in concurrence with building regulations and functional regulations are precautionary measures that should be looked into as well.
Extreme temperature	Extreme temperatures, especially heat, can cause some sensitive hardware components to melt and degrade, resulting in data loss. You can avoid this threat by implementing controls that keep the temperature in your data center within acceptable ranges.
Extreme humidity	Extreme humidity can cause computer components, data storage media, and other devices to rust, deteriorate, and degrade and results in data loss. You can avoid this threat by ensuring that there is enough ventilation in your data centers and storage locations, and by using temperature and humidity controls and monitors.

ACTIVITY 2-2
Identifying Physical Threats and Vulnerabilities

Scenario:

Your manager, the security administrator in your organization, has asked that you help complete a report for senior management about the possible security risks you face and some suggested solutions. You have been presented with a list of scenarios and have been asked to identify whether the type of attack described in each scenario is a physical security attack.

1. **A disgruntled employee removes the UPS on a critical server system and then cuts power to the system, causing costly downtime. This physical threat is a(n): (Select all that apply.)**

   a) Internal threat.

   b) External threat.

   c) Man-made threat.

   d) False alarm.

2. **A power failure has occurred due to a tree branch falling on a power line outside your facility, and there is no UPS, or a generator. This physical threat is a(n):**

   a) Internal threat.

   b) External threat.

   c) Man-made threat.

   d) False alarm.

3. **A backhoe operator on a nearby construction site has accidently dug up fiber optic cables, thus disabling remote network access. This physical threat is a(n): (Select all that apply.)**

   a) Internal threat.

   b) External threat.

   c) Man-made threat.

   d) False alarm.

4. **While entering the building through the rear security door, an employee realizes he has left his car keys in his car door lock. He has already swiped his badge to open the door, so he props it open with his briefcase while he returns to his car to retrieve his keys. He has the door in view at all times and no one else enters while the door is propped open. He locks the door behind him once he is in the building. This is a(n):**

   a) Internal attack.

   b) External attack.

   c) Man-made attack.

   d) False alarm.

TOPIC C
Network-Based Threats

You reviewed the physical aspects of security. Now you will focus on the different network-based threats to be aware of and how they can be targeted towards getting access to and breaking through network technologies to access information. In this topic, you will identify the types of attacks that target networks and how you can guard against specific types of network-based threats.

The network is the lifeblood of today's business, whether it is your company's local area network (LAN) or your e-commerce connection to the Internet. Most businesses today rely on their networks to be the base of all operations. A network allows people to stay connected to each other in an organized way and allows businesses to access and share information as quickly and securely as possible. A network-based threat can compromise daily business interactions and can be detrimental to keeping information private and secure. This topic will help you identify the network attacks that you will need to be aware of in order to protect your networks.

TCP/IP Basics

Because Transmission Control Protocol/Internet Protocol (TCP/IP) is the standard network protocol used today, understanding some TCP/IP basics is a good start to understanding how network attacks may be launched. TCP/IP is a layered suite of many protocols. By adding header information to the data in a network packet, a protocol at a given layer on the sending host can communicate with the protocol at the corresponding layer at the receiving host.

The logical endpoints of a connection between hosts are called *ports,* and a given port can be open, to allow communication of a certain type, or closed, to prevent it. Each host on a TCP/IP network receives a numeric address as well as a descriptive name. Names are organized hierarchically in domains and mapped to hosts through the *Domain Name System (DNS)* service.

TCP/IP Layers
The following table describes the layered architecture of TCP/IP in more detail.

Layer	Description	Major Protocols and Utilities
Application	Provides utilities that enable client applications on an individual system to access the networking software.	Network Basic Input/Output System (NetBIOS): A simple, broadcast-based naming service.
		Sockets: A piece of software within an operating system that connects an application with a network protocol, so that the application can request network services from the operating system.
		File Transfer Protocol (FTP): Enables the transfer of files between a user's workstation and a remote host.

Layer	Description	Major Protocols and Utilities
Transport	Provides connection and communication services.	Transmission Control Protocol (TCP): A connection-oriented, guaranteed-delivery protocol. This means that it not only sends data, but also waits for acknowledgement (ACK) and fixes errors when possible. User Datagram Protocol (UDP): Like TCP but connectionless and based on best-effort delivery; data is sent without waiting for acknowledgement and there is no attempt to fix errors.
Internet	Provides addressing, naming, and routing.	IP: Manages numeric host addresses. Address assignment is typically done automatically through a separate service called Dynamic Host Configuration Protocol (DHCP). Internet Control Message Protocol (ICMP): Tests for communication between devices.
Physical	Enables the network software to transmit data on the physical network, via the network adapter cards and network media.	Various Ethernet and wireless specifications, not specific to TCP/IP.

Port Scanning Attacks

Definition:

A *port scanning attack* is a type of network attack where a potential attacker scans the computers and devices that are connected to the Internet or other networks to see which TCP and UDP ports are listening and which services on the system are active. Port scans can be easily automated, so almost any system on the Internet will be scanned almost constantly. Some monitoring software can detect port scans, or they might happen without your knowledge.

Example:

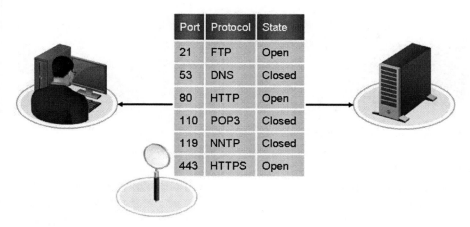

Port	Protocol	State
21	FTP	Open
53	DNS	Closed
80	HTTP	Open
110	POP3	Closed
119	NNTP	Closed
443	HTTPS	Open

Figure 2-4: A port scanning attack.

Port Scanning Utilities

There are many utilities available that potential attackers can use to scan ports on networks, including Nmap, SuperScan, and Strobe. Many utilities can be downloaded for free from the Internet. Performing port scanning attacks is often the first step an attacker takes to identify live systems and open ports to launch further attacks with other tools.

Example: Xmas Attack

The Xmas Scan is available in popular port scanners such as Nmap. It is mainly used to check which machines are alive or reachable, and subsequently what ports are open or responding, so that those machines or ports can be used as an avenue for a follow-up attack. The type of port scanning attack uses an Xmas packet with all the flags turned on in the TCP header of the packet. The name "Xmas" refers to all the flags being "on" (like lights) and so a packet is "lit up like a Christmas tree."

This scan is commonly known as a stealth scan due to its ability to hide the scan in progress, and its ability to pass undetected through some popular firewalls, intrusion detection systems (IDSes), and systems. However, most modern-day intrusion prevention systems (IPSes) can detect this type of scan.

Eavesdropping Attacks

Definition:

An *eavesdropping attack* or *sniffing attack* uses special monitoring software to gain access to private network communications, either to steal the content of the communication itself or to obtain user names and passwords for future software attacks. Attackers can eavesdrop on both wired and wireless network communications. On a wired network, the attacker must have physical access to the network or tap in to the network cable. On a wireless network, an attacker needs a device capable of receiving signals from the wireless network. Eavesdropping is very hard to detect, unless you spot an unknown computer leasing an IP address from a DHCP server.

Example:

Figure 2-5: An eavesdropping attack.

Eavesdropping Utilities

Many utilities are available that will monitor and capture network traffic. Some of these tools can only sniff the traffic that is sent to or received by the computer on which they are installed. Other tools are capable of scaling up to scan very large corporate networks. Examples of these tools include: Wireshark, the Microsoft Network Monitor Capture utility, tcpdump, and dsniff.

Replay Attacks

Definition:

A *replay attack* is a network attack where an attacker captures network traffic and stores it for retransmitting at a later time to gain unauthorized access to a specific host or a network. This attack is particularly successful when an attacker captures packets that contain user names, passwords, or other authentication data. In most cases, replay attacks are never discovered.

Example:

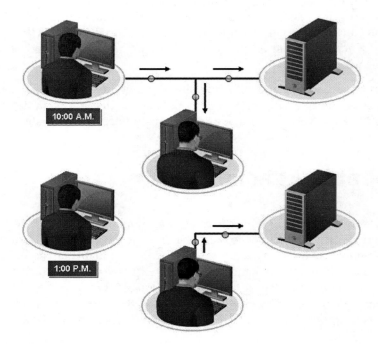

Figure 2-6: A replay attack.

Social Network Attacks

Social network attacks are attacks that are targeted towards social networking sites such as Facebook, Twitter, and MySpace.

Social Network Attack	Description
Evil twin attack and *account phishing*	An evil twin attack on a social networking site is an attack where an attacker creates a social network account to impersonate a genuine user. Then, when the friends of that user allow the attacker to become friends with them or join a group, the attacker can gain access to various personal details and even company information if a company has a page on the site. This is often preceded by account phishing, in which an attacker creates an account and joins the friends list of an individual just to try to obtain information about the individual and his circle of friends or colleagues.
Drive-by download	A program that is automatically installed on a computer when a user accesses a malicious site, even without clicking on a link or giving consent. This often happens when a user searches for a social networking site and selects a site using a fraudulent link. Sometimes a drive-by download may be packaged invisibly together with a program that a user requests to download.
Clickjacking	An attack that forces a user to unintentionally click a link. The attacker uses opaque layers or multiple transparent layers to trick the user. This happens when a user is going through a fraudulent networking site or a site that has been hijacked by an attacker.
Password stealer	A type of software that, when installed on a system, will be able to capture all the passwords and user names entered into the *instant messaging (IM)* application or social network site that it was designed for. This information is sent back to the attacker who can use it for fraudulent purposes.
Spamming	Within social networking, spamming refers to sending unsolicited bulk messages by misusing the electronic messaging services inside the social networking site.

 Social networking sites are also subject to various general attack types such as Denial of Service (DoS) attacks.

URL Shortening Service

A *URL shortening service* makes it easier to share links on social networking sites by abbreviating the Uniform Resource Locators (URLs). Though they are usually benign, this creates a vulnerability that attackers can exploit because the shortened URL hides the true target of the link. A user may be directed to a fraudulent site that is a source of malware or other threats.

Man-in-the-Middle Attacks

Definition:

A *man-in-the-middle attack* is a form of eavesdropping where the attacker makes an independent connection between two victims (two clients or a client and a server) and relays information between the two victims as if they are directly talking to each other over a closed connection, when in reality the attacker is controlling the information that travels between the two victims. During the process, the attacker can view or steal information to use it fraudulently.

Example:

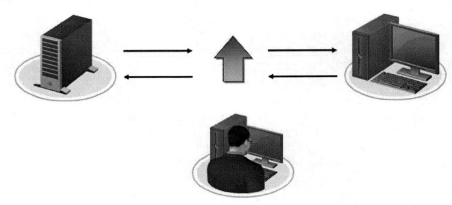

Figure 2-7: A man-in-the-middle attack.

Example: A Man-in-the-Middle Attack

In a typical man-in-the-middle attack, the attacker sets up a host on a network with IP forwarding enabled and a network-monitoring utility installed to capture and analyze packets. After analyzing network traffic to determine which server would make an attractive target:

1. The attacker intercepts packets from a legitimate client that are destined for the server.

2. The attacker's computer sends a fake reply to the client.

3. The attacker's computer forwards a fake packet to the server, which is modified so the attacker's computer looks like the original sender.

4. The server replies to the attacker's computer.

5. The attacker's computer replies to the server as it if were the original client.

6. The attacker stores any valuable information contained in the packets, such as sensitive data or user credentials, for use in future attacks.

Purpose of a Man-in-the-Middle Attack

Man-in-the-middle attacks are used to gain access to authentication and network infrastructure information for future attacks, or to gain direct access to the packet contents. Generally, there will be no signs that a man-in-the-middle attack is in progress or has just taken place.

DoS Attacks

Definition:

A denial of service *(DoS) attack* is a type of network attack in which an attacker attempts to disrupt or disable systems that provide network services by various means, including:

- Flooding a network link with data to consume all available bandwidth.
- Sending data designed to exploit known flaws in an application.
- Sending multiple service requests to consume a system's resources.
- And, flooding a user's email inbox with spam messages, causing the genuine messages to get bounced back to the sender.

 Nearly anything can cause a DoS attack if it interrupts or disables a system. For example, pulling a plug from a server will cause a DoS condition.

Example:

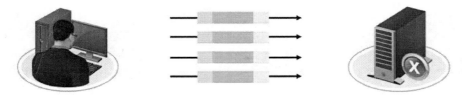

Figure 2-8: A DoS attack.

DoS Targets

The attack can target any service or network device, but is usually mounted against servers or routers, preventing them from responding to legitimate network requests. A DoS attack can also be caused by something as simple as disconnecting a network cable.

DDoS Attacks

Definition:

A *Distributed Denial of Service (DDoS) attack* is a type of DoS attack that uses multiple computers on disparate networks to launch the attack from many simultaneous sources. The attacker introduces unauthorized software that turns the computer into a *zombie* or *drone* that directs the computers to launch the attack.

Example:

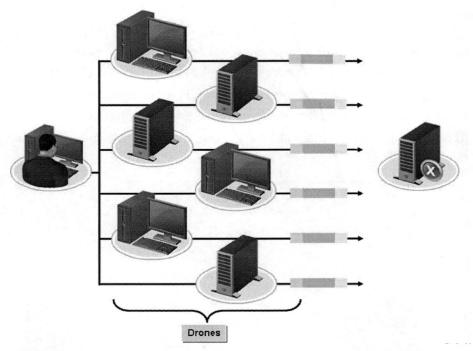

Figure 2-9: A DDoS attack.

Symptoms of DoS and DDoS Attacks

DoS attacks manifest themselves in a variety of ways, including:

- Sudden and overwhelming service requests from hosts outside your network.
- A sudden and unexplained drop in the amount of available Internet bandwidth.
- A sudden and overwhelming drain on a specific resource in a system, causing unusual behavior or freezes.

Types of DoS Attacks

There are many types of DoS attacks.

DoS Attack Type	Description
ICMP flood	This attack is based on sending high volumes of ICMP ping packets to a target. Common names for ICMP flood attacks are *Smurf attacks* and *ping floods*. Modern systems and networks are usually well-protected against these types of attacks.
UDP flood	In this attack, the attacker attempts to overwhelm the target system with UDP ping requests. Often the source IP address is spoofed, creating a DoS condition for the spoofed IP.

DoS Attack Type	Description
SYN flood	In this attack, an attacker sends countless requests for a TCP connection (SYN messages) to an FTP server, web server, or any other target system attached to the Internet. The target server then responds to each request with a SYN-ACK message and, in doing so, creates a space in memory that will be used for the TCP session when the remote host (in this case, the attacker) responds with its own SYN-ACK message. However, the attacker has crafted the SYN message (usually through IP spoofing) so that the target server sends its initial SYN-ACK response to a computer that will never reply. So, the target server has reserved memory for numerous TCP connections that will never be completed. Eventually, the target server will stop responding to legitimate requests because its memory resources are flooded with incomplete TCP connections.
Buffer overflow	Many systems and services are vulnerable to a buffer overflow condition, in which too much data is fed into a fixed-length memory buffer, resulting in adjacent areas of memory being overwritten. Attackers can exploit buffer overflow vulnerabilities by deliberately invoking buffer overflow conditions, introducing bad data into memory, thus opening the door for any number of subsequent attack methods or simply causing the system to cease to function or respond. A buffer overflow can also occur when there is an excessive amount of incomplete fragmented traffic on a network. In this case, an attacker may attempt to pass through security systems or IDSes.
Reflected DoS attack	In reflected DOS and DDoS attacks, a forged source IP address is used when sending requests to a large number of computers. This causes those systems to send a reply to the target system, causing a DoS condition.

Session Hijacking

Definition:

A *session hijacking attack* involves exploiting a computer in session to obtain unauthorized access to an organization's network or services. It involves stealing an active session cookie that is used to authenticate a user to a remote server and using that to control the session thereafter. The main intent in session hijacking attacks is to execute denial of service to either the client's system or the server system, or in some cases, both systems.

Example:

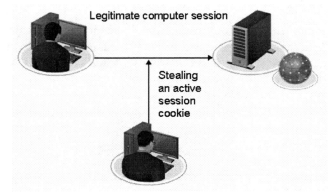

Figure 2-10: Session hijacking.

P2P Attacks

Definition:

Peer-to-peer (P2P) attacks are launched by malware propagating through *P2P* networks. P2P networks typically have a shared command and control architecture, making it harder to detect an attacker. A P2P attack can be used to launch huge DoS attacks. Within a P2P network, personal computers with high-speed connections can be compromised by malware such as viruses and Trojans. An attacker can then control all these compromised computers to launch a DDoS attack.

 Some famous P2P programs are Napster, Kazaa, Vuze, and Tixati, which enable fast transfers of files between computers and networks.

Example:

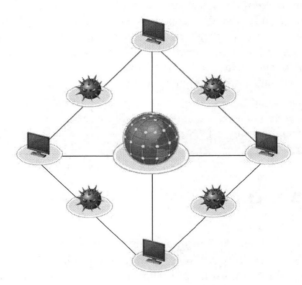

Figure 2-11: A P2P attack.

ARP Poisoning

Address Resolution Protocol (ARP) is the mechanism by which individual hardware Media Access Control (MAC) addresses are matched to an IP address on a network. *ARP poisoning* occurs when an attacker with access to the target network redirects an IP address to the MAC address of a computer that is not the intended recipient. At this point, the attacker could choose to capture and alter network traffic before forwarding it to the correct destination, or create a DoS condition by pointing the selected IP address at a non-existent MAC address.

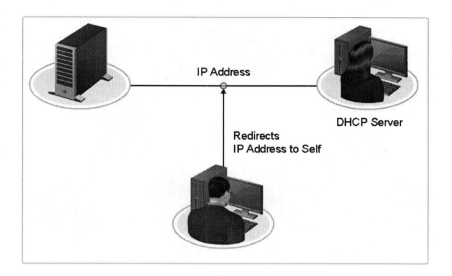

Figure 2-12: ARP poisoning.

The Physical Network Address

Switches generally deliver packets based on a unique physical address that is individually assigned to every network adapter board by the adapter's manufacturer. No two network adapters in the world are supposed to have the same physical address. This address is also referred to as the *MAC* address because these addresses operate at the Media Access Control sub-layer of the Data Link layer of the OSI network model. For more information on the OSI network model, see **http://www.webopedia.com/quick_ref/OSI_Layers.asp**

Transitive Access Attacks

Transitive access is the access given to certain members in an organization to use data on a system without the need for authenticating themselves. The information regarding the list of members that have transitive access is usually saved in a log or host file. If an attacker can access and modify the file, then that will give transitive access to all data and programs to the attacker. Therefore a *transitive access attack* is an attack that takes advantage of the transitive access given in order to steal or destroy data on a system.

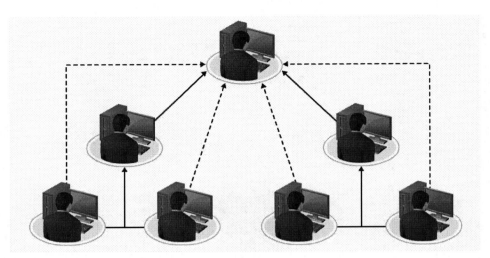

Figure 2-13: *Transitive access attack.*

DNS Vulnerabilities

A DNS system keeps tables of which IP addresses should be associated with a particular domain name. There are some DNS vulnerabilities.

DNS Vulnerability	Description
DNS poisoning	In this technique, an attacker exploits the traditionally open nature of the DNS system to redirect a domain name to an IP address of the attacker's choosing. Once the domain name has been redirected, the attacker can capture data from or serve malware to visitors to the target domain name. A DoS condition could also be created by directing the target domain name to a non-existent IP address.
DNS hijacking	In this technique, an attacker sets up a rogue DNS server. This rogue DNS server responds to legitimate requests with IP addresses for malicious or non-existent websites. In some cases, Internet Service Providers (ISPs) have implemented DNS hijacking to serve advertisements to users who attempt to navigate to non-existent domain names.

Legitimate Use of DNS Spoofing

Some network hardware has DNS spoofing capabilities built in to allow routers to act as proxy DNS servers in the event that designated primary DNS servers are unavailable, which could occur in an Internet connection outage.

ACTIVITY 2-3
Classifying Network-Based Threats

Scenario:
You and Ronald, your IT administrator, have been investigating poor performance on the company network. You are certain that your systems are under attack, but now you need to know the types of attacks that are occurring so that you can devise an appropriate response. To determine the exact attack methods, you review incidents.

1. **While you are connected to another host on your network, the connection is suddenly dropped. When you review the logs at the other host, it appears as if the connection is still active. This could be a(n):**

    a) IP spoofing attack.

    b) Replay attack.

    c) Man-in-the-middle attack.

    d) Session hijacking attack.

2. **Your e-commerce web server is getting extremely slow. Customers are calling stating that it is taking a long time to place an order on your site. This could be a(n):**

    a) DNS poisoning attack.

    b) DoS attack.

    c) Backdoor attack.

    d) ARP poisoning attack.

3. **Tina, the network analysis guru in your organization, analyzes a network trace capture file and discovers that packets have been intercepted and retransmitted to both a sender and a receiver during an active session. This could be a(n):**

    a) IP spoofing attack.

    b) Session hijacking attack.

    c) Replay attack.

    d) Man-in-the-middle attack.

4. **Your intranet webmaster, Tim, has noticed an entry in a log file from an IP address that is within the range of addresses used on your network. But, Tim does not recognize the computer name as valid. Your network administrator, Deb, checks the DHCP server and finds out that the IP address is not similar to any in their list of IP addresses in that particular domain. This could be a(n):**

   a) IP spoofing attack.

   b) Replay attack.

   c) Man-in-the-middle attack.

   d) Session hijacking attack.

5. **Match the network-based attack with the corresponding description.**

___ Social network attack	a.	An attack that is launched by malware propagating through peer-to-peer networks.
___ P2P attack	b.	A network attack where an attacker inserts himself between two hosts to gain access to their data transmissions.
___ Eavesdropping attack	c.	An attack that uses special monitoring software to gain access to private network communications to steal the content of the communication.
___ Man-in-the-middle attack	d.	A network attack where an attacker captures network traffic and stores it for retransmitting at a later time.
___ Replay attack	e.	An attack that is targeted towards popular websites and services like Facebook, Twitter, and MySpace.

6. **True or False? A DNS poisoning attack can be used to cause a DoS condition.**

   ___ True

   ___ False

TOPIC D

Wireless Threats and Vulnerabilities

You identified the network-based threats that can affect information systems. Now, you will focus on the wireless threats and vulnerabilities that can cause damage to your internal systems. Wireless networks are everywhere, and protecting devices against wireless vulnerabilities is crucial to protect sensitive data from unauthorized access.

Wireless networks have quickly become the norm in business today. Most organizations have both a wired and a wireless network for employees to access while on the move within their facilities. Because of this trend, securing an organization's wireless network against common threats and vulnerabilities is just as important as securing the physical network systems and devices. Understanding the potential threats and vulnerabilities will allow you to successfully secure the wireless components of an organization's information systems infrastructure.

Wireless Security

Definition:

Wireless security is any method of securing your wireless LAN network to prevent unauthorized network access and network data theft. You need to ensure that authorized users can connect to the network without any hindrances. Wireless networks are more vulnerable to attacks than any other network system. For one thing, most wireless devices such as laptops, mobile phones, and personal digital assistants (PDAs) search and connect automatically to the access point offering the best signal, which can be coming from an attacker. Wireless transmissions can also be scanned or sniffed out of the air, with no need to access physical network media. Such attacks can be avoided by using relevant security protocols.

Example:

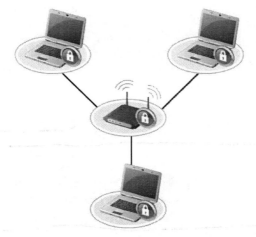

Figure 2-14: *A wireless security design.*

Wireless Threats and Vulnerabilities

Wireless networks have an increasing number of specific vulnerabilities.

Wireless Threat and Vulnerability	Description
Rogue access point	This is an unauthorized wireless access point on a corporate or private network. Rogue access points can cause considerable damage to an organization's data. They are not detected easily, and can allow private network access to many unauthorized users with the proper devices. A rogue access point can allow man-in-the-middle attacks and access to private information. Organizations should protect themselves from this type of attack by implementing techniques to constantly monitor the system, such as installing an IDS.
Evil twins	These are rogue access points on a network that appear to be legitimate. Although they can be installed both in corporate or private networks, typically they are found in public Wi-Fi hotspots where users do not connect transparently and automatically as they do in a corporate network, but rather select available networks from a list. Evil twins can be more dangerous than other rogue access points because the user thinks that the wireless signal is genuine, making it difficult to differentiate from a valid access point with the same name.
Interference	In wireless networking, this is the phenomenon by which radio waves interfere with the 802.11 wireless signals. It usually occurs at home because of various electronic devices, such as microwaves, operating in a bandwidth close to that of the wireless network. When this occurs, it causes the 802.11 signals to wait before transmitting and the wait can be indefinite at times.
Bluejacking	This is a method used by attackers to send out unwanted *Bluetooth* signals from PDAs, mobile phones, and laptops to other Bluetooth-enabled devices. Because Bluetooth has a 30-foot transmission limit, this is a very close-range attack. With the advanced technology available today, attackers can send out unsolicited messages along with images and video. These types of signals can lead to many different types of threats. They can lead to device malfunctions, or even propagate viruses, including Trojan horses. Users should reject anonymous contacts, and should configure their mobile devices to non-discoverable mode.
Bluesnarfing	This is a method in which attackers gain access to unauthorized information on a wireless device using a Bluetooth connection within the 30-foot Bluetooth transmission limit. Unlike bluejacking, access to wireless devices such as PDAs, mobile phones, and laptops by bluesnarfing can lead to the exploitation of private information including email messages, contact information, calendar entries, images, videos, and any data stored on the device.
War driving and *war chalking*	War driving is the act of searching for instances of wireless networks using wireless tracking devices such as PDAs, mobile phones, or laptops. It locates wireless access points while traveling, which can be exploited to obtain unauthorized Internet access and potentially steal data. This process can be automated using a GPS device and war driving software. War chalking is the act of using symbols to mark off a sidewalk or wall to indicate that there is an open wireless network which may be offering Internet access.

Wireless Threat and Vulnerability	Description
IV attack	In this attack, the attacker is able to predict or control the *initialization vector (IV)* of an encryption process. This gives the attacker access to view the encrypted data that is supposed to be hidden from everyone else except the authentic user or network.
Packet sniffing	This can be used as an attack on wireless networks where an attacker captures data and registers data flows, which allow the attacker to analyze the data contained in a packet. In its benign form, it also helps organizations monitor their own networks against attackers.

Wireless Security Tools

There are common tools that can be used for war driving and war chalking:

- NetStumbler
- Kismet
- Aircrack
- Airsnort

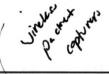

 In the terms war driving and war chalking, "war" stands for wireless access receiver.

ACTIVITY 2-4
Discussing Wireless Security, Threats, and Vulnerabilities

Scenario:
You are the administrator for a large organization and your manager has asked you to look into setting up the wireless network. During the setup, you are faced with certain issues which relate to attacks that you have learned about. How well can you identify the types of wireless attacks you are facing?

1. John is given a laptop for official use and is on a business trip. When he arrives at his hotel, he turns on his laptop and finds a wireless access point with the name of the hotel, which he connects to for sending official communications. He may become a victim of which wireless threat?

    a) Interference

    b) War driving

    c) Bluesnarfing

    d) Rogue access point

2. A new administrator in your company is in the process of installing a new wireless device. He is called away to attend an urgent meeting before he can secure the wireless network, and without realizing it, he forgot to switch the device off. A person with a mobile device who is passing the building takes advantage of the open network and hacks the network. Your company may become vulnerable to which type of wireless threat?

    a) Interference

    b) War driving

    c) Bluesnarfing

    d) Rogue access point

3. Every time Margaret decided to work at home, she would get frustrated with the poor wireless connection. But when she gets to her office, the wireless connection seems normal. What might have been one of the factors affecting Margaret's wireless connection when she worked at home?

    a) Bluesnarfing

    b) Interference

    c) IV attack

    d) Evil twins attack

4. **Chuck, a sales executive, is attending meetings at a professional conference that is also being attended by representatives of other companies in his field. At the conference, he uses his smartphone with a Bluetooth headset to stay in touch with clients. A few days after the conference, he finds that competitors' sales representatives are getting in touch with his key contacts and influencing them by revealing what he thought was private information from his email and calendar. Chuck is a victim of which wireless threat?**

   a) Packet sniffing

   b) Bluejacking

   c) Bluesnarfing

   d) Rogue access point

5. **Match the wireless threat with its description.**

   ___ Interference

   ___ Evil twins

   ___ War chalking

   ___ Packet sniffing

   ___ Bluejacking

   a. A threat where a rogue access point in a public access location has been configured so that it appears to be genuine.

   b. A threat where the attacker sends out unwanted signals from a mobile device with unsolicited content.

   c. A threat where an attacker captures data and registers data flows to analyze what data is contained in a packet.

   d. A threat where symbols are used to mark off a sidewalk or wall to indicate that there is an open wireless network which may be offering Internet access.

   e. A threat where the wireless signal is jammed due to other wireless signals operating in the area.

TOPIC E
Software-Based Threats

You have learned about attacks against the human component of information systems, as well as the physical and network components, but there are many other types of security threats that can be aimed directly against the software elements of the system. In this topic, you will identify the types of attacks that target your operating systems and other software.

A software attack against the computers in your organization can bring your company to its knees, and part of your job as a security professional is to prevent that. But, as you know, you cannot protect against what you cannot recognize. This topic will help you identify the software attacks that you will need to be on guard against.

Software Attacks

Definition:

A *software attack* is any attack against software resources including operating systems, applications, protocols, and files. The goal of a software attack is to disrupt or disable the software running on the target system, or to somehow exploit the target system to gain access to the target system, to other systems, or to a network. Many software attacks are designed to surreptitiously gain control of a computer so that the attacker can use that computer in the future, often for profit or further malicious activity.

Example:

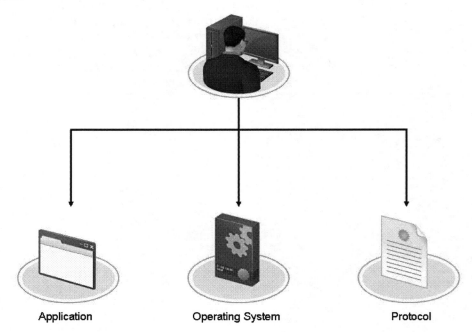

Figure 2-15: A software attack.

Software Attack Combinations

A software attack might be used by itself or in combination with another type of attack, such as a social engineering attack.

Malicious Code Attacks

Definition:

A *malicious code attack* is a type of software attack where an attacker inserts some type of undesired or unauthorized software, or malware, into a target system. In the past, many malicious code attacks were intended to disrupt or disable an operating system or an application, or force the target system to disrupt or disable other systems. More recent malicious code attacks attempt to remain hidden on the target system, utilizing available resources to the attacker's advantage.

Potential uses of malicious code include launching DoS attacks on other systems; hosting illicit or illegal data; skimming personal or business information for the purposes of identity theft, profit, or extortion; or displaying unsolicited advertisements.

Example:

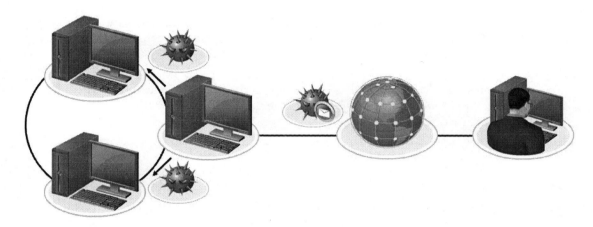

Figure 2-16: *A malicious code attack.*

Example: Viruses

Virus attacks are the most well-known type of malicious code attacks.

Evidence of a Malicious Code Attack

Malicious code is often combined with social engineering to convince a user that the malware is from a trusted or benign source. Typically, you will see the results of malicious code in corrupted applications, data files, and system files, unsolicited pop-up advertisements, counterfeit virus scan or software update notifications, or reduced system performance or increased network traffic. Any of these could result in malfunctioning applications and operating systems.

Types of Malicious Code Attacks

There are various types of malicious code attacks that target a system.

Malicious Code Type	Description
Virus	A sample of code that spreads from one computer to another by attaching itself to other files. The code in a virus executes when the file it is attached to is opened. Frequently, viruses are intended to enable further attacks, send data back to the attacker, or even corrupt or destroy data.
Worm	A piece of code that spreads from one computer to another on its own, not by attaching itself to another file. Like a virus, a worm can enable further attacks, transmit data, or corrupt or erase files.
Trojan horse	An insidious type of malware that is itself a software attack and can pave the way for a number of other types of attacks. There is a social engineering component to a Trojan horse attack since the user has to be fooled into executing it.
Logic bomb	A piece of code that sits dormant on a target computer until it is triggered by a specific event, such as a specific date. Once the code is triggered, the logic bomb "detonates," and performs whatever actions it was programed to do. Often, this includes erasing and corrupting data on the target system.
Spyware	Surreptitiously installed malicious software that is intended to track and report the usage of a target system, or collect other data the author wishes to obtain. Data collected can include web browsing history, personal information, banking and other financial information, and user names and passwords.
Adware	Software that automatically displays or downloads advertisements when it is used. While not all adware is malicious, many adware programs have been associated with spyware and other types of malicious software. Also, it can reduce user productivity by slowing down systems and simply by creating annoyances.
Rootkit	Code that is intended to take full or partial control of a system at the lowest levels. Rootkits often attempt to hide themselves from monitoring or detection, and modify low-level system files when integrating themselves into a system. Rootkits can be used for non-malicious purposes such as virtualization; however, most rootkit infections install backdoors, spyware, or other malicious code once they have control of the target system.
Botnet	A set of computers that has been infected by a control program called a bot that enables attackers to exploit them to mount attacks. Typically, black hats use botnets for DDoS attacks, sending spam email, and mining for personal information or passwords.
Spam	Typically, black hats use spam to deliver malware.

[Handwritten annotations:]

multiport virus — attack both system and non system files

retro virus — Not based off of on other virus. They attack anti virus software

boot sector virus — alter the bootrecord and boot files

Armored virus — wrp itself in protection code

Password Attacks

Definition:

A *password attack* is any type of attack in which the attacker attempts to obtain and make use of passwords illegitimately. The attacker can guess or steal passwords, or crack encrypted password files. A password attack can show up in audit logs as repeatedly failed logons and then a successful logon, or as several successful logon attempts at unusual times or locations.

Example:

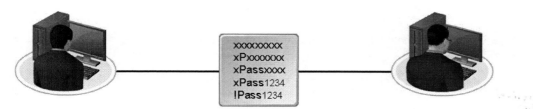

Figure 2-17: A password attack.

Protecting Password Databases

Attackers know the storage locations of encrypted passwords on common systems, such as the Security Accounts Manager (SAM) database on standalone Windows® systems. Password-cracking tools take advantage of known weaknesses in the security of these password databases, so security might need to be increased.

Types of Password Attacks

There are different types of password attacks that attackers use to crack passwords.

Password Attack Type	Description
Guessing	The simplest type of password attack is making individual, repeated attempts to guess a password by entering different common password values, such as the user's name, spouse's name, or a significant date. Most systems have a feature that will lock out an account after a specified number of incorrect password attempts.
Stealing	Passwords can be stolen by various means, including sniffing network communications, reading handwritten password notes, or observing a user in the act of entering a password.
Dictionary attack	This attack type automates password guessing by comparing encrypted passwords against a predetermined list of possible password values. Dictionary attacks are only successful against fairly simple and obvious passwords, because they rely on a dictionary of common words and predictable variations, such as adding a single digit to the end of a word.
Brute force attack	In this attack method, the attacker uses password-cracking software to attempt every possible alphanumeric password combination.

Password Attack Type	Description
Rainbow tables	These are sets of related plaintext passwords and their hashes. The underlying principle of rainbow tables is to do the central processing unit (CPU)-intensive work of generating hashes in advance, trading time saved during the attack for the disk space to store the tables. Beginning with a base word such as "password" the table then progresses through a large number of possible variations on that root word, such as "passw0rd" or "p@ssw0rd." Rainbow table attacks are executed by comparing the target password hash to the password hashes stored in the tables, then working backward in an attempt to determine the actual password from the known hash.
Hybrid password attack	This attack type utilizes multiple attack methods including dictionary, rainbow table, and brute force attacks when trying to crack a password.
Birthday attack	This attack type exploits weaknesses in the mathematical algorithms used to generate hashes. This type of attack takes advantage of the probability of different inputs producing the same encrypted outputs, given a large enough set of inputs.
	It is named after the surprising statistical fact that there is a 50 percent chance that two people in a group of 23 will share a birthday.

aka mathematical probability

Password-Cracking Utilities

Commonly available password-cracking utilities include Ophcrack, L0phtCrack, John the Ripper, Cain & Abel, THC Hydra, RainbowCrack, Aircrack, Airsnort, Pwdump, and Brutus.

Backdoor Attacks

Definition:

A *backdoor attack* is a type of software attack where an attacker creates a software mechanism called a *backdoor* to gain access to a computer. The backdoor can be a software utility or an illegitimate user account. Typically, a backdoor is delivered through use of a Trojan horse or other malware. Backdoor software typically listens for commands from the attacker on an open port. The backdoor mechanism often survives even after the initial intrusion has been discovered and resolved.

Example:

Backdoor
Account

Figure 2-18: A backdoor attack.

Backdoor Detection

Backdoor attacks can be difficult to spot because they may not leave any obvious evidence behind.

Takeover Attacks

Backdoor attacks can be the first step in a *takeover attack* in which an attacker assumes complete control over a system. A takeover attack will manifest itself in the loss of local control over the system under attack. Other attack methods are often used as first steps in a system takeover.

Application Attacks

Definition:

Application attacks are software attacks that are targeted at web-based and other client-server applications. They can threaten application and web servers, users, other back-end systems, and the application code itself. These attacks can lead to an authentication breach, customer impersonation, information disclosure, *source code* disclosure or tampering, and further network breaches.

Example:

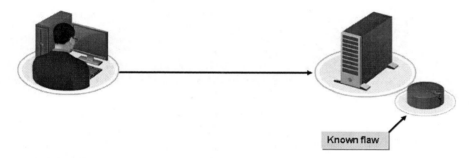

Figure 2-19: *An application attack.*

Types of Application Attacks

Attackers target applications that are vulnerable and exploit these vulnerabilities for their personal or financial gain.

Application Attack	Description
Cross-site scripting	An attack that is directed towards sites with dynamic content. This is done by introducing malicious scripts or by taking over the session before the user session *cookies* expire.

Application Attack	Description
Command injection attacks	Command injection attacks include several types: • *SQL injection* is an attack that injects a *Structured Query Language (SQL)* query into the input data intended for the server by accessing the client side of the application. The query typically exploits and reads data in the database, modifies data in the database, or executes administrative operations such as shutting down or recovering content off the database. It can also affect the operating system of the SQL server. • *LDAP injection* is an attack that targets web-based applications by fabricating *Lightweight Directory Access Protocol (LDAP)* statements that typically are created from user input. A system is vulnerable to this attack when the application fails to filter user input properly. • An *XML injection* is an attack that injects corrupted *eXtensible Markup Language (XML)* query data so that an attacker can gain access to the XML data structure and input malicious code or read private data stored on a server. • *Directory traversal* is an attack that allows access to commands, files, and directories that may or may not be connected to the web document root directory. It usually affects the Hypertext Transfer Protocol (HTTP)-based interface.
Zero day exploit	An attack that occurs when the security level of a system is at its lowest, immediately after the discovery of a vulnerability. These attacks are very effective against relatively secure networks because they are difficult to detect even after the attacks are launched.
Cookie manipulation	An attack where an attacker injects a meta tag in an HTTP header, making it possible to modify a cookie stored in a browser. This is often done to impersonate a genuine user or authenticate an attacker to gain access to a website fraudulently.
Attachment attack	An attack where the attacker can merge malicious software or code into a downloadable file or attachment on a web server so that users download and execute it on client systems.
Malicious add-on	An add-on that is meant to look like a normal add-on, except that when a user installs it, malicious content will be injected to target the security loopholes that are present in a web browser.
Header manipulation	An attack where the attacker manipulates the header information passed between the web servers and clients in HTTP requests. An attacker will either write his own code for this request or go through a free proxy which allows modification to any data request from a browser.

 Web applications and other client-server applications are also vulnerable to various general attack types such as buffer overflows and session hijacking.

ACTIVITY 2-5
Identifying Software Attacks

Scenario:

Your IT department wants to know why the performance of some of your computer systems is degrading. In all the cases of poor performance, your IT administrator, Ronald, has already used existing network baseline data to rule out the possibility of this performance degradation being caused by a temporary spike in traffic or insufficient hardware resources. You and Ronald believe your systems are under attack, but now you need to discover the types of attacks so that you can devise an appropriate response.

1. **Kim, a help desk staffer, gets a phone call from Alex in human resources stating that he cannot log on. Kim looks up the account information for Alex and sees that the account is locked. This is the third time the account has locked this week. Alex insists that he was typing in his password correctly. Kim notices that the account was locked at 6 A.M.; Alex says he was in a meeting at a client's site until 10 A.M. today. This could be a(n):**

   a) Password attack.

   b) Backdoor attack.

   c) Malicious code attack.

   d) Application attack.

2. **Which of the following is the best example of a malicious code attack?**

   a) Your password has been changed without your knowledge.

   b) Your antivirus software has detected the Stuxnet worm.

   c) Your software keeps coming up with errors every time you click the Menu button.

   d) In a system audit, you notice a foreign system accessing your files on a daily basis without proper permissions.

3. **Which are the traits of a backdoor attack? (Select all that apply.)**

   a) It can be the first step in a takeover attack which completely controls a system.

   b) It typically generates unsolicited pop-up advertisements, counterfeit virus scans, or software update notifications.

   c) A backdoor attack is typically delivered through the use of a Trojan horse or other malware.

   d) It is a mechanism for gaining access to a computer that bypasses or subverts the normal methods of authentication.

4. **Match the following malicious code types with their descriptions.**

___	Virus	a.	A piece of code that spreads from one computer to another on its own, not by attaching itself to another file.
___	Worm	b.	A sample of code that spreads from one computer to another by attaching itself to other files.
___	Logic bomb	c.	Software that is intended to take full or partial control of a system at the lowest levels.
___	Rootkit	d.	A piece of code that sits dormant on a target computer until it is triggered by the occurrence of specific conditions, such as a specific date and time.

5. **Match the following application attacks to their descriptions.**

___	Cross-site scripting	a.	An attack where the attacker manipulates the information that is passed between web servers and clients in HTTP requests.
___	LDAP injection	b.	An attack that submits invalid query data to a database server by accessing the client side of the application.
___	SQL injection	c.	An attack that targets web-based applications by fabricating directory service statements that depend on user input.
___	Header manipulation	d.	An attack that is directed towards sites with dynamic content by introducing malicious scripts or by taking over the session before the user session cookies expire.

Lesson 2 Follow-up

In this lesson, you identified the main types of security threats you will face: social engineering attacks, software attacks, network attacks, application attacks, wireless attacks, and physical security attacks. Understanding the types of threats you face is an important first step in learning how to protect your network and respond to an intrusion.

1. **What type of attack is of the most concern in your environment?**

2. **Which type of attack do you think might be the most difficult to guard against?**

3 | Network Security

Lesson Time: 4 hour(s)

Lesson Objectives:

In this lesson, you will examine network security.

You will:

- Identify network devices and technologies.

- Identify network design elements and components.

- Implement network protocols.

- Apply network security administration principles.

- Secure wireless traffic.

Introduction

Now that you have reviewed all the threats and vulnerabilities that can cause damage to your organization, it is time to focus on the components that contribute to network security. Understanding network components and knowing how to properly secure an organization's network is one of the most important steps in becoming a successful Security+ certified professional.

Securing your networks against intruders is not that different from securing your own home. You can secure the perimeter of your home by locking the doors and installing alarm systems, but if intruders get past those, they will have access to everything. So, you cannot just secure from the outside in; you need to secure from the inside out, by doing things like locking up your valuables in a home safe. Securing your internal network and components accomplishes the same goal; it prevents intruders who get in from stealing your valuable hardware, software, and data.

This lesson covers all or part of the following CompTIA® Security+® (Exam SY0-301) certification objectives:

- Topic A:
  - Objective 1.1 Explain the security function and purpose of network devices and technologies
  - Objective 2.7 Execute disaster recovery plans and procedures
  - Objective 3.6 Analyze and differentiate among types of mitigation and deterrent techniques
- Topic B:

- Objective 1.3 Distinguish and differentiate network design elements and compounds
- Objective 4.2 Carry out appropriate procedures to establish host security
- Objective 4.3 Explain the importance of data security
- Topic C:
  - Objective 1.3 Distinguish and differentiate network design elements and compounds
  - Objective 1.4 Implement and use common protocols
  - Objective 1.5 Identify commonly used default network ports
  - Objective 6.1 Summarize general cryptography concepts
  - Objective 6.2 Use and apply appropriate cryptographic tools and products
- Topic D:
  - Objective 1.2 Apply and implement secure network administration principles
- Topic E:
  - Objective 1.2 Apply and implement secure network administration principles
  - Objective 1.6 Implement wireless network in a secure manner
  - Objective 6.2 Use and apply appropriate cryptographic tools and products

TOPIC A

Network Devices and Technologies

In this lesson, you will examine network security and the devices and technologies that are used. You cannot fully secure a network without first understanding the devices and technologies that make the network function. In this topic, you will examine the devices and technologies that are used in a network.

In order to fully understand how network security principles are applied and managed, you must first understand how the network devices and technologies operate. This is the key to successfully securing a network's components and operations. As a Security+ professional, you may have to not only secure the network as a whole, but also manage security settings for specific devices that are used within a network.

Network Components

There are several common components that make up a network.

Network Component	Description
Device	Any piece of hardware such as a computer, server, printer, or smartphone.
Media	Connects devices to the network and carries the data between devices.
Network adapter	Hardware that translates the data between the network and a device.
Network operating system	Software that controls network traffic and access to network resources.
Protocol	Software that controls network communications using a set of rules.

Network Devices

Different types of internetwork devices provide different levels of connectivity and security between network interconnections and network segments.

Device	Description
Router	A device that connects multiple networks that use the same protocol. Routers can examine the protocol-based addressing information in the network packets and determine the most efficient path for data to take. They can also filter network traffic based on other criteria. Most routers will not forward broadcast network traffic.
Switch	A device that has multiple network ports and combines multiple physical network segments into a single logical network. It controls network traffic on the logical network by creating dedicated, or "switched," connections that contain only the two hosts involved in a transmission. Standard switches generally forward broadcasts to all ports on the switch, but will send individual packets to the specific destination host based on the unique physical address assigned to each network adapter. Some switches can perform routing functions based on protocol addresses.

Device	Description
Proxy server	A system that can isolate internal networks from the Internet by downloading and storing Internet files on behalf of internal clients. It intercepts requests for web-based or other external resources that come from internal clients, and, if it does not have the data in its cache, generates a completely new request packet using itself as the source. In addition to providing security, the data cache can also improve client response time and reduce Internet traffic by providing frequently used pages to clients from a local source. A proxy server can also include Network Address Translation (NAT) and firewall functionality.
Firewall	Any software or hardware device that protects a system or network by blocking unwanted network traffic. Firewalls generally are configured to stop suspicious or unsolicited incoming traffic, but permit most types of outgoing traffic. Information about the incoming or outgoing connections can be saved to a log, and used for network monitoring or hardening purposes. There are three common types of firewalls: ● *Host or personal firewalls* are installed on a single computer and are used to secure most home computers. ● *Network-based firewalls* are dedicated hardware/software combinations that protect all the computers on a network behind the firewall. ● *Web application-based firewalls* are specifically deployed to secure an organization's web-based applications and transactions from attackers.
Load balancer	A network device that performs load balancing as its primary function. *Load balancing* is the practice of spreading out the work among the devices in a network. By sharing the work, more resources are available and data is processed faster. By balancing the workload between devices, all the devices in the network perform more efficiently. Often, a dedicated program or hardware device is used to provide the balancing service.
All-in-one security appliance	A single network security device that is used to perform a number of security functions to secure a network. Most devices will contain firewall, intrusion prevention, load balancing, filtering, and reporting functionalities.

Multifunction Network Devices

A *multifunction network device* is any piece of network hardware that is meant to perform more than one networking task without having to be reconfigured. An excellent example of a multifunction network device is a combination switch, router, Dynamic Host Configuration Protocol (DHCP) server, and firewall that is installed in many small office or home networks. In larger corporate networks, multifunction devices are available in a wide variety of configurations including switch and router, or router and load balancer configurations.

Router Discovery Protocols

Router discovery protocols are the language that routers use to talk to each other.

Protocol	Description
Routing Information Protocol (RIP)	This is a simple distance-vector protocol that is easy to configure, works well inside simple autonomous systems, and is best deployed in small networks with only a few routers in an environment that does not change much. Most equipment that supports RIP costs less than those that support more complicated routing protocols.

Protocol	Description
RIPv2	RIPv2 enhances RIP by supporting the following features: ● Next Hop Addressing: Includes Internet Protocol (IP) address information in routing tables for every router in a given path to avoid sending packets through extra routers. ● Authentication: Enables password authentication and the use of a key to authenticate routing information to a router. ● Subnet mask: Supports more subnets and hosts on an internetwork by supporting Variable Length Subnet Masks (VLSMs) and including length information in routing information. ● Multicast packet: Decreases the workload of non–RIPv2 hosts by communicating only with RIPv2 routers. RIPv2 packets use 224.0.0.9 as their IP multicast address.
Interior Gateway Routing Protocol (IGRP)	This is a distance-vector routing protocol developed by Cisco as an improvement over RIP and RIPv2. It was designated as a protocol best deployed on interior routers within an autonomous system (AS).
Enhanced Interior Gateway Routing Protocol (EIGRP)	This is a proprietary routing protocol by Cisco and is considered a hybrid type protocol. It includes features that support VLSM and classful and classless subnet masks. Additional updates reduce convergence times and improve network stability during changes.

LEGACY (handwritten)

Network Technologies

There are a number of network technologies used within a network that function as security measures.

Network Technology	Description
Sniffer	A device or program that monitors network communications on the network wire or across a wireless network and captures data. A sniffer can be used to gather information passed through a network, or selectively record specific types of transactions based on devices, protocols, or applications used.
Spam filters	Programs used to read and reject incoming messages that contain target words and phrases used in known spam messages.
Protocol analyzer	Also known as a *network analyzer,* this is a type of diagnostic software that can examine and display data packets that are being transmitted over a network. Protocol analyzers can gather all the information passed through a network, or selectively record certain types of transactions based on various filtering mechanisms. On a wired network, it is possible to gather information on all or just part of the network. On a wireless network, traffic can be captured on one wireless channel at a time.

IDSes

Definition:

An *intrusion detection system (IDS)* is a detection control system that scans, audits, and monitors the security infrastructure for signs of attacks in progress. IDS software can also analyze data and alert security administrators to potential infrastructure problems. An IDS can comprise a variety of hardware sensors, intrusion detection software, and IDS management software. Each implementation is unique, and depends on an organization's security needs and the components chosen.

Example:

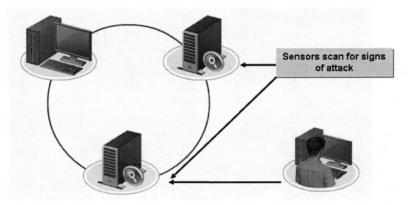

Figure 3-1: An IDS.

NIDS

A *network intrusion detection system (NIDS)* primarily uses passive hardware sensors to monitor traffic on a specific segment of the network. It cannot analyze encrypted packets because it has no method for decrypting the data. It can sniff traffic and send alerts about anomalies or concerns.

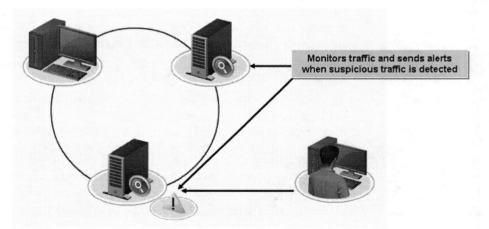

Figure 3-2: NIDS.

NIPS

A *network intrusion prevention system (NIPS)*, also referred to as an *intrusion prevention system (IPS)*, is an inline prevention control security device that monitors suspicious network and system traffic and reacts in real time to block it. One advantage of using an IPS is that it can regulate traffic according to specific content, because it examines packets as they travel through the IPS. This is in contrast to the way a firewall behaves, which blocks IP addresses or entire ports.

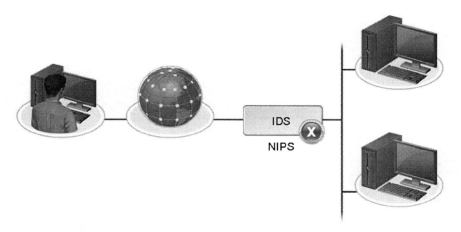

Figure 3-3: *NIPS.*

Types of Network Monitoring Systems

If you want to monitor network activity, there are various methods you can use to obtain the kind of information you want to collect.

Monitoring System	Description
Behavior-based monitoring	This system detects changes in normal operating data sequences and identifies abnormal sequences. When behavior-based systems are installed, they have no performance baseline or acceptable traffic pattern defined. Initially, these systems will report all traffic as a threat. Over time, however, they learn which traffic is allowed and which is not with the assistance of an administrator.
Signature-based monitoring	This solution uses a predefined set of rules provided by a software vendor to identify traffic that is unacceptable.
Anomaly-based monitoring	This system uses a database of unacceptable traffic patterns identified by analyzing traffic flows. Anomaly-based systems are dynamic and create a performance baseline of acceptable traffic flows during their implementation process.
Heuristic monitoring	This system is set up using known best practices and characteristics in order to identify and fix issues within the network.

VPNs

Definition:

A *virtual private network (VPN)* is a private network that is configured by tunneling through a public network, such as the Internet. VPNs provide secure connections between endpoints, such as routers, clients, or servers, by using tunneling to encapsulate and encrypt data. Special *VPN protocols* are required to provide the VPN tunneling, security, and data encryption services.

Example:

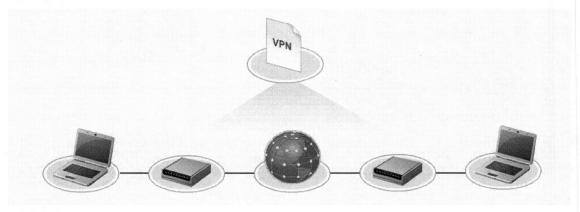

Figure 3-4: A VPN.

VPN Concentrator

Definition:

A *VPN concentrator* is a single device that incorporates advanced encryption and authentication methods in order to handle a large number of VPN tunnels. It is geared specifically towards secure remote access or site-to-site VPNs. VPN concentrators provide high performance, high availability, and impressive scalability.

Example:

Figure 3-5: A VPN concentrator.

Web Security Gateways

Definition:

A *web security gateway* is a utility used primarily to intentionally block internal Internet access to a predefined list of websites or categories of websites. The utility is configured by administrators to deny access to a specified list of Uniform Resource Locators (URLs). This type of software can also be used for tracking and reporting a business' Internet usage and activity. Web security gateways can provide a number of functions, including *URL filtering*, which is based on blacklist settings; malware inspection, which is used to identify infected packets; and content inspection, which is used to scan the contents of a packet for abnormalities.

Example:

Figure 3-6: A web security gateway.

 An example of a common web security gateway used is Microsoft® Forefront®.

Blacklists

Blacklists contain addresses that are automatically blocked. URL filtering functions use the entries in a blacklist to allow or deny access to a particular website. Some organizations may use a whitelist or greylist, depending on their access control specifications. When a URL is specified on a whitelist, access is allowed, and when a URL is specified on a greylist, temporary access is granted.

ACTIVITY 3-1
Examining Network Devices and Technologies

Scenario:

In this activity, you will examine the various network devices and technologies commonly used within an organization.

1. **What is the correct description for each network technology?**

    ___ Router

    ___ Switch

    ___ Proxy server

    ___ Firewall

    ___ Load balancer

    ___ All-in-one security appliance

    a. Has multiple network ports and combines multiple physical network segments into a single logical network.

    b. Protects a system or network by blocking unwanted network traffic.

    c. Can isolate internal networks from the Internet by downloading and storing Internet files on behalf of internal clients.

    d. Spreads out the work among the devices in a network.

    e. Contains firewall, intrusion prevention, load balancing, filtering, and reporting functionalities.

    f. Connects multiple networks that use the same protocol.

2. **Which technology is only used for monitoring and capturing the content of data communications on a network?**

    a) IDS

    b) NIPS

    c) Spam filter

    d) Sniffer

3. **What is the difference between a host-based, network-based, and web application-based firewall?**

4. **Your organization is in the process of implementing security controls throughout the corporate network. A security device is needed to actively scan and monitor network activity and then alert and block any access that is suspicious. What device is the best option in this scenario?**

   a) IDS

   b) NIPS

   c) Sniffer

   d) Spam filter

TOPIC B

Network Design Elements and Components

Now that you have learned what devices and technologies make up a network's architecture, you can move onto the security design elements and components of a network. The design elements and components of a network are just as important as the devices and technologies used to set up that network. This topic examines the network design elements and components of a successful network.

Many factors can go into properly setting up and securing a network from common threats and vulnerabilities, but understanding how the design elements and components work within that network enables you to easily manage and make necessary security-related adjustments.

NAC

Definition:

Network Access Control (NAC) is a general term for the collected protocols, policies, and hardware that govern access on device network interconnections. NAC provides an additional security layer that scans systems for conformance and allows or quarantines updates to meet policy standards. Security professionals will deploy a NAC policy according to an organization's needs based on three main elements: authentication method, endpoint vulnerability assessment, and network security enforcement. Once the NAC policy is determined, professionals must determine where NAC will be deployed within their network structure.

Example:

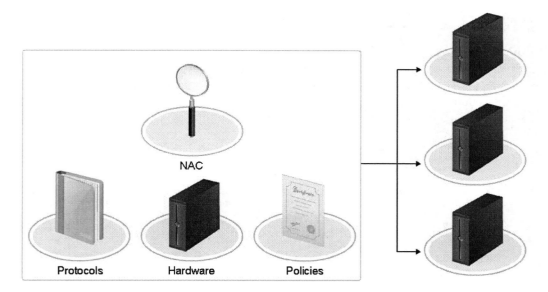

Figure 3-7: NAC.

DMZs

Definition:

A *demilitarized zone (DMZ)* is a small section of a private network that is located between two firewalls and made available for public access. A DMZ enables external clients to access data on private systems, such as web servers, without compromising the security of the internal network as a whole. The external firewall enables public clients to access the service; the internal firewall prevents them from connecting to protected internal hosts.

Example:

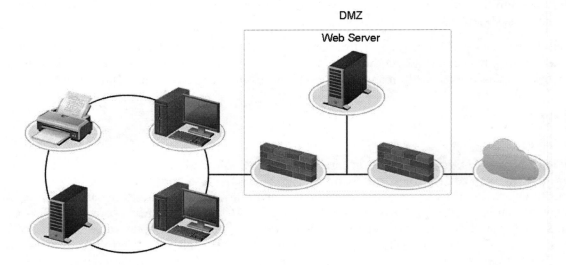

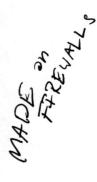

Figure 3-8: A DMZ.

VLANs

Definition:

A *virtual local area network (VLAN)* is a point-to-point logical network that is created by grouping selected hosts together, regardless of their physical location. A VLAN uses a switch or router that controls the groups of hosts that receive network broadcasts. VLANs can provide network security by enabling administrators to segment groups of hosts within the larger physical network.

Example:

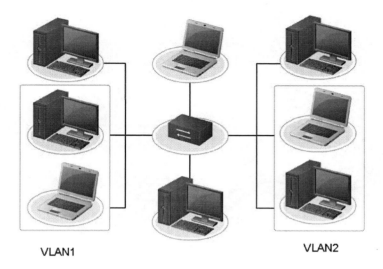

VLAN1   VLAN2

Figure 3-9: A VLAN.

VLAN Vulnerabilities

Improperly configured VLAN devices and associated switches give attackers the opportunity to redirect packets from one VLAN to another (through VLAN hopping) and to capture those packets and the data they contain.

Some VLAN switch configurations can also be open to other attacks such as Denial of Service (DoS), traffic flooding, and Mandatory Access Control (MAC) address spoofing. Being aware of these types of attacks and correctly configuring a VLAN implementation can eliminate these types of attacks.

Subnetting

Definition:

Subnetting is a network design element that is used to divide a large network into smaller logical networks. Each node is configured with an IP address and a subnet address in order to segment a network into subnetworks and to create a routing structure. By creating logical groupings of network devices based on an addressing scheme, data flow and security measures can be managed more easily on a smaller scale than on a large network.

Example:

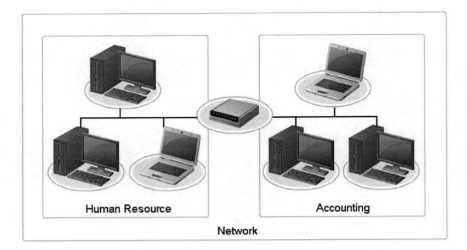

Figure 3-10: *A subnet.*

NAT

Network Address Translation (NAT) is a simple form of Internet security that conceals internal addressing schemes from the public Internet. A router is configured with a single public IP address on its external interface and a private, non-routable address on its internal interface. A NAT service translates between the two addressing schemes. Packets sent to the Internet from internal hosts all appear as if they came from a single IP address, preventing external hosts from identifying and connecting directly to internal systems.

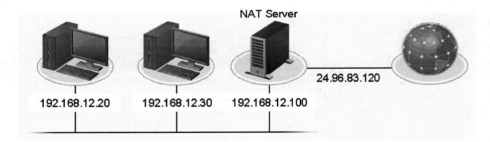

Figure 3-11: *NAT.*

Remote Access

Definition:

Remote access is the ability to connect to network systems and services from an offsite or remote location using a remote access method. Remote access enables authorized users to access and use systems and services through a secure Internet connection.

Example:

Offsite Employee

Figure 3-12: A remote access connection.

Telephony

Telephony provides voice communications through devices over a distance. Modern networks are designed to handle more than just the traditional networking components and, in some cases, may also be expected to carry converged data. Common telephony components include:

- Voice over Internet Protocol (VoIP) implementations, in which voice traffic is transmitted over the IP network.

- Private branch exchange implementations.

- And, computer telephony integration (CTI), which incorporates telephone, email, web, and computing infrastructures.

Virtualization

Definition:

Virtualization technology separates computing software from the hardware it runs on via an additional software layer. This enables a great deal of additional flexibility and increases hardware utilization by running multiple operating systems on a single computer, each thinking it is the only system present. In addition, virtualization allows hardware resources in an organization to be pooled and leveraged as part of a virtual infrastructure, increasing available processing and storage capacity. Virtualization has many uses in the modern IT environment:

- Running multiple operating systems on one computer, reducing hardware requirements.

- Separating software applications within a single operating system to prevent conflicts.

- And, increasing utilization of processing and storage resources throughout the organization by creating a "virtual infrastructure."

Example:

Figure 3-13: Running multiple operating systems on one computer.

Cloud Computing

Definition:

Cloud computing is a method of computing that relies on the Internet to provide the resources, software, data, and media needs of a user, business, or organization. This method of computing relies on the Internet to provide computing capabilities that a single machine cannot. "The cloud" refers to anything available on the Internet. This could include business websites, consumer websites, storage services, IT-related services, file editing applications, and social networking websites. The main idea behind cloud computing is that you can access and manage your data and applications from any computer anywhere in the world while the storage method and location is hidden.

Example:

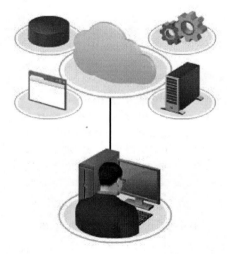

Figure 3-14: A cloud computing architecture.

Cloud Computing Service Types

Cloud computing provides three main services to users.

Service	Description
Software	*Software as a Service (SaaS)* refers to using the cloud to provide applications to users. This service eliminates the need for users to have the software installed on their computers and for organizations to purchase and maintain software versions.
Platform	*Platform as a Service (PaaS)* refers to using the cloud to provide virtual systems, such as operating systems, to customers.
Infrastructure	*Infrastructure as a Service (IaaS)* refers to using the cloud to provide access to any or all infrastructure needs a client may have. This can include data centers, servers, or any networking devices needed. IaaS can guarantee quality of service (QoS) for clients.

ACTIVITY 3-2
Examining Network Design Components

Scenario:

In this activity, you will examine the network design elements of a network.

1. **What is the role of NAT on a network?**

2. **Which telephony technology allows telephone, email, fax, web, and computer actions to be integrated to work together?**

   a) PBX

   b) VoIP

   c) CTI

   d) NAT

3. **What is the correct cloud computing service type for each description?**

   ___ Software   a. An organization uses the cloud to pro-vide Microsoft® Windows® 7 access to all their employees.

   ___ Platform   b. An organization uses the cloud to pro-vide photo editing applications to their employees.

   ___ Infrastructure   c. An organization uses the cloud to pro-vide access to data center functionalities.

4. **Your organization is in the testing phase of a new accounting application and needs to verify its functionality on various operating systems before deploying it to customers, but is dealing with hardware availability issues. What network design component would you suggest in this scenario?**

TOPIC C

Implement Networking Protocols

As you continue to explore the realm of network security, you will need to understand how networking protocols are used within a network. In this topic, you will implement common networking protocols.

You may be able to successfully design and set up a network, but it will not function without the proper protocols applied. There are a number of different protocols designed to operate within different types of networks. Depending on the type of network you are securing, you may come across a number of different protocols, and it is your job to understand how they function within the network.

Internet Protocols

There are a number of protocols used to provide access to the Internet.

Internet Protocol	Description
Transmission Control Protocol/Internet Protocol (TCP/IP)	This is a non-proprietary, routable network protocol suite that enables computers to communicate over all types of networks. TCP/IP is the native protocol of the Internet and is required for Internet connectivity.
IP version 4 (IPv4)	This is an Internet standard that uses a 32-bit number assigned to a computer on a TCP/IP network. Some of the bits in the address represent the network segment; the other bits represent the computer, or node, itself. For readability, the 32-bit IPv4 address is usually separated by dots into four 8-bit octets, 10101100.00010000.11110000.00000001 and each octet is converted to a single decimal value. Each decimal number can range from 0 to 255, but the first number cannot be 0. In addition, all four numbers in a host address cannot be 0 (0.0.0.0) or 255 (255.255.255.255).
IP version 6 (IPv6)	This is an Internet standard that increases the available pool of IP addresses by implementing a 128-bit binary address space. IPv6 also includes new efficiency features, such as simplified address headers, hierarchical addressing, support for time-sensitive network traffic, and a new structure for unicast addressing.
	IPv6 addresses are usually separated by colons into eight groups of four hexadecimal digits: 2001:0db8:85a3:0000:0000:8a2e:0370:7334. While all eight groups must have four digits, leading zeros can be omitted, such as 2001:db8:85a3:0:0:8a2e:370:7334, and groups of consecutive zeros can be replaced with two colons, such as 2001:db8:85a3::8a2e:370:7334.
	IPv6 is not compatible with IPv4, so now it is narrowly deployed on a limited number of test and production networks. Full adoption of the IPv6 standard will require a general conversion of IP routers to support interoperability. IPv6 uses an Institute of Electrical and Electronics Engineers (IEEE) standard called Extended Unique Identifier (EUI). A host computer implemented with EUI-64 can assign itself a 64-bit IPv6 interface identifier automatically.

Internet Protocol	Description
Dynamic Host Configuration Protocol (DHCP)	This is a protocol used to automatically assign IP addressing information to IP network computers. Except for a few systems that have manually assigned static IP addresses, most IP systems obtain addressing information dynamically from a central DHCP server or a router configured to provide DHCP functions. Therefore, a DHCP service is a critical component of an IP implementation in most corporate environments.

The IEEE

The Institute of Electrical and Electronics Engineers (IEEE) is an organization dedicated to advancing theory and technology in the electrical sciences. The standards wing of IEEE issues standards in areas such as electronic communications, circuitry, computer engineering, electromagnetics, and nuclear science. See **www.ieee.org** for more information.

APIPA

Automatic Private IP Addressing (APIPA) is a Microsoft® Windows® service that enables DHCP client computers to initialize TCP/IP when DHCP is unavailable. With APIPA, DHCP clients can get IP addresses when the DHCP servers malfunction or when the computer does not have connectivity. APIPA self allocates addresses randomly from a small range of 169.254.0.1 to 169.254.255.254.

Simple TCP/IP Services

Simple TCP/IP Services is a Microsoft implementation that supports several TCP/IP services such as Character Generator, Daytime, Discard, and Quote of the Day. For more information on the Simple TCP/IP Services, visit **http://technet.microsoft.com/en-us/library/cc725973.aspx**.

DNS

Definition:

The *Domain Name System (DNS)* is the primary name resolution service on the Internet and private IP networks. DNS is a hierarchal system of databases that map computer names to their associated IP addresses. DNS servers store, maintain, and update databases and respond to DNS client name resolution requests to translate host names to IP addresses. The DNS servers on the Internet work together to provide global name resolution for all Internet hosts.

Example:

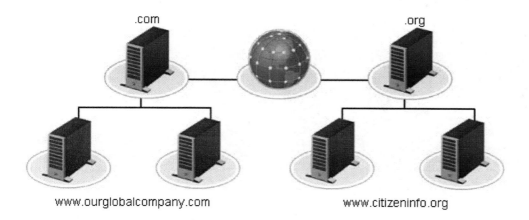

Figure 3-15: The DNS.

DNS Security Measures

In any corporate network, the DNS is the most likely target that is attacked first. There are several applications available in the IT market that help secure a DNS. Some of the measures that can be taken to secure a DNS are:

- Placing the DNS server in the DMZ and within the firewall perimeter.
- Setting firewall rules to block incoming non-essential services requests.
- Exposing only essential ports.
- Strengthening DHCP filtering.
- Preventing buffer overflows.
- Using Secure Sockets Layer (SSL).
- Keeping the DNS updated regularly. Security patches are issued by the operating system vendors to update the DNS.
- Backing up the DNS and saving the backups in different geographical locations.

HTTP

Hypertext Transfer Protocol (HTTP) is the TCP/IP protocol that enables clients to connect to and interact with websites. It is responsible for transferring the data on web pages between systems. HTTP defines how messages are formatted and transmitted, as well as what actions web servers and the client's browser should take in response to different commands.

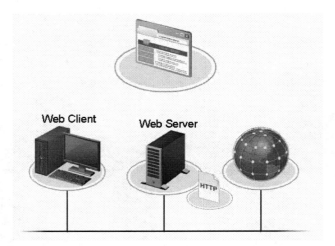

Figure 3-16: HTTP.

Web Server Security

Hackers primarily try to break into the web servers of organizations. The moment the security of web servers is breached, the hacker gets direct access to all the sensitive data stored on the web servers. Securing web servers remains one of the toughest challenges security administrators face. To effectively secure web servers, you should:

- Remove unnecessary services running in the background. Most often, services such as remote registry services, print server service, and RAS, which are not required for web servers, run in the background.

- Avoid remote access to web servers. Administrators should try to log on locally.

- Web applications, website logs that contain user information, and other related files should be securely stored in another drive.

- Install security patches regularly.

- Unused user accounts should be deleted or disabled.

- Use the appropriate security tools. There are several useful security tools available to secure web servers.

- Use port scanners to scan the web servers regularly.

SSL

Secure Sockets Layer (SSL) is a security protocol that combines digital certificates for authentication with public key data encryption. SSL is a server-driven process; any web client that supports SSL, including all current web browsers, can connect securely to an SSL-enabled server.

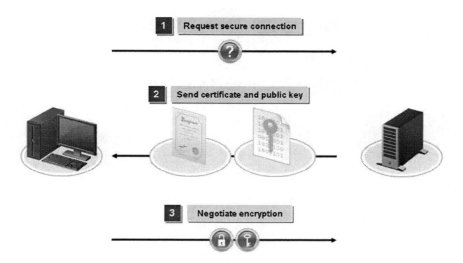

Figure 3-17: SSL.

TLS

Transport Layer Security (TLS) protects sensitive communication from eavesdropping and tampering by using a secure, encrypted, and authenticated channel over a TCP/IP connection. TLS uses certificates and public key cryptography for mutual authentication and data encryption using negotiated secret keys.

TCP/IP

Figure 3-18: TLS.

TLS and SSL

TLS is very similar to SSL, but the two protocols are not compatible.

HTTPS

Hypertext Transfer Protocol Secure (HTTPS) is a secure version of HTTP that supports web commerce by providing a secure connection between a web browser and a server. HTTPS uses SSL to encrypt data. Virtually all web browsers and servers today support HTTPS. An SSL-enabled web address begins with the protocol identifier *https://.*

 HTTPS is also referred to as Hypertext Transfer Protocol over Secure Sockets Layer or HTTP over SSL.

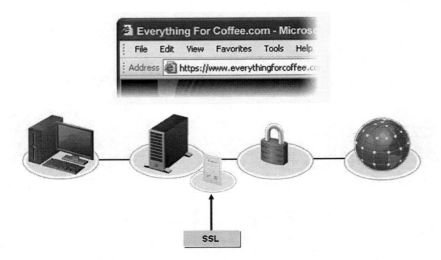

Figure 3-19: *HTTPS.*

SSH

Secure Shell (SSH) is a protocol used for secure remote login and secure transfer of data. SSH consists of a server and a client. Most SSH clients also implement login terminal-emulation software to open secure terminal sessions on remote servers. To ensure security, the entire SSH session, including authentication, is encrypted using a variety of encryption methods. SSH is the preferred protocol to File Transfer Protocol (FTP) and is used primarily on Linux and Unix systems to access shell accounts. Microsoft Windows does not offer native support for SSH, but it can be implemented by using a third-party tool.

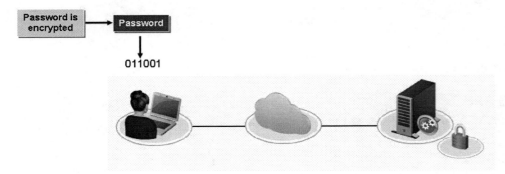

Figure 3-20: *SSH.*

SNMP

Definition:

Simple Network Management Protocol (SNMP) is a service used to collect information from network devices for diagnostic and maintenance purposes. SNMP includes two components: management systems and agent software, which is installed on network devices such as servers, routers, and printers. The agents send information to an SNMP manager. The SNMP manager can then notify an administrator of problems, run a corrective program or script, store the information for later review, or ask the agent about a specific network device.

Example:

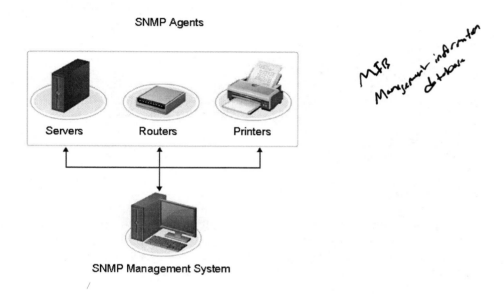

Figure 3-21: SNMP.

ICMP

Definition:

Internet Control Message Protocol (ICMP) is an IP network service that reports on connections between two hosts. It is often used for simple functions, such as the `ping` command that checks for a response from a particular target host. Attackers can use redirected ICMP packets in two ways: to flood a router and cause a DoS attack by consuming resources, and to reconfigure routing tables by using forged packets.

Example:

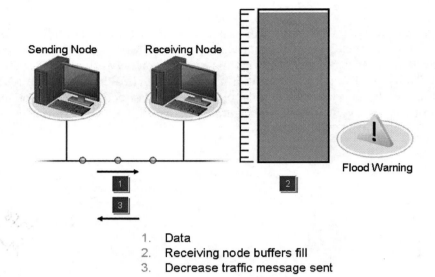

1. Data
2. Receiving node buffers fill
3. Decrease traffic message sent

Figure 3-22: ICMP.

IPSec

Internet Protocol Security (IPSec) is a set of open, non-proprietary standards that you can use to secure data as it travels across the network or the Internet. IPSec uses an array of protocols and services to provide data authenticity and integrity, anti-replay protection, non-repudiation, and protection against eavesdropping and sniffing.

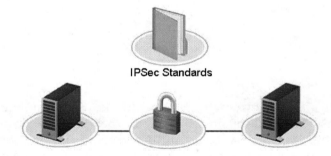

IPSec Standards

Figure 3-23: IPSec.

IPSec System Support

Many operating systems support IPSec, including Windows Server 2008 and 2003, Microsoft® Windows® XP and later, Linux, Unix, and Sun Solaris. Internetworking devices, such as most routers, also support IPSec. While IPSec is an industry standard, it is implemented differently in each operating system and device.

IPSec Policies

An IPSec policy is a set of security configuration settings that define how an IPSec-enabled system will respond to IP network traffic. The policy determines the security level and other characteristics for an IPSec connection. Each computer that uses IPSec must have an assigned policy. Policies work in pairs; each of the endpoints in a network communication must have an IPSec policy with at least one matching security method in order for the communication to succeed. Some default IPSec policies include secure server, server, client, IP filters, filter action, authentication method, tunnel setting, and connection type.

File Transfer Protocols

There are many protocols that are used to support file transfers within a network.

Protocol	Description
File Transfer Protocol (FTP)	This protocol enables the transfer of files between a user's workstation and a remote host. With FTP, a user can access the directory structure on a remote host, change directories, search and rename files and directories, and download and upload files.
Simple File Transfer Protocol (SFTP)	This protocol was an early unsecured file transfer protocol that has since been declared obsolete.
Secure Copy Protocol (SCP)	This protocol uses SSH to securely transfer computer files between a local and a remote host, or between two remote hosts. SCP can also be implemented as a command-line utility that uses either SCP or SFTP to perform secure copying.
File Transfer Protocol Secure (FTPS)	This protocol, also known as FTP-SSL, combines the use of FTP with additional support for TLS and SSL.

Ports

In networks, a *port* is the endpoint of a logical connection. Client computers connect to specific server programs through a designated port. All ports are assigned a number in a range from 0 to 65,535. The Internet Assigned Numbers Authority (IANA) separates port numbers into three blocks: well-known ports, which are preassigned to system processes by IANA; registered ports, which are available to user processes and are listed as a convenience by IANA; and dynamic ports, which are assigned by a client operating system as needed when there is a request for service.

IANA

The Internet Assigned Numbers Authority (IANA) manages the registration of well-known ports, and also lists registered ports as a convenience. For a complete list of TCP and User Datagram Protocol (UDP) ports, see the IANA website at **www.iana.org/assignments/port-numbers**.

Vulnerable Port Ranges

TCP and UDP ports are assigned in one of three ranges. Hackers will target commonly used, well-known ports for attack, but may scan for open registered or dynamic ports as well.

Range	Numbers	Description
Well-known ports	0 to 1,023	Specific port numbers are most vulnerable to attack.
Registered ports	1,024 to 49,151	Too system-specific for direct target by attackers, but they might scan for open ports in this range.
Dynamic or private ports	49,152 to 65,535	Constantly changing; cannot be targeted by number, but attackers might scan for open ports in this range.

Common Default Network Ports

This table lists some of the most common network port numbers. Well-known ports and other port number assignments are available online at **www.iana.org/assignments/port-numbers**.

Service	Port Number
HTTP	80
HTTPS	443
FTP	21
SFTP	115
FTPS	989
TFTP	69
TELNET	23
SCP	22
SSH	22
NetBIOS	137

NetBIOS

NetBIOS is a simple, broadcast-based naming service. A NetBIOS name can be any combination of alphanumeric characters excluding spaces and the following characters: \\:*?";|. The length of the name cannot exceed 15 characters. The sixteenth character is reserved.

WINS

Windows Internet Name Service (WINS) is a Windows implementation of NetBIOS. It contains two components: a server service and a TCP/IP client component. The server service manages server-to-server replication and service requests. The TCP/IP client component manages the client's registration and renewal of names.

How to Implement Networking Protocols

Procedure Reference: Implement Networking Protocols Securely

The steps you will follow to securely implement a given network protocol will vary depending upon the system you are using and the protocol itself. General steps to install and secure a network protocol are:

1. Verify that the protocol is supported on your system, and update the systems, if necessary.

    For example, to implement DNS in a Windows network environment, you can perform a Server Core installation of Windows Server 2008 R2.

2. Perform the appropriate installation routine on that system for the given protocol.

    For example, in Windows Server 2008 R2, some protocols, such as IPv6, are implemented by modifying the network properties; others, such as DNS, are implemented as server roles that you can add using the Server Manager tool.

3. Perform the security procedures appropriate for that protocol in your environment.

    For example, for DNS on Windows Server, some typical security procedures are:

    *   Store the DNS zone databases in the Active Directory so that they are protected by Active Directory security and replication.

    *   Allow only secure dynamic updates so that only approved clients can register in the zone database.

    *   Restrict zone transfers to approved DNS servers only so that zone information is contained within your approved infrastructure.

    *   Secure the DNS cache against pollution to protect it from accepting records from non-authoritative servers during the DNS query process.

Procedure Reference: Install and Secure a Web Server on Windows Server 2008 R2

To install and secure a web server on Windows Server 2008 R2:

1. Choose **Start→Administrative Tools→Server Manager.**
2. In **Server Manager,** in the left pane, select **Roles** and click the **Add roles** link.
3. In the **Add Roles Wizard,** on the **Before You Begin** page, click **Next.**
4. On the **Select Server Roles** page, check the **Web Server (IIS)** check box and click **Next.**
5. In the **Add Roles Wizard** dialog box, click **Add Required Features** to add all the suggested features. Click **Next.**
6. On the **Web Server (IIS)** page, click **Next.**
7. On the **Select Role Services** page, scroll down and check the **FTP Server.** check box. Click **Next.**
8. On the **Confirm Installation Selections** page, click **Install.**
9. Wait for the installation to complete the process and display the results.
10. On the **Installation Results** page, click **Close.**

11. Enable logging.

   a. From the **Administrative Tools** menu, choose **Internet Information Services (IIS) Manager.**

   b. Expand the IIS server object.

   c. Expand **Sites.**

   d. Select **Default Web Site.**

   e. On the **Default Web Site Home** page, double-click **Logging.**

   f. Set the required logging settings.

   g. From the console tree, select **Default Web Site.**

12. Set file access and execution permissions on websites.

   a. On the **Default Website Home** page, double-click **Directory Browsing.**

   b. In the **Actions** pane, click **Edit Permissions.**

   c. On the **Security** page, set the appropriate permissions.

   d. From the console tree, select **Default Web Site.**

13. Configure website authentication.

   a. On the **Default Web Site Home** page, double-click **Authentication.**

   b. On the **Authentication** page, select **Anonymous Authentication.**

   c. On the **Actions** pane, perform the appropriate actions.

   d. From the console tree, select **Default Web Site.**

14. Restrict website access by domain or IP address.

   a. On the **Default Web Site Home** page, double-click **IP Address and Domain Restrictions.**

   b. On the **Actions** pane, perform the appropriate actions.

   c. From the console tree, select **Default Web Site.**

15. Set NT File System (NTFS) permissions by configuring the properties of the website's folder in **Computer** or Windows Explorer.

16. Use **Server Manager** to add additional security options.

Procedure Reference: Configure IPSec on Windows Server 2008 R2

There are several ways to configure IPSec on Windows Server 2008 R2. One method to configure IPSec is:

1. Configure the policy for the local computer.

   a. Open the **IP Security Policy Management** snap-in.

   b. Choose **Local Computer** for the snap-in.

   c. Select **IP Security Policies on Local Computer** and choose **Action→Create IP Security Policy.**

   d. Use the **IP Security Policy Wizard** to create a new IP security policy.

2. Configure the policy at the domain level.

    a. Open the **IP Security Policy Management** snap-in.

    b. Choose the Active Directory domain for the snap-in.

    c. Double-click **IP Security policies** on Active Directory to display the default IPSec policies.

    d. Open the properties for the appropriate security policy.

    e. In the **Properties** dialog box, modify the policy according to your security policy guidelines.

3. Assign the policy:

    ● To assign a policy to the local computer, select the policy you want to assign and choose **Action→Assign.**

    ● To deploy IPSec policies using Group Policy, assign the appropriate IPSec policy at the site, domain, or OU level using **Group Policy Management Editor.**

4. Test the communications to verify that only secured hosts can communicate with each other.

5. Verify the secure communications for the local computer by using **Windows IP Security Monitor:**

    a. In **Windows IP Security Monitor,** expand your computer object.

    b. Expand the **Main Mode** folder and select the **Security Associations** folder.

    c. Open the properties for the security association object to see the authentication mode as well as the encryption and data integrity algorithms negotiated for the security association.

6. Verify the active IP security policy for your domain:

    a. In **Windows IP Security Monitor,** expand your computer object.

    b. Select the **Active Policy** folder.

    c. Verify the details of the active policy assigned to your domain.

MMC

Microsoft Management Console (MMC) is an interface that provides a standard framework for a wide variety of administrative tools within Windows, so that tools with many different functions have a similar look and feel and so that you can access them from within a common application. MMC in Windows Server 2008 R2 has a multi-pane view. MMC allows you to create custom MMC consoles by adding snap-in tools into the MMC interface. See Windows Help for more information on creating and saving a custom MMC console.

NTFS

In Windows operating systems, file-level security is supported on drives that are formatted to use the Windows NT file system. NTFS permissions can be applied either to folders or to individual files. NTFS permissions on a folder are inherited by the files and subfolders within it. There are several levels of NTFS permissions, which can determine, for example, whether users can read files or run applications; write to existing files; and modify, create, or delete files. NTFS also supports file system encryption at the file and folder level.

ACTIVITY 3-3
Installing an IIS Web Server

 There is a simulated version of this activity available on the CD-ROM that shipped with this course. You can run this simulation on any Windows computer to review the activity after class, or as an alternative to performing the activity as a group in class. The activity simulation can be launched either directly from the CD-ROM by clicking the **Interactives** link and navigating to the appropriate one, or from the installed data file location by opening the C:\SPlus\Simulations\Lesson#\Activity# folder and double-clicking the executable (.exe) file.

 Microsoft Windows is the platform used to practice the security concepts presented in this course. There are also Windows-specific procedures included throughout the course to help you perform the guided activities. Be aware that there may be other methods for performing the tasks included in the activities.

Data Files:

Register.htm, dac10001.gif

Setup:

You are logged on as **Administrator** to a server with Windows Server 2008 R2 installed. Your password is **!Pass1234.** The computer name is **Server##,** where **##** is a unique student number. The server is a domain controller for domain##.internal.com.

Scenario:

You are the security administrator of a state university in the United States. The university is expected to start a web portal where students can enroll themselves. Before hosting the site live, the IT team has planned to test the functionality on a test server. You have been assigned the task of creating a web server for the test team and to set up a default web page. You also need to establish file transfer services for students and faculty in your offline learning programs to exchange large files quickly and efficiently.

1. Install **Web Server (IIS).**

    a. Choose **Start→Administrative Tools→Server Manager.**

    b. From the console tree on the left side of the window, select **Roles.**

c. In the right pane, click **Add Roles.**

d. On the **Before You Begin** page, click **Next.**

e. On the **Select Server Roles** page, check the **Web Server (IIS)** check box and click **Next.**

f. Read the content on the **Introduction to Web Server (IIS)** page and then click **Next.**

g. On the **Select Role Services** page, scroll down in the **Role Services** section, check **FTP Server,** and click **Next.**

h. Review the web server services and click **Install.**

i. Click **Close.**

j. In the Server Manager window, expand **Roles** and select **Web Server (IIS).**

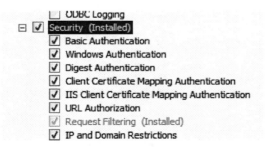

k. Scroll down and click **Add Role Services.**

l. On the **Select Role Services** page, scroll down and check the **Security (Installed)** check box.

m. Click **Next.**

n. Click **Install.**

o. Once the installation has completed, click **Close,** and then close **Server Manager.**

2. Enable IIS logging on the default website.

a. Choose **Start→Administrative Tools→Internet Information Services (IIS) Manager.**

b. In the **Connections** pane, expand the IIS server object.

c. Expand **Sites.**

d. Select **Default Web Site.**

e. In the **Default Web Site Home** pane, double-click **Logging.**

f. In the **Logging** pane, in the **Log File Rollover** section, verify that the IIS logging is enabled and will create a new log file daily.

---

3. Enable the appropriate file permissions and execution settings on the default public website.

a. In the **Connections** pane, select **Default Web Site.**

b. In the **Default Web Site Home** pane, click **Directory Browsing** once to select it.

c. In the **Actions** pane, click **Edit Permissions.**

d. In the **wwwroot Properties** dialog box, select the **Security** tab.

e. In the **Group or user names** list, scroll down and select **Users (DOMAIN##\Users).**

f.   Verify that users have **Read & execute, List folder contents,** and **Read** permissions to the local website files.

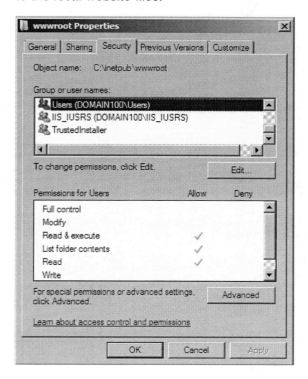

g.   Close the **wwwroot Properties** dialog box.

h.   If necessary, in the **Connections** pane, select **Default Web Site.**

i.   On the **Default Web Site Home** page, double-click **Authentication.**

j.   On the **Authentication** page, select **Anonymous Authentication.**

k.   In the **Actions** pane, click **Disable.**

l.   On the **Authentication** page, select **Windows Authentication.**

m.   In the **Actions** pane, click **Enable.**

4.   Set up the default website.

a.   Navigate to the C:\SPlus folder.

b.   Copy the files **Register.htm** and **dac10001.gif.**

c.   Navigate to the C:\inetpub\wwwroot folder.

d.   Paste the **Register.htm** and **dac10001.gif** files in the **wwwroot** folder.

e.   Rename the **Register.htm** as *Default.htm*

f.   Close Windows Explorer.

5.   Verify the authentication credentials of the website.

a.   Choose **Start→Internet Explorer.**

b.   In the address bar, type ***http://server##*** and then press **Enter.**

      c.   In the **Windows Security** dialog box, in the **User name** text box, click and type *Administrator*

      d.   Press **Tab.**

      e.   In the **Password** text box, type *!Pass1234* and press **Enter.**

      f.   Observe that you have to enter the authentication credentials to view the website. Close Internet Explorer.

---

6.   Set up the FTP connection.

      a.   If necessary, on the Windows taskbar, click the **Internet Information Services (IIS) Manager** button.

      b.   Right-click on **Sites** and choose **Add FTP Site.**

      c.   In the **Add FTP Site** dialog box, on the **Site Information** page, in the **FTP site name** text box, type *Default FTP Site*

      d.   In the **Physical path** text box, click and type *C:\inetpub\ftproot* as the path.

      e.   Click **Next.**

      f.   On the **Binding and SSL Settings** page, in the **SSL** section, select the **Allow SSL** option, and click **Next.**

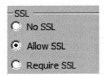

      g.   On the **Authentication and Authorization Information** page, in the **Authentication** section, check the **Basic** check box and click **Finish.**

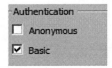

      h.   Verify that in the left pane **Default FTP site** is selected and from the **Default FTP Site Home** pane, double-click **FTP Authorization Rules.**

      i.   In the **Actions** pane, click the **Add Allow Rule** link.

      j.   Verify that all users are allowed access to the FTP site. In the **Permissions** section, check the **Read** check box and click **OK.**

      k.   Close the Internet Information Services (IIS) Manager window.

---

7.   Verify the FTP connection.

      a.   Choose **Start→Command Prompt.**

      b.   In the command line, enter *ftp server##* where *##* is the number assigned to your partner's computer.

      c.   When the system prompts you to enter a user name, enter *Administrator*

      d.   When the system prompts you to enter the password, enter *!Pass1234*

e. Observe that you are logged in. Close the Command Prompt window.

```
Microsoft Windows [Version 6.1.7600]
Copyright (c) 2009 Microsoft Corporation.  All rights reserved.

C:\Users\Administrator>ftp server01
Connected to server01.
220 Microsoft FTP Service
User (server01:(none)): Administrator
331 Password required for Administrator.
Password:
230 User logged in.
ftp>
```

ACTIVITY 3-4
Securing Network Traffic Using IPSec

 There is a simulated version of this activity available on the CD-ROM that shipped with this course. You can run this simulation on any Windows computer to review the activity after class, or as an alternative to performing the activity as a group in class. The activity simulation can be launched either directly from the CD-ROM by clicking the **Interactives** link and navigating to the appropriate one, or from the installed data file location by opening the C:\SPlus\ Simulations\Lesson#\Activity# folder and double-clicking the executable (.exe) file.

Setup:

You will work with a partner in this exercise.

Scenario:

You are the security administrator for an organization called MultiCor International, which does consulting for military personnel. As the organization begins the process of adopting a security policy, you want to be sure you understand some basic ideas about the Windows IPSec policies and management tools.

Most of MultiCor's consulting is done on site at military bases throughout the world that are in different domains. It is your responsibility to set up computers in each site, so that consultants can fill out background check applications and send them to a security officer for review. The consultants will then be granted or denied the appropriate clearance to enter the military installations. You want to transfer the data securely between the computers in different domains by using IPSec. Because you do not have Kerberos-based authentication in your workgroup, or have a Certificate Authority (CA) available at the various military sites, IPSec security will be based on the use of pre-shared keys. For your implementation of IPSec, you will use a pre-shared key of *key123.*

---

1. Create a custom MMC console containing **IP Security Policy Management** and **IP Security Monitor**.

   a. Click **Start.**

   b. Enter *mmc*

   c. Maximize the Console1 - [Console Root] window.

   d. Choose **File→Add/Remove Snap-in.**

   e. In the **Available snap-ins** list, select **IP Security Monitor** and click **Add.**

   f. Select **IP Security Policy Management** and click **Add.**

   g. In the **Select Computer or Domain** dialog box, select **The Active Directory domain of which this computer is a member** and click **Finish.**

   ⦿ The Active Directory domain of which this computer is a member

h. Click **OK** to close the **Add or Remove Snap-ins** dialog box.

i. Choose **File→Save As.**

j. Type *IPSec Management* as the file name.

k. Click **Save** to save the console to the default location.

---

2. Modify the appropriate IPSec policy for your computer to use a pre-shared key of *key123.*

    a. If necessary, in the console tree pane of the IPSec Management console window, select **IP Security Policies on Active Directory.**

    b. In the console tree pane of the IPSec Management console window, select **IP Security Policies on Active Directory**, and double-click the **Secure Server (Require Security)** policy.

    c. In the **IP Filter List,** verify that the **All IP Traffic** filter is selected and click **Edit.**

    d. In the **Edit Rule Properties** dialog box, select the **Authentication Methods** tab.

    e. In the **Authentication method preference order** section, click **Add.**

    f. In the **New Authentication Method Properties** dialog box, select **Use this string (preshared key).**

 Enter the key exactly as it appears here. IPSec is case-sensitive.

    g. In the **Use this string (preshared key)** text box, click and type *key123*

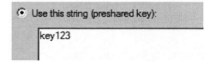

    h. Click **OK.**

    i. In the **Authentication method preference order** list, verify that **Preshared Key** is selected and click **Move up.**

    j. Verify that **Preshared Key** is now first in the list. Click **OK.**

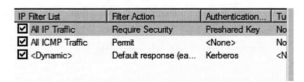

IP Filter List	Filter Action	Authentication...	Tu
☑ All IP Traffic	Require Security	Preshared Key	No
☑ All ICMP Traffic	Permit	<None>	No
☑ <Dynamic>	Default response (ea...	Kerberos	<N

    k. In the **Secure Server (Require Security) Properties** dialog box, click **OK.**

---

3. Assign the policy to your domain.

 After you assign the policy, you need to wait for your partner before proceeding to the next step.

---

a. Choose **Start→Administrative Tools→Group Policy Management.**

b. In the console tree, select **Default Domain Policy.**

c. In the **Group Policy Management Console** dialog box, click **OK.**

d. Choose **Action→Edit.**

e. In the **Group Policy Management Editor,** in the console tree under **Computer Configuration,** expand **Policies, Windows Settings, Security Settings,** and select **IP Security Policies on Active Directory (domain##.internal)** where **##** is your domain number.

 It may take a moment for the security settings to expand.

f. In the right pane, select **Secure Server (Require Security)** policy and choose **Action→Assign.**

 All students in the classroom must have this policy assigned.

g. Verify that the **Policy Assigned** value for the **Secure Server (Require Security)** policy is **Yes.**

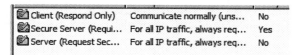

4. Make sure the IPSec Policy Agent service starts automatically.

   a. Choose **Start→Administrative Tools→Services.**

   b. Scroll down and double-click **IPsec Policy Agent.**

   c. If necessary, from the **Startup type** drop-down list, select **Automatic.**

   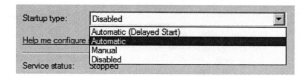

   d. To apply the changes, click **Apply.**

   e. Click **OK** and then close the Services window.

5. Verify that you have the **Secure Server (Require Security)** policy active in your domain.

   a. On the Windows taskbar, click **IPSec Management - [Console Root\IP Security Policies on Active Directory].**

   b. In the tree pane of the IPSec Management console window, expand **IP Security Monitor** and expand the server object.

   c. If necessary, select the server object and choose **Action→Reconnect.**

   d. Verify that your computer object appears with a green upward-pointing arrow. Select **Active Policy.**

   e. Verify that the **Policy Name** shows **Secure Server (Require Security),** indicating that the policy is active in your domain. This may take a moment.

6. Test the connection to your partner's machine.

   a. Click **Start.**

   b. Type **\\Server##** and press **Enter.**

   c. Close your partner's computer window.

   d. In the IPSec Management [Console Root\IP Security Policies on Active Directory] window, expand **Main Mode.**

   e. Select the **Security Associations** folder.

    f.   In the middle pane, verify that your partner's IP address is listed in the **Peer** column, and then expand **Quick Mode.**

    g.   Select the **Statistics** folder, and observe the data sent back and forth with your partner's computer and then close the IPSec Management window without saving.

---

7.   To prevent connection problems with other classroom hosts, unassign the IPSec policy.

    a.   In the Group Policy Management Editor window, verify that **IP Security Policies on Active Directory (domain#.internal)** is selected.

    b.   Select the **Secure Server (Require Security)** policy and choose **Action→Unassign.**

    c.   Close all open windows.

TOPIC D

Apply Network Security Administration Principles

In the previous topics, you covered the networking components, devices, and protocols. With this knowledge and understanding, you are prepared to apply the security administration principles used to govern network security. In this topic, you will explore the various administration principles applied to network security.

It is not only important to understand what makes up a network, and how it is designed, but it is just as important to understand the principles applied to managing the network's day-to-day operations and security. How a network is managed can not only affect its security, but can also affect its availability to the users who need to access it. With the proper security administration principles applied, a business can ensure that systems and applications are available to the users who rely on them.

Rule-Based Management

Definition:

Rule-based management is the use of operational rules or restrictions to govern the security of an organization's infrastructure. Typically, rules are incorporated into organizational policies that get disseminated throughout an organization.

Example:

A company that uses a security policy to determine how employees can access the Internet and other network resources is an example of a rule-based management approach.

Network Administration Security Methods

There are many tools that can be implemented within an organization to secure the networking infrastructure.

Security Method	Description
Flood guards	This is a tool used by network administrators and security professionals to protect resources from flooding attacks, such as Distributed Denial of Service (DDoS) attacks. Flood guards can be implemented at the enterprise level and are designed to protect an organization's entire network. The tool includes detectors that are distributed throughout a network at points that are susceptible to DDoS attacks. The detectors will react when an attack occurs and will apply appropriate mitigation techniques. As a security professional, you may need to advise organizations if and when they need to consider a flood guard installation.

Security Method	Description
Loop protection	Network loops can occur when one or more pathways exist between the endpoints in a network and packets get forwarded over and over again. This can be of concern in complex networks with many networking devices and can cause flooding issues within the network. Security professionals must assess and determine what loop protection methods are needed, such as applying proper router configurations and verifying that proper manufacturer configurations are also applied.
Port security	Properly securing ports on a network includes: • Disabling unnecessary services. • Closing ports that are by default open or have limited functionality. • Regularly applying the appropriate patches. • Hiding responses from ports that indicate their status and allow access to pre-configured connections only.
Secure router configuration	Ensuring that all routers on the network are properly secured will protect your network from attacks and can also prevent routing loops, which are caused by a routing algorithm error that creates a looping pattern.
Network separation	Splitting your network into two or more logically separated networks helps separate critical network functions from lower-priority functions so that security can be managed on a critical versus non-critical basis. It can also prevent intruders from getting to other systems, and helps enforce access control efforts.
VLAN management	VLAN configurations can be very complicated. With proper management procedures in place, security measures can be implemented and managed quickly. Most organizations will keep track of VLAN configurations using diagrams and documentation.
Implicit deny	Use the principle of implicit deny when granting access to network resources within a network.
Log analysis	Regular monitoring and analyzing of security logs helps detect any unauthorized intrusion attempts on the network. It is also wise to regularly review logs and assess any data leaks and insider threats that may be present.

How to Apply Network Security Administration Principles

Almost all security administrators are faced with the challenge of securing their networks to prevent attacks from external and internal sources. In order to do this efficiently, every organization facing this issue should have a well-defined network security administration model. This model should contain best practices and guidelines that any new security administrator can follow as he or she takes up the responsibility of securing the network.

Guidelines

To apply network security administration principles, you should:

- Manage the network devices such as firewalls, routers, switches, load balancers, proxies, and other all-in-one appliances to ensure that configurations conform with your security policies.

- Maintain documentation about all current server configurations.

- Establish and document baselines that suit your organization.

- Set up strong access control lists (ACLs) in sensitive resources on your network, and use the principle of implicit deny to ensure that unauthorized users and groups cannot inadvertently access information when they do not have specific rights to do so.

- Update antivirus software regularly. If possible, this task should be automated.

- Configure the required network services only. Configuring too many network services creates additional exploit points.

- Have a good backup strategy and disaster recovery plan (DRP) in place.

- Apply security updates and patches regularly.

- Ensure that sensitive data is well encrypted.

- Regularly check event logs for unusual activities.

- Monitor network activities on a regular basis.

Example:

Ralph, the newly hired network administrator in a multinational corporation, is familiarizing himself with the company's security policies with the help of his senior administrator, Angela. Angela explains to Ralph that the company's network hardware maintenance is critical to keep the network operational. She shows him the server configurations and server baselines that are optimally set to suit the company's operations.

A few weeks later, one of the wireless routers in the company fails. Angela takes this opportunity to show Ralph how to configure and set up the wireless router so that the company's sensitive data will not be compromised.

Ralph learns how to monitor network activities and he makes it a habit to check the event logs for unusual activities on a regular basis. He also refers to the company's DRPs and backup strategies so that he can act quickly when disaster strikes.

ACTIVITY 3-5
Securing a Windows Server 2008 R2 Router

 There is a simulated version of this activity available on the CD-ROM that shipped with this course. You can run this simulation on any Windows computer to review the activity after class, or as an alternative to performing the activity as a group in class. The activity simulation can be launched either directly from the CD-ROM by clicking the **Interactives** link and navigating to the appropriate one, or from the installed data file location by opening the C:\SPlus\ Simulations\Lesson#\Activity# folder and double-clicking the executable (.exe) file.

Setup:

You will work with a partner in this exercise. The two peer routers will represent the two routers in the DMZ.

Scenario:

As the security administrator for a small regional bank, you have the task of ensuring that the bank's routers are secure. In the past, the bank had problems with attackers accessing services and data that they were not supposed to have access to through the routers. Before connecting the new Windows Server 2008 routers behind a firewall on your network, you want to make sure that your routers are hardened to minimize the likelihood of attacks, especially DDoS and spoofing attacks from external users. After you configure the routers, the bank's desktop team will test the connections from laptops to make sure the security is not too restrictive.

To prevent users from accessing restricted information and to prevent attackers from getting data, the bank's IT department has decided to create a DMZ by implementing two software-based routers using the Windows Server 2008 Routing and Remote Access Servers. These routers will be installed behind the existing hardware-based firewall, which has already been hardened. To help ensure security on these software-based routers, they will run RIPv2 and will communicate with each other securely through RIP peer security. The bank also wants to implement packet filters to drop incoming external packets with internal private IP addresses as the source addresses to prevent attackers from spoofing internal IP addresses on the private subnet.

---

1. Install RIPv2 for IP, using the Local Area Connection as the RIP protocol interface.

    a. Choose **Start→Administrative Tools→Routing and Remote Access.**

b.   If necessary, expand the server object and then expand IPv4, select the **General** object, and choose **Action→New Routing Protocol.**

c.   In the **New Routing Protocol** dialog box, in the **Routing protocols** list, select **RIP Version 2 for Internet Protocol** and click **OK.**

d.   Under **IPv4,** select the **RIP** object and choose **Action→New Interface.**

e.   In the **Interfaces** list, verify that **Local Area Connection** is selected and click **OK** twice.

---

2.   Modify the RIP protocol's security properties with the appropriate peer router settings.

a.   In the tree pane, if necessary, select the **RIP object** and choose **Action→ Properties.**

b.   In the **RIP Properties** dialog box, select the **Security** tab.

c.   Select **Accept announcements from listed routers only.**

d.   In the **Router IP Address** text box, type your partner router's IP address.

e.   Click **Add.**

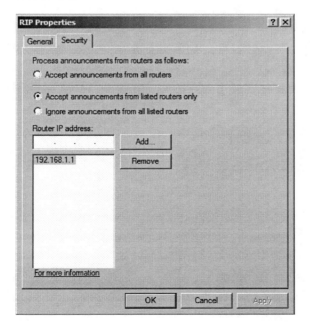

    f.   Click **OK.**

3.   Verify filtering on the external router interface.

    a.   In **Routing and Remote Access,** under **IPv4,** select **General.**

    b.   In the right pane, select **Loopback Adapter.**

    c.   Choose **Action→Properties.**

    d.   On the **General** tab, click **Inbound Filters.**

    e.   Click **New.**

    f.   Check the **Source network** check box.

    g.   Under **Source Network,** in the **IP address** text box, type *192.168.0.0*

    h.   In the **Subnet mask** text box, click and type *255.255.0.0*

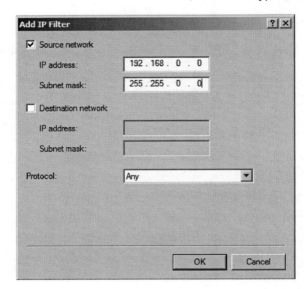

    i.   Click **OK.**

    j.   Under **Filter action,** select **Receive all packets except those that meet the criteria below** and click **OK.**

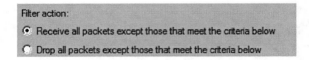

    k.   Click **OK.**

4.   Verify the connection.

    a.   If necessary, under **IPv4,** select **General.**

    b.   In the right pane, under the **Incoming bytes** and **Outgoing bytes** sections, verify that data packets are received and sent.

    c.   In the tree in the left pane, select **RIP.**

d. On the right pane, under the **Responses sent** and **Responses received** sections, verify that responses are sent and received.

e. Close the Routing and Remote Access window.

ACTIVITY 3-6
Securing a File Server

 There is a simulated version of this activity available on the CD-ROM that shipped with this course. You can run this simulation on any Windows computer to review the activity after class, or as an alternative to performing the activity as a group in class. The activity simulation can be launched either directly from the CD-ROM by clicking the **Interactives** link and navigating to the appropriate one, or from the installed data file location by opening the C:\SPlus\Simulations\Lesson#\Activity# folder and double-clicking the executable (.exe) file.

Scenario:

Your next task as the bank's security administrator is to make sure your file servers are secure. As the security administrator, you will implement the following system-wide security measures:

- Disable any unnecessary services.
- Convert any File Allocation Table (FAT) or FAT32 volumes to NT File System (NTFS).
- Securely share the ITData folder on each server. Only members of the Administrators group and individually designated users should be able to access this folder.
- Enable encryption on the ITData folder.

---

1. Turn off unnecessary services.

    a. Choose **Start→Administrative Tools→Services.**

    b. In the Services window, on the right pane, scroll down and double-click **Print Spooler.**

    c. In the **Print Spooler Properties (Local Computer)** dialog box, from the **Startup type** drop-down list, select **Disabled** and click **Stop.**

    d. Click **OK.**

    e. In the Services window, on the right pane, scroll down and double-click **Smart Card.**

    f. In the **Smart Card Properties (Local Computer)** dialog box, from the **Startup type** drop-down list, select **Disabled** and click **Apply.**

    g. Click **OK.**

    h. Close the Services window.

---

2. Convert the S drive to NTFS.

    a. Choose **Start→Computer.**

    b. Select the **S drive** and choose **Organize→Properties.**

    c. Verify that the file system is **FAT32** and the volume label is **STORAGE.** Click **OK.**

    d. Close the **Computer** window.

---

e. Choose **Start→Command Prompt.**

f. Enter ***convert s:/fs:ntfs***

g. When prompted for the volume label for drive S, enter ***storage***

h. After the file system conversion, close the command prompt window.

3. Verify the conversion of the S drive to NTFS.

a. Select the **S drive** and choose **Organize→Properties.**

b. Verify that the file system is NTFS. Click **OK** to close the **STORAGE (S:) Properties** dialog box.

4. Share the S:\ITData folder.

a. From the navigation bar on the left side, select the **STORAGE (S:)** drive and then select the **ITData** folder on the right-pane.

b. With the **ITData** folder selected, choose **Organize→Properties.**

c. Select the **Sharing** tab and click **Share.**

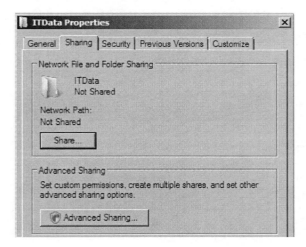

d. In the **Choose people on your network to share with** section, from the drop-down list, select **Find people.**

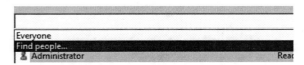

e. In the **Enter the object names to select** field, type ***John*** and then click **Check Names.**

f. Click **OK,** and then in the **Permission Level** drop-down list for **John E. Greg,** select **Read/Write.**

g. Click **Share** to share the folder.

h. In the **File Sharing** message box, verify that your folder is shared. Click **Done.**

     i.   In the **ITData Properties** dialog box, click **Advanced Sharing** to display the **Advanced Sharing** dialog box.

     j.   In the **Advanced Sharing** dialog box, click **Permissions.**

     k.   In the **Permissions for ITData** dialog box, click **Add.**

     l.   Type *John* and click the **Check Names** button.

     m.   Click **OK.**

     n.   In the **Permissions for John E. Greg** section, check the **Allow** check box for **Full Control** and click **OK.**

     o.   Click **OK** to close the Advanced Sharing window.

5.   Encrypt the S:\ITData folder.

     a.   Select the **General** tab.

     b.   Click **Advanced.**

     c.   In the **Advanced Attributes** dialog box, check the **Encrypt contents to secure data** check box.

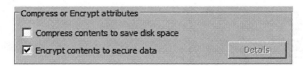

     d.   Click **OK** to close the **Advanced Attributes** dialog box.

     e.   Click **Apply** to encrypt the folder.

     f.   In the **Confirm Attribute Changes** dialog box, click **OK.**

     g.   Click **Close.**

 This process may take a few moments to complete.

     h.   Verify the encryption is applied by clicking outside the folder. Observe that the folder has changed to a green color.

     i.   Close Windows Explorer.

TOPIC E

Secure Wireless Traffic

In the previous topics, you examined the devices, components, protocols, and security administration principles used in network security, and now you will examine how to secure the wireless components of a network. Wireless networking is common in all local area network (LAN) environments, and wireless devices and protocols pose their own security challenges. In this topic, you will learn to secure traffic over wireless LAN connections.

Wireless networking has become a standard in most networks because of the mobility it gives to network users and the simplicity of connecting components to a local area network (LAN). However, that very simplicity creates security problems, because any attacker with physical access and a laptop with a wireless network adapter can attach to your wireless LAN, and once an attacker is on your network, you have trouble. If you know the right security procedures, you can provide the convenience of wireless connections to your users without compromising network security.

802.11 Standards

There are various 802.11 standards that you may encounter in networking implementations in your role as a security professional. Each of the approved standards in the 802.11 family has different characteristics.

Wireless Protocol	Description
802.11	A family of specifications developed by the IEEE for wireless local area network (LAN) communications between wireless devices or between wireless devices and a base station. The standard is supported by various working groups, known collectively as 802.11x. It specifies wireless data transfer rates of up to 2 megabits per second (Mbps) in the 2.4 gigahertz (GHz) frequency band.
802.11a	The approved specification for a fast, secure, but relatively expensive wireless protocol. 802.11a supports speeds up to 54 Mbps in the 5 GHz frequency band. Unfortunately, that speed has a limited range of only 60 feet, which, depending on how you arrange your access points, could severely limit user mobility.
802.11b	Also called Wi-Fi, short for "wired fidelity," 802.11b is probably the most common and certainly the least expensive wireless network protocol. 802.11b provides for an 11 Mbps transfer rate in the 2.4 GHz frequency. (Some vendors, such as D-Link, have increased the rate on their devices to 22 Mbps.) 802.11b has a range up to 1,000 feet in an open area and a range of 200 to 400 feet in an enclosed space (where walls might hamper the signal). It is backwards compatible with 802.11, but is not interoperable with 802.11a.
802.11g	The specification for wireless data throughput at the rate of up to 54 Mbps in the 2.4 GHz band. It is compatible with 802.11b and may operate at a much faster speed.
802.11n	A recent specification for wireless data throughput. Even before approval, many "Draft N" or "Pre-N" products were already being produced and sold, which were compliant with the specification. The specification increased speeds dramatically, with data throughput up to 600 Mbps in the 2.4 GHz or 5 GHz ranges.

Wireless Security Protocols

There are several major wireless security protocols.

Security Protocol	Description
Wired Equivalent Privacy (WEP)	Provides 64-bit, 128-bit, and 256-bit encryption using the Rivest Cipher 4 (RC4) algorithm for wireless communication that uses the 802.11a and 802.11b protocols. While WEP might sound like a good solution at first, it ironically is not as secure as it should be. The problem stems from the way WEP produces the keys that are used to encrypt data. Because of a flaw in the method, attackers could easily generate their own keys using a wireless network capture tool, such as Kismet, to capture and analyze as little as 10 MB of data transferred through the air.
Wireless Transport Layer Security (WTLS)	The security layer of the Wireless Application Protocol (WAP) that uses public key cryptography for mutual authentication and data encryption. In most cases, WTLS is meant to provide secure WAP communications, but if it is improperly configured or implemented, it can expose wireless devices to attacks that include email forgery and sniffing data that has been sent in plaintext.
802.1x	An IEEE standard used to provide a port-based authentication mechanism for wireless communications using the 802.11a and 802.11b protocols. 802.1x uses the Extensible Authentication Protocol (EAP) to provide user authentication against a directory service.
Wi-Fi Protected Access (WPA/WPA2)	The security protocol introduced to address some of the shortcomings in WEP. WPA was introduced during the development of the 802.11i IEEE standard, and WPA2 implemented all the mandatory components of the standard. It provides for dynamic reassignment of keys to prevent the key-attack vulnerabilities of WEP. • WPA provides improved data encryption through the *Temporal Key Integrity Protocol (TKIP),* which is a security protocol created by the IEEE 802.11i task group to replace WEP. It is combined with the existing WEP encryption to provide a 128-bit encryption key that fixes the key length issues of WEP. • In addition to TKIP, WPA2 adds Advanced Encryption Standard (AES) cipher-based *Counter Mode with Cipher Block Chaining Message Authentication Code Protocol (CCMP)* encryption for even greater security and to replace TKIP. It provides a 128-bit encryption key. • Both standards have been extended to include several types of user authentication through EAP, which is considered poor in WEP. WEP regulates access to a wireless network based on a computer's hardware-specific MAC address, which is relatively easy to figure out, steal, and use (that is, sniff and spoof). EAP is built on a more secure public key encryption system to ensure that only authorized network users can access the network.

Security Protocol	Description
EAP	A framework that allows clients and servers to authenticate with each other using one of a variety of plug-ins. Because EAP does not specify which authentication method should be used, it enables the choice of a wide range of current authentication methods, and allows for the implementation of future authentication methods. EAP is often utilized in wireless networks and can also be used in wired implementations. Two common EAP implementations include: • *Protected Extensible Authentication Protocol (PEAP)*, which is an open standard developed by a coalition made up of Cisco Systems, Microsoft, and RSA Security. • *Lightweight Extensible Authentication Protocol (LEAP)*, which is Cisco Systems' proprietary EAP implementation.

WAP

Wireless Application Protocol (WAP) is a protocol designed to transmit data such as web pages, email, and newsgroup postings to and from wireless devices such as mobile phones, smartphones, and handheld computers over very long distances, and display the data on small screens in a web-like interface.

WAP uses the proprietary Wireless Markup Language (WML) rather than native Hypertext Markup Language (HTML). WAP has five layers: Wireless Application Environment, Wireless Session Protocol, Wireless Transport Protocol, Wireless Transport Layer Security (WTLS), and the Wireless Datagram Protocol. The WAP standard was developed by companies such as Ericsson, Motorola, and Nokia. The standard is currently maintained by the Open Mobile Alliance (OMA), on the web at **www.openmobilealliance.org**.

Wireless Security Methods

There are a number of security methods you can use to ensure that your wireless network is secure from unauthorized access.

Security Method	Countermeasures
Configuration	• Secure your wireless router or access point administration interface. • Change default administrator passwords (and user names). • Disable remote administration. • Secure/disable the reset switch/function. • Change the default SNMP parameter. • Change the default channel. • Regularly upgrade the Wi-Fi router firmware to ensure you have the latest security patches and critical fixes. • Apply MAC address filtering. By configuring a wireless access point (WAP) to filter MAC addresses, you can control which wireless clients may join your network.
SSID	• Don't broadcast your Service Set Identifier (SSID). • Change the default SSID broadcast.

Security Method	Countermeasures
Encryption	• Enable WPA2 encryption instead of WEP. • Change the default encryption keys. • Avoid using pre-shared keys (PSK).
Network	• Assign static IP addresses to devices. • Use MAC filtering for access control. • Use the Remote Authentication Dial-In User Service Plus (RADIUS+) network directory authentication where feasible. • Use a VPN. • Perform periodic rogue wireless access point scans. • Perform periodic security assessments.
Antennae placement and power level configuration	• Reduce your wireless LAN transmitter power. • Position the router or access point safely. The radio frequency range of each access point should not extend beyond the physical boundaries of the organization's facilities. • Adjust the power level controls on routers and access points as needed to help minimize power consumption within the wireless network. It can be difficult to manage the power of wireless to reduce the power used, while providing the right level of power to operate the network.
Client	• Do not auto-connect to open Wi-Fi networks. • Enable firewalls on each computer and the router.

How to Secure Wireless Traffic

When you secure wireless traffic, you must prevent unauthorized network access and the theft of network data while ensuring that authorized users can connect to the network.

Guidelines

Some steps you might take to secure wireless traffic include:

- Keep sensitive data private. Do not include any data on a wireless device, such as a smartphone, that you are not willing to lose if the device is lost or stolen.

- Install antivirus software if it is available for your wireless devices.

- Update the software on wireless devices and routers to provide additional functionality as well as to close security holes in wireless devices such as:

  - To prevent bluejacking and bluesnarfing attacks, disable the discovery setting on Bluetooth connections.

  - Set Bluetooth connections to hidden.

- Implement a security protocol.

- Implement appropriate authentication and access control, such as MAC address filtering or user authentication, against a directory service to prevent authentication attacks such as war driving.

- To protect against rogue access point attacks and data emanation, implement an intrusion detection system (IDS) on the wireless network for monitoring network activity.

- Implement your hardware and software manufacturers' security recommendations.

- Test the functionality of systems after hardening them to make sure that required services and resources are accessible to legitimate users.
- Document your changes.

Example: AFR Travel's Wireless Network

AFR Travel is a small regional travel company with a central office and several branch locations in shopping malls and other venues. AFR Travel has many travel consultants and agents who use wireless laptops to work in different locations within the main office or in branch offices. They also use mobile devices to check email and web-based travel data from any location. All wireless devices have antivirus software installed, and all software patches are kept up to date.

Wireless routers are also patched with the latest firmware updates. AFR Travel employs the 802.11i security protocol for data encryption. All authentication is performed through EAP against the Active Directory accounts database.

ACTIVITY 3-7
Securing Wireless Traffic

 This is a simulated activity that is available on the CD-ROM that shipped with this course. In addition to using the simulation in class, you can run it on any Windows computer to review the activity after class. The activity simulation can be launched directly from the CD-ROM by clicking the **Interactives** button and navigating to the appropriate one, or from the default installed datafile location by opening the C:\SPlus\Simulations\Lesson#\Activity# folder and double-clicking the executable (.exe) file.

Setup:

This is a simulated activity using a Cisco Linksys Wireless-G broadband router, model WRT54G2. The simulation file is available in the course Data folder.

Scenario:

You have been assigned the task of tightening security for the sales department of MultiCor International. Many of the employees in this department are mobile users, and it is your responsibility to set up Windows laptop and desktop computers with wireless cards so that users can communicate with each other without having to run any cables. The department manager is concerned that attackers may steal client information. He says that employees run applications and transfer customer data and sales information on Windows client systems configured in a workgroup. He wants to make sure that only valid computers can communicate with each other. You have successfully tested Internet access through the router on the first desktop computer. Now, you need to configure the router's security features.

---

1.   Configure the wireless security on your wireless router.

     a.   Browse to the C:\SPlus\Simulations\Lesson3\Activity7 folder.

     b.   Double-click the executable file.

     c.   In the **Open File - Security Warning** message box, click **Run.**

     d.   Follow the on-screen steps for the simulation.

     e.   Close the C:\SPlus\Simulations folder.

Lesson 3 Follow-up

In this lesson, you examined the many different components that play a role in securing a network against threats and vulnerabilities. Having a good, basic network security understanding will enable you to evaluate an organization's security infrastructure as well as to provide valuable advice on network security management.

1. **Were there any network security components you were familiar with? What experience do you have with them?**

2. **Do you have any experience with securing a wireless network? If so, then what security measures have you applied?**

4 Managing Application, Data, and Host Security

Lesson Time: 3 hour(s)

Lesson Objectives:

In this lesson, you will manage application, data, and host security.

You will:

- Establish device/host security.

- Identify application security issues and methods.

- Analyze components of data security.

- Identify components of mobile security.

Introduction

In previous lessons, you reviewed the most common threats and attacks that can affect people, devices, and networks. With that knowledge, you can transition to applying security measures to applications, data, and devices to prevent threats and vulnerabilities that are targeted to user end computing components. In this lesson, you will manage application, data, and host security.

Organizations are made up of many different computing devices that use a number of applications and services on a daily basis. As a security professional, it is your job to properly secure all user end devices, as well as the software and data used on these devices. Security must be applied to all levels of an organization. Without the proper security controls implemented at the level of individual hosts, data storage areas, and applications, then all other security controls applied within the organization will be wasted.

This lesson covers all or part of the following CompTIA® Security+® (Exam SY0-301) certification objectives:

- Topic A:

    - Objective 1.1 Explain the security function and purpose of network devices and technologies

    - Objective 1.2 Apply and implement secure network administration principles

    - Objective 1.3 Distinguish and differentiate network design elements and compounds

- Objective 5.2 Explain the fundamental concepts and best practices related to authentication, authorization and access control
- Objective 5.3 Implement appropriate security controls when performing account management
- Topic B:
  - Objective 1.1 Explain the security function and purpose of network devices and technologies
  - Objective 4.1 Explain the importance of application security
  - Objective 4.2 Carry out appropriate procedures to establish host security
- Topic C:
  - Objective 4.3 Explain the importance of data security
  - Objective 6.2 Use and apply appropriate cryptographic tools and products
- Topic D:
  - Objective 1.2 Apply and implement secure network administration principles
  - Objective 4.2 Carry out appropriate procedures to establish host security

TOPIC A
Establish Device/Host Security

In the previous lesson, network-related security issues and controls were introduced, and in this lesson you will go a step further to make sure that the devices and hosts connecting to the network are also secure. In this topic, you will implement security measures for devices.

In order to properly protect an organization's assets as a whole, you must be able to secure its networks, devices, and end user systems. Most viruses today start from an individual machine first, then spread to other devices through a network. In order to prevent this type of infiltration, you must be able to establish necessary security measures on all the devices within an organization.

Hardening

Definition:

Hardening is a general term for any security technique in which the default configuration of a system is altered in an attempt to close vulnerabilities and generally protect the system against attacks. Typically, hardening is implemented to conform with the security requirements in a defined security policy. Many different hardening techniques can be employed, depending on the type of system and the desired level of security. When hardening a system, it is important to keep in mind its intended use because hardening a system can also restrict the system's access and capabilities. The need for hardening must be balanced against the access requirements and usability in a particular situation.

Example:

Figure 4-1: Hardening a system.

Operating System Security

Each type of operating system has unique vulnerabilities that present opportunities for would-be attackers. Systems from different vendors have different weaknesses, as do client and server systems. As soon as a vulnerability is identified, vendors will try to correct it while, at the same time, attackers will try to exploit it. There can never be a single comprehensive list of vulnerabilities for each operating system, so security professionals must stay up-to-date with the system security information posted on vendor websites and in other security references.

Operating System Security Settings

General operating system security settings include:

- Managing services running on the operating system.
- Configuring the operating system's built-in firewall.
- Configuring Internet security options.
- Managing all automatic updates and patches for software and services.
- And, enabling necessary auditing and logging functions when applicable.

TCB

Definition:

The *Trusted Computing Base (TCB)* is a hardware, firmware, and software component of a computer system that is responsible for ensuring that the security policy is implemented and the system is secure. This means that the security properties of an entire system could be jeopardized should defects occur inside the TCB. The TCB is implemented in the hardware through processor rings or privileges, in the firmware through driver and resource protection, and in the operating system's isolation of resources and services from applications, which is referred to as a *Trusted Operating System (TOS)*.

Example:

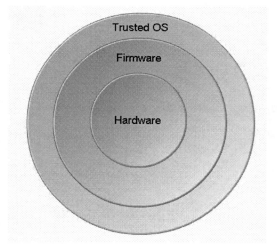

Figure 4-2: *A TCB.*

Trusted OS Certification

To meet government requirements and to be designated as a trusted OS, systems must adhere to the relevant set of standards accepted by that government. The Common Criteria (CC) certification is an international standard recognized by many governments. For more information, see **www.commoncriteriaportal.org**.

Security Baselines

Definition:

A *security baseline* is a collection of security and configuration settings that are to be applied to a particular host in the enterprise. The host software baseline is a benchmark against which you can compare other hosts in your network. When creating a baseline for a particular computer, the settings you decide to include will depend on its operating system and its function in your organization, and should include manufacturer recommendations.

Because each baseline configuration is specific to a particular type of system, you will have separate baselines defined for desktop clients, file and print servers, Domain Name System (DNS)/BIND servers, application servers, directory services servers, and other types of systems. You will also have different baselines for all those same types of systems, depending on the operating system in use.

Example:

Figure 4-3: Security baselines.

Security Analyzers

When establishing a security baseline for your host(s), you may find it helpful to make use of the many software tools that are available. Tools can be found to scan for and detect a very wide range of vulnerabilities ranging from port scanners to password analyzers to tools that scan for specific hard-to-detect vulnerabilities. For Unix-based systems, check to see if your software vendor provides any analysis tools that you could make use of, as they will likely make the analysis process far easier. Two such tools for Unix are Nessus® and Nmap. When dealing with Microsoft®-based systems, tools such as the Microsoft Baseline Security Analyzer (MBSA) and the **Security Configuration Wizard (SCW)** are good places to start.

Software Updates

Software manufacturers regularly issue different types of system updates that can include security-related changes to the software.

Update Type	Description
Patch	A small unit of supplemental code meant to address either a security problem or a functionality flaw in a software package or operating system.
Hotfix	A patch that is often issued on an emergency basis to address a specific security flaw.
Rollup	A collection of previously issued patches and hotfixes, usually meant to be applied to one component of a system, such as the web browser or a particular service.
Service Pack	A larger compilation of system updates that can include functionality enhancements, new features, and typically all patches, updates, and hotfixes issued up to the point of the release of the Service Pack.

Patch Management

Patch management is the practice of monitoring for, obtaining, evaluating, testing, and deploying software patches and updates. As the number of computer systems in use has grown over recent years, so has the volume of vulnerabilities and corresponding patches and updates intended to address those vulnerabilities. So, the task of managing and applying them can be very time-consuming and inefficient without an organized patch management system. In typical patch management, software updates are evaluated for their applicability to an environment and then tested in a safe way on non-production systems. Finally, an organized plan for rolling out a valid patch across the organization is executed.

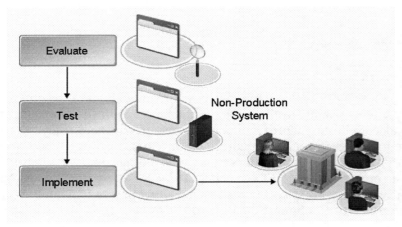

Figure 4-4: Patch management.

Patch Management Policies

Many organizations have taken to creating official patch management policies that define the who, what, where, when, why, and how of patch management for that organization.

Patch Management Example

A patch management program might include:

- An individual responsible for subscribing to and reviewing vendor and security patches and updating newsletters.

- A review and triage of the updates into urgent, important, and non-critical categories.

- An offline patch-test environment where urgent and important patches can be installed and tested for functionality and impact.

- Immediate administrative "push" delivery of approved urgent patches.

- Weekly administrative "push" delivery of approved important patches.

- A periodic evaluation phase and "pull" rollout for non-critical patches.

Logging

Definition:

In computing terms, *logging* is using an operating system or application to record data about activity on a computer. The resulting *log* files are usually stored as text files in known locations. The level of detail available in log files can vary from showing only significant errors, to the recording of every keystroke, mouse movement, and network packet. Use care when enabling logging features—detailed logging, or even simple logging on a high-volume system, can rapidly consume a large amount of storage space. Reviewing the activity recorded in log files can be difficult due to the variations in formatting and detail, but is worthwhile because the review may reveal a great deal about a suspected attack. Log files themselves can be the target of an attack; therefore, for security purposes, it is recommended that you restrict access to and back up important logs.

Example:

Log Files Are
Stored

Log Files Are
Generated from the
System

Figure 4-5: Logging.

Auditing

Definition:

Computer *security auditing* is the process of performing an organized technical assessment of the security strengths and weaknesses of a system. Computer security audits can include reviewing log files, either manually or via software, testing the strength of passwords, network scanning for open ports or rogue servers and workstations, reviewing user and group permissions, and reviewing the physical security related to the system or systems in question.

Example:

Figure 4-6: Auditing.

Anti-Malware Software

Definition:

Anti-malware software is protective software that scans individual computers and entire enterprise networks for known viruses, Trojans, worms, and other malicious programs. Some programs attempt to scan for unknown harmful software. It is advisable to install anti-malware software on all computers, and keep it updated according to your organization's patch management policy.

Example:

Figure 4-7: Anti-malware software.

Types of Anti-Malware Software

Many types of anti-malware software are commonly used to protect systems from specific threats and attacks.

Type	Description
Antivirus software	An application that scans files for executable code that matches specific patterns that are known to be common to viruses. Antivirus software also monitors systems for activity that is associated with viruses, such as accessing the boot sector. Antivirus software should be deployed on various network systems as well as on individual computers, and the signature database and program updates should be downloaded and installed on a regular basis as well as whenever a new threat is active.

Type	Description
Anti-spam	Spam detection has become an important task for end users. There are many different ways end users can protect themselves against spammers. Detection can include an anti-spam filtering program that will detect specific words that are commonly used in spam messages. The message may be rejected once the words are found. This can cause issues if the detection system rejects legitimate messages that may contain one of the keywords. Other detection methods are used to block Internet Protocol (IP) addresses of known spammers or to pose an email address that is not in use or is too old to collect spam. These methods can help reduce the number of spam messages in your inbox. Some examples of anti-spam software include SPAMfighter, iHateSpam, Cloudmark for Microsoft® Outlook®, and BullGuard™ Internet Security Suite.
Anti-spyware	This software is specifically designed to protect systems against spyware attacks. Some antivirus software packages include protection against adware and spyware, but in most cases it is necessary to maintain anti-spyware protection in addition to antivirus protection. Some examples of anti-spyware include Webroot's Spy Sweeper and STOPzilla Anti-Spyware.
Pop-up blockers	Malicious software can be attached to *pop-up* ads or other pop-up content on websites.(Pop-ups are windows or frames that load and appear automatically when a user connects to a particular web page.) Pop-up blockers prevent pop-ups from sites that are unknown or untrusted and prevent the transfer of unwanted code to the local system. Most Internet browsers include some type of pop-up blocking feature.
Host-based firewalls	This is software that is installed on a single system to specifically guard against networking attacks. The software is configured to monitor incoming and outgoing network packets in order to control and prevent unauthorized access.

Windows® Firewall Configuration

Windows® Firewall is a software-based firewall that is included with all current Windows operating system client and server versions. You can configure the firewall by using the Windows Firewall program in **Control Panel,** or through **Group Policy Settings,** although most versions of Windows will provide a wizard. You can use the Windows Firewall with Advanced Security console to monitor the rules that control the flow of information to and from the system, specify new rules, modify existing rules, or delete rules. For more information, see the Windows Firewall entries in the Help and Support Center, and the Windows Firewall Technical Reference on the Microsoft Technet website.

Types of Firewall Rules

There are three types of firewall rules that you can set using the Windows Firewall with Advanced Security console:

- Inbound rules: These rules define the action to be performed by the firewall on the data that enters the system from another system.

- Outbound rules: These rules define the action to be performed by the firewall on the data that flows out of the system.

- Connection security rules: These rules define the type of authentication that is needed to allow communication between the systems.

For more information about the Windows Firewall with Advanced Security console, refer to the Overview of Windows Firewall with Advanced Security at **http://technet.microsoft.com/en-us/library/dd448535(WS.10).aspx**.

Virtualization Security Techniques

The overall security of a system that is hosting a virtualization environment is crucial to ensuring the security of the network and devices connected to it. There are a number of security techniques available to properly secure a virtual host machine.

Security Technique	Description
Patch management	A patch management system must be in place to ensure that all patches are installed. This is especially important for any patches released that apply to the virtualization software itself. Careful analysis must be done to determine when and if general operating system patches should also be installed on the host. In some cases, these patches can threaten the security of the virtualization environment.
Least privilege	The concept of least privilege should be applied when determining access control assignments to any virtual environment. Access to all environments must be monitored on a regular basis to prevent unauthorized access.
Logging	User activities in the virtual environment should be logged and reviewed to check for irregular activity and any possible security breaches.
Design	Applying good security measures to all virtualization environments starts with a good design. By planning carefully and determining what security controls should be used on each component of the virtual environment, you can prevent many security-related issues once the virtualization environment is launched.

Hardware Security Controls

Because security is most often breached at the end user level, hardware security controls can be applied to help prevent security issues:

- Proper log off and shut down procedures must be enforced for all systems when not in use.
- Wireless communication devices must be approved by the IT department and installed properly.
- Mobile devices, such as laptops, mobile phones, and smartphones, must be properly stored and secured in a cabinet or safe when not in use.
- Cable locks should be installed and used on all end user hardware components.
- And, strong password policies should be enforced on all user end devices.

Strong Passwords

Definition:

A *strong password* is a password that meets the complexity requirements that are set by a system administrator and documented in a security policy or password policy. Strong passwords increase the security of systems that use password-based authentication by protecting against password guessing and brute force password attacks.

Password complexity requirements should meet the security needs of an individual organization, and can specify:

● The minimum length of the password.

● Required characters, such as a combination of letters, numbers, and symbols.

● And, forbidden character strings, such as the user account name or dictionary words.

Example:

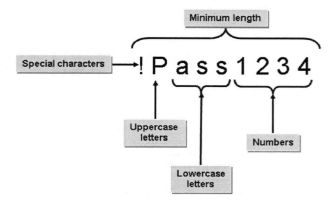

Figure 4-8: *Strong passwords.*

How to Establish Device/Host Security

In order to establish device and host security, you must implement security measures that protect the devices themselves from attack, and that prevent unauthorized access to your network, while ensuring that legitimate users continue to have the appropriate level of connectivity between internal and external networks.

Guidelines

Some steps for establishing host security include:

● Require strong passwords to protect against password-cracking utilities, to keep passwords secure, and to protect password databases.

● Implement your hardware and software manufacturers' security recommendations.

● Implement antivirus, anti-spyware, and anti-adware software to protect against malicious code.

● Disable unnecessary services to prevent attackers from exploiting them.

● Restrict access permissions so that only those users who absolutely need access are allowed into the system.

● Implement security policies to control, limit, or restrict user interaction with the system.

- Physically secure mission-critical servers and devices by installing them in locked rooms to which only trusted administrators have access.

- Plan backup strategies to protect sensitive data and provide methods to restore the data in the event of data loss or corruption. Backup media should be stored offsite. Backups help ensure business continuity in the event of an attack.

- Test the functionality of systems after hardening to make sure that required services and resources are accessible to legitimate users.

- Utilize scanning and auditing tools to detect potential vulnerabilities in your systems.

- Document your changes.

Some steps for establishing device security include:

- For software-based systems, harden the base operating system to close security holes in running services.

  For hardware-based systems, install the latest firmware updates to address known security issues.

- Implement your hardware and software manufacturers' security recommendations.

- Implement strict access control and use strong, robust passwords so that unauthorized persons cannot access and reconfigure the systems.

- Secure router configuration files to keep configuration details secret.

- Configure appropriate ingress and egress filters to help prevent IP spoofing and Denial of Service (DoS) attacks.

- Disable IP source routing to prevent attackers from gaining information about the internal network.

- Implement a routing protocol that supports authentication, such as Routing Information Protocol (RIP) version 2 (RIPv2), Enhanced Interior Gateway Routing Protocol (EIGRP), or Open Shortest Path First (OSPF), to enable a greater level of security and authentication and to help prevent unauthorized changes to routing tables.

- Protect routers, virtual local area networks (VLANs), Network Address Translation (NAT) devices, and other internetworking devices with properly configured firewalls.

- To protect against Address Resolution Protocol (ARP) poisoning, verify all routers are configured properly and are set up with notifications and appropriate monitoring software.

- Implement NAT to hide the true IP scheme of your network.

- Close unused well-known Transmission Control Protocol (TCP) and User Datagram Protocol (UDP) ports.

- Place appropriate servers in a demilitarized zone (DMZ).

- Disable IP directed broadcasts on routers.

- Protect all internetwork devices and network media from unauthorized physical access to prevent wiretapping, vandalism, and theft.

- Test the functionality of systems after hardening to make sure that required services and resources are accessible to legitimate users.

- Document your changes.

Example: AFR Travel's Servers

AFR Travel is a large travel company with a central office and several branch locations in shopping malls and other venues. AFR Travel wants to protect the base operating system security for all of its internal servers. When the servers are installed, all running services are evaluated, and unneeded services or applications are uninstalled or disabled.

Each branch office administrator must check for and apply all current operating system updates weekly. In addition, applications running on each server must be patched individually. The servers all have antivirus software installed, and the software is configured to automatically check for and download updated virus definitions weekly as well as perform regular virus scans.

Define New Firewall Rules

You can use the wizard-based interface to define new firewall rules for Windows Firewall.

To define a new inbound rule, perform the following steps:

a. Launch the **New Inbound Rule Wizard.**

b. Select the type of object to which the rule will apply: program, port, or service. You can also select a custom rule, which allows you to specify all the three objects listed earlier.

c. Based on the object type selected, specify the program path, port number (local port or remote), or service name.

d. Select whether the rule is to allow or block traffic.

e. Specify an appropriate name for the rule.

f. After ensuring the rule is active, enforce the rule using the command `gpupdate /force`.

g. Check whether the rule is enforced by launching the relevant application or performing the required actions.

The **Outbound Rule Wizard** is similar.

ACTIVITY 4-1
Implementing Auditing

 There is a simulated version of this activity available on the CD-ROM that shipped with this course. You can run this simulation on any Windows computer to review the activity after class, or as an alternative to performing the activity as a group in class. The activity simulation can be launched either directly from the CD-ROM by clicking the **Interactives** link and navigating to the appropriate one, or from the installed data file location by opening the C:\SPlus\Simulations\Lesson#\Activity# folder and double-clicking the executable (.exe) file.

Scenario:

As the security administrator for a small regional bank, you have been asked to configure your domain controllers to detect any unauthorized logon attempts.

1. Enable the auditing of all failed account logon events on your domain controllers.

    a. From the **Start** menu, choose **Group Policy Management.**

    b. If necessary, in the console tree, expand your domain object.

    c. If necessary, expand **Domain Controllers** and select **Default Domain Controllers Policy.**

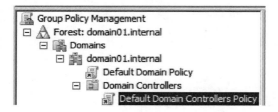

    d. If necessary, in the **Group Policy Management Console** message box, click **OK.**

    e. From the menu bar, choose **Action→Edit.**

f.   In the console tree, under **Computer Configuration,** expand **Policies, Windows Settings, Security Settings,** and **Local Policies.**

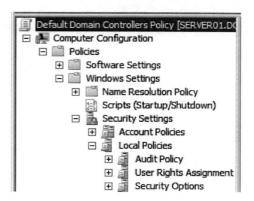

g.   Under **Local Policies,** select **Audit Policy.**

h.   In the details pane, double-click **Audit account logon events.**

i.   On the **Security Policy Setting** tab, check the **Define these policy settings** check box, verify that the **Success** check box is checked, and check the **Failure** check box to enable auditing of failed logon attempts.

j.   Click **OK.**

k.   Verify that the **Policy Setting** for **Audit account logon events** policy is changed to **Success, Failure.**

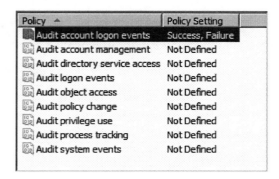

2.   Force a group policy update.

a. Open a Command Prompt window.

b. Enter **gpupdate /force**

c. Verify that the computer policy update has been completed successfully, and close the Command Prompt window.

d. Close the Group Policy Management Editor and Group Policy Management windows.

3. Generate auditing entries in the security log.

a. Log off and attempt to log back on as **Administrator** with an incorrect password.

b. Click **OK** and in the **Password** text box, enter **!Pass1234**

4. Verify that your auditing changes obtain the desired results.

a. Choose **Start→Administrative Tools→Event Viewer.**

b. Maximize the Event Viewer window.

c. In the console tree, expand **Windows Logs** and select the **Security** log.

d. In the **Actions** pane, in the **Security** section, click **Filter Current Log.**

e. In the **Filter Current Log** dialog box, in the **Keywords** drop-down list, check the **Audit Failure** check box and click **OK.**

f. The latest filtered event with **Logon** in the **Task Category** column represents your failed logon attempt. Double-click the log entry to review its content.

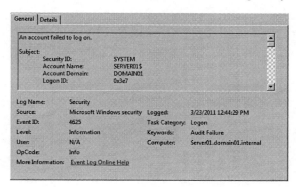

g. Close the log file.

h. Close the Event Viewer window.

ACTIVITY 4-2
Manually Harden a Windows Server 2008 R2 System

 There is a simulated version of this activity available on the CD-ROM that shipped with this course. You can run this simulation on any Windows computer to review the activity after class, or as an alternative to performing the activity as a group in class. The activity simulation can be launched either directly from the CD-ROM by clicking the **Interactives** link and navigating to the appropriate one, or from the installed data file location by opening the C:\SPlus\ Simulations\Lesson#\Activity# folder and double-clicking the executable (.exe) file.

Setup:
The Security Update for Windows Server 2008 R2 (KB2259539) is available in the C:\SPlus\ Security Update folder.

The MBSA installation files are available in C:\SPlus\MBSA. The Microsoft Windows Malicious Software Removal Tool installation files are available at C:\SPlus\SWRemove.

Scenario:
As the bank's security administrator, one of your primary responsibilities is to make sure all network computers are secured in accordance with the bank's security policy. The bank's security policy recommends applying the newest security updates and applying any additional security parameters defined in the bank's security policy. A recent audit has revealed that there is a machine that needs to have an update installed, as well as some additional security features.

Once you have installed the Service Pack, you must configure additional security parameters defined in the bank's security policy. These steps include:

- Install the Windows Server update.
- Run the MBSA to scan for security vulnerabilities.
- Scan for and remove any malware by using the Malicious Software Removal Tool.

---

1. Install Windows Server 2008 R2 Security Update (KB2259539).

    a. Browse to C:\SPlus\Security Update and double-click the Security Update executable file **Windows6. 1–KB2259539–x64.msu.**

    b. In the **Windows Update Standalone Installer** dialog box, click **Yes** to install the Security Update.

    c. When the installation is complete, click **Restart Now** to restart the computer.

    d. Log on as **Administrator.**

---

2. Verify the Security Update installation.

    a. While logged on as **Administrator,** choose **Start→Control Panel** and click **Programs** to open the Programs window.

---

b. In the Programs window, in the **Programs and Features** section, click the **View installed updates** link.

c. Observe that **Update for Microsoft Windows (KB2259539)** is shown as the update installed.

d. Close the Installed Updates window.

---

3. Install the MBSA.

a. Choose **Start→Run.**

b. In the **Open** text box, type *C:\SPlus\MBSA\MBSASetup-x64–EN.msi* and click **OK.**

c. In the **Open File - Security Warning** dialog box, click **Run.**

d. In the **MBSA Setup Wizard,** click **Next.**

e. Select **I accept the license agreement** and click **Next.**

f. Click **Next** to accept the destination folder.

g. Click **Install.**

h. After the installation process is completed, click **OK.**

---

4. Use the MBSA to scan your system to establish baseline security values.

a. On the desktop, double-click the **Microsoft Baseline Security Analyzer 2.2** short-cut.

b. In the **Check computers for common security misconfigurations** section, click the **Scan a computer** link.

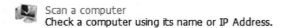

c. Verify that your computer name appears in the **Computer name** drop-down list, and uncheck the **Check for SQL administrative vulnerabilities** and **Check for security updates** check boxes.

d. Click **Start Scan.**

---

e.   Review the scan results and click any **What was scanned** or **How to correct this** links to view the security recommendations reported by MBSA.

f.   After you have reviewed the report, close the Microsoft Baseline Security Analyzer 2.2 window.

---

5.   Run the Malicious Software Removal Tool.

a.   Choose **Start→Run.**

b.   Type *C:\SPlus\SWRemove* and click **OK.**

c.   Double-click the installation application.

d.   In the **Open File - Security Warning** dialog box, click **Run.**

e.   If necessary, in the **Malicious Software Removal Tool** message box, click **OK** to continue with the current version of the tool.

f.   Check the **Accept all terms of the preceding license agreement** check box and click **Next.**

g.   Click the **View a list of malicious software that this tool detects and removes** link to view the malicious software list.

h.   Click **OK** to close the **Malicious Software Removal Tool** dialog box.

i.   Click **Next** to continue.

j.   On the **Scan type** page, verify that **Quick scan** is selected and click **Next.**

k.   Click the link **View detailed results of the scan** to view the scan results.

l.   Click **OK** and then click **Finish.**

m.   Close the SWRemove window.

---

6.   **According to general system hardening guidelines, what additional software should you install to combat malware on all systems?**

   a) Security Configuration Wizard

   b) Antivirus software

   c) A firewall

   d) Database software

ACTIVITY 4-3

Using the Security Configuration Wizard to Harden a Server

 There is a simulated version of this activity available on the CD-ROM that shipped with this course. You can run this simulation on any Windows computer to review the activity after class, or as an alternative to performing the activity as a group in class. The activity simulation can be launched either directly from the CD-ROM by clicking the **Interactives** link and navigating to the appropriate one, or from the installed data file location by opening the C:\SPlus\ Simulations\Lesson#\Activity# folder and double-clicking the executable (.exe) file.

Scenario:

In addition to the manual hardening tasks you completed to secure the bank's server machines, you must also use the **Security Configuration Wizard** to perform all suggested security configuration settings.

---

1. Use the **Security Configuration Wizard** to configure services settings.

   a. From the **Start** menu, choose **Administrative Tools→Security Configuration Wizard.**

   b. On the **Welcome to the Security Configuration Wizard** page, click **Next.**

   c. Verify that **Create a new security policy** option is selected and click **Next.**

   > Select the action you want to perform:
   >
   > ⦿ Create a new security policy
   > ○ Edit an existing security policy
   > ○ Apply an existing security policy
   > ○ Rollback the last applied security policy

   d. Verify that your server name appears in the **Server** text box and click **Next.**

   e. After the wizard builds the security configuration database, click **Next** twice.

   f. On the **Select Server Roles** page, scroll down two times to review the roles for which you can use the **Security Configuration Wizard** to harden your server. The **Security Configuration Wizard** uses this list to determine which services to leave running on your server. Click **Next.**

   g. On the **Select Client Features** page, scroll down to review the client features list. The **Security Configuration Wizard** also uses this list to determine which services it should leave running on your server.

   h. Uncheck the **Windows Update** check box and click **Next.**

    i.   On the **Select Administration and Other Options** page, scroll down four times to review the installed options. Click **Next**.

    j.   On the **Select Additional Services** page, click **Next**.

    k.   On the **Handling Unspecified Services** page, verify that **Do not change the startup mode of the service** is selected. You can use this page to configure the **Security Configuration Wizard** to automatically disable any services not specified within the wizard. Click **Next**.

    l.   On the **Confirm Service Changes** page, review the changes the **Security Configuration Wizard** proposes to your server's services. As you can see, the **Security Configuration Wizard** disables all services it identifies as unnecessary for the roles your server will now perform. From the **View** drop-down list, select **All services.**

    m.   Scroll down to verify that the **Windows Update** service is disabled at startup and then click **Next**.

2.   Skip the options for securing network communications and for configuring registry settings.

    a.   On the **Network Security** page, check the **Skip this section** check box and click **Next**.

    b.   On the **Registry Settings** page, check the **Skip this section** check box, and click **Next**.

3.   Use the **Security Configuration Wizard** to configure **Audit Policy** settings.

    a.   On the **Audit Policy** page, verify that the **Skip this section** check box is unchecked and click **Next**.

    b.   Review the **System Audit Policy** page. By default, the **Security Configuration Wizard** enables various auditing settings on your server. Click **Next**.

    c.   Review the **Audit Policy Summary** page. This page summarizes the changes the **Security Configuration Wizard** will make. Scroll down to review them and click **Next**.

4.   Save the security policy generated by the **Security Configuration Wizard.**

    a.   On the **Save Security Policy** page, click **Next**.

    b.   In the **Security policy file name** text box, at the end of the current path, type ***BankSCW1***

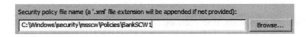

    c.   Click in the **Description** field and type ***Services and auditing as recommended by SCW.***

    d.   Click **Next** and then select **Apply now.**

    e.   To apply the template, click **Next**.

    f.   Once the application is complete, click **Next**.

    g.   Click **Finish.**

TOPIC B
Application Security

You established security measures for devices in the last topic. Now you will focus on the applications that run on these systems. Insecure applications can easily undermine the hardening efforts on the systems and network level if their security flaws are exploited. In this topic, you will identify application security methods.

Applications run on nearly every system in an organization, and are increasingly being delivered to those systems over the web. Insecure web-based applications can be vulnerable to a wide range of attacks, leaving your business at great risk. Employee or customer data could be stolen or damaged, or DoS conditions could be created. If your organization creates applications, unchecked vulnerabilities could result in dissatisfied customers and lost business. Even if you personally are not responsible for the application development functions in your organization, knowing some of the ways in which applications can be secured and how to mitigate threats can make you a more effective security professional.

What Is Application Security?

Application security ensures that the proper development, deployment, and maintenance of software is in place to protect applications from threats and vulnerabilities. Application security is applied in every phase of the software development process and should be incorporated into the initial design of all applications. With threats and attacks to applications on the rise, attackers will attempt to access and steal sensitive information through any vulnerability that exists in an application.

Application Security Methods

Several common application security methods are implemented to prevent and treat possible security threats and attacks.

Application Security Method	Description
Configuration baseline	An application configuration baseline is created at many points during the application development life cycle. A baseline is comprised of the minimum security requirements needed for an application to be complete. Organizations should determine a security baseline at the start of application development and track changes to make updates as needed. The baseline is also helpful when updates and changes are proposed.
Application hardening	The process used to configure a default application to prevent security threats and vulnerabilities. Each type of application will have its own configurations and methods used to increase security.
Patch management	Utilize a patch management system for your third-party software to ensure that every application is running with the latest security requirements and updates issued by manufacturers. Organizations should have an application patch management system in place to ensure that all patches are analyzed and installed as necessary.

Input Validation

Definition:

Input validation involves ensuring that the data entered into a field or variable in an application is within acceptable bounds for the object that will receive the data. Input data should be within the size constraints of the memory location that will store it, be formatted in the expected way, and make sense in the context for which it will be used. If a given piece of input data cannot meet these standards, it should be considered invalid and should not be processed.

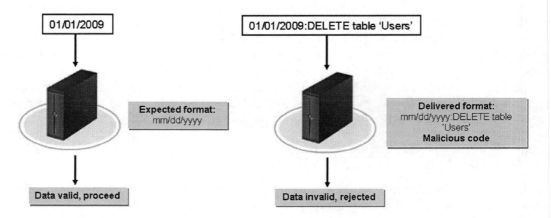

Figure 4-9: *Input validation.*

Example:

An input field on a web page asks for a date. An unvalidated input could allow an attacker to submit a chunk of text that is actually malicious code intended to exploit a vulnerability in the server or operating system software. Proper input validation would check to see if the submitted value is in the expected format (for example, mm/dd/yyyy for a date input). If the format is not correct, validation fails and the value is not recorded.

Input Validation Vulnerabilities

Input validation vulnerabilities can occur in any type of software. Websites and web-based applications are tempting targets for attackers to use input validation attacks because they are often developed by inexperienced coders, or put together in a hurry, with little thought to application or data security. All input fields from any source should be validated before processing.

Command Injection

Command injection, which is when an attacker sends additional commands to an application through an unchecked input field, is one way to exploit input validation vulnerabilities. For example, an attacker may use an Structured Query Language (SQL) injection attack to send extra SQL commands to a database through a web form or Uniform Resource Locator (URL). When the commands are successfully executed, that attacker could gain the ability to access, change, or delete data in the target database.

Error and Exception Handling

Error and exception handling is a strategy used by organizations to design and develop security measures that are targeted at possible errors in an application. This type of development strategy is used to prevent attackers from gathering and using sensitive data that may be presented in an error message when the application fails under normal working conditions. For example, in some cases when an attacker enters a user name and password, he or she may get an error message back stating that the password does not match the registered user name. In this case, the attacker now knows a valid user name, and can attempt to use that information to learn the valid password.

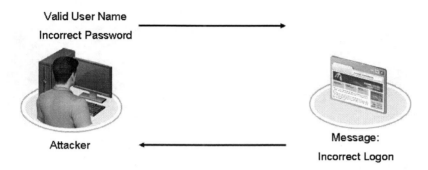

Figure 4-10: *Error and exception handling.*

XSS

In a cross-site scripting (XSS) attack, the attacker takes advantage of scripting and input validation vulnerabilities in an interactive website to attack legitimate users in two different ways. In a *stored attack,* the attacker injects malicious code or links into a website's forums, databases, or other data. When a user views the stored malicious code, or clicks a malicious link, an attack is perpetrated against the user.

In a *reflected attack,* the attacker poses as a legitimate user and sends information to a web server in the form of a page request or form submission. This "information" is in fact an attack, and when the web server responds to the request, the attack is directed at the targeted user or users. In this way, the attack is "reflected" off the server to users.

XSRF

In a cross-site request forgery (XSRF) attack, an attacker takes advantage of the trust established between an authorized user of a website and the website itself. This type of attack exploits a web browser's trust in a user's unexpired browser cookies. Websites that are at the most risk are those that perform functions based on input from trusted authenticated users who authenticate automatically using a saved browser cookie stored on their machines. The attacker takes advantage of the saved authentication data stored inside the cookie to gain access to a web browser's sensitive data.

This functionality is found on most web pages and is allowed when a user logs in to access account information. If, when logging in, the user selects the **Remember Me** option, then a cookie is saved and accessed the next time they visit that web page.

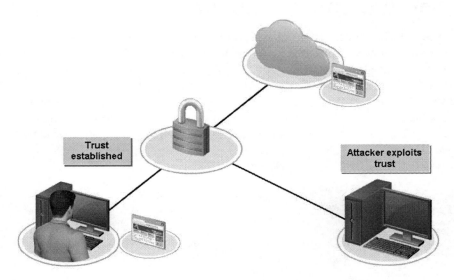

Figure 4-11: XSRF.

Cross-Site Attack Prevention Methods

To protect systems from XSS and XSRF attacks, you must verify that the proper security controls and development guidelines are implemented in applications you develop and run or that you purchase from third parties:

- Do not allow Hypertext Markup Language (HTML) formatting in form fields.
- Use input validation on all fields, strings, variables, and cookies.
- Do not unnecessarily store data in cookies and limit the expiration time for cookies.
- Encrypt data communications between clients and servers.
- Inform end users to not use the **Remember Me** option when authenticating on websites.

Fuzzing

Definition:

Fuzzing is a testing method used to identify vulnerabilities and weaknesses in applications by sending the application a range of random or unusual input data and noting any failures and crashes that result. Fuzzing is used to identify potential security issues and areas that may be vulnerable to attacks within an application. This type of testing is usually performed in the final phases of the application development process. Organizations may consider this type of testing on any application that transmits sensitive data and performs online transactions.

Example:

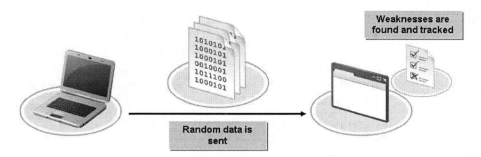

Figure 4-12: Fuzzing.

Fuzzing Tools

There are various pre-built fuzzing tools available to help generate the fuzzy input data for testing procedures. Some of the best-known ones include SPIKE Proxy and Peach Fuzzer Framework.

Web Browser Security

Because many applications are implemented through web browser interfaces, it is very important to ensure proper security within individual web browser installations. There are some general security guidelines that can be implemented to ensure web browser security:

● Harden the host machine or device.

● Install all the latest software versions and patches.

● Configure the security settings built in to the software.

● Disable scripting when appropriate.

● Disable auto-complete and password saving features.

● And, install anti-malware software.

Common Web Browser Security Features

Specific security features will vary depending on the browser, but most browsers offer some common features. Popular web browsers include Microsoft® Internet Explorer®, Mozilla® Firefox®, Apple® Safari®, and Google Chrome™.

Security Feature	Description
Pop-up blocker	In most browsers, the pop-up blocking feature is enabled by default to prevent websites from displaying pop-up windows without user authorization. It can be configured to specify sites that are allowed to open pop-up windows.
Parental controls	Most browsers will have some sort of parental controls to manage Internet access. For example, Mozilla Firefox works with Windows' built-in parental controls.
Automated updating	Most browsers can be configured to automatically check for updates and request the user to install them.
Encryption	Support for current strong encryption standards includes Secure Sockets Layer 2 (SSL2), SSL3, and Transport Layer Security (TLS).

Security Feature	Description
Proxy support	Many popular browsers support proxy mechanisms, including Hypertext Transfer Protocol (HTTP), Hypertext Transfer Protocol Secure (HTTPS), File Transfer Protocol (FTP) SOCKS, Gopher, and Rapid Spanning Tree Protocol (RSTP).
Web content	All browsers provides options to enable or disable JavaScript, with options for some specific features.
Advanced security	Most browsers have options provided to remove: • Cookies • Web cache • Download and browsing history • Saved form and search history • Offline website data • Saved passwords • Authenticated sessions

ACTIVITY 4-4

Configuring the Microsoft Internet Explorer Web Browser

 There is a simulated version of this activity available on the CD-ROM that shipped with this course. You can run this simulation on any Windows computer to review the activity after class, or as an alternative to performing the activity as a group in class. The activity simulation can be launched either directly from the CD-ROM by clicking the **Interactives** link and navigating to the appropriate one, or from the installed data file location by opening the C:\SPlus\ Simulations\Lesson#\Activity# folder and double-clicking the executable (.exe) file.

Data Files:

IESecurity.rtf

Setup:

There is an unrated website available on the network at http://Server100.

Scenario:

You are the security administrator for a nuclear power plant, and you need to make sure your new Windows Server 2008 R2 computers with Microsoft Internet Explorer are secure. In the past, the plant's IT department has had problems with users storing passwords in their Internet browsers. They have also had problems with users visiting sites that contain inappropriate content, and users have also downloaded unauthorized programs to their computers. Before connecting the new Windows Server 2008 R2 computers to your network, you need to make sure that the browser is configured properly to minimize the likelihood of attacks.

The IT department has designed a security deployment plan for all new systems, including the new Windows Server 2008 R2 computers with Internet Explorer, and documented it as IESecurity.rtf. Before the IT department deploys the browser to all users, this security configuration needs to be set up manually on a test system to verify that clients will still have the appropriate level of web access.

---

1. Review the security specifications in the IESecurity.rtf file.

   a. Choose **Start→Run.**

   b. Type **C:\SPlus\IESecurity.rtf** and click **OK.**

   c. The file opens in WordPad. Review the security specifications in the document and close WordPad.

---

2. Verify that Internet Explorer Advanced Security Configuration is installed.

   a. Choose **Start→Internet Explorer.**

   b. Verify that the **Internet Explorer Enhanced Security Configuration** screen appears as the home page.

   c. Click the **Effects of Internet Explorer Enhanced Security Configuration** link.

d.   Review the specifications and click the  **Home** button to return to the main page.

3.   Configure Internet Explorer with the appropriate zone level for the Internet zone.

a.   Choose **Tools→Internet Options.**

b.   In the **Internet Options** dialog box, select the **Security** tab.

c.   With the Internet zone selected, click **Custom level.**

d.   In the **Security Settings - Internet Zone** dialog box, scroll down to the **ActiveX controls and plug-ins** section.

e.   Verify that **Allow Scriptlets** and **Automatic prompting for ActiveX controls** are disabled.

f.   Press **End** to scroll down to the end of the list.

g.   Verify that the **Scripting of Java applets** is disabled and the **Logon** is set to **Prompt for user name and password.**

h.   From the **Reset to** drop-down list, verify that **High (default)** is selected.

i.   Click **OK.**

4.   Block insecure cookies.

a.   Select the **Privacy** tab.

b.   Move the **Settings** slider to **High** to block insecure cookies from the Internet zone.

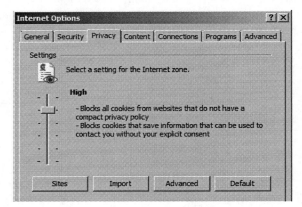

c.   Click **Apply.**

5.   Configure the appropriate websites to allow use of cookies.

a.   Click **Sites.**

b.   In the **Address of website** text box, type *nrc.gov* and click **Allow.**

c.   In the **Address of website** text box, type *anl.gov* and click **Allow.**

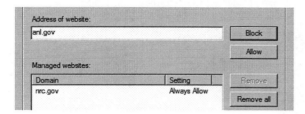

d.   Click **OK.**

6.   Set the appropriate Content Advisor rating levels without blocking approved, unrated sites.

a.   Select the **Content** tab.

b.   In the **Content Advisor** section, click **Enable.**

c.   In the **Content Advisor** dialog box, on the **Ratings** page, in the **Select a category to view the rating levels** list, scroll down and select **Language.**

d.   Adjust the rating slider to **Limited.**

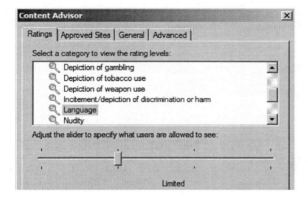

e.   Press **End** to scroll down to the end of the list.

f.   Set the rating level for **Violence** category to **Limited.**

g.   Click **Apply.**

h.   Click **OK.**

i.   In the **Create Supervisor Password** dialog box, in the **Password** text box, type *!Pass1234* and press **Tab.** In the **Confirm password** text box, type *!Pass1234*

j.   In the **Hint** text box, click and type *same as Administrator*

k.   Click **OK.**

l.   In the **Content Advisor** message box, click **OK.**

7.   Configure the appropriate forms settings.

a.   On the **Content** page, in the **AutoComplete** section, click **Settings.**

b. In the **AutoComplete Settings** dialog box, in the **Use AutoComplete for** section, uncheck the **User names and passwords on forms** check box.

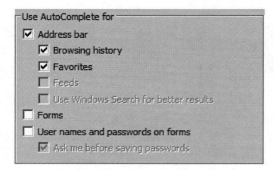

c. Click **OK.**

d. On the **General** page, in the **Browsing history** section, click **Delete.**

e. In the **Delete Browsing History** dialog box, check the **Passwords** check box and click **Delete.**

f. When the browsing history has been deleted, click **OK** to close the **Internet Options** dialog box.

8. Verify that you can connect to the http://Server100 website.

a. Click the Internet Explorer **Address** bar, type *http://Server100* and press **Enter.**

b. Log in with your Administrator name and password.

c. In the **Content Advisor** dialog box, select **Always allow this website to be viewed.**

d. In the **Password** text box, click and type *!Pass1234* and click **OK.**

e. You should see the default University Registration web page on the Server100 website.

9. Turn off Content Advisor to avoid issues later.

a. Choose **Tools→Internet Options.**

b. Click **Content.**

c. In the **Content Advisor** section, click **Disable.**

d. In the **Password** text box, type *!Pass1234* and click **OK.**

e. Click **OK** to confirm your change.

f. Click **OK** to close the **Internet Options** dialog box.

g. Close Internet Explorer.

TOPIC C
Data Security

You identified methods to secure applications that run on an organization's devices and systems. Now, you will focus on the data being exchanged through those applications. Data security is crucial in keeping a business' data from being exposed. In this topic, you will explore data security techniques.

Understanding the possible threats and vulnerabilities that can impact data security will help you to manage data security at the corporate level. A successful business depends on the privacy of its data and client data. Without the proper security measures in place, a business cannot guarantee the security of its customers, and this may result in business loss.

What Is Data Security?

Data security refers to the security controls and measures taken in order keep an organization's data safe and accessible and to prevent unauthorized access. Today's workforce is more mobile than ever before, and the need for enhanced data security is on the rise. Since data now is stored and accessed in many locations, organizations must consider not only the physical access to data storage systems, but also the devices that access them. Data security must be applied at every level of an organization, including to the physical environment, to all devices and systems, and to all mobile devices used for business, especially as the use of smartphones for business continues to grow. Data security must be a priority for every business and it should be incorporated into all security policies.

Data Security Vulnerabilities

Data security vulnerabilities can include the increased use of cloud computing to perform job functions, the lack of restricted physical access to data storage systems, and the lack of user awareness. Any one of these vulnerabilities can lead to unauthorized access to data and data leakage possibilities. *Data leakage* refers to gaining access to data through unintentional user methods such as email and instant messaging, and the use of mobile devices. Data leakage through any of these methods can lead to malicious activity, and possible data loss.

Data Encryption Methods

In order to protect data from security vulnerabilities, apply a data encryption method that is appropriate to the data level, including:

- Full disk encryption, to encrypt an entire disk and all the data stored in it.
- Database encryption, to encrypt sensitive data stored in the database. Some organizations may need to comply with regulatory guidelines that require database encryption for specific types of data.
- File encryption, to protect individual files that contain private or confidential data.
- Removable media encryption, on Secure Digital (SD) cards, CDs, and DVDs, to protect data stored on the media.
- Mobile device encryption to protect any data stored on smartphones or other mobile devices.

- Email encryption to encrypt and protect emails and attachments from being read by unauthorized users. Secure/Multipurpose Internet Mail Extensions (S/MIME), Pretty Good Privacy (PGP) and GNU Privacy Guard (GPG) are utilities that provide this functionality.

- And, voice encryption to protect voice communications and data across a network.

Hardware-Based Encryption Devices

In *hardware-based encryption devices*, encryption, decryption, and access control are enforced by a cryptographic module called a *Hardware Security Module (HSM)*. Hardware-based encryption devices do not allow the execution of external programs, which attempt either to reset any counters or access their memory. The lockdown in the event of unauthenticated use can also destroy data and encryption keys that are present on a universal serial bus (USB) flash drive or hard drive, based on the level of security enforced in the HSMs.

Benefits of Hardware-Based Encryption Devices

Hardware-based encryption devices provide benefits such as:

- Preventing storage mapping from the drive to the file system until a user inserts a plug-in smart card into a slot connected to the hard drive.

- Preventing attackers from copying the drive contents without the assigned HSM.

- Providing security controls that are self governed and not dependent on the operating system; therefore, the hard drive is not affected by malicious code.

- Providing an organization with the proof that each machine is encrypted. In the event of a machine being lost due to a security attack, this will act as an assurance to customers that none of the data has been lost or compromised.

Types of Hardware-Based Encryption Devices

To secure data from unauthorized access, there are a number of hardware-based encryption devices used.

Device	Description
Trusted Platform Module (TPM)	This specification includes the use of *cryptoprocessors* to create a secure computing environment. A TPM can generate cryptographic keys securely and can be used to authenticate hardware, for disk encryption, for digital rights management, or for any other encryption-enabled application. TPM can be used as a basic input/output system (BIOS) security method by using full disk encryption such as BitLocker to secure the operating system's volume.
HSM	A cryptoprocessor device that can be attached to servers and computers to provide digital key security. The modules can provide a number of security functions including enhancing cryptoprocesses and providing strong authentication services.
USB	Users who store sensitive data on USB devices should take care to protect the devices physically. However, because of their small size and extreme portability, these devices can easily be lost or stolen. USB encryption can be implemented on USB devices to provide an additional way to protect sensitive data stored on the device.

Device	Description
Hard drive	Hard drive encryption is a full disk encryption method used to encrypt and protect data on the entire disk. This type of encryption can be a very effective security measure to protect mobile devices and laptops, which can be misplaced, stolen, or damaged simply because they are moved around.

ACTIVITY 4-5
Examining Data Security

Scenario:
In this activity, you will examine data security methods and techniques.

1. **Why should organizations invest in data security?**

2. **What is the correct description for each hardware-based encryption device?**

___	TPM	a.	Cryptoprocessor device that can be attached to servers and computers to provide digital key security.
___	HSM	b.	Encryption that can be implemented specifically to provide additional security for removable data storage.
___	USB	c.	A specification that includes the use of cryptoprocessors to create a secure computing environment.
___	Hard drive	d.	Encryption that is applied to protect every bit of data stored in the disk.

3. **What data encryption method should you implement when you need to send data for the company's annual earnings report as an attachment in an email from your mobile device to the board of directors of your organization?**

   a) Database encryption

   b) Email encryption

   c) Mobile device encryption

   d) Full disk encryption

4. **How can data leakage affect your organization, and how could it be prevented?**

TOPIC D
Mobile Security

In the last topic, you identified the general importance of securing data on all devices, including mobile devices. Mobile security goes beyond basic data security, however. Today, mobile devices are used everywhere and are deployed by many companies for employees' business use. In this topic, you will explore the components of mobile security.

Mobile devices are everywhere today. Organizations deploy mobile devices to their employees to use for work-related purposes and will most likely include mobile security measures in their security policies. With this in mind, it is important to understand the most common devices used today and what threats and vulnerabilities apply. As a security professional, it is also your job to understand what techniques are used to secure mobile devices and how they prevent unauthorized access to mobile devices and sensitive data.

Mobile Device Types

A mobile device is a small handheld computing device. There are a number of common mobile devices used for work purposes today:

- Smartphones: Examples include Apple® iPhones®, BlackBerry® devices, Windows® Mobile devices, and Android™ phones.
- And, Wi-Fi enabled devices: Examples include Apple® iPads®, the Apple® iPod touch®, and Android-based tablets such as the Barnes & Noble NOOK Color™.

Mobile Device Vulnerabilities

Modern mobile phones have the ability to transfer voice data, emails, photos, and videos, and can access the Internet. Some may have remote network access. With these functions, users can assume all the same threats related to desktop computers and mobile devices will apply. For example, viruses and spam can infect mobile devices as they would desktop and wireless devices by email or downloaded programs. If a mobile device is lost or stolen, it is not only an inconvenience to the user who lost access to his information, but attackers can hack into the device as they would a desktop or laptop computer.

Mobile Device Security Controls

Organizational security policies should implement and enforce mobile security controls on all mobile devices used for business. There are a number of controls used to provide mobile device security.

Security Control	Description
Enable screen lock	The screen lock option on all mobile devices should be enabled with strict requirements on when the device will be locked. Once the device is locked, it can only be accessed by entering the code that has been set up by the user.

Security Control	Description
Require a strong password	A strong password should be set up by the user to access the device once it has been turned on. Password requirements will be different for every organization and should be documented in the organization's security policy.
Configure device encryption	When possible, all mobile devices should be configured to use data encryption to protect company-specific data that may be stored and accessed on the device.
Require remote wipe/ sanitization	*Data wiping* is a method used to remove any sensitive data from a mobile device and permanently delete it. *Data sanitization* is the method used to repeatedly delete and overwrite any traces or bits of sensitive data that may remain on the device after data wiping has been done. Remote options are available, so you can perform these functions remotely in case the phone is lost or stolen. Wipe and sanitization guidelines and requirements should be included in the security policies for companies that uses mobile devices.
Enable global positioning system (GPS)	GPS tracking service functionality is available on a number of mobile devices and can be added in most cases when required for business reasons. This feature is used as a security measure to protect mobile devices that may be lost or stolen.

ACTIVITY 4-6
Examining Mobile Security

Scenario:

In this activity, you will examine mobile security components and measures.

1. **What are some of the security concerns you have about the common mobile devices you use or support?**

2. **Your organization requires that you ensure your BlackBerry is secured from unauthorized access in case it is lost or stolen. To prevent someone from accessing data on the device immediately after it has been turned on, what security control should be used?**

   a) GPS tracking

   b) Device encryption

   c) Screen lock

   d) Sanitization

3. **How can the use of mobile devices by employees affect the security of an organization?**

4. Pair up with a partner who has a different mobile device and examine the security features on that mobile device. Use the main menu to open the security settings.

5. Look at the specific security settings for each device such as the screen lock feature, device encryption options, and GPS tracking features. Compare the available settings on each device.

Lesson 4 Follow-up

In this lesson, you managed the security of applications, data, and hosts. These components are vital to an organization's operations, and must be secured properly in order to control access. The skills and information in this lesson should help you to implement the right controls at the application, data, and host levels.

1. **What experience have you had securing applications, data, or hosts for your organization?**

2. **Have you ever dealt with mobile security issues for your organization? Are there any security controls that would have prevented these issues?**

5 Access Control, Authentication, and Account Management

Lesson Time: 2 hour(s), 15 minutes

Lesson Objectives:

In this lesson, you will identify access control and account management security measures.

You will:

- Describe common authentication services.

- Implement account management security controls.

Introduction

In previous lessons, you examined network security as well as data, host, and device security. User access control, authentication, and user account management form the next logical steps in ensuring the security of an organization. In this lesson, you will identify how access control methods, authentication services, and account management security measures and best practices are applied to protect the identity of users within a system.

The way users access and log in to systems can be like a doorway into an organization's applications, data, and services. Because of this, it is crucial to apply appropriate access control and authentication services to your information systems infrastructure. You are also responsible for securing the identity of the individuals accessing systems and services within the organization. In order to properly implement the right security measures, you will need to be able to implement access control, authentication services, and account management controls properly.

This lesson covers all or part of the following CompTIA® Security+® (Exam SY0-301) certification objectives:

- Topic A:

  - Objective 1.3 Distinguish and differentiate network design elements and compounds

  - Objective 5.1 Explain the function and purpose of authentication services

- Objective 5.2 Explain the fundamental concepts and best practices related to authentication, authorization and access control
- Objective 5.3 Implement appropriate security controls when performing account management
- Objective 6.2 Use and apply appropriate cryptographic tools and products
- Topic B:
  - Objective 2.1 Explain risk related concepts
  - Objective 2.4 Explain the importance of security related awareness and training
  - Objective 3.2 Analyze and differentiate among types of attacks
  - Objective 5.3 Implement appropriate security controls when performing account management

TOPIC A
Access Control and Authentication Services

You have learned that access control and authentication are among the primary factors in computer security. Although access control and authentication always have the same goal, there are many different approaches to accomplishing both. In this topic, you will discuss some of the primary authentication services and access control mechanisms used today.

Strong authentication and access control are the first lines of defense in the battle to secure network resources. But applying access control and authentication is not a single process; there are many different methods and mechanisms, some of which can even be combined into more complex schemes. As a network professional, you will need to be familiar with the major access control and authentication services used today so you can implement and support the ones that are appropriate for your environment.

Directory Services

Definition:

A *directory service* is a network service that stores identity information about all the objects in a particular network, including users, groups, servers, clients, printers, and network services. The directory also provides user access control to directory objects and network resources. Directory services can also be used to centralize security and to control access to individual network resources.

Example:

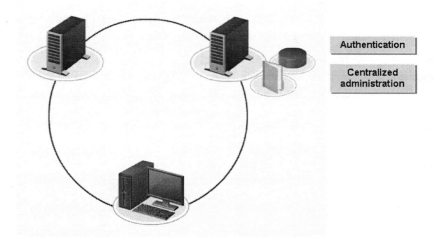

Figure 5-1: A directory service.

Directory Schema

The structure of the directory is controlled by a *schema* that defines rules for how objects are created and what their characteristics can be. Most schemas are extensible, so they can be modified to support the specific needs of an organization.

LDAP

The *Lightweight Directory Access Protocol (LDAP)* is a standard authentication protocol that is used on Transmission Control Protocol/Internet Protocol (TCP/IP) networks to access an LDAP-compliant directory service or directory database. LDAP has a schema that defines the tasks you can and cannot perform while accessing a directory database, the form your directory query must take, and how the directory server will respond. The LDAP schema is extensible, which means you can make changes or add on to it.

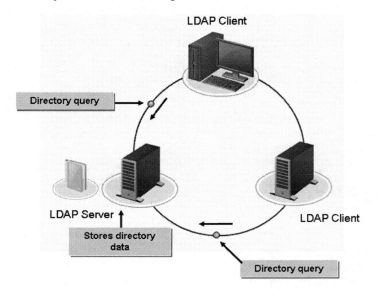

Figure 5-2: LDAP.

Directory Management Tools

Most directory services implementations ship with some management tools of their own. In addition, there are a wide variety of third-party LDAP browsing and administration tools available from both open- and closed-source vendors.

While a plaintext editor might be useful in troubleshooting situations, graphical user interface (GUI) utilities are generally easier to work with. In addition to preconfigured tools, you can create scripts that use LDAP to automate routine directory maintenance tasks, such as adding large numbers of users or groups, and checking for blank passwords or disabled or obsolete user accounts.

Common Directory Services

There are a variety of robust directory servers available, both paid and free, open and closed source.

Directory Service	Description
Microsoft *Active Directory*	A directory service that holds information about all network objects for a single domain or multiple domains. Active Directory allows administrators to centrally manage and control access to resources using access control lists (ACLs). It allows users to find resources anywhere on the network. Active Directory also has a schema that controls how accounts are created and what attributes an Administrator may assign to them. Active Directory Application Mode (ADAM) is a lightweight version of Active Directory.
Sun Java System Directory Server	This is the latest version of Sun Microsystems' Directory Server. It was formerly known as Sun ONE Directory Server and iPlanet Directory Server. Sun Java System Directory Server is built with 64-bit technology and marketed towards large installations that require reliable scaling. The software is free, and paid support is available from Sun.
OpenDS	An open source directory server that runs on Linux, Unix, Microsoft® Windows®, and Mac OS® X. OpenDS is written by Sun in Java. It supports LDAPv3 and Directory Service Markup Language version 2 (DSMLv2).
OpenLDAP	A free, open source LDAP implementation with distributions available for many operating systems.
Open Directory	Apple's customized implementation of OpenLDAP that is included with Mac OS X Server. Open Directory is somewhat compatible with both Active Directory and Novell's eDirectory and integrates both the LDAP and Kerberos standards.

Directory Service Vulnerabilities

Each directory service has its own vulnerabilities; however, like any other server or service, there are some common vulnerability areas to be aware of:

- All categories of network-based attacks, including:
    - Denial of Service (DoS)/Distributed Denial of Service (DDoS) attacks.
    - Unencrypted transmission of data.
    - Man-in-the-middle attacks.
    - Packet sniffing/capture attacks.
- Buffer overflow attacks.
- Security of user and administrator accounts and passwords.

Backing Up Active Directory

Before you harden Active Directory, you should back it up in case anything goes wrong. You back up Active Directory by backing up the computer's System State Data within the Windows® Backup utility. In addition to Active Directory, backing up the computer's System State Data also backs up the following components:

- Registry
- COM+ Class Registration database
- Boot and system files
- Certificate Services database (if you have installed Certificate Services on the server)
- The SYSVOL folder (if the server is a domain controller)
- The IIS Metabase (if you have installed IIS)

ACTIVITY 5-1
Backing Up Active Directory

 There is a simulated version of this activity available on the CD-ROM that shipped with this course. You can run this simulation on any Windows computer to review the activity after class, or as an alternative to performing the activity as a group in class. The activity simulation can be launched either directly from the CD-ROM by clicking the **Interactives** link and navigating to the appropriate one, or from the installed data file location by opening the C:\SPlus\ Simulations\Lesson#\Activity# folder and double-clicking the executable (.exe) file.

Scenario:

As the bank's security administrator, your boss has asked you to make sure that Active Directory is secure. You want to make sure that you have a current backup of Active Directory in case you encounter any problems. You have a D drive in your server to save your backup.

1. Observe the components of **Active Directory Users and Computers.**

    a. Choose **Start→Administrative Tools→Active Directory Users and Computers.**

    b. In the Active Directory Users and Computers window, if necessary, expand the domain object.

    c. Select **Users.**

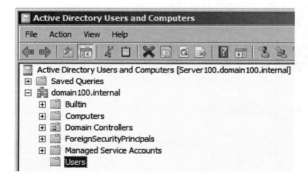

    d. There are various user and group objects such as **Administrator, Guest,** and **Domain Admins.** In the console tree, select **Domain Controllers.**

e. Observe that the domain controller's name is **Server##,** where **##** is the number assigned to your computer. Close **Active Directory Users and Computers.**

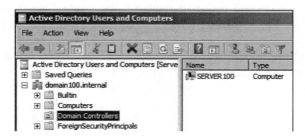

2. Back up your domain controller's system state data.

a. Choose **Start→Administrative Tools→Windows Server Backup.**

b. In the **Actions** pane on the right side, click **Backup Once.**

c. On the **Backup Options** page, verify that **Different options** is selected and click **Next.**

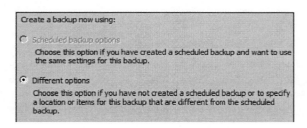

d. On the **Select Backup Configuration** page, select the **Custom** option and then click **Next.**

e. On the **Select Items for Backup** page, click **Add Items.**

f. Check the **System state** check box and click **OK.**

g. On the **Select Items for Backup** page, click **Next.**

h. On the **Specify Destination Type** page, verify that the **Local drives** option is selected and click **Next.**

i. On the **Select Backup Destination** page, click **Next.**

j. On the **Confirmation** page, click **Backup.**

k. Click the **Close** button to close the wizard.

l. Close the Windows Server Backup window.

Remote Access Methods

With today's mobile workforce, there are several different methods that organizations can use to provide remote employees and customers with access to their network resources. Companies that require privacy may connect to a gateway remote access server (RAS) that provides access control services to all or part of the internal network. Also, remote access from a remote system or a wireless device to a private network can be provided through an intermediate network, such as the Internet. Especially in this case, care must be taken to secure transmissions as they pass over the public network.

Figure 5-3: RAS.

Tunneling

Definition:

Tunneling is a data-transport technique that can be used to provide remote access in which a data packet is encrypted and encapsulated in another data packet in order to conceal the information of the packet inside. This enables data from one network to travel through another network. The tunnel can provide additional security by hiding user-encrypted data from the carrier network.

Example:

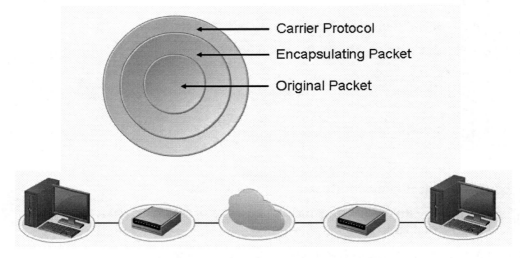

Figure 5-4: Tunneling.

Remote Access Protocols

There are a number of common protocols used to provide remote access to networks.

Protocol	Description
Point-to-Point Protocol (PPP)	This is an Internet standard for sending IP datagram packets over serial point-to-point links. Its most common use is for dial-up Internet access. It can be used in synchronous and asynchronous connections. Point-to-Point Protocol over Ethernet (PPPoE) and Point-to-Point Protocol over ATM (PPPoA) are more recent PPP implementations used by many Digital Subscriber Line (DSL) broadband Internet connections.
	PPP can dynamically configure and test remote network connections, and is often used by clients to connect to networks and the Internet. It also provides encryption for passwords, paving the way for secure authentication of remote users.
Point-to-Point Tunneling Protocol (PPTP)	A Microsoft VPN Layer 2 protocol that increases the security of PPP by providing tunneling and data encryption for PPP packets. It uses the same authentication types as PPP, and is the most widely supported VPN method among older Windows clients. PPTP encapsulates any type of network protocol and transports it over IP networks.
Layer Two Tunneling Protocol (L2TP)	An Internet-standard protocol combination of PPTP and Layer 2 Forwarding (L2F) that enables the tunneling of PPP sessions across a variety of network protocols, such as IP, frame relay, or Asynchronous Transfer Mode (ATM). L2TP was specifically designed to provide tunneling and security interoperability for client-to-gateway and gateway-to-gateway connections. L2TP does not provide any encryption on its own and L2TP tunnels appear as IP packets, so L2TP employs IP Security (IPSec) Transport Mode for authentication, integrity, and confidentiality.
Secure Socket Tunneling Protocol (SSTP)	This protocol uses the Hypertext Transfer Protocol over Secure Sockets Layer (HTTP over SSL) protocol and encapsulates an IP packet with a PPP header and then with an SSTP header. The IP packet, PPP header, and SSTP header are encrypted by the SSL session. An IP header containing the destination addresses is then added to the packet. It is supported in all current Windows operating systems.

 L2TP has wide vendor support because it addresses the IPSec shortcomings of client-to-gateway and gateway-to-gateway connections.

CHAP

Challenge Handshake Authentication Protocol (CHAP) is an encrypted authentication protocol that is often used to provide access control for remote access servers. CHAP was developed so that passwords would not have to be sent in plaintext. It is generally used to connect to non-Microsoft servers. CHAP uses a combination of Message Digest 5 (MD5) hashing and a challenge-response mechanism, and accomplishes authentication without ever sending passwords over the network. It can accept connections from any authentication method except for certain unencrypted schemes.

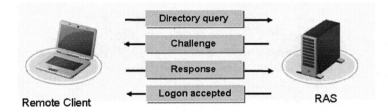

Remote Client — Directory query → — Challenge ← — Response → — Logon accepted ← — RAS

Figure 5-5: *CHAP.*

The CHAP Process

In the challenge-response authentication process, a user's password is never sent across the network.

Step	Description
Step 1	The remote client requests a connection to the RAS.
Step 2	The remote server sends a challenge sequence, which is usually a random value.
Step 3	The remote client uses its password as an encryption key to encrypt the challenge sequence and sends the modified sequence to the server.
Step 4	The server encrypts the original challenge sequence with the password stored in its local credentials list and compares the results with the modified sequence received from the client. • If the two sequences do not match, the server closes the connection. • If the two sequences match, the server allows the client to access resources.

PAP

Definition:

Password Authentication Protocol (PAP) is an authentication protocol that sends user IDs and passwords as cleartext. It is generally used when a remote client is connecting to a non-Windows server that does not support a stronger password encryption, such as CHAP. When the server receives a user ID and password pair, it compares them to its local list of credentials. If a match is found, the server accepts the credentials and allows the remote client to access resources. If no match is found, the connection is terminated.

Example:

Figure 5-6: PAP.

ACTIVITY 5-2
Securing a Remote Access Server

 There is a simulated version of this activity available on the CD-ROM that shipped with this course. You can run this simulation on any Windows computer to review the activity after class, or as an alternative to performing the activity as a group in class. The activity simulation can be launched either directly from the CD-ROM by clicking the **Interactives** link and navigating to the appropriate one, or from the installed data file location by opening the C:\SPlus\ Simulations\Lesson#\Activity# folder and double-clicking the executable (.exe) file.

Setup:
The Microsoft® Windows Server® 2008 R2 Server computer has a physical local area network (LAN) adapter and also a virtual Microsoft Loopback Adapter to simulate the presence of an external connection object. The Microsoft Loopback Adapter has been configured with default IP settings. The Routing and Remote Access Server (RRAS) is configured to use Dynamic Host Configuration Protocol (DHCP) to distribute IP addresses to remote access clients.

Scenario:
One of the next tasks as the bank's security administrator is to make sure your remote access servers are secure. In the past, the bank has had problems with attackers accessing services and data that they were not supposed to have access to through VPN connections. You will now provide VPN services through new Windows Server 2008 R2 RRAS servers, which you will secure before connecting them to the network. The bank's IT department will install the new VPN RRAS server in the demilitarized zone (DMZ). The DMZ has already been secured. Also, the Active Directory team has already created a remote access security policy to determine who will have VPN access to RRAS servers in your domain.

You need to configure the VPN server with system-wide security settings that include:

● Permitting only L2TP clients with IPSec encryption to connect.

● Blocking PPTP packets from external networks.

---

1. Use the SCW to enable and configure security on the **Remote Access Server.**

   a. Choose **Start→Security Configuration Wizard.**

   b. On the **Welcome** page, click **Next.**

   c. Verify that **Create a new security policy** is selected and click **Next.**

   > Select the action you want to perform:
   > ⦿ Create a new security policy
   > ○ Edit an existing security policy
   > ○ Apply an existing security policy
   > ○ Rollback the last applied security policy

   d. Click **Next** to accept the server name.

e.   When the processing is complete, click **Next** twice.

f.   Scroll down and check the **Remote access/VPN server** check box and click **Next.**

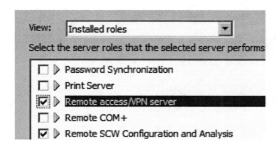

g.   On the **Select Client Features** page, click **Next.**

h.   On the **Select Administration and Other Options** page, click **Next.**

i.   On the **Select Additional Services** page, click **Next.**

j.   On the **Handling Unspecified Services** page, verify that **Do not change the startup mode of the service** is selected, and click **Next.**

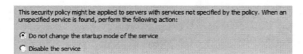

k.   Confirm the service changes and click **Next.**

l.   On the **Network Security** page, click **Next.**

m.   Scroll down, and uncheck the **Routing and Remote Access (PPTP-In)** and **Routing and Remote Access (PPTP-Out)** check boxes.

n.   Select **Routing and Remote Access (L2TP-In)** and click **Edit.**

o.   In the **Action** section, select **Allow only secure connections** and check the **Require encryption** check box.

p.   Click **OK** and then click **Next.**

q.   On the **Registry Settings** page, check the **Skip this section** check box and click **Next.**

r.   On the **Audit Policy** page, check the **Skip this section** check box and click **Next.**

s.   On the **Save Security Policy** page, click **Next.**

t.   On the **Security Policy File Name** page, in the file name text box, at the end of the path, type *RA Security*

u.   In the **Description** field, click and type *Configure Remote Access* and click **Next.**

v.   On the **Apply Security Policy** page, select **Apply now** and click **Next.**

w.   When the process is complete, click **Next,** and click **Finish.**

2. Start the RRAS server.

    a. Choose **Start→Routing and Remote Access.**

    b. Select the server and choose **Action→All Tasks→Start.**

    c. In the message box, click **Yes** to re-enable the service and start the server.

    d. After the server arrow turns green, close the Routing and Remote Access window.

PGP

Pretty Good Privacy (PGP) is a publicly available email security and authentication utility that uses a variation of public key cryptography to encrypt emails: the sender encrypts the contents of the email message and then encrypts the key that was used to encrypt the contents. The encrypted key is sent with the email, and the receiver decrypts the key and then uses the key to decrypt the contents. PGP also uses public key cryptography to digitally sign emails to authenticate the sender and the contents.

 For more information about PGP implementations and other similar security schemes, see **http://en.wikipedia.org/wiki/Pretty_Good_Privacy**.

GPG

GNU Privacy Guard (GPG) is a free open-source version of PGP that provides equivalent encryption and authentication services. GPG is compliant with current PGP services and meets the latest standards issued by the Internet Engineering Task Force (IETF).

RADIUS

Remote Authentication Dial-In User Service (RADIUS) is an Internet standard protocol that provides centralized remote access authentication, authorization, and auditing services. When a network contains several remote access servers, you can configure one of the servers to be a RADIUS server, and all of the other servers as RADIUS clients. The RADIUS clients will pass all authentication requests to the RADIUS server for verification. User configuration, remote access policies, and usage logging can be centralized on the RADIUS server. In this configuration, the remote access server is generically known as the *Network Access Server (NAS)*.

Diameter

Diameter is a authentication protocol that improves upon RADIUS by strengthening some of its weaknesses. Diameter is backward-compatible with RADIUS.

The name "Diameter" comes from the claim that Diameter is twice as good as RADIUS. Diameter is a stronger protocol in many ways but is not as widespread in its implementation due to the lack of products using it.

NPS

Network Policy Server (NPS) is a Microsoft Server 2008 implementation of a RADIUS server. It helps in administrating VPNs and wireless networks. NPS was known as Internet Authentication Service (IAS) in Windows Server 2003.

TACACS

Terminal Access Controller Access Control System (TACACS) and *TACACS Plus (TACACS+)* protocols provide centralized authentication and authorization services for remote users. TACACS+ also supports multi-factor authentication. TACACS+ is considered more secure and more scalable than RADIUS because it accepts login requests and authenticates the access credentials of the user. TACACS includes process-wide encryption for authentication while RADIUS encrypts only passwords. Extensions to the TACACS protocols exist, such as Cisco's TACACS+ and XTACACS. XTACACS was created to extend the original TACACS protocol.

Kerberos

Kerberos is an authentication service that is based on a time-sensitive ticket-granting system. It was developed by Massachusetts Institute of Technology (MIT) to use a single sign-on (SSO) method where the user enters access credentials that are then passed to the authentication server, which contains an access list and allowed access credentials. Kerberos can be used to manage access control to many different services using one centralized authentication server.

The Kerberos Process

In the Kerberos process:

1. A user logs on to the domain.

2. The user requests a ticket granting ticket (TGT) from the authenticating server.

3. The authenticating server responds with a time-stamped TGT.

4. The user presents the TGT back to the authenticating server and requests a service ticket to access a specific resource.

5. The authenticating server responds with a service ticket.

6. The user presents the service ticket to the resource.

7. The resource authenticates the user and allows access.

ACTIVITY 5-3
Setting Up Remote Access Authentication

 There is a simulated version of this activity available on the CD-ROM that shipped with this course. You can run this simulation on any Windows computer to review the activity after class, or as an alternative to performing the activity as a group in class. The activity simulation can be launched either directly from the CD-ROM by clicking the **Interactives** link and navigating to the appropriate one, or from the installed data file location by opening the C:\SPlus\ Simulations\Lesson#\Activity# folder and double-clicking the executable (.exe) file.

Scenario:

As part of your remote access implementation, the senior network administrator in your organization favors implementing NPS so that the administrators can obtain detailed authentication information and use a single remote access policy for all RRAS servers. She also recommends configuring the policy to automatically disconnect users if their connections are idle for 15 minutes.

1. Set up the Network Policy Server.

    In this case, the NPS and RRAS servers are the same computer. In a production environment, however, you would typically use at least one NPS server separate from the RRAS servers.

   a. Choose **Start→Administrative Tools→Network Policy Server.**

   b. In the Network Policy Server window, select **RADIUS Clients and Servers.**

   c. In the right pane, click **Configure RADIUS Clients.**

   d. Choose **Action→New.**

   e. In the **New RADIUS Client** dialog box, in the **Friendly name** text box, type the name of your server.

   f. In the **Address (IP or DNS)** text box, type your server's IP address.

   g. In the **Shared Secret** section, in the **Shared secret** and **Confirm shared secret** text boxes, type *!Pass1234* and click **OK.**

   h. Minimize the Network Policy Server window.

2. Configure your RRAS server to use Network Policy Server for authentication.

   a. Open **Routing and Remote Access.**

b. In the Routing and Remote Access window, if necessary, select your server and choose **Action→Properties.**

c. In the Server## (local) Properties window, select the **Security** tab.

d. From the **Authentication provider** drop-down list, select **RADIUS Authentication.**

e. Click **Configure** to display the **RADIUS Authentication** dialog box. You use this dialog box to define the name of the NPS server.

f. In the **RADIUS Authentication** dialog box, click **Add.**

g. In the **Add RADIUS Server** dialog box, in the **Server name** text box, type the name of your server to match the friendly name (*Server##*), and click **Change.**

h. In the **New Secret** and **Confirm New Secret** text boxes, type *!Pass1234* and then click **OK.**

i. In the **Add RADIUS Server** dialog box, click **OK.**

j. In the **RADIUS Authentication** dialog box, click **OK.**

k. In the **Server Properties** dialog box, click **OK.** If necessary, click **OK** to confirm the service restart.

---

3. Configure the NPS and RRAS servers to report all successful and failed authentication attempts using accounting.

a. On the Windows taskbar, click **Network Policy Server.**

b. In the Network Policy Server window, select **NPS (Local)** and choose **Action→ Properties.**

c. In the **Network Policy Server (Local) Properties** dialog box, verify that the **Rejected authentication requests** check box and **Successful authentication requests** check box are checked and click **OK.**

d. On the Windows taskbar, select **Routing and Remote Access.**

e. In the Routing and Remote Access window, verify your server is selected and choose **Action→Properties.**

f. In the Server## (local) Properties window, select the **Security** tab.

g. From the **Accounting provider** drop-down list, select **RADIUS Accounting** and click **Configure.**

h. In the **RADIUS Accounting** dialog box, click **Add.**

i. In the **Add RADIUS Server** dialog box, in the **Server name** text box, type the name of the RRAS server.

j. Click **Change.**

k. In the **Change Secret** dialog box, in the **New secret** and **Confirm new secret** text boxes, type *!Pass1234* and click **OK.**

l. Click **OK** three times.

m. In the Routing and Remote Access window, if necessary, select your server object.

n. Choose **Action→All Tasks→Restart** to restart the server.

o. The RRAS will now report successful and failed user authentication attempts to the NPS server. Close the Routing and Remote Access window.

By default, NPS stores the accounting information it receives in the C:\Windows\ System32\LogFiles\Iaslog file.

4. Create a policy to automatically disconnect idle VPN connections after 15 minutes.

    a.   In the Network Policy Server window, expand **Policies.**

    b.   Select **Connection Request Policies** and choose **Action→New.**

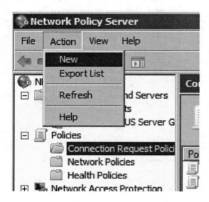

    c.   In the New Connection Request Policy Wizard window, in the **Policy name** text box, type *Disconnect Idle Connections*

    d.   From the **Type of network access server** drop-down list, select **Remote Access Server(VPN-Dial up)** and click **Next.**

    e.   On the **Specify Conditions** page, click **Add.**

    f.   In the **Select condition** dialog box, click **End,** and in the **Gateway** section, verify that **NAS Port Type** is selected.

    g.   In the **Select condition** dialog box, click **Add.**

    h.   In the **NAS Port Type** dialog box, in the **Common dial-up and VPN tunnel types** list, check the **Virtual (VPN)** check box, and click **OK.**

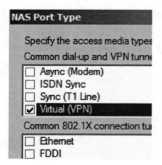

    i.   Click **Next.**

j. On the **Specify Connection Request Forwarding** page, verify that **Authenticate requests on this server** is selected and click **Next**.

⦿ Authenticate requests on this server

⦾ Forward requests to the following remote RADIUS server group for authentication:

k. On the **Specify Authentication Methods** page, click **Next**.

l. On the **Configure Settings** page, in the **RADIUS Attributes** section, select **Standard**.

m. Click **Add**.

n. In the **Add Standard RADIUS Attribute** dialog box, in the **Attributes** list, scroll down and select **Session-Timeout**.

o. Click **Add**.

p. In the **Attribute Information** dialog box, in the **Attribute value** text box, type *15* and click **OK**.

q. Click **Close**.

r. Click **Next** and then click **Finish**.

s. Close the Network Policy Server window.

 Because the VPN has been configured on a virtual adapter, the policy cannot be tested.

TOPIC B

Implement Account Management Security Controls

In the previous topic, you identified the various access control and authentication services used to manage access to systems and hardware. Account management security controls are similar in that they are implemented to control how accounts are managed within an organization. In this topic, you will implement account management security controls.

A single organization can contain a number of different account types that are assigned to its employees. With this in mind, you need to be able to implement proper controls that will guard against unauthorized access to user and group account information. As a security professional, it is your job to know what controls should be implemented and what policies should be enforced to effectively manage account security.

Identity Management

Identity management is an area of information security that is used to identify individuals within a computer system or network. Identities are created with specific characteristics and information specific for each individual or resource in a system. When pertaining to security, restrictions and access controls are assigned using an individual's identity within a system, network, or organization. Security professionals need to apply proper security controls to protect the identities of all individuals within a system, and to prevent *identity theft* by unauthorized users.

PII

Personally Identifying Information (PII) refers to the pieces of information that a company uses or prefers to use to identify or contact an employee. PII can include a user's full name, fingerprints, license plate number, phone numbers, street address, driver's license number, and so on.

Information Classification

To adequately protect information from disclosure and other threats, you need to understand the risks associated with the release or modification of the information. Determining the risk of loss or modification is often measured by labeling the information. Labeling schemes are often known as classifications. The classifications will depend on the type of business and how the data is stored. Classified data can be either hard or soft. Hard data refers to concrete information, such as measurements and facts about an organization. Soft data refers to the organization's ideas, thoughts, and views. All data should be classified and protected accordingly. Common information classifications include the following.

Classification Scheme Level	Description
Corporate Confidential	Information that should not be provided to individuals outside of the enterprise.
Personal and Confidential	Information of a personal nature that should be protected.

Classification Scheme Level	Description
Private	Correspondence of a private nature between two people that should be safeguarded.
Trade Secret	Corporate intellectual property that, if released, will present serious damage to the company's ability to protect patents and processes.
Client Confidential	• Client personal information that, if released, may result in the identity theft of the individual. • Client corporate information or intellectual property. You may need to sign a non-disclosure agreement (NDA) to keep an organization's information about a client confidential.

Account Management

Account management is a common term used to refer to the processes, functions, and policies used to effectively manage user accounts within an organization. Account management job functions should follow the appropriate processes and security guidelines documented in an organizational security policy or account management policy. User accounts allow or deny access to an organization's information systems and resources; therefore, with the proper controls in place, accounts can be properly managed.

Account Privileges

Account privileges are permissions granted to users that allow them to perform various actions such as creating, deleting, and editing files, and also accessing systems and services on the network. Privileges can be assigned by user or by group. *User assigned privileges* are unique to each system user and can be configured to meet the needs of a specific job function or task. *Group based privileges* are assigned to an entire group of users within an organization. Each user within the group will have the same permissions applied. This can be very effective for large organizations with many users where privileges can be assigned at a departmental level. It is a universal best practice to assign privileges by group. User and group privileges should be well-documented in an organization's account policy. A user who has unique user assigned privileges and who is also a member of a group will be granted both sets of privileges.

Account Policy

An *account policy* is a document that includes an organization's requirements for account creation, account monitoring, and account removal. Policies can include user specific guidelines or group management guidelines.

 User account policies will vary and can be customized to meet the needs of the business. As a security professional, you will need to research and analyze your organization's policy needs based on business requirements.

Multiple Accounts

Multiple user accounts occur when one individual has multiple accounts for a system or resource. Accounts may differ depending on the level of access applied, such as a user level account versus an administrator account. It is common within an organization for an individual user to have more than one account for a number of systems. There are issues related to assigning and managing multiple accounts, such as:

- Lack of user awareness of the various accounts.

- Assigning the right level of data access and permissions to the appropriate accounts.

- And, managing the privileges, permissions, and data replication for each individual's accounts.

Using Multiple Accounts

A common use case for multiple accounts is for system administrators who have a user level account with typical user privileges for daily work such as preparing documents, using the Internet, and sending email, and an administrator-level account for use only to perform system procedures such as managing users or configuring servers. A user in this situation typically prefers to be able to use the same environment configuration, such as Windows desktop settings, document history, and web browser favorites lists, when switching between accounts. The management challenge is to enable the user to be able to access the elevated privileges of the administrative account when needed, without losing all the other environment settings that support productivity.

Account Management Security Controls

To maintain and enforce the security needs of an organization, strict account management security controls should be implemented and enforced.

Security Control	Description
User ID and password requirements	User IDs and passwords should be implemented and managed with a number of strict guidelines: • User IDs and passwords should be required to access all data systems and services within a network, or when accessing services on the Internet. • Unique user IDs should be required for each system user and documented. • Strong passwords should be required and documented for every system user, along with the character length requirements. • Password and user account recovery procedures should be documented and followed by all administrators.
Account access restrictions	Account access guidelines should be documented for each type of account used within an organization. For example, user account and group account privileges and systems access information should be documented. The concept of least privilege should be used when granting or denying access.
Account management guidelines	Account management can include a number of different tasks. The most common security guidelines include account creation, disablement, lockout, and expiration. Security guidelines should include organizational procedures for each account action and what specific conditions must be present to allow for an account change or deletion.

Security Control	Description
Multiple account guidelines	There can be many issues revolving around multiple user accounts. Users may have access to many different systems, or have more than one user account for an individual system. When managing multiple accounts: • Ensure proper documentation of all accounts assigned to an individual, including privileges, permissions, and data access rights assigned to each type of account. • Verify that user accounts are assigned properly, and that each individual only has the necessary accounts assigned to perform his or her job. • Verify that the proper level of access is assigned to each account.

Group Policy

Definition:

A *group policy* is a centralized account management feature available for Active Directory on Windows Server systems. A group policy can be used to control certain desktop workstation features within an enterprise, such as specifying that all workstations display the company logo as their wallpaper, or that the default browser should have pre-loaded settings. It is also used to control security features, such as limiting the desktop icons that get displayed, granting permission to access certain servers but not others, or totally locking down a desktop.

Example:

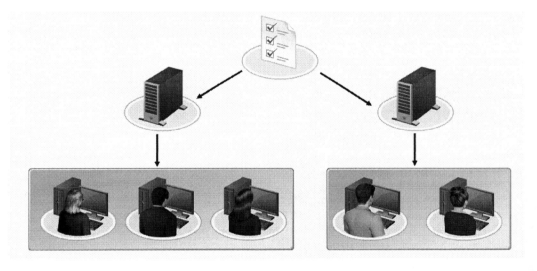

Figure 5-7: Group Policy.

How to Implement Account Management Security Controls

With proper account management security controls in place, you can ensure that the identity and log on information for all individuals within an organization is fully protected from unauthorized access or theft.

Guidelines

To implement account management security controls:

- Implement the principle of least privilege when assigning user and group account access.
- Ensure an account policy exists and includes all account policy guidelines.
- Verify that account request and approval procedures exist and are enforced.
- Verify that account modification procedures exist and are enforced.
- Verify that strong user name and password guidelines exist and are documented.
- Verify account usage guidelines exist and are documented, such as how to manage inactive accounts.

Example:

Our Global Company is revising their user account policy to include new stricter guidelines pertaining to the management of user accounts. Additions to the policy will include the account creation process stating that before an account is created or granted access to any systems, the direct manager for the user must approve the request, and verify that the access rights are directly related to the job role of the user.

The user name guidelines state that the first two letters of the user's first name along with the user's last name will be used to log in to all systems within the organization. Password guidelines in the policy state that each password must include a minimum of eight characters, with at least one number, and one special character.

Create Group Policy Objects in Windows Server 2008 R2

To create group policy objects in Windows Server 2008 R2:

1. Choose **Start→Administrative Tools→Group Policy Management.**
2. In the console tree, right-click on the domain object and choose **Create a GPO in this domain, and Link it here.**
3. In the **New GPO** dialog box, enter a name for the policy object you are going to create.
4. Close **GPMC.**

Edit Group Policy Objects in Windows Server 2008 R2

To edit group policy objects in Windows Server 2008 R2:

1. Choose **Start→Administrative Tools→Group Policy Management.**
2. Right-click the policy object you want to edit and choose **Edit.**
3. Edit the appropriate settings.
4. Close **GPMC.**

ACTIVITY 5-4
Implementing Account Management Security Controls

There is a simulated version of this activity available on the CD-ROM that shipped with this course. You can run this simulation on any Windows computer to review the activity after class, or as an alternative to performing the activity as a group in class. The activity simulation can be launched either directly from the CD-ROM by clicking the **Interactives** link and navigating to the appropriate one, or from the installed data file location by opening the C:\SPlus\ Simulations\Lesson#\Activity# folder and double-clicking the executable (.exe) file.

Scenario:
Without proper security controls, any network is vulnerable to threats and attacks. As a security administrator of a bank, you cannot risk the sensitive information stored on the network. As a part of organizational policies, you should implement account management security controls.

---

1. Create and link a new **Group Policy Object.**

    a. Choose **Start→Group Policy Management.**

    b. In the console tree, select the domain object and choose **Action→Create a GPO in this domain, and Link it here.**

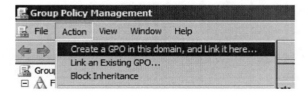

    c. In the **New GPO** dialog box, in the **Name** text box, type *My Policy*

    d. Click **OK.**

---

2. Enforce password history in the new policy.

    a. Under the domain, right-click on the policy **My Policy,** and choose **Edit.**

    b. In the console tree, under **Computer Configuration,** expand **Policies, Windows Settings, Security Settings,** and **Account Policies,** and then select **Password Policy.**

    c. In the right pane, double-click **Enforce password history.**

    d. Check the **Define this policy setting** check box.

    e.   In the **passwords remembered** text box, type **24**

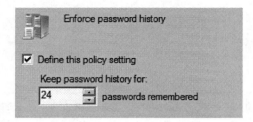

    f.   Click **Apply** and then click **OK.**

---

3.   Set a minimum password length and complexity.

    a.   In the right pane, double-click **Minimum password length.**

    b.   Check the **Define this policy setting** check box.

    c.   In the **characters** text box, type **7**

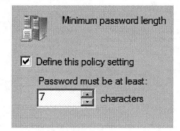

    d.   Click **Apply** and then click **OK.**

    e.   Double-click **Password must meet complexity requirements.**

    f.   Check the **Define this policy setting** check box and select the **Enabled** option.

    g.   Click **Apply** and then click **OK.**

---

4.   Change the account lockout duration.

    a.   In the console tree, select **Account Lockout Policy.**

    b.   In the right pane, double-click **Account lockout duration.**

    c.   Check the **Define this policy setting** check box.

    d.   In the **minutes** text box, double-click to select the text and then type **15**

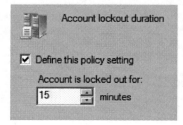

    e.   Click **Apply.**

f. In the **Suggested Value Changes** dialog box, click **OK** to accept the suggested changes.

g. Click **OK** to close the **Account lockout duration Properties** dialog box.

h. Open a Command Prompt window.

i. Enter **gpupdate /force**

```
C:\Users\Administrator.SERVER1.001>gpupdate /force
Updating Policy...

User Policy update has completed successfully.
Computer Policy update has completed successfully.
```

j. Close the Command Prompt.

5. Test the policy.

a. Choose **Start→Active Directory Users and Computers.**

b. Select **Users.**

c. Choose **Action→New→User.**

d. In the **New Object - User** dialog box, provide the following information.

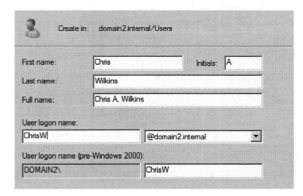

First name: *Chris*

Initials: *A*

Last name: *Wilkins*

User logon name: *ChrisW*

e. Click **Next.**

f. In the **Password** and **Confirm password** text boxes, type ***chris1***

g. Click **Next.**

h. Click **Finish.**

i. Verify that the policy does not allow a password that is less than seven characters. This confirms that the policy is active. Click **OK.**

j. Click **Back.**

k. In the **Password** and **Confirm password** text boxes, type ***!Pass1234***

l.   Click **Next.**

m.   Click **Finish.**

n.   Close all open windows.

Lesson 5 Follow-up

In this lesson, you identified how access control, authentication, and account management methods and services are used within organizations. Managing how users access resources is key to not only protecting unauthorized access to systems, but to also protect the identity of users connecting to systems. Implementing the proper services and security controls can help ensure that the organization as a whole is protected from attacks.

1. **What experience do you have with access control? What types of access control services are you familiar with?**

2. **What account management security controls have you come across in your current job role? Do you think they are sufficient in properly protecting employees' personal information?**

6 Managing Certificates

Lesson Time: 3 hour(s)

Lesson Objectives:

In this lesson, you will manage certificates.

You will:

- Install a CA hierarchy.
- Enroll certificates for entities.
- Secure network traffic using certificates.
- Renew certificates.
- Revoke certificates.
- Back up certificates and private keys.

Introduction

In the last lesson, you applied access control, authentication, and account management to protect the identity of users within a system. Once that is in place, you can begin installing certificate authorities to provide secure network communications between services and clients on your network. In this lesson, you will manage certificate-based security.

Certificates enable users, servers, clients, and applications to prove their identities and validate their communications across almost any network connection. As a security professional, you should be able to manage all the phases of the certificate process, from installation or enrollment to revocation, to ensure certificates are available and used properly.

This lesson covers all or part of the following CompTIA® Security+® (Exam SY0-301) certification objectives:

- Topic A:
  - Objective 6.1 Summarize general cryptography concepts
  - Objective 6.3 Explain the core concepts of public key infrastructure
  - Objective 6.4 Implement PKI, certificate management and associated components
- Topic B:
  - Objective 1.4 Implement and use common protocols
  - Objective 6.3 Explain the core concepts of public key infrastructure

- Topic C:
  - Objective 6.2 Use and apply appropriate cryptographic tools and products
  - Objective 6.3 Explain the core concepts of public key infrastructure
- Topic D:
  - Objective 6.4 Implement PKI, certificate management and associated components
- Topic E:
  - Objective 6.3 Explain the core concepts of public key infrastructure
  - Objective 6.4 Implement PKI, certificate management and associated components
- Topic F:
  - Objective 6.1 Summarize general cryptography concepts
  - Objective 6.3 Explain the core concepts of public key infrastructure
  - Objective 6.4 Implement PKI, certificate management and associated components

TOPIC A

Install a CA Hierarchy

You can implement certificate-based security either by obtaining certificates from a public Certificate Authority (CA) or by establishing your own CA. If you plan to use your own CA servers to issue certificates on your network, then the first step in the process of setting up public key security is installing the CA servers. In this topic, you will install CA servers into a CA hierarchy.

You can trust a certificate only if you can trust the CA that issued it, and you can trust that CA only if you can trust the CA above it in the chain. The entire certificate security system will fail if the basic CA hierarchy is not properly established and authorized. If your job as a security professional requires you to implement a CA design by installing CAs, you can use the skills in this topic to make sure it is done properly.

Digital Certificates

Definition:

A *digital certificate* is an electronic document that associates credentials with a public key. Both users and devices can hold certificates. The certificate validates the certificate holder's identity and is also a way to distribute the holder's public key. A server called a *Certificate Authority (CA)* issues certificates and the associated public/private key pairs.

Example:

User with Certificate   Device with Certificate

Figure 6-1: Digital certificates.

Certificate Authentication

When a user authenticates using a certificate, the user presents a digital certificate in place of a user name and password. A user is authenticated if the certificate is validated by a CA.

Certificate authentication is therefore the process of identifying end users in a transaction that involves a series of steps to be carried out before the user's identity is confirmed. These can include initiating a secure transaction such as a client requesting access to a secure site. The secure site presents its digital certificate to the client enclosing its public key and verified digital signature. The client browser validates the signature against its cache of trusted and acknowledged certificates, comparing it to a library of certificate authorities.

Once the digital signature is accepted, then certificate authentication is successful. If the issuing CA does not match the library of certificate authorities, then certificate authentication is unsuccessful and the user obtains a notification that the digital certificate supplied is invalid.

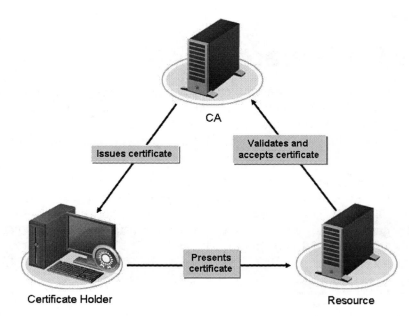

Figure 6-2: Certificate authentication.

PKI

Definition:

A *Public Key Infrastructure (PKI)* is a system that is composed of a CA, certificates, software, services, and other cryptographic components, for the purpose of enabling authenticity and validation of data and entities. The PKI can be implemented in various hierarchical structures, and can be publicly available or maintained privately by an organization. A PKI can be used to secure transactions over the Internet.

Example:

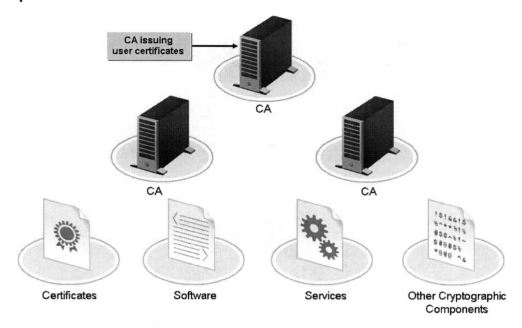

Figure 6-3: PKI.

PKI Components

A PKI contains several components:

- Digital certificates, to verify the identity of entities.

- One or more CAs, to issue digital certificates to computers, users, or applications.

- A *Registration Authority (RA),* responsible for verifying users' identities and approving or denying requests for digital certificates.

- A *certificate repository database,* to store the digital certificates.

- A *certificate management system,* to provide software tools to perform the day-to-day functions of the PKI.

PKCS

Public Key Cryptography Standards (PKCS) are a set of protocol standards developed by a consortium of vendors to send information over the Internet in a secure manner using a PKI. Important PKCS standards include:

- *PKCS #7—Cryptographic Message Syntax Standard:* A PKCS that describes the general syntax used for cryptographic data, such as digital signatures.

- *PKCS #10—Certification Request Syntax Standard:* A PKCS that describes the syntax used to request certification of a public key and other information.

For more information on PKCS, visit **www.rsa.com/rsalabs/node.asp?id=2124**

CA Hierarchies (Trust Models)

Definition:

A *CA hierarchy* or *trust model* is a single CA or group of CAs that work together to issue digital certificates. Each CA in the hierarchy has a parent-child relationship with the CA directly above it. A CA hierarchy provides a way for multiple CAs to distribute the certificate workload and provide certificate services more efficiently. If a CA is compromised, only those certificates issued by that particular CA and its children are invalid. The remaining CAs in the hierarchy will continue to function.

Example:

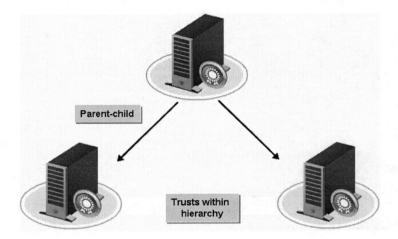

Figure 6-4: CA hierarchies.

The Root CA

Definition:

The *root CA* is the top-most CA in the hierarchy and, consequently, the most trusted authority. The root CA issues and self-signs the first certificate in the hierarchy. The root CA must be secured, because if it is compromised, all other certificates become invalid.

Example:

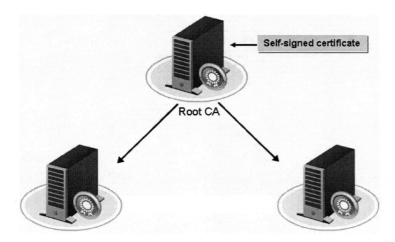

Figure 6-5: The root CA.

Microsoft® CA Terminology

If a Microsoft® CA is integrated with Active Directory, it is called an enterprise CA, but it is considered a standalone CA if it is not.

Public and Private Roots

Root CAs can be designated as either public or private.

- A *private root CA* is created by a company for use primarily within the company itself. The root can be set up and configured in-house or contracted to a third-party vendor.

- And, a *public root CA* is created by a third-party or commercial vendor for general access by the public.

Figure 6-6: Public and private roots.

Commercial CAs

VeriSign® is a well-known provider of public certificate services, along with Comodo™, GlobalSign®, and Entrust®.

Subordinate CAs

Definition:

Subordinate CAs are any CAs below the root in the hierarchy. Subordinate CAs issue certificates and provide day-to-day management of the certificates including renewal, suspension, and revocation.

Example:

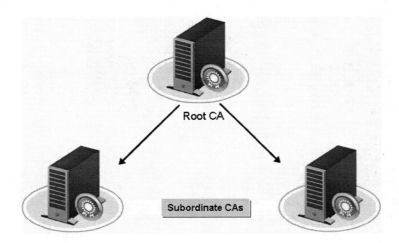

Figure 6-7: Subordinate CAs.

Offline Root CAs

To provide the most secure environment possible for the root CA, companies will often set up the root CA and then take it offline, allowing the subordinate CAs to issue all certificates. The root CA remains offline, and is not patched again once it is taken offline. All updates are installed physically on all subordinate CAs. This strategy ensures that the root CA is not accessible by anyone on the network and thus, it is much less likely to be compromised.

CA Hierarchy Design Options

The design of your CA hierarchy will depend on your organization's business and security requirements.

Company Profile	CA Hierarchy Implementation
Thousands of employees worldwide.	The subordinate CAs are designated by geographic location to balance the number of issued certificates among the individual CAs.
Individuals need to access specific applications only.	The subordinate CAs are designated by function or department so the individual CAs serve groups of people with specific resource needs.
Tight security allows individuals to have differing levels of access to the same resources.	The subordinate CAs are designated by the security required to obtain a certificate. Some CAs may be set up to issue a certificate with a network ID and password; other CAs may require a person to present a valid driver's license.

How to Install a CA Hierarchy

Procedure Reference: Install a CA Hierarchy

To install a CA hierarchy:

1. Set up the root CA or contract with a third-party vendor to provide root CA services.
2. Secure the root CA by taking it offline.
3. Install subordinate CAs.
4. Install further levels of issuing CAs according to your trust model design plan.

Procedure Reference: Install a Microsoft® Windows Server® 2008 R2 CA Hierarchy

For detailed instructions on planning and installing Microsoft® Windows Server® 2008 R2 CAs, see the Help and Support system in Windows Server 2008 R2.

To install a Windows Server 2008 R2 CA hierarchy:

1. Verify that all CAs in the hierarchy can locate each other by Domain Name System (DNS) name. The CA hierarchy uses DNS naming to publish and locate critical CA information, including the Certificate Revocation List (CRL).
2. Install the root CA.

   a. Choose **Start→Administrative Tools→Server Manager.**

   b. In the left pane, under the **Server Manager (Server#)** object, select **Roles.**

   c. In the **Roles Summary** section, click the **Add Roles** link.

   d. In the **Add Roles Wizard,** on the **Before You Begin** page, click **Next.**

   e. On the **Select Server Roles** page, in the **Roles** section, check the **Active Directory Certificate Services** check box and click **Next.**

   f. On the **Introduction to Active Directory Certificate Services** page, click **Next.**

   g. On the **Select Role Services** page, check the **Certification Authority** and **Certification Authority Web Enrollment** check boxes. Click **Next.**

   h. In the **Add Role Services** dialog box, click **Add Required Role Services.**

   i. On the **Specify Setup Type** page, select the **Standalone** option. Click **Next.**

   j. On the **Specify CA Type** page, with the **Root CA** option selected, click **Next.**

   k. On the **Set Up Private Key** page, with the **Create a new private key** option selected, click **Next.**

   l. On the **Configure Cryptography for CA** page, accept the default values, and click **Next.**

   m. On the **Configure CA Name** page, in the **Common name for this CA** text box, enter the CA name. Click **Next.**

   n. On the **Set Validity Period** page, set the validity period for the certificate. Click **Next.**

   o. On the **Configure Certificate Database** page, select the storage location for the CA database and log. Click **Next.**

   p. On the **Web Server (IIS)** page, click **Next.**

   q. On the **Select Role Services** page, click **Next.**

   r. On the **Confirm Installation Selections** page, click **Install.**

   s. On the **Installation Results** page, click **Close.**

3. Install the subordinate CAs.

    a. Retrieve the root server certificate from **http://** *root-server* **/certsrv**, where *root-server* is your server name. Install the certification path into the Root Store on the server where you will install the subordinate CA.

    b. Install the subordinate CA using the **Add Roles Wizard** in the same manner that you installed the root server.

    c. During the installation, request a server certificate from the root CA. (If the root CA is offline, you will have to save the request as a file, take the file to the root CA, and request the certificate.)

    d. At the root CA, issue the certificate for the subordinate CA. If the root CA is offline, save the certificate as a file and take the file to the new subordinate CA.

    e. Start the CA service at the subordinate CA and install the new CA server certificate.

 In a production environment, always run the **Security Configuration Wizard** when you add services to a Windows 2008 R2 server.

Procedure Reference: Secure a Windows Server 2008 R2 CA

To secure a Windows Server 2008 R2 CA:

1. Choose **Start→Administrative Tools→Active Directory Sites and Services.**
2. If necessary, choose **View→Show Services Node.**
3. Expand **Services,** then **Public Key Services,** and select **Certificate Templates.**
4. Double-click the template you want to secure, and configure security as necessary.

Procedure Reference: Back up the CA

To back up the CA:

1. Open **Certification Authority.**
2. Select your CA object and choose **Action→All Tasks→Back up CA.**
3. Use the **Certification Authority Backup Wizard** to back up the CA's private key, CA certificate, certificate database, log, and request queue.
4. To restore components of the CAs, select your CA object and choose **Action→All Tasks→Restore CA.**
5. Use the **Certification Authority Restore Wizard** to restore the CA's private key, CA certificate, certificate database, log, and request queue from the backup location.

ACTIVITY 6-1
Installing a CA

 There is a simulated version of this activity available on the CD-ROM that shipped with this course. You can run this simulation on any Windows computer to review the activity after class, or as an alternative to performing the activity as a group in class. The activity simulation can be launched either directly from the CD-ROM by clicking the **Interactives** link and navigating to the appropriate one, or from the installed data file location by opening the C:\SPlus\ Simulations\Lesson#\Activity# folder and double-clicking the executable (.exe) file.

Scenario:

As the security administrator for a private university located in Rochester, New York, USA, one of your job functions is to make sure the CA hierarchy designed by the IT department is implemented correctly. To prevent users from receiving unapproved certificates and accessing information that they are not supposed to, and also to prevent attackers from getting data, the university has decided to implement a new secure CA using Windows Server 2008 R2 CAs. The IT design team has created and documented a CA implementation plan that calls for installing a root CA for the entire university. The Windows Server 2008 R2 systems on which you will install certificate services have already been hardened to minimize the likelihood of attacks against the operating system itself from external users.

---

1. Install **Active Directory Certificate Services** on the CA.

   a. Choose **Start→Administrative Tools→Server Manager.**

   b. In the left pane, under the **Server Manager (SERVER##)** object, select **Roles.**

   c. In the **Roles Summary** section, click the **Add Roles** link.

   d. In the **Add Roles Wizard,** on the **Before You Begin** page, click **Next.**

   e. On the **Select Server Roles** page, in the **Roles** section, check the **Active Directory Certificate Services** check box and click **Next.**

   f. On the **Introduction to Active Directory Certificate Services** page, click **Next.**

   g. On the **Select Role Services** page, check the **Certification Authority Web Enrollment** check box.

   h. In the **Add Roles Wizard** dialog box, click **Add Required Role Services.** Click **Next.**

   i. On the **Specify Setup Type** page, select the **Standalone** option. Click **Next.**

   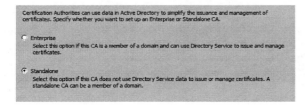

j. On the **Specify CA Type** page, with the **Root CA** option selected, click **Next**.

k. On the **Set Up Private Key** page, with the **Create a new private key** option selected, click **Next**.

l. On the **Configure Cryptography for CA** page, click **Next** to accept the default values.

m. On the **Configure CA Name** page, in the **Common name for this CA** text box, type *UniversityCA##* as the common name for the CA. Click **Next**.

n. On the **Set Validity Period** page, click **Next** to accept the default validity period for the certificate.

o. On the **Configure Certificate Database** page, click **Next** to accept the default storage location for the CA database and log.

p. On the **Web Server (IIS)** page, click **Next**.

q. On the **Select Role Services** page, click **Next**.

r. On the **Confirm Installation Selections** page, click **Install**.

s. On the **Installation Results** page, click **Close** and then close **Server Manager**.

2. Verify that Active Directory Certificate Services was installed properly.

a. Choose **Start→Administrative Tools→Certification Authority**.

b. The CA object should appear in the Microsoft Management Console (MMC). Select the CA object and choose **Action→Properties**.

c. In the **UniversityCA# Properties** dialog box, the name should appear as you configured it during installation. Click **View Certificate**.

d.   The certificate should expire in five years. Click **OK** to close the **Certificate** dialog box.

e.   Click **OK** to close the **UniversityCA# Properties** dialog box, and leave the Certification Authority window open.

ACTIVITY 6-2

Securing a Windows Server 2008 R2 Certificate Authority

 There is a simulated version of this activity available on the CD-ROM that shipped with this course. You can run this simulation on any Windows computer to review the activity after class, or as an alternative to performing the activity as a group in class. The activity simulation can be launched either directly from the CD-ROM by clicking the **Interactives** link and navigating to the appropriate one, or from the installed data file location by opening the C:\SPlus\ Simulations\Lesson#\Activity# folder and double-clicking the executable (.exe) file.

Scenario:

One of the next tasks as the university's security administrator is to make sure the CA server is secured such that Public Key Services is configured to give Authenticated Users Read and Enroll permissions to both the User Certificate Template and Web Server Certificate Templates. In the past, the university has had problems with unauthorized users being granted certificates. You have installed new Windows Server 2008 R2 CAs in your domain so that you have the ability to configure the CA server to restrict authenticated user access to certificate templates.

 In the classroom, your CA is actually installed as a standalone CA. You will still be able to perform the required permissions configurations in the Active Directory.

---

1. Create an Active Directory group containing all the faculty user accounts.

    a. Choose **Start→Active Directory Users and Computers.**

    b. Expand the **domain#.internal** object.

    c. Select the **Users** folder.

    d. Choose **Action→New→Group.**

    e. In the **New Object - Group** dialog box, in the **Group name** text box, type *Faculty*

    f. In the **Group scope** section, select the **Domain local** option.

    g. Verify that in the **Group type** section, the **Security** option is selected.

    h. In the **New Object - Group** dialog box, click **OK.**

---

2. Create a new **Faculty User** account and add it to the **Faculty** group.

    a. Choose **Action→New→User.**

    b. In the **New Object - User** dialog box, in the **First name** text box, type *Faculty* and press **Tab** twice.

    c. In the **Last name** text box, type *User*

d. Verify that **Faculty User** is displayed as the full user name.

e. Press **Tab** twice and in the **User logon name** text box, type *facultyuser*

f. Click **Next.**

g. In the **Password** text box, type *!Pass1234* as the password, and press **Tab.**

h. In the **Confirm password** text box, type *!Pass1234* to confirm the password.

i. Uncheck the **User must change password at next logon** check box.

j. Check the **User cannot change password** check box and click **Next.**

k. Click **Finish.**

l. Select the **Faculty User** account.

m. Choose **Action→Add to a group.**

n. In the **Select Groups** dialog box, in the **Enter the object names to select** text box, type *Faculty* and click **Check Names,** and then click **OK.**

o. In the **Active Directory Domain Services** message box, click **OK.**

p. Close the Active Directory Users and Computers window.

---

3. Use Active Directory to grant the **Faculty** group **Read** and **Enroll** permissions to the **User** template.

a. Choose **Start→Administrative Tools→Active Directory Sites and Services.**

b. If necessary, select **Active Directory Sites and Services.**

c. Choose **View→Show Services Node.**

d. Expand **Services** and **Public Key Services,** and select **Certificate Templates.**

e. In the templates list, double-click **User.**

f. In the **User Properties** dialog box, select the **Security** tab.

g. With **Authenticated Users** selected, verify that the **Allow** box for **Read** is checked.

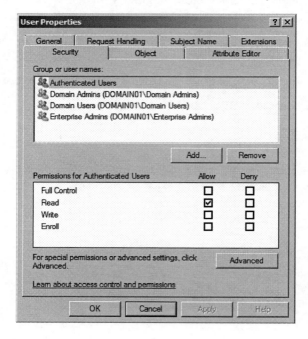

h. Click **Add.**

i. In the **Select Users, Computers, Service Accounts, or Groups** dialog box, in the **Enter the object names to select** text box, type *Faculty* and click **Check Names.**

j. In the **Multiple Names Found** dialog box, verify that the **Faculty** group is selected and click **OK** twice.

k. In the **User Properties** dialog box, with the **Faculty** group selected, verify that the **Allow** box for **Read** is checked. Check the **Allow** box for **Enroll** and click **OK.**

4. Use Active Directory Public Key Services to configure the appropriate faculty permission on the **WebServer** template.

  a.   In the templates list, double-click **WebServer.**

  b.   In the **WebServer Properties** dialog box, select the **Security** tab.

  c.   With **Authenticated Users** selected, verify that the **Allow** box for **Read** is checked.

  d.   Click **Add.**

  e.   In the **Select Users, Computers, Service Accounts, or Groups** dialog box, in the **Enter the object names to select** text box, type *Faculty* and click **OK.**

  f.   In the **Multiple Names Found** dialog box, verify that the **Faculty** group is selected and click **OK.**

  g.   In the **WebServer Properties** dialog box, with the **Faculty** group selected, verify that the **Allow** box for **Read** is checked. Check the **Allow** box for **Enroll** and click **OK.**

  h.   Close the Active Directory Sites and Services window.

TOPIC B
Enroll Certificates

Using certificates is a process that has several stages. The first stage is enrolling and installing certificates for the entities (such as users, devices, and services) that need them. In this topic, you will enroll certificates for various entities that require them.

A CA by itself does not do you any good. You have to get the certificates enrolled properly for the appropriate entities in order to implement certificate-based security. If a user, server, or client machine does not have the right certificate, there is nothing you can do to secure communications to or from that entity. The skills you will learn in this topic will help you request and install the proper certificates for each security situation.

The Certificate Enrollment Process

Users and other entities obtain certificates from the CA through the certificate enrollment process.

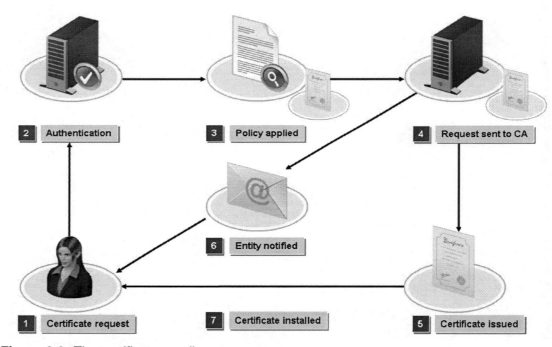

Figure 6-8: *The certificate enrollment process.*

Enrollment Step	Explanation
1. Entity requests certificate	An entity follows the procedure (for example, filling out an online form) to obtain a certificate.
2. RA authenticates entity	Authentication is determined by the certificate policy requirements (for example, a network user ID and password, driver's license, or other unique identifier).

Enrollment Step	Explanation
3. Policy applied to request	The RA applies the certificate policy that pertains to the particular CA that will issue the certificate.
4. Request sent to CA	If the identity of the entity is authenticated successfully and the policy requirements are met, the RA sends the certificate request on to the CA.
5. CA issues certificate	The CA creates the certificate and puts it in the repository.
6. Entity notified	The CA notifies the entity that the certificate is available, and the certificate is delivered.
7. Certificate installed	Once the certificate is obtained, it can be installed using the appropriate tool.

The Certificate Life Cycle

There are several main phases in the certificate life cycle.

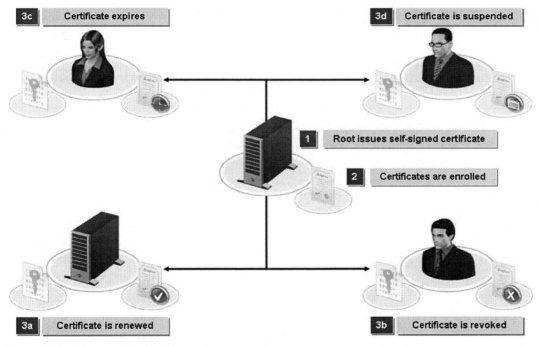

Figure 6-9: *The certificate life cycle.*

Certificate Life Cycle Phase	Description
Issuance	The life cycle begins when the root CA has issued its self-signed key pair. The root CA then begins issuing certificates to other CAs and end users.
Enrollment	Users and other entities obtain certificates from the CA through certificate enrollment.

Certificate Life Cycle Phase	Description
Expiration	Certificates expire after a given length of time, which is established in the certificate policy and configured in the issuing CA. The expiration parameter is part of the certificate data. If the root CA's certificate expires, the entire CA becomes inactive.
Revocation	Certificates can be revoked before their expiration date, which renders them permanently invalid. Certificates can be revoked for a variety of reasons, including misuse, loss, or compromise.
Suspension	Some CAs support temporary suspension of certificates, in addition to permanent revocation.
Renewal	Certificates can be renewed more than once—again, depending on the certificate policy parameters.

Certificate Life Cycle Management

As a general rule, the longer the life cycle is, the less administrative overhead is involved. This could pose a higher security risk, however, because a longer life cycle also gives attackers more time to break the cryptography of the key pair or otherwise compromise the system. Also, with a shortened lifetime, new developments in cryptography could allow you to have entities renew certificates that are more secure. The actual life cycle of your certificates will be based on your business requirements and security needs.

Balancing Certificate Life Cycle Needs

Although it would seem that a long key pair combined with a very complex algorithm would provide the longest life cycle and less administrative overhead, this combination can increase the time it takes to encrypt and decrypt data on the network. A long life cycle also allows attackers more time to break the code. You must balance the needs for security and accessibility when you design your certificate hierarchy.

Certificate Life Cycle Factors

The following table shows the most common factors that affect a certificate's life cycle, although this is not a comprehensive list.

Factor	Variables	Implications
The length of the private key	What length key is appropriate? 56 bit, 128 bit, 256 bit, 1024 bit, or 2048 bit?	The longer the key, the more data bits there are to work with. Long keys require more resources (more central processing unit [CPU] cycles or memory, more computers, more time, and so on) to break. Attackers may not think it is worth the effort.
Strength of the cryptography used	How complex will the algorithm be? Will it be created by a programmer or developed by algorithm software?	The more complex the mathematical functions are that are used in the algorithm, the harder it is for an attacker to decrypt. But it means that the time taken to generate the keys will also be higher.

Factor	Variables	Implications
Physical security of the CA and private key	Where is the CA kept? Is it in a locked area or just protected by a password? Who has access to it?	Higher physical security is essential for longer life cycles. All the policies in the world will not protect a private key if it is not physically secure. Keep in mind that physical security may be expensive.
Security of issued certificates and their private keys	Where is the private key stored? On a smart card? On the desktop? Is a password required?	The more secure the user's private keys are, the better they are for the security of the overall system. Conversely, users can forget passwords or lose smart cards, and that means more work for administrators.
Risk of attack	Is your CA offline or online? Is your root CA within your company or handled by a third-party company? What type of business are you in? Does your company have an intranet?	Your CA may be secure, but an attacker can use another access point that is not as secure on your network to gain access to the CA.
User trust	Who is using the issued certificates? External or internal users?	You can generally trust internal users (employees on the corporate network) more than external users (individuals accessing through the Internet).
Administrative involvement	Long life cycles require less administrative work. Short life cycles require more administrative work.	Although a long life cycle requires less administrative work (renewals, revocations, and so on), it also gives attackers more time to gain access.

How to Enroll Certificates

Procedure Reference: Enroll a Certificate for a Windows Server 2008 R2 Web Server

The exact procedures you will follow to enroll certificates depend upon your CA software, its configuration, and the type of certificate you are enrolling.

To enroll a certificate for a Windows Server 2008 R2 web server:

1. Request the certificate. The certificate request can be saved as a file or submitted across the network.

   - You can request certificates for users by using the web-based enrollment form on your certificate server's home page at **http://servername/certsrv**.

   - Or, you can request a web server certificate by using the **Web Server Certificate Wizard** in Internet Information Services (IIS) Manager.

     a. In Internet Information Services (IIS) Manager, select the **Server** object.

     b. On the **Server Home** page, in the **IIS** section, click **Server Certificates.**

     c. Complete the wizard with all the appropriate information.

2. If the certificate request is saved as a file, take the file to the issuing CA and submit it manually. If the CA is not configured to issue certificates automatically, the CA administrator will issue the certificate manually.

3.   After the certificate has been issued, install it. To install a certificate on a web server:

    a.   Download and save the certificate.

    b.   In Internet Information Services (IIS) Manager, select the **Server** object.

    c.   Click **Server Certificates.**

    d.   Click the **Complete Certificate Request** link and follow the wizard steps.

    e.   Verify that the correct certificate is selected.

    f.   Open the certificate and click **Install Certificate** to import it.

ACTIVITY 6-3
Enrolling Certificates

 There is a simulated version of this activity available on the CD-ROM that shipped with this course. You can run this simulation on any Windows computer to review the activity after class, or as an alternative to performing the activity as a group in class. The activity simulation can be launched either directly from the CD-ROM by clicking the **Interactives** link and navigating to the appropriate one, or from the installed data file location by opening the C:\SPlus\ Simulations\Lesson#\Activity# folder and double-clicking the executable (.exe) file.

Scenario:

Now that your CA server is functional, one of the next tasks as the university's security administrator is to enroll certificates for entities that require them. The university maintains a web-based student registration system. Internet Information Services (IIS) has already been hardened on your CAs and all university web servers. One of the first implementations of using certificates will be to make sure the data being transferred is secure on the student registration web servers. Before you can enable the secure web communications, you will need to enroll a certificate for the web server.

 The focus of this activity is on enrolling a certificate for a website, not using the certificate to enable secure web communications.

---

1. Create a file-based request for a new web server certificate from your CA.

   a. Choose **Start→Internet Information Services (IIS) Manager.**

   b. Maximize the window.

   c. Select your **Web Server** object.

   d. In the **SERVER## Home** pane, in the **IIS** section, double-click **Server Certificates.**

   e. On the **Server Certificates** page, in the **Actions** pane, click the **Create Certificate Request** link.

   f. In the **Request Certificate Wizard,** on the **Distinguished Name Properties** page, type *Server##* as the **Common name.**

   g. In the **Organization** text box, type *Registrar* and press **Tab.** In the **Organizational unit** text box, type *University* and press **Tab.**

    h.   In the **City/locality** text box, type *Rochester* and press **Tab.** In the **State/province** text box, type *New York*

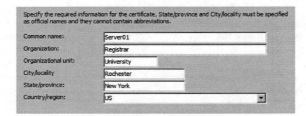

    i.   Click **Next** to move to the next page of the wizard.

    j.   On the **Cryptographic Service Provider Properties** page, click **Next** to accept the default **Cryptographic service provider** and **Bit length** settings.

    k.   As the file name, type *C:\Certreq.txt* and click **Finish** to generate and save the request file.

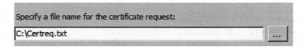

2.   Submit the request to your CA server.

    a.   Choose **Start→Computer,** and double-click the **C drive.**

    b.   Double-click the **Certreq.txt** file.

    c.   The file opens in **Notepad.** Choose **Edit→Select All,** and then choose **Edit→Copy.**

    d.   Close the Notepad and C drive windows.

    e.   Choose **Start→Internet Explorer.**

    f.   Connect to *http://server#/certsrv* where *#* is your student number.

    g.   If necessary, add the certificate server to the **Trusted Sites** zone.

    h.   On the **Welcome** web page, in the **Select a task** section, click the **Request a certificate** link.

    i.   On the **Request a Certificate** web page, click the **advanced certificate request** link.

    j.   On the **Advanced Certificate Request** web page, click the **Submit a certificate request by using a base–64–encoded CMC or PKCS #10 file, or submit a renewal request by using a base–64–encoded PKCS #7 file** link.

    k.   On the **Submit a Certificate Request or Renewal Request** web page, click in the **Saved Request** text area and choose **Page→Paste.**

    l.   Click **Submit.**

    m.   On the **Certificate Pending** web page, in the upper-right corner, click the **Home** link.

    n.   Minimize the Windows Internet Explorer window.

3.   Issue the requested server certificate.

    a.   Switch to **Certification Authority.**

    b.   In the Certification Authority window, expand your certificate server and select the **Pending Requests** folder.

    c.   Select the pending request with a **Request Common Name** of *Server#* and choose **Action→All Tasks→Issue.** You may have to scroll to the right to view the **Request Common Name** column.

    d.   Select the **Issued Certificates** folder.

    e.   Verify that the newly issued certificate appears in the details pane and minimize the Certification Authority window.

4.   Download the newly issued certificate as a file.

    a.   Click the **Microsoft Active Directory Certificate Services – Windows Internet Explorer** taskbar button.

    b.   Click the **View the status of a pending certificate request** link.

    c.   Click the **Saved-Request Certificate** link.

    d.   If necessary, in the **Information Bar** message box, click **Close.**

    e.   On the **Certificate Issued** web page, click the **Download certificate** link.

    f.   In the **File Download - Security Warning** dialog box, click **Save.**

    g.   In the **Save As** dialog box, in the **File name** text box, type *C:\Webcert.cer* and then click **Save.**

5.   Install and verify the certificate.

    a.   In the **Download complete** dialog box, click **Open.**

    b.   In the **Certificate** dialog box, click **Install Certificate.**

    c.   In the **Certificate Import Wizard,** on the **Welcome to the Certificate Import Wizard** page, click **Next.**

    d.   On the **Certificate Store** page, click **Next** to allow Windows to automatically select the store location based on the file certificate type.

    e.   On the **Completing the Certificate Import Wizard** page, click **Finish** to complete the wizard steps.

    f.   In the **Certificate Import Wizard** message box, click **OK.**

    g.   In the **Certificate** dialog box, click **OK** to close it.

    h.   Close the Internet Explorer window.

    i.   If necessary, in the Internet Information Services (IIS) Manager window, verify that the **Server** object is selected, and in the **IIS** section, double-click **Server Certificates.**

    j.   In the Internet Information Services (IIS) Manager window, on the **Server Certificates** web page, in the **Actions** pane, click the **Complete Certificate Request** link.

    k.   In the **Complete Certificate Request** dialog box, in the **File name containing the certification authority's response** text box, type *C:\Webcert.cer* as the file name and press **Tab.**

l.   In the **Friendly name** text box, type *WebCert* and click **OK.**

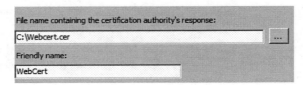

m.   Verify that the certificate is displayed in the list of server certificates.

n.   Close all open windows.

TOPIC C

Secure Network Traffic by Using Certificates

Once an entity has a certificate enrolled, you can use the certificate to secure network traffic flowing to and from that entity. Setting up the security is the next step in the process, so, in this topic, you will use certificates to secure network communications.

The end result of all your PKI planning, installation, and configuration is a mechanism for securing network communications. As you know by now, unsecure network communication is open to a variety of attacks, including eavesdropping. Attackers can use simple tools to steal data as it travels across the network and, most importantly, capture user names and passwords to get into your most sensitive systems. If you secure data using certificates, you will have another method for keeping attackers out of the critical components in your network.

The SSL Enrollment Process

You can use certificates to implement Secure Sockets Layer (SSL). The process has several steps.

SSL Enrollment Step	Explanation
1. Request	The client requests a session with the server.
2. Response	The server responds by sending its digital certificate and public key to the client.
3. Negotiation	The server and client then negotiate an encryption level.
4. Encryption	Once they agree on an encryption level, the client generates a session key, encrypts it, and sends it with the public key from the server.
5. Communication	The session key then becomes the key used in the conversation.

How to Secure Network Traffic by Using Certificates

Procedure Reference: Secure Network Traffic with Certificates

The exact procedures you will follow to secure network traffic will depend on the software you are using and the purpose of the certificate. To secure a Windows Server 2008 R2 website with certificates:

1. In Internet Information Services (IIS) Manager, select the website or virtual directory.
2. Double-click **SSL Settings.**
3. Check **Require SSL.**
4. Click **Apply.**
5. If this website has subordinate virtual directories, select the directories you want to inherit the new security configuration and click **OK.**

ACTIVITY 6-4
Securing Network Traffic With Certificates

 There is a simulated version of this activity available on the CD-ROM that shipped with this course. You can run this simulation on any Windows computer to review the activity after class, or as an alternative to performing the activity as a group in class. The activity simulation can be launched either directly from the CD-ROM by clicking the **Interactives** link and navigating to the appropriate one, or from the installed data file location by opening the C:\SPlus\ Simulations\Lesson#\Activity# folder and double-clicking the executable (.exe) file.

Setup:
A certificate has been installed on the web server. There is a home page for a student registration website on the server at the Uniform Resource Locator (URL) http://server##.

Scenario:
Now that you have obtained and installed the required certificate, your next task as the university's security administrator is to enable secure communications on the student registration website, which the university's webmaster has created on the web server. You need to ensure that the enrollment data being transferred to and from the registration website is secured.

---

1. Verify that you can connect to the student registration website.

   a. Choose **Start→Internet Explorer.**

   b. In the **Address** text box, type **http://server##** where **##** is your student number.

   c. In the **Windows Security** dialog box, in the first text box, click and type **Administrator** and press **Tab.** Type **!Pass1234** as the password and click **OK.**

   d. Verify that you can see the home page of the online enrollment system and then close Internet Explorer.

---

2. Bind the secure communication protocol to the **Default Web Site** object.

   a. Switch to Internet Information Services (IIS) Manager, and with your server expanded, expand **Sites,** and then select the **Default Web Site** object.

   b. In the **Actions** pane, click **Bindings.**

   c. In the **Site Bindings** dialog box, click **Add.**

   d. In the **Add Site Binding** dialog box, from the **Type** drop-down list, select the **https** option.

   e. From the **SSL certificate** drop-down list, select the **WebCert** certificate.

   f. Click **OK.**

   g. If necessary, in the **Add Site Binding** dialog box, click **Yes** to allow overwriting of existing SSL certificate.

> h. In the **Site Bindings** dialog box, click **Close.**

3. Enable the appropriate secure communications method and encryption level for the student registration website.

> a. Select the **Default Web Site** object.

> b. On the **Default Web Site Home** page, in the **IIS** section, double-click the **SSL Settings** option.
>
> c. On the **SSL Settings** page, check the **Require SSL** check box.
>
> d. In the **Actions** pane, click **Apply.**
>
> e. Verify that a message appears indicating that the change was successful.
>
> f. Minimize the Internet Information Services (IIS) Manager window.

4. Test unsecure communications with the student enrollment website.

> a. Open Internet Explorer.
>
> b. In the **Address** text box, type ***http://server##***
>
> c. Verify that you receive a message that the page must be viewed over a secure channel.

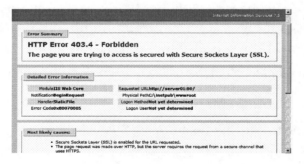

5. **Why did the connection fail?**

> a) Because the server now requires secure communications
>
> b) Because you typed an invalid URL
>
> c) Because you did not log on
>
> d) Because the certificate has expired

6. **How can you connect successfully?**

    a) By using the SFTP protocol.

    b) By using the HTTPS protocol.

    c) By using a certificate to authenticate the user.

    d) By logging on as a different user.

---

7. Test secure communication with the student enrollment website.

    a. In the **Address** text box, type *https://server##*

    b. In the **Security Alert** message box, click **OK** to acknowledge that you are making a secure connection.

    c. Log on as **Administrator** with a password of *!Pass1234* and click **OK.**

    d. If necessary, in the Internet Explorer message box, click **Add** to add the URL to the list of trusted sites.

    e. If necessary, in the **Trusted sites** dialog box, verify that in the **Add this website to the zone** text box, the URL is displayed and click **Close.**

    f. Verify that you are able to connect to the enrollment site.

    g. Next to the address bar, click the **Security Report** icon.

    h. A message, "Website Identification," is displayed. Click the **View certificates** link.

    i. As the name on the certificate matched the site name, you can see that it is the web server certificate you issued for this server. You should not accept certificates without verification. Click **OK** to close the certificate.

    j. Close the Internet Explorer window.

TOPIC D
Renew Certificates

After you initially configure certificate-based security, the remainder of your certificate management tasks have to do with maintaining the certificates over the rest of their life cycle. Because certificates are temporary and can expire, your first concern will be renewing existing certificates at the appropriate intervals. In this topic, you will learn to renew certificates.

Just like a driver's license, certificates are designed to expire at regular intervals. If a driver's license was good indefinitely, society would have no way to verify over time that the driver was still qualified to drive. And if certificates did not expire, an entity on the network could use one indefinitely even if its job role or function had changed. So that drivers can keep their licenses past the expiration period, most motor vehicle departments have a renewal process in place that does not interrupt a driver's right to be on the road. It is the same way with certificates. You should renew certificates appropriately so that you do not have any interruptions in your security services.

How to Renew Certificates

Procedure Reference: Renew Certificates

The procedures for renewing a certificate will vary depending upon the entity for whom you are renewing and upon your CA software. To renew a CA certificate in Windows Server 2008 R2:

1. Open **Certification Authority.**
2. Select your CA object and choose **Action→All Tasks→Renew CA Certificate.**
3. Stop the **Active Directory Certificate Services** when prompted.
4. Choose whether or not to generate a new key pair when prompted.
5. View the new certificate to verify that the expiration date has been extended.

ACTIVITY 6-5
Renewing a CA Certificate

 There is a simulated version of this activity available on the CD-ROM that shipped with this course. You can run this simulation on any Windows computer to review the activity after class, or as an alternative to performing the activity as a group in class. The activity simulation can be launched either directly from the CD-ROM by clicking the **Interactives** link and navigating to the appropriate one, or from the installed data file location by opening the C:\SPlus\Simulations\Lesson#\Activity# folder and double-clicking the executable (.exe) file.

Scenario:

Your root CA certificate is nearing its expiration. To maintain the integrity of your CA hierarchy, you need to renew the certificate.

1. Renew the root CA certificate at the root CA server.

   a. Open Certification Authority, select the CA object, and choose **Action→All Tasks→ Renew CA Certificate.**

   b. In the **Install CA Certificate** dialog box, click **Yes** to stop **Active Directory Certificate Services.**

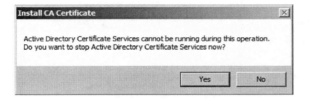

   c. In the **Renew CA Certificate** dialog box, verify that **Yes** is selected and click **OK** to renew the certificate and generate a new key pair.

2. Verify the certificate renewal.

   a. With the CA object selected, choose **Action→Properties.**

b. With **Certificate #1** selected, click **View Certificate.**

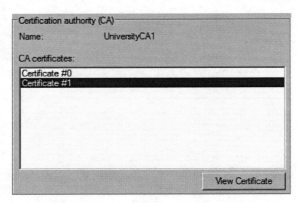

c. The renewed certificate should expire five years from the current date. In the **Certificate** dialog box, click **OK** to close the certificate.

d. In the **UniversityCA# Properties** dialog box, click **Cancel** to close the property sheet.

ACTIVITY 6-6

Renewing a Web Server Certificate

 There is a simulated version of this activity available on the CD-ROM that shipped with this course. You can run this simulation on any Windows computer to review the activity after class, or as an alternative to performing the activity as a group in class. The activity simulation can be launched either directly from the CD-ROM by clicking the **Interactives** link and navigating to the appropriate one, or from the installed data file location by opening the C:\SPlus\ Simulations\Lesson#\Activity# folder and double-clicking the executable (.exe) file.

Scenario:

Your web server's certificate is about to expire. You must renew it immediately so that it can continue to support SSL communications.

---

1. Renew the web server's certificate.

   a. Click **Internet Information Services Manager** on the taskbar. In the Internet Information Services (IIS) Manager window, select the **SERVER#** object.

   b. In the **SERVER## Home** pane, in the **IIS** section, double-click **Server Certificates.**

   c. On the **Server Certificates** page, select the **WebCert** certificate.

   d. In the **Actions** pane, click **Renew.**

   e. In the **Renew an Existing Certificate Wizard,** select the **Create a renewal certificate request** option and click **Next.**

   f. On the **Specify save as file name** page, in the **Specify a file name for the certificate renewal request** text box, type **C:\Certrenewal.txt** to name the certificate renewal request file and its location. Click **Finish.**

---

2. Submit the request to your CA server.

   a. Choose **Start→Computer,** and double-click the C drive.

   b. Double-click the **Certrenewal.txt** file.

   c. The file opens in **Notepad.** Choose **Edit→Select All,** and then choose **Edit→Copy.**

   d. Close the Notepad and C drive windows.

   e. Choose **Start→Internet Explorer.**

   f. In the **Address** text box, enter **https://server#/certsrv** where **#** is your student number.

   g. If necessary, in the **Security Alert** dialog box, click **OK,** click **Add** twice, and click **Close.**

   h. Click the **Request a certificate** link.

   i. Click the **advanced certificate request** link.

---

j.   Click the **Submit a certificate request by using a base–64–encoded CMC or PKCS #10 file, or submit a renewal request by using a base–64–encoded PKCS #7 file** link.

k.   Click in the **Saved Request** text box and choose **Page→Paste.**

l.   Click **Submit.**

m.   On the **Certificate Pending** web page, click the **Home** link.

3.   Issue the requested renewal of the web server certificate.

a.   In the Certification Authority window, in the right pane, double-click the **Pending Requests** folder.

b.   Select the pending request with a **Request Common Name** of **Server#** and choose **Action→All Tasks→Issue.** You may have to scroll to the right a little in order to view the **Request Common Name.**

c.   Select the **Issued Certificates** folder.

d.   Verify that the renewed certificate appears in the details pane and minimize Certification Authority.

4.   Download the newly issued certificate as a file.

a.   In Internet Explorer, click the **View the status of a pending certificate request** link.

b.   Click the **Saved-Request Certificate** link.

c.   If necessary, in the **Web Access Confirmation** dialog box, click **Yes.**

d.   If necessary, in the **Information Bar** message box, click **Close.**

e.   On the **Certificate Issued** web page, click **Download certificate.**

f.   In the **File Download - Security Warning** dialog box, click **Save.**

g.   In the **Save As** dialog box, in the **File name** text box, type *C:\Webcertrenew.cer* and click **Save.**

5.   Install and verify the certificate.

a.   In the **Download complete** dialog box, click **Open.**

b.   In the **Certificate** dialog box, click **Install Certificate.**

c.   In the **Certificate Import Wizard,** on the **Welcome to the Certificate Import Wizard** page, click **Next.**

d.   On the **Certificate Store** page, click **Next** to allow Windows to automatically select the store location based on the file certificate type.

e.   On the **Completing the Certificate Import Wizard** page, click **Finish** to complete the wizard steps.

f.   In the **Certificate Import Wizard** message box, click **OK.**

g.   In the **Certificate** dialog box, click **OK** to close it.

h.   Close the Internet Explorer window.

i.   In the Internet Information Services (IIS) Manager window, select the **Server** object, and in the **IIS** section, double-click **Server Certificates.**

j.   In the Internet Information Services (IIS) Manager window, on the **Server Certificates** web page, in the **Actions** pane, click **Complete Certificate Request.**

k.   In the **Complete Certificate Request** dialog box, in the **File name containing the certification authority's response** text box, type *C:\Webcertrenew.cer* as the file name.

l.   In the **Friendly name** text box, click and type *WebCertRenew* and click **OK.**

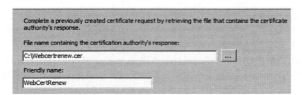

m.   Verify that the certificate is displayed in the list of server certificates.

n.   Minimize the Internet Information Services (IIS) Manager window.

TOPIC E
Revoke Certificates

You have performed certificate renewal, which is necessary when you want a security entity to be able to continue using a certificate past its original expiration period. You might sometimes encounter the opposite case, when you want a security entity to stop using a certificate for a specified period of time. To do that, you must revoke the certificate, which will be covered in this topic.

Remember that certificates are sort of like driver's licenses; although they are only good for a limited period, most people can simply renew theirs to keep it valid past the original expiration date. But sometimes, a driver loses the right to drive. In the same way, sometimes a security principal no longer needs a certificate or should no longer be able to authenticate with a certificate. Just like the driver's license, the certificate has to be revoked to prevent its further use.

Certificate Revocation

Certificates can be revoked before expiration for one of several reasons:

- The certificate owner's private key has been compromised or lost.
- The certificate was obtained by fraudulent means.
- Or, the certificate holder is no longer trusted. This can occur in normal circumstances, such as when an employee leaves a company, or it can be due to a system intrusion, such as when a subordinate CA is attacked.

The CRL

Definition:

A *Certificate Revocation List (CRL)* is a list of certificates that were revoked before the expiration date. Each CA has its own CRL that can be accessed through the directory services of the network operating system or a website. The CRL generally contains the requester's name, the request ID number, the reason why the certificate was revoked, and other pertinent information.

Example:

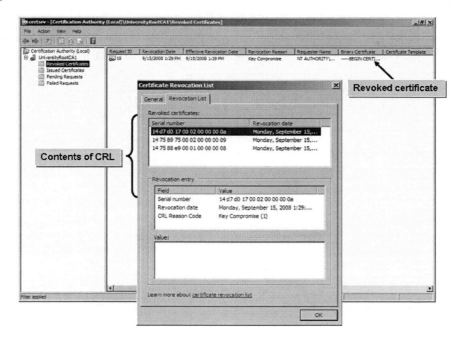

Figure 6-10: A CRL.

CRL Checked By Software

Many software programs, such as email applications, will check the CRL for the status of a certificate before accepting it, and will reject revoked certificates.

Status Checking and Suspensions

In certificate systems that support temporary certificate suspensions as well as permanent certificate revocations, the certificate clients will check for both suspended and revoked certificates and will reject certificates that have been either suspended or revoked.

How to Revoke Certificates

Procedure Reference: Revoke Certificates

No matter what type of CA software you use, there are three main steps in revoking certificates:

1. Revoke the certificate itself.

2. Publish the CRL.

3. Physically destroy the old certificate if it has been stored as a file. If the certificate was stored on a smart card, destroy or reprogram the card.

Procedure Reference: Revoke a Certificate in Windows Server 2008 R2

To revoke a certificate in Windows Server 2008 R2:

1. In the Certification Authority window, select the **Issued Certificates** folder, select the certificate you want to revoke, and choose **Action→All Tasks→Revoke Certificate.** You can specify a reason why the certificate was revoked.

2. Publish the CRL manually or automatically.
  - To publish the CRL automatically, wait for the automatic CRL publication interval.
  - To publish the CRL manually, in the Certification Authority window, select the **Revoked Certificates** folder and choose **Action→All Tasks→Publish.**

Procedure Reference: Modify the CRL Publication Schedule

To modify the CRL publication schedule in Windows Server 2008 R2:

1. Open the properties of the **Revoked Certificates** folder.
2. Set the publication interval to the desired interval.
3. Republish the list to change the update schedule for clients.

ACTIVITY 6-7
Revoking Certificates

There is a simulated version of this activity available on the CD-ROM that shipped with this course. You can run this simulation on any Windows computer to review the activity after class, or as an alternative to performing the activity as a group in class. The activity simulation can be launched either directly from the CD-ROM by clicking the **Interactives** link and navigating to the appropriate one, or from the installed data file location by opening the C:\SPlus\ Simulations\Lesson#\Activity# folder and double-clicking the executable (.exe) file.

Scenario:

One of your colleagues in IT thinks that a student has compromised the public and private key pairs on the student registration web server. IT wants to make sure the suspect keys are no longer used. In cases like this, the university's CA security guidelines call for revocation of the compromised certificate and immediate publication of the CRL.

---

1. Revoke the certificate for the web server.

    a. In the Certification Authority window, select the **Issued Certificates** folder.

    b. Select the certificate that was most recently issued to the web server and choose **Action→All Tasks→Revoke Certificate.**

    c. In the **Certificate Revocation** dialog box, from the **Reason code** drop-down list, select the **Key Compromise** option.

    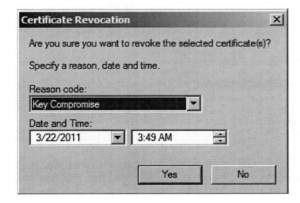

    d. Click **Yes** to revoke the certificate.

    e. Select the **Revoked Certificates** folder.

    f. Verify that the revoked certificate appears in the **Revoked Certificates** folder.

    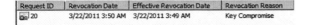

2. **When will clients know that the certificate has been revoked?**

   a) When the certificate expires

   b) When they connect to the website

   c) When the CRL is published

   d) When the client requests a new certificate

3. **If an attacker maliciously revokes certificates, how could they be recovered?**

   a) By renewing the CA certificates

   b) By republishing the CRL

   c) By reissuing the certificates

   d) By restoring the CA from a backup

4. Publish the CRL manually.

   a. In the Certification Authority window, with the **Revoked Certificates** folder selected, choose **Action→All Tasks→Publish.**

   b. In the **Publish CRL** dialog box, click **OK** to confirm that you want to publish a new CRL.

5. Verify that the CRL is current.

   a. Choose **Action→Properties** to open the properties for the Revoked Certificates folder.

   b. In the **Revoked Certificates Properties** dialog box, select the **View CRLs** tab.

   c. In the **CRLs** section, verify that the CRL with the highest key index is selected.

   d. Click **View CRL.**

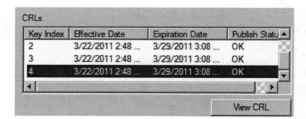

   e. The **Effective date** for the current CRL should be the current date and time. The next automatic update is scheduled on the default weekly update schedule. Select the **Revocation List** tab.

   f. The certificate you revoked should be in the list. Select the certificate.

   > If the certificate you revoked does not display, select another CRL.

   g. The **Revocation entry** section displays details about the certificate. Click **OK** to close the **Certificate Revocation List** dialog box.

h. In the **Revoked Certificates Properties** dialog box, click **OK** to close the revoked certificates property sheet.

ACTIVITY 6-8
Modifying the CRL Publication Interval

 There is a simulated version of this activity available on the CD-ROM that shipped with this course. You can run this simulation on any Windows computer to review the activity after class, or as an alternative to performing the activity as a group in class. The activity simulation can be launched either directly from the CD-ROM by clicking the **Interactives** link and navigating to the appropriate one, or from the installed data file location by opening the C:\SPlus\ Simulations\Lesson#\Activity# folder and double-clicking the executable (.exe) file.

Scenario:

Your CA is configured with the default publication interval for the CRL. The university's CA security guidelines call for daily publication of the CRL. You are responsible for configuring your CA in accordance with the guidelines.

1. Change the publication interval for the CRL.

    a. In the Certification Authority window, open the properties of the **Revoked Certificates** folder.

    b. In the **Revoked Certificates Properties** dialog box, in the **CRL publication interval** section, from the drop-down list, select the **Days** option.

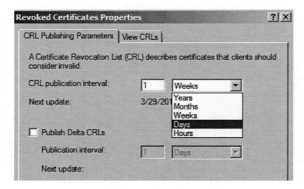

    c. Click **Apply.**

    d. The **Next update** schedule will change the next time the list is published. Click **OK** to close the property sheet.

2. Publish the CRL.

    a. With the **Revoked Certificates** folder selected, choose **Action→All Tasks→Publish.**

    b. In the **Publish CRL** dialog box, click **OK** to confirm that you want to publish a new CRL.

c.   Open the properties of the Revoked Certificates folder.

d.   Verify that the **Next update** is scheduled for one day from the current date and click **Cancel.**

e.   Minimize the Certification Authority window.

TOPIC F

Back Up and Restore Certificates and Private Keys

Previously, you recovered a failed CA server to restore your certificate infrastructure. A failed CA server is only one of the problems that can affect your CA infrastructure. Other major problem that can arise are the loss or destruction of certificates and their associated private keys or the need for a backup to be restored. In this topic, you will learn methods to back up certificates and keys so that you can restore them if they are lost or compromised.

Without keys, public key security simply cannot function. Due to their necessity, keys should be safeguarded closely. However, despite the best precautions, keys are occasionally damaged or lost. You need to have backup procedures for certificates and keys so that you can restore them when needed.

Private Key Protection Methods

Private keys are crucial to the security of a CA hierarchy and must be protected from loss, theft, or compromise. To secure a private key:

● Back it up to removable media and store the media securely.

● Delete it from insecure media.

● Require a password to restore the private key.

● Never share a key.

● Never transmit a key on the network or across the Internet after it is issued.

● And, consider using key escrow to store a private key with trusted third parties.

Key Escrow

Key escrow, an alternative to key backups, can be used to store private keys securely, while allowing one or more trusted third parties access to the keys under predefined conditions. The third party is called the *key escrow agent.* For example, in certain situations, a government agency might require private keys to be placed in escrow with the agency. Commercial CAs can also act as escrow agents on a contract basis for organizations that do not want to back up and manage their own private keys.

M of N Control

In a key escrow scheme, there are only a certain number of agents or trustees that have the authority to recover a key. To determine how many agents are required, the *M of N scheme* is commonly used. The M of N scheme is a mathematical control that takes into account the total number of key recovery agents (N) along with the number of agents required to perform a key recovery (M). The exact values of M and N will vary with the implementation.

Private Key Restoration Methods

If a private key is lost or damaged, you must restore the key from a backup or from escrow before you can recover any encrypted data.

- If you are using key escrow, the key is divided among escrow agents. The agents can use the parts to reconstruct the lost key or decrypt the information directly.

- And, if the key has been backed up to removable media, it can be restored from the backup location.

Private Key Replacement

If a private key is lost, you might wish to replace the key entirely after you recover any encrypted data:

1. First, recover the private key.
2. Decrypt any encrypted data.
3. Destroy the original private key.
4. Obtain a new key pair.
5. Finally, re-encrypt the data using the new private key.

How to Back Up and Restore Certificates and Private Keys

Procedure Reference: Back Up Certificates and Private Keys in Windows Server 2008 R2

To back up user certificates and private keys in Windows Server 2008 R2:

1. As the user, create a custom MMC console containing the **Certificates** snap-in.
2. In the **Certificates** console, expand **Certificates** and **Current User.**
3. Expand the **Personal store** and select the **Certificates** folder.
4. Select the certificate with the appropriate intended purpose.
5. Select the certificate and choose **Action→All Tasks→Export.**
6. Complete the appropriate steps in the **Export Wizard.** For maximum security, use a strong password and export the certificate to a flash drive or other external storage medium. Store the drive in a secure location.

Procedure Reference: Restore a Certificate and Private Key

Certificate and key restoration procedures will vary depending upon the type of certificate you need to restore and the software you are using.

To restore a user's certificate and private key in Windows Server 2008 R2:

1. Open a **Certificates** console for the affected user account.
2. Open the **Personal store,** select the **Certificates** folder, and choose **Action→All Tasks→ Import.**
3. In the **Certificate Import Wizard,** on the **File to Import** page, in the **File name** text box, specify the location of the backup certificate.
4. On the **Password** page, in the **Password** text box, enter the password. Check the **Mark this key as exportable** check box. This will allow you to back up or transport your keys at a later time.

The EFS Recovery Agent

The *Encrypting File System (EFS)* uses public key encryption. Windows Server 2008 automatically creates encryption certificates and public keys based on a user's credentials; or, you can use Windows Server 2008 Certificate Services to distribute certificates and keys. File encryption keys, which are used to encrypt the files, are stored by the public key. The files are then accessible only by using the file owner's private key. The file encryption keys are then stored in the Windows operating system kernel and are never copied to the paging file, thus providing another level of security.

The problem you can encounter with encryption is how to recover encrypted files in the event the user account under which files were encrypted no longer exists. For example, this problem can occur if you delete a user account after the user leaves your organization. Windows Server 2008 R2 enables you to define an EFS recovery agent. This individual has the necessary credentials to recover files that were encrypted by another user. By default, Windows Server 2008 R2 designates the domain administrator as an EFS recovery agent. You can add other EFS recovery agents in the group policy by modifying the **Add Data Recovery Agent** policy setting within the Computer Configuration\Windows Settings\Security Settings\Public Key Policies\Encrypting File System.

To recover an encrypted file, the EFS recovery agent must complete the following steps:

1. Back up the encrypted files.

2. Move the backup of the encrypted files to a secure server.

3. Import the recovery certificate and private keys to the secure server. Use steps 1 and 2 to export the recovery certificate and keys.

4. Restore the backup of the encrypted files.

5. Decrypt the files using Windows Explorer.

ACTIVITY 6-9
Backing Up a Certificate and Private Key

 There is a simulated version of this activity available on the CD-ROM that shipped with this course. You can run this simulation on any Windows computer to review the activity after class, or as an alternative to performing the activity as a group in class. The activity simulation can be launched either directly from the CD-ROM by clicking the **Interactives** link and navigating to the appropriate one, or from the installed data file location by opening the C:\SPlus\ Simulations\Lesson#\Activity# folder and double-clicking the executable (.exe) file.

Setup:

You will need a flash drive or another external storage device for this activity.

Scenario:

The university has decided to secure email communications through the use of individual email certificates for all students and staff members. The security design team has developed recommendations for the strength of the email certificates. The team has also developed recommendations for maintaining backup copies of the email certificates and their associated private keys to guard against loss or compromise of the certificates. As the security administrator, your job is to support enrollment for email certificates and to maintain backups of each issued certificate. You will need an email certificate enrolled and backed up for your own personal Administrator user account.

1. Request a certificate for email protection for the Administrator user.

   a. Open Internet Explorer.

   b. Connect to **https://server##/certsrv** where ## is your student number.

   c. In the **Security Alert** message box, click **OK** to acknowledge that you are making a secure connection.

   d. If necessary, click **Add** twice.

   e. Click **Close.**

   f. Click the **Request a certificate** link.

   g. Click the **advanced certificate request** link.

   h. Click the **Create and submit a request to this CA** link.

   i. In the **Web Access Confirmation** dialog box, click **Yes** to verify the certificate request.

   j. Type *Administrator* as the **Name** and *administrator@domain##.internal* as the **E-Mail.**

   k. From the **Type of Certificate Needed** drop-down list, select **E-Mail Protection Certificate.**

   l. Scroll to the **Key Options** section.

m.   If necessary, double-click and enter **1024** for the value in the **Key Size** text box.

n.   Check the **Mark keys as exportable** check box.

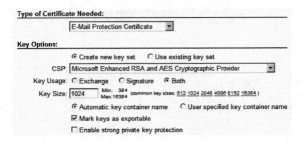

o.   Scroll down and click **Submit.**

p.   If necessary, in the **Web Access Confirmation** dialog box, click **Yes** to verify the certificate request.

q.   On the **Certificate Pending** web page, click the **Home** link.

---

2.   Issue the pending user certificate.

a.   On the taskbar, click **Certification Authority.**

b.   In the Certification Authority window, select the **Pending Requests** folder.

c.   Scroll to the right to confirm that the **Request Common Name** for the certificate is **Administrator.** Select the pending request and choose **Action→All Tasks→Issue.**

---

3.   Install the new email certificate for the Administrator user.

a.   On the taskbar, click **Internet Explorer.**

b.   In Internet Explorer, click the **View the status of a pending certificate request** link.

c.   Click the **E-Mail Protection Certificate** link.

d.   In the **Web Access Confirmation** dialog box, click **Yes.**

e.   Click **Install this certificate.**

f.   Observe that a message "Your new certificate has been successfully installed" is displayed and close the Internet Explorer window.

---

4.   Create a Certificates MMC console for the Administrator user.

a.   Choose **Start→Run.**

b.   Type **mmc** and click **OK.**

c.   Maximize the Console1 - [Console Root] window.

d.   Choose **File→Add/Remove Snap-in.**

e.   Select **Certificates** and click **Add.**

f.   In the **Certificates snap-in** dialog box, verify that **My user account** is selected and click **Finish.**

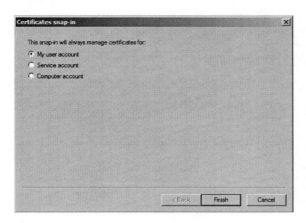

g.   Click **OK.**

h.   Choose **File→Save As.**

i.   In the **Save As** dialog box, in the **File name** text box, type **Certificates.msc** and click **Save.**

---

5.   Export the certificate and its private key to removable backup media.

a.   Insert your flash drive or other media in the USB port.

b.   In the **Certificates** console, expand **Certificates - Current User.**

c.   Expand the **Personal** folder and select the **Certificates** folder.

d.   Select the certificate with an intended purpose of **Secure Email.**

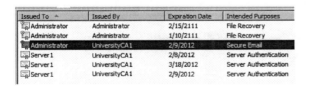

e.   Choose **Action→All Tasks→Export.**

f.   In the **Certificate Export Wizard,** on the **Welcome to the Certificate Export Wizard** page, click **Next.**

g.   Select **Yes, export the private key,** and click **Next.**

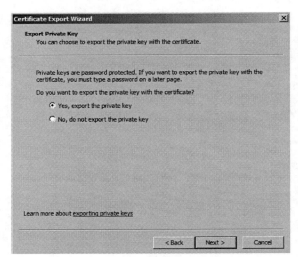

h.   On the **Export File Format** page, click **Next** to accept the default file format.

i.   In the **Password** and **Type and confirm password (mandatory)** text boxes, type ***!Pass1234*** and click **Next.**

j.   In the **File name** text box, type ***(drive):\mailcert*** where ***(drive)*** represents the drive letter of your flash drive (it should be E), and click **Next.**

k.   Click **Finish.**

l.   Click **OK** to close the message box.

---

6.   Verify that the certificate was exported.

a.   Choose **Start→Computer.**

b.   Double-click the **E drive.**

c.   Verify that the mailcert.pfx file appears and close the E drive window.

d.   Remove the flash drive.

---

7.   **What should you do with the removable backup media?**

a) Store it in the server room with the CA.

b) Store it in a separate secure location.

c) Leave it in the drive for convenient access.

OPTIONAL ACTIVITY 6-10
Restoring a Certificate and Private Key

 There is a simulated version of this activity available on the CD-ROM that shipped with this course. You can run this simulation on any Windows computer to review the activity after class, or as an alternative to performing the activity as a group in class. The activity simulation can be launched either directly from the CD-ROM by clicking the **Interactives** link and navigating to the appropriate one, or from the installed data file location by opening the C:\SPlus\ Simulations\Lesson#\Activity# folder and double-clicking the executable (.exe) file.

Setup:
There is a backup copy of the Administrator user's email certificate and private key on a flash drive. There is a Certificates MMC console for the Administrator user.

Scenario:
A staff member's email certificate and private key have become corrupted. Fortunately, you have followed the procedures in your security policy document and maintain backup copies of all user certificates and private keys. You can use these backups to correct the user's problem.

---

1. Create a key-compromise situation by deleting the Administrator user's email certificate.

   a. In the Certificates console, with the **Secure Email** certificate selected, choose **Action→Delete.**

   b. In the **Certificates** dialog box, click **Yes** to confirm the deletion.

---

2. Restore the certificate and private key from the backup.

   a. Insert the flash drive containing the backup copy of the Administrator's email certificate into the USB port.

   b. In the **Certificates** console, in the **Personal** folder, verify that the **Certificates** folder is selected and choose **Action→All Tasks→Import.**

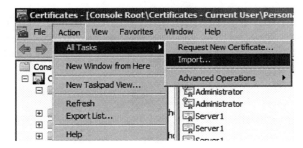

   c. In the **Certificate Import Wizard,** on the **Welcome to the Certificate Import Wizard** page, click **Next.**

   d. On the **File to Import** page, in the **File name** text box, type *E:\mailcert.pfx* and click **Next.**

e. On the **Password** page, type *!Pass1234* as the password.

f. Check the **Mark this key as exportable. This will allow you to back up or transport your keys at a later time** check box. Click **Next**.

g. On the **Certificate Store** page, click **Next** to place the certificate in the **Personal** store.

h. On the **Completing the Certificate Import Wizard** page, click **Finish**.

i. Click **OK** in the message box.

j. Verify that the restored certificate appears in the **Certificates** folder in the **Personal** store. Close the Certificates window and click **Yes** when prompted to save console settings.

k. Close all open windows.

Lesson 6 Follow-up

In this lesson, you performed the tasks involved in the day-to-day management of certificates. Regardless of how simple or complex your certificate hierarchy is, you will still need to do different tasks such as install, issue, revoke, renew, and eventually expire certificates. Each of these tasks plays an equally important role in managing certificates.

1. **What type of CAs are you familiar with?**

2. **What types of certificate management functions have you performed?**

7 Compliance and Operational Security

Lesson Time: 1 hour(s), 30 minutes

Lesson Objectives:

In this lesson, you will identify compliance and operational security measures.

You will:

- Describe physical security issues and principles.
- Describe legal compliance issues and principles.
- Identify security awareness and training requirements.

Introduction

Now that you have implemented and managed your basic security infrastructure, you will need to make sure that appropriate security procedures and policies are enforced, and rules and regulations are followed. In this lesson, you will identify common compliance issues and related security controls.

Although system and network security are key concerns, you still need to know what areas of the organization are vulnerable to threats. Enforcing operational security across an organization will provide you with the first defense against security threats and will enable regulatory compliance. It is your responsibility as a security professional to provide the right level of support to organizations. Having a strong compliance framework is crucial to gaining the level of security control required to properly protect the employees, systems, and networks within an organization.

This lesson covers all or part of the following CompTIA® Security+® (Exam SY0-301) certification objectives:

- Topic A:
    - Objective 2.4 Explain the importance of security related awareness and training
    - Objective 2.6 Explain the impact and proper use of environmental controls
    - Objective 3.6 Analyze and differentiate among types of mitigation and deterrent techniques
- Topic B:
    - Objective 2.3 Execute appropriate incident response procedures

- Objective 2.4 Explain the importance of security related awareness and training
- Topic C:
  - Objective 2.1 Explain risk related concepts
  - Objective 2.4 Explain the importance of security related awareness and training

TOPIC A
Physical Security

You now have the skills to verify your company's compliance with internal and external policies on an ongoing basis. There is one more piece to maintaining a complete security infrastructure, and that is to make sure that the physical components of your company's security plan are in place. In this topic, you will explore the security measures used to ensure the physical security for an organization.

You can make sure that servers have been secured, access control mechanisms are in place, and all network connections are protected, but all of that effort is wasted if the physical security to those systems is not also properly secured. Part of completely securing an organization's assets is also securing all physical components.

Physical Security Controls

Physical security controls are security measures that restrict, detect, and monitor access to specific physical areas or assets. They can control access to a building, to equipment, or to specific areas, such as server rooms, finance or legal areas, data centers, network cable runs, or any other area that has hardware or information that is considered to have important value and sensitivity. Determining where to use physical access controls requires a risk/benefit analysis and must include the consideration of any regulations or other compliance requirements for the specific types of data that are being safeguarded.

Physical Security Control Types

There are a number of physical access controls available to ensure the protection of an organization's physical environment.

Physical Security Control	Description
Locks	There are a number of different locks that can be used to restrict unauthorized access to information resources:
	• Bolting door locks are a traditional lock-and-key method that requires a non-duplicate policy for keys to access a door.
	• Combination door locks, or cipher locks, use a keypad or dial system with a code or numeric combination to access a door.
	• Electronic door locks use an access ID card, with an electronic chip or token that is read by the electronic sensor attached to a door.
	• Biometric door locks are commonly used in highly secure environments. This method uses an individual's unique body features to scan and identify the access permissions for a particular door.
	• Hardware locks can be attached to a laptop, hard drive, or file cabinet to secure it from being opened or turned on.

Physical Security Control	Description
Logging and visitor access	Logging should be used at all entrances that are open to the general public. This method requires all visitors to sign in and out when entering and leaving the building. Logging requirements will vary depending on the organization, but should include the following: ● Name and company being represented. ● Date, time of entry, and time of departure. ● Reason for visiting. ● Contact within the organization. When possible, one single entry point should be used for all incoming visitors. This decreases the risk of unauthorized individuals gaining access to the building.
Identification systems	Security cards, such as swipe cards or proximity cards, provide identity information about the bearer, which is then checked against an appropriate access list for that location. The cards can be used along with a proximity reader to verify identification and grant access. A security card can also include a picture or some other identification code for a second authentication factor. Security cards should be required for all employees and should be visible at all times.
Video surveillance	Video or still-image surveillance can be put in place to deter or help in the prosecution of unwanted access. These systems can be placed inside and outside the building. All video recording should be saved and stored in a secure environment.
Security guards	Human security guards, armed or unarmed, can be placed in front of and around a location to protect it. They can monitor critical checkpoints and verify identification, allow or disallow access, and log physical entry occurrences. They also provide a visual deterrent and can apply their own knowledge and intuition to potential security breaches.
Bonded personnel	Contracted services personnel, such as cleaning services, should be bonded to protect an organization from financial exposures.
Mantrap doors	A mantrap door system, also referred to as a deadman door, is a system with a door at each end of a secure chamber. An individual enters a secure area through an outer door. The outer door must be closed before an inner door can open. An individual's identity is sometimes verified before they enter the secure area through the first door, and other times while they are confined to the secure area between the two doors. This system also requires that one person enter at a time. This system typically requires two separate authentication processes, with the second one being done while the authenticated person is isolated inside a reinforced enclosure.
Physical barriers	The location of highly secure resources, such as a server room, should not have windows or be visible from the outside of a building. This creates a more secure barrier from the outside. Examples of physical barriers include fencing and true floor-to-ceiling wall architectures.
Alarms	Alarms activated by an unauthorized access attempt require a quick response. Locally stationed security guards or police may respond to alarms. These responding individuals may trigger access control devices in the facility to automatically lock.

Environmental Exposures

Environmental exposures must be considered when evaluating the overall security of a building. Exposures can include lightning, hurricanes, earthquakes, volcanic eruptions, high winds, and other extreme weather conditions. As a result of any of these exposures, a number of issues may arise:

● Power fluctuations and failures.

● Water damage and flooding.

● Fires.

● And, structural damage to the building leading to unauthorized access.

Environmental Controls

There are certain *environmental controls* that can be implemented to help control a facility's physical environment.

Environmental Control	Description
Heating, ventilation, and air conditioning (HVAC) system	An HVAC system controls the environment inside a building. ● Humidity and temperature control: Most experts recommend that temperatures in a computer facility should be in the range of 72°–76° Fahrenheit. The relative humidity in the facility should be between 40 percent and 60 percent. High and low temperatures can damage equipment. Low humidity causes static electricity; high humidity causes corrosion. ● Positive air pressure is a must. Air should be forced from the facility to keep contaminants out. Filters on HVAC systems keep dust to a minimum and must be changed regularly. ● To ensure that HVAC systems are running properly, it is important to monitor them both locally and remotely.
Hot and cold aisle	A method used within data centers and computer rooms to control the temperature and humidity. A hot and cold aisle layout is designed to control the flow of air to or from systems using strategically placed vents and exhaust fans in order to keep the hardware and room at the desired temperature and humidity.
Electromagnetic interference (EMI) shielding	EMI occurs when a magnetic field builds up around one electrical circuit and interferes with the signal being carried on an adjacent circuit, causing network interference issues resulting in signal noise or errors. EMI shielding is used to prevent electromagnetic transfers from cables and devices by creating a conductive material protective barrier. For example, a shielded cable contains an electromagnetic covering within the cable that directly protects the inner core conductor from producing an electromagnetic discharge.
Alarm control panel	The main control panel for an organization's alarm system should be protected and secured from any type of exposure. The panel must be in a separate location and protected from unauthorized access, and be accessible by the fire department, encased in a waterproof and climate-controlled box, powered by a dedicated circuit, and programmed to function by zone within an organization.

Environmental Control	Description
Fire prevention	The first rule of fire protection is fire prevention. Fires can be prevented by: ● Eliminating unnecessary storage items and clutter. ● Conducting annual inspections by the fire department, which include an extensive review of computer room controls, all fire suppression systems, and extinguishers within the building. ● Installing fireproof walls, and a fireproof floor and ceiling in the computer room, which all have at least a two-hour fire resistance rating. ● Using fire-resistant office materials, such as garbage bins, desks, chairs, and window treatments.
Fire detection	Various fire detection systems are used to identify the threat of a fire: ● Smoke detectors sense the presence of smoke using various scientific methods, such as testing for particles in the air. ● Heat sensors are triggered either when a target temperature is reached or when there is a high rate of increase in temperature. ● Flame detectors use optical sensors to record incoming radiation at selected wavelengths. ● Commercial fire detection systems should be connected to a central reporting station where the location of the suspected fire is indicated. In some cases, the detection system or monitoring station is connected directly to a fire department.
Fire suppression	Fires in computer facilities are especially dangerous. The damage done to computing systems is extremely expensive, and the chemicals used in the machines may emit toxic substances during fires. In some cases, small fires may be extinguished using hand-held fire extinguishers. These systems must be placed in the appropriate locations within a facility and should be inspected regularly. When it is not practical to fight these fires with small extinguishers or to douse fires with water, then special gases should be used to extinguish fires in areas with a large number of computers or servers. Frequently, local jurisdictions mandate water-based fire extinguishing systems, even though gaseous systems often provide more appropriate protection for computer equipment. To satisfy each requirement, organizations are outfitted with both. Here is what occurs: if the gas system does not suppress the fire, the sprinkler system will then activate, but is otherwise maintained as the official back-up extinguisher. The best practice is to contact your local fire authorities when designing a fire suppression system.

Environmental Monitoring

Regularly monitoring the environmental conditions and controls surrounding a building and the hardware stored inside it is important to properly secure and prevent damage to resources. Conditions that can threaten security should be monitored regularly, along with the implementation of necessary security controls. In some instances, constant video monitoring is used to look for environmental issues such as overheating, water, or electricity issues.

ACTIVITY 7-1
Examining the Components of Physical Security

Scenario:

InfiniTrade Financial is relocating its main headquarters to a new building. The head of information security has asked for your input on the physical security needed to protect the main server room at the new location.

1. **What types of physical security controls would you suggest for the main server room?**

2. **What are some common environmental exposures that InfiniTrade may consider when evaluating the overall security of its new building?**

3. **What type of environmental controls should InfiniTrade Financial consider as part of their relocation?**

TOPIC B

Legal Compliance

Previously in the course, you identified corporate policies that are designed to meet the internal needs of your organization. But, as a security professional, you may be responsible for meeting the security needs of outside legal authorities as well. In this topic, you will identify security requirements that your company might legally be required to meet.

Legal security compliance requirements can affect your company in a variety of situations. You might work for a company in a publicly regulated industry, such as the nuclear power industry. Your company might have business partnerships with or provide services or products to any one of a number of government agencies. You also have responsibilities to your local municipality for safety and security. As a security professional, you will need to be able to demonstrate that your company is compliant with any or all of these entities' security requirements.

Compliance Laws and Regulations

The effect of laws and regulations on applying security measures can be substantial. Security professionals must review all laws and regulations relevant to the type of business and operation that needs to be secured. Most organizations will have legal requirements that apply to their data systems, processes, controls, and infrastructure. Regulations can affect the way businesses store, transmit, and process data. When securing an organization as a whole, you must review the business' privacy policy and other legal documents that convey business requirements.

Legal Requirements

All organizations must consider their legal obligations, rights, liabilities, and limitations when creating security policies. Because security incidents can potentially be prosecuted as technology crimes, organizations must be prepared to work with civil authorities when investigating, reporting, and resolving each incident. Information security practices must comply with legal requirements that are documented in other departmental policies, such as human resources. A company's response to a security incident must conform to the company's legal limitations as well as the civil rights of the individuals involved.

Requirements of Regulated Industries

In addition to the various local, state, federal, and international legal considerations, organizations in regulated industries, such as utility companies, hazardous material manufacturers, and medical professions, will have to comply with the additional standards and requirements imposed by governmental authorities and professional oversight bodies for each industry. The requirements can vary widely, depending on the industry involved, and are specific for every organization.

Industry Best Practices

When applying security measures to an organization, it is always a good idea to consider industry best practices. Depending on the type of business, best practices will vary.

Types of Legal Requirements

Legal issues can affect different parties within each organization.

Affected Party	Legal Considerations
Employees	• Who is liable for the misuse of email and Internet resources? The organization, the employee, or both? • What is the extent of liability for an organization for criminal acts committed by its employees? • What rights to privacy do employees have regarding electronic communications?
Customers	• What customer data is considered private and what is considered public? • How will a company protect the privacy and confidentiality of customer information?
Business partners	• Who is liable if data resides in one location (country) and the processing takes place in another location? • Who is responsible for the security and privacy of the information transmitted between an organization and a business partner? The sender or the receiver?

Forensic Requirements

Information security professionals must observe generally accepted forensic practices when investigating security incidents.

Forensics Requirement	Description
Evidence collection	Following the correct procedures for collecting evidence from floppy disks, hard drives, smart cards, and other media ensures the integrity of the evidence and prevents tampering. As in any other case, evidence that is improperly collected may not be admissible in court.
Evidence preservation	Criminal cases or even internal security incidents can take months or years to resolve. The company must be able to properly preserve all gathered evidence for a lengthy period of time.
Chain of custody	Whoever gathers and preserves the evidence must also maintain a complete inventory that shows who handled specific items and where they have been stored. This document must be kept secure at all times to prevent tampering. If the chain of custody is broken, it can be difficult, if not impossible, to prosecute a technology crime.
Jurisdiction	Determining exactly who has the right to investigate and prosecute an information technology criminal case can be extremely difficult due to overlapping laws for copyright, computer fraud, and mail tampering. In addition, each country has its own laws and these laws may vary depending on what part of the country is involved. Organizations are obliged to use due care to determine the appropriate jurisdiction for a security investigation.

ACTIVITY 7-2
Examining Legal Compliance

Data Files:

InfiniTradeFinancialAcceptableUsePolicy.rtf

Scenario:

As the security administrator for InfiniTrade Financial Group, you have been assigned the task of determining when appropriate legal action should be taken based on the acceptable use policy (AUP). Use the AUP document to determine if your security policy calls for legal action in the following situations.

1. **An employee unintentionally opens an attachment that causes a virus to spread within the organization. Does the policy call for legal action?**

2. **An employee emails a copy of a new type of encryption software program to a user in a foreign country for testing. Does the policy call for legal action?**

3. **An employee scans your network for open ports. Does the policy call for legal action?**

4. **An employee forwards an email that appears to be a Ponzi or Pyramid scheme. Does the policy call for legal action?**

5. **Two employees have an argument at lunchtime. During the afternoon, one user sends a threatening email to the other. The second employee is afraid to leave the building unescorted that evening. Does the policy call for legal action?**

TOPIC C
Security Awareness and Training

Throughout this course, you have acquired the skills you need to keep your security infrastructure healthy. But security is the responsibility of all the individuals in the organization, not just the professional security team. In this topic, you will learn how to give users the information they need to follow appropriate security practices in their day-to-day work.

Attackers are smart and will take advantage of employees that may not be savvy enough to know they are being solicited for information. Because of this, it is your responsibility to educate or coach your users about their individual security responsibilities. An educated user is the security professional's best partner in preventing security breaches.

Security Policy Awareness

An organization's security policy is created to ensure that all system users comply with the security guidelines and procedures enforced by management. Security professionals should verify that the security policy is accessible and that users are trained in the importance of security awareness within an organization. Regular training sessions and security policy documentation will ensure that users follow the correct procedures when accessing and using system resources and services.

Employee Education

Information security is not the exclusive responsibility of information professionals. A comprehensive security plan can only succeed when all members of an organization understand the necessary security practices and comply with them. Security professionals are often the ones responsible for educating employees and encouraging their compliance with security policies.

There are three important components that work together in order to ensure proper employee security education.

Step	Explanation
Awareness	Employees must understand the importance of information security and security policies, and have an awareness of the potential threats to security. Threats can include new and upcoming viruses, types of phishing attacks, and zero day exploits.
	Employees also need to be aware of the role they play to protect an organization's assets and resources. A security professional can create awareness through seminars, email, or information on a company intranet.
Communication	The lines of communication between employees and the security team must remain open. Security professionals can accomplish this by encouraging employees to ask questions and provide feedback on security issues. Also, the security team must take responsibility for keeping the workforce informed of ongoing security concerns and updated best practices and standards.

Step	Explanation
Education	Employees should be trained and educated in security procedures, practices, and expectations from the moment they walk through the door. Employees are responsible for organizational security the second they join an organization and have access to the physical building and resources, and the intellectual property inside. Education should continue as technology changes and new information become available. Education takes many forms, from training sessions to online courses employees can take at work. Educated users are one of your best defenses against social engineering attacks.

Online Resources

A common way to promote employee awareness and training is to provide employees with online access to security-related resources and information. You can provide proprietary, private security information, such as your corporate security policy document, through an organization's intranet. You can also point employees to a number of reputable and valuable security resources on the Internet. However, both you and the employee should be cautious whenever researching information on the Internet. Just because information is posted on a website does not mean it is factual or reliable. Monitor the websites you recommend to your employees periodically to make sure that they are providing worthwhile information, and encourage employees to verify any technical or security-related information with a reliable third party before acting on the information or passing it along to others.

Here are just a few of the valuable information security resources from technology vendors and other organizations that you can find on the Internet:

- **http://www.microsoft.com/security/default.mspx**
- **http://www.oracle.com/technetwork/topics/security/whatsnew/index.html**
- **http://tools.cisco.com/security/center/home.x**
- **http://www.sans.org**
- **http://www.openssh.org**
- **http://www.rsa.com**
- **http://www.cert.org**
- **http://searchsecurity.techtarget.com/**
- **http://www.securityfocus.com**
- **http://www.entrust.com**
- **http://www.ruskwig.com**
- **http://www.symantec.com/security_response/index.jsp**
- **http://www.mcafee.com**
- **http://project.honeynet.org**
- **http://web.mit.edu/kerberos**
- **http://hoaxbusters.org**
- **http://vmyths.com**
- **http://snopes.com**

User Security Responsibilities

Because security is most often breached at the end-user level, users need to be aware of their specific security responsibilities and habits.

Security Area	Employee Responsibilities
Physical security	Employees should not allow anyone in the building without an ID badge. Employees should not allow other individuals to "tailgate" on a single ID badge. Employees should be comfortable approaching and challenging unknown or unidentified persons in a work area. Access within the building should be restricted to only those areas an employee needs to access for job purposes. Data handling procedures of confidential files must be followed. Employees must also follow clean desk policies to ensure that confidential documents and private corporate information are secured and filed away from plain sight.
System security	Proper password behaviors can be crucial in keeping systems resources secure from unauthorized users. Employees must use their user IDs and passwords properly and comply with the ID and password requirements set forth by management. Password information should never be shared or written down where it is accessible to others. All confidential files should be saved to an appropriate location on the network where they can be secured and backed up, not on a hard drive or removable media device.
Device security	Employees must use correct procedures to log off all systems and shut down computers when not in use. Wireless communication and personally owned devices must be approved by the IT department and installed properly. These devices can be a gateway for attackers to access corporate information and sensitive data. Portable devices, such as laptops and mobile devices, must be properly stored and secured when not in use.
Social networking security	Employees must be made aware of the potential threats and attacks that target social networking and peer-to-peer (P2P) applications and websites. The use of these applications can lead to potential breaches in security on an organization's network. Security policies should include guidelines and restrictions for users of any social networking application or website.

ACTIVITY 7-3
Examining Security Awareness and Training

Scenario:

As the security administrator for a new military subcontractor, one of your responsibilities is to coordinate the employee security training and awareness program. The plant has recently experienced several security incidents involving improper user behavior. IT staff and plant management have come to you for recommendations on how to implement proper employee training procedures to prevent similar problems in the future.

1. A virus has spread throughout your organization, causing expensive system down-time and corrupted data. You find that the virus sent to many users was an email attachment that was forwarded by an employee. The employee that received the original email was fooled into believing the link it contained was a legitimate marketing survey. You quickly determine that this is a well-known email hoax that had already been posted on several hoax-related websites. When questioned, the employee said that he thought it sounded as if it could be legitimate, and he could not see any harm in "just trying it." How could better user training and awareness have helped this situation?

2. What specific training steps do you recommend taking in response to this incident?

3. You come in on a Monday morning to find laptops have been stolen from several employees' desks over the weekend. After reviewing videotapes from the security cameras, you find that as an employee exited the building through the secure rear door on Friday night, she held the door open to admit another individual. You suspect this individual was the thief. When you question the employee, she states that the individual told her that he was a new employee who had not yet received his employee badge, that he only needed to be in the building for a few minutes, and that it would save him some time if she could let him in the back door rather than having to walk around to the receptionist entrance. Your security policy states that no one without identification should be admitted through the security doors at any time, but the employee says she was unaware of this policy. You ask her to locate the security policy documents on the network, and she is unable to do so. How could better user education have helped this situation?

4. What user training steps do you recommend taking in response to this incident?

5. One of your competitors has somehow obtained confidential data about your organization. There have been no obvious security breaches or physical break-ins, and you are puzzled as to the source of the leak. You begin to ask questions about any suspicious or unusual employee activity, and you begin to hear stories about a sales representative from out of town who did not have a desk in the office and was sitting down in open cubes and plugging her laptop in to the corporate network. You suspect that the sales representative was really an industrial spy for your competitor. When you ask other employees why they did not ask the sales representative for identification or report the incident to security, the other employees said that, giving their understanding of company policies, they did not see anything unusual or problematic in the situation. You review your security policy documents and, in fact, none of them refer to a situation like this one. How could better user education have helped this situation?

6. What user training steps do you recommend taking in response to this incident?

Lesson 7 Follow-up

In this lesson, you examined the components of compliance and operational security, including the best practices and user awareness guidelines used to achieve operational security. With this knowledge, you are better prepared to tackle the common security issues related to physical and environmental security, and also to properly support security policy implementations.

1. **In your work experience, what types of physical security controls have you come across?**

2. **How do you think security awareness and training can impact an organization?**

8 | Risk Management

Lesson Time: 3 hour(s), 45 minutes

Lesson Objectives:

In this lesson, you will manage risk.

You will:

- Analyze risk.

- Implement vulnerability assessment tools and techniques.

- Scan for vulnerabilities.

- Identify mitigation and deterrent techniques.

Introduction

Now that you have taken the steps to secure your system and network, you will need to properly manage the risk surrounding those systems and networks. In this lesson, you will analyze the risks, assess vulnerabilities, scan systems, and implement mitigation strategies.

Managing risk plays a major role in ensuring a secure environment for an organization. By assessing and identifying specific risks that can cause damage to network components, hardware, and personnel, you can mitigate possible threats and establish the right corrective measures to avoid possible damage to people or systems.

This lesson covers all or part of the following CompTIA® Security+® (Exam SY0-301) certification objectives:

- Topic A:

    - Objective 1.1 Explain the security function and purpose of network devices and technologies

    - Objective 2.1 Explain risk related concepts

    - Objective 2.2 Carry out appropriate risk mitigation strategies

    - Objective 3.7 Implement assessment tools and techniques to discover security threats and vulnerabilities

- Topic B:

    - Objective 1.1 Explain the security function and purpose of network devices and technologies

    - Objective 2.4 Explain the importance of security related awareness and training

- Objective 3.7 Implement assessment tools and techniques to discover security threats and vulnerabilities
- Topic C:
  - Objective 3.7 Implement assessment tools and techniques to discover security threats and vulnerabilities
  - Objective 3.8 Within the realm of vulnerability assessments, explain the proper use of penetration testing versus vulnerability scanning
- Topic D:
  - Objective 1.2 Apply and implement secure network administration principles
  - Objective 2.1 Explain risk related concepts
  - Objective 2.2 Carry out appropriate risk mitigation strategies
  - Objective 3.6 Analyze and differentiate among types of mitigation and deterrent techniques

TOPIC A
Risk Analysis

In the early phases of applying security controls, the focus has been on securing an organization as a whole. You have covered all the main hardware, network, and infrastructure components, and now will review the risk assessment process.

How do you know what to protect your organization against? What constitutes a risk? You need to find out what exactly will help you determine what a risk is on your system or network. If you can foresee and analyze some of those risks, then you can avoid some major issues that can come up later. Risk analysis helps you achieve this milestone.

Risk Management

In the information management world, risks come in many different forms. If a risk is not managed correctly, it could result in disclosure, modification, loss, destruction, or interruption of a critical asset. *Risk management* is a cyclical process that includes four phases:

● Identification.

● Mitigation.

● Response.

● And, recovery.

Security Assessment Types

Assessing an organization's security infrastructure will determine whether current security measures are acceptable. There are three general categories of assessment.

Assessment Type	Description
Risk	A risk assessment is a evaluation of an organization, a portion of an organization, an information system, or system components to assess the security risk. Risk assessments are usually performed as part of the risk analysis process to identify what parts or functions of the business propose the highest risk.
Threat	A threat assessment is an evaluation of known threats to an organization and the potential damage to business operations and systems. Threat assessment is usually performed as part of the risk analysis process, but could be performed at any time to verify that current security controls are still operating successfully, and are detecting and managing threats.
Vulnerability	A vulnerability assessment is an evaluation used to find security weaknesses within an organization. Vulnerability assessments can be performed on an organization's physical security implementations and all networks, hardware, and software.

Types of Risk

Security risks are often categorized as natural, man-made, or system risks, depending on their source.

Risk Type	Description
Natural	Natural risks are related to weather or other non-controllable events that are residual occurrences of the activities of nature. Different types of natural disasters include: • Earthquakes. • Wildfires. • Flooding. • Excessive snowfalls. • Tsunamis. • Hurricanes. • Tornados. • Landslides.
Man-made	Man-made risks are residual occurrences of individual or collective human activity. Man-made events can be caused intentionally or unintentionally. Intentional man-made attacks include: • Arson. • Terrorist attacks. • Political unrest. • Break-ins. • Theft of equipment and/or data. • Equipment damage. • File destruction. • Information disclosure. Unintentional man-made risks include: • User computing mistakes. • Social networking and cloud computing. • Excessive employee illnesses or epidemics. • Information disclosure.
System	System risks are related to any weakness or vulnerability found within a network, service, application, or device. System risks include: • Unsecured mobile devices. • Unstable virtualization environments. • Unsecured network devices. • Email vulnerabilities, such as viruses and spam. • Account management vulnerabilities, such as unassigned privileges.

Components of Risk Analysis

Risk is the likelihood that a threat can exploit a vulnerability to cause some type of damage. Therefore, when you perform an analysis to determine if a risk exists, you need to not only identify potential threats, but also determine if there are vulnerabilities in your systems that those threats could exploit. Once you are sure that a risk exists, you can determine the severity of the risk based on how much damage the risk could cause and how likely it is to occur.

Vulnerability-Assessed Threats

Some examples of vulnerability-assessed threats may include the following:

- If a business is located next to railroad tracks and a train derails, leaking toxic fluids, the business might be forced into inactivity for a number of days.

- If key manufacturing staff express their plans to strike, they may threaten to damage equipment beforehand to heighten the impact of their impending actions.

- A key supplier may be unable to provide raw materials for the production of an organization's principal products.

- Overly hardened servers.

Phases of Risk Analysis

When determining how to protect computer networks, computer installations, and information, *risk analysis* is the security process used for assessing risk damages that can affect an organization.

There are six phases in the risk analysis process.

Risk Analysis Process Phase	Description
Asset identification	Identifying the assets that require protection and determining the value of the assets.
Vulnerability identification	Identifying vulnerabilities so the analyst can confirm where asset protection problems exist. Locating weaknesses exposes the critical areas that are most susceptible to vulnerabilities. Vulnerability scanning is a method used to determine weaknesses in systems. This method can, however, produce false positives which tend to initiate reasons for concern, even when there are no actual issues or weaknesses in the system.
Threat assessment	Once vulnerabilities are understood, the threats that may take advantage of or exploit those vulnerabilities are determined.
Probability quantification	Quantifying the likelihood or probability that threats will exploit vulnerabilities.
Impact analysis	Once the probabilities are determined, the impact of these potential threats need to be evaluated. This can include either the impact of recovering from the damage, or the impact of implementing possible preventive measures.
Countermeasures determination	Determining and developing countermeasures to eliminate or reduce risks. The countermeasures must be economically sound and provide the expected level of protection. In other words, the countermeasures must not cost more than the expected loss caused by threats that exploit vulnerabilities.

Risk Analysis Methods

A number of methods are used to analyze risk.

Method	Description
Qualitative	Qualitative analysis methods use descriptions and words to measure the amount and impact of risk. For example, ratings can be high, medium, or low based on the criteria used to analyze the impact. Qualitative analysis is generally scenario based.
Quantitative	Quantitative analysis is based completely on numeric values. Data is analyzed using historic records, experiences, industry best practices and records, statistical theories, testing, and experiments.
Semi-quantitative	The semi-quantitative analysis method uses a description that is associated with a numeric value. It is neither fully qualitative nor quantitative.

Risk Calculation

Risk calculation focuses on financial and operational loss impact and locates threat exploitation indicators in an organization. Risk calculation can be viewed as a formula that takes into account the worth of each asset, the potential impact of each risk, and the likelihood of each threat, and then weighs that against the potential costs of alleviating system vulnerabilities. Organizations may use this process to determine the *annual loss expectancy (ALE)* for each risk identified. The ALE value is the total cost of a risk to an organization on an annual basis.

Calculating Risk

A company might calculate that a certain system in its demilitarized zone (DMZ) has almost a 90 percent probability of experiencing a port scan attack on a daily basis. However, although the threat level is high, the company does not consider the system to be at much risk of damage from the threat of a scan. The cost of hardening the system to completely prevent the scan far outweighs the potential losses due to the identified risk.

On the other hand, a company might determine that its server room is at a high risk of complete loss due to a natural disaster and that the cost of such a loss would be catastrophic for the organization. Although the likelihood of the disaster threat is quite low, the overall impact is so great that the company maintains an expensive alternate site that it can switch operations to in the event of such an emergency.

Vulnerability Tables

A simple vulnerability table is often a strategic tool for completing a vulnerability assessment.

Vulnerability	Identification Source	Risk of Occurrence (1 = Low; 5 = High)	Impact Estimate (US Dollars)	Mitigation
Flood damage	Physical plant	5	$95,000	Physical adjustments and flood insurance

Vulnerability	Identification Source	Risk of Occurrence (1 = Low; 5 = High)	Impact Estimate (US Dollars)	Mitigation
Electrical failure	Physical plant	2	$100,000	Generator, Uninterruptible Power Supply (UPS)
Flu epidemic	Personnel	4	$200,000	Flu shots

Using a table allows planners to identify the likelihood of threats or vulnerabilities, record the possible impact, and then prioritize mitigation efforts. Mitigation helps reduce the impact of an exploited vulnerability. A loss of power has a relatively high risk with a reasonable mitigation effort, consisting of a one-time expenditure to purchase a backup generator.

If there were two additional columns in the table, the assessment would be more useful.

Vulnerability	Cost of Mitigation	Vulnerability Impact Post Mitigation
Electrical failure	$500 for generator	$0

By adding these extra columns, business continuity planners would be able to evaluate the vulnerabilities, propose mitigation, and evaluate the vulnerabilities by the residual risks after mitigation.

Risk Response Strategies

Once a risk is identified, a response strategy will be examined to determine the appropriate action to take. There are five common strategies used.

Response Strategy	Description
Avoidance	This is used to eliminate the risk altogether by eliminating the cause.
Transference	This is used to allocate the responsibility of risk with another agency, or to a third party, such as an insurance company.
Acceptance	This is the acknowledgement and acceptance of the risk and consequences that come with it, if that risk were to materialize.
Mitigation	These techniques protect against possible attacks and are implemented when the impact of a potential risk is substantial.
Deterrence	This involves applying changes to the conditions to make it less likely or enticing for an attacker to launch an attack.

Risk Control Types

Risk can be controlled and monitored closely by implementing the appropriate security controls.

Control Type	Description
Technical controls	Hardware or software installations that are implemented to monitor and prevent threats and attacks to computer systems and services. For example, installing and configuring a network firewall is a type of technical control.
Management controls	Procedures implemented to monitor the adherence to organizational security policies. These controls are specifically designed to control the operational efficiencies of a particular area and to monitor security policy compliance. For example, annual or regularly scheduled security scans and audits to check for compliance with security policies.
Operational controls	Security measures implemented to safeguard all aspects of day-to-day operations, functions, and activities. For example, door locks and guards at entrances are controls used to permit only authorized personnel into a building.

ACTIVITY 8-1
Examining Risk Analysis

Scenario:

InfiniTrade Financial is a well-known financial consulting firm, with many offices worldwide. Lately, there have been concerns regarding the security of the computer room located on the first floor within the main headquarters building. The high-business-value assets identified in this room are the human resources servers with sensitive employee identification data, and the client financial data server. The room is situated next to the main lobby, contains no windows, and is access-controlled with a numeric keypad. You have been asked to conduct a full risk analysis of the computer room's physical security.

1. **What are some obvious vulnerabilities surrounding the InfiniTrade Financial computer room and what others would you investigate?**

2. **Based on the known vulnerabilities for the computer room, what potential threats exist?**

3. **What do you think the potential impact would be if an unauthorized access attempt was successful?**

4. **What risk mitigation strategies would you use in this situation to reduce the risks surrounding the physical access of the computer room?**

TOPIC B

Implement Vulnerability Assessment Tools and Techniques

To properly assess threats and vulnerabilities, you will have to familiarize yourself with the various tools and techniques required to protect the organization from these threats. In this topic, you will assess threats and vulnerabilities using various tools and techniques.

The first step in building a strong security infrastructure is for you to assess the various threats and vulnerabilities the organization faces. Then, you will be better able to identify and implement the ideal tools and techniques to handle these situations.

Vulnerability Assessment Techniques

Assessing the current state of security implementations for an organization is crucial to ensuring all threats and vulnerabilities have been addressed. Common techniques can be used to carry out security assessments.

Technique	Description
Review *baseline report*	A baseline report is a collection of security and configuration settings that are to be applied to a particular system or network in the organization. The baseline report is a benchmark against which you can compare other systems in your network. When creating a baseline for a particular computer, the settings you decide to include will depend on its operating system and its function in your organization, and should include manufacturer recommendations.
Perform *code reviews*	Regular code reviews should be conducted for all applications in development. Reviews may be carried out manually by a developer, or automatically using a source code analysis tool. Both methods are useful in identifying potential weaknesses in an application that may eventually lead to an attack if not corrected.
Determine *attack surface*	The attack surface is the portion of a system or application that is exposed and available to attackers. By reducing the attack surface you will be less vulnerable to possible attacks.
Review the security architecture	A *security architecture review* is an evaluation of an organization's current security infrastructure model and measures. Regular reviews are important to determine if current systems and critical assets are secured properly and if potential threats and vulnerabilities have been addressed. During this review, areas of concern are targeted and further evaluated to make sure security measures meet the current needs.
Review the security design	Security design reviews are completed before a security implementation is applied. Using the architectural review results, the reviewer can determine if the security solution will in fact fulfill the needs of an organization.

Vulnerability Assessment Tools

When assessing security for your system or systems, there are many software tools that are available. Tools can be found to scan for and detect a very wide range of vulnerabilities and specific hard-to-detect vulnerabilities. By running these tools, you can see exactly what potential attackers would see if they assessed your systems.

There are a number of tools available for assessing your systems.

Tool	Use
Protocol analyzer	Implement to assess data on a network.
Sniffer	Implement to regularly assess and monitor data passed on your network.
Vulnerability scanner	Implement this application to assess your systems, networks, and applications for weaknesses.
Port scanner	Implement to assess the current state of all ports on your network, and to detect potential open ports that may pose risks to your organization.
Honeypot	Implement this environment to assess any suspicious activity and redirect it away from legitimate network systems.

Honeypots

A *honeypot* is a security tool that lures attackers away from legitimate network resources while tracking their activities. Honeypots appear and act as a legitimate component of the network but are actually secure lockboxes where security professionals can block the intrusion and begin logging activity for use in court or even launch a counterattack. The act of luring individuals in could potentially be perceived as entrapment or violate the code of ethics of your organization. These legal and ethical issues should be discussed with your organization's legal counsel and human resources department.

Honeypots can be software emulation programs, hardware decoys, or an entire dummy network, known as a *honeynet*. A honeypot implementation often includes some kind of intrusion detection system (IDS) to facilitate monitoring and tracking of intruders. Some dedicated honeypot software packages can be specialized types of IDSes.

How to Implement Vulnerability Assessment Tools and Techniques

Procedure Reference: Identify Vulnerability Tools and Techniques

To identify vulnerability assessment tools and techniques:

1. Identify potential assessment tools by preparing a list from the Internet or from your software vendor.

2. Thoroughly study the details of each of the assessment tool on the list.

3. Select the tools and techniques that are the best fit for your organization. Initiate the process for procuring them.

4. Suitably upgrade systems per the requirements of the new software and roll out an implementation plan.

Procedure Reference: Implement Vulnerability Tools and Techniques

To implement vulnerability assessment tools and techniques:

1. Install the software on the systems per the implementation plan. If necessary, run suitable patches to ensure that the latest version of the tool is implemented.

2. Study the software's help manual. Enable options that will allow the software to be automatically updated. Register the software to receive its full benefits.

3. Perform an initial scan of the system.

4. Save the initial scan results as the baseline.

5. Analyze the scan reports.

6. Take suitable corrective actions based on the reported findings.

7. Install additional software as required.

8. Save the results and compare them with the baseline scan results.

9. Document your findings and prepare suitable reports to be presented to upper management.

10. Ensure that your perform this vulnerability scan on all systems in your organization.

ACTIVITY 8-2

Capturing Network Data with Windows® Network Monitor

 There is a simulated version of this activity available on the CD-ROM that shipped with this course. You can run this simulation on any Windows computer to review the activity after class, or as an alternative to performing the activity as a group in class. The activity simulation can be launched either directly from the CD-ROM by clicking the **Interactives** link and navigating to the appropriate one, or from the installed data file location by opening the C:\SPlus\ Simulations\Lesson#\Activity# folder and double-clicking the executable (.exe) file.

Scenario:

You want to use Windows® Network Monitor to capture baseline data about local network traffic under normal conditions. You do not need to capture data sent to and from other stations on the network. Network Monitor has not yet been installed on the system.

---

1. Install Network Monitor.

    a. Choose **Start→Run.**

    b. Type **C:\SPlus\SMS** and then click **OK.**

    c. Double-click the **NM34_x64.exe** file.

    d. In the **Open File - Security Warning** dialog box, click **Run.**

    e. In the **Microsoft Network Monitor** dialog box, click **Yes.**

    f. In the **Microsoft Network Monitor 3.4 Setup - 3.4.2350.0 Wizard,** on the **Welcome** page, click **Next.**

    g. On the **End-User License Agreement** page, select the **I accept the terms in the License Agreement** option and click **Next.**

    h. If necessary, on the **Microsoft Update** page, select **I do not want to use Microsoft Update** and click **Next.**

    i. Verify that the **I do not want to use Microsoft Update** option is selected and click **Next.**

    j. If necessary, select **I do not want to participate in the program at this time** and click **Next.**

    k. On the **Choose Setup Type** page, click **Complete.**

    l. On the **Ready to Install** page, after verifying that the check box is checked, click **Install.**

    m. On the **Completing the Setup Wizard** page, click **Finish.**

    n. Wait for Windows to configure Network Monitor. Close the SMS window.

2. Perform a sample capture.

    a. On the desktop, double-click the **Microsoft Network Monitor 3.4** shortcut.

    b. If necessary, in the message box, click **No.**

    c. In the Microsoft Network Monitor 3.4 window, click **New Capture.** `New Capture`

    d. Maximize the Network Monitor window.

    e. Click **Start.** `▶ Start`

    f. Observe in the **Network Conversations** section, the system displays a status message, "Waiting for network traffic."

3. Generate network traffic.

    a. Choose **Start→Command Prompt.**

    b. Ping another student's Internet Protocol (IP) address in the classroom.

    c. Choose **Start→Internet Explorer** to launch the web browser.

    d. In the **Address** bar, click and enter ***https://server100***

    e. In the **Security Alert** dialog box, click **OK.**

    f. In the **Windows Security** dialog box, log on as **Administrator** with a password of ***!Pass1234*** and click **OK.**

    g. Verify that you are able to connect to the enrollment site.

4. Stop the capture and review the capture log.

    a. On the taskbar, click **Microsoft Network Monitor 3.4** to display the window.

    b. Click **Stop.** `■ Stop`

    c. Select a few frames and view the contents in the **Details** pane.

    d. In the **Display Filter** text field, click and type ***TLS*** and then click **Apply.**

    e. View the details of the Transport Layer Security (TLS) frames. When you have finished, close the Microsoft Network Monitor 3.4 window without saving the capture.

    f. Close all open windows.

TOPIC C
Scan for Vulnerabilities

You just performed the threat and vulnerability assessment for your business. Based on the findings of the assessment, you may have to intensify your security policies to reduce vulnerabilities. In this topic, you will scan for vulnerabilities.

IT departments in businesses today strive to defend themselves against threats and vulnerabilities to protect the valuable information and intellectual property they possess. When valuable information falls into the wrong hands, it may result in major disruptions to the business. To avoid losing valuable information, IT departments should continually scan for vulnerabilities and threats inside and outside their organizations.

The Hacking Process

Understanding the general steps of the hacking process will help you recognize attacks in progress and stop them before they cause damage.

Hacking Step	Description
Footprinting	Also known as *profiling,* in this step, the attacker chooses a target and begins to gather information that is publicly or readily available. With basic tools, such as a web browser and an Internet connection, an attacker can often determine the IP addresses of a company's Domain Name System (DNS) servers; the range of addresses assigned to the company; names, email addresses, and phone numbers of contacts within the company; and the company's physical address. Attackers use dumpster diving, or searching through garbage, to find sensitive information in paper form. The names and titles of people within the organization enable the attacker to begin social engineering to gain even more private information. The Hypertext Markup Language (HTML) code of a company's web page can provide information, such as IP addresses and names of web servers, operating system versions, file paths, and names of developers or administrators. DNS servers are common footprinting targets because, if not properly secured, they can provide a detailed map of an organization's entire network infrastructure.
Scanning	The second step is scanning an organization's infrastructure or systems to see where vulnerabilities might lie. In this step, the attacker may use a network mapping tool such as Nmap or perform a *ping sweep* to determine which host IP addresses in the company's IP address range are active. The attacker will scan the target's border routers, firewalls, web servers, and other systems that are directly connected to the Internet to see which services are listening on which ports and to determine the operating systems and manufacturers of each system. Additionally, the attacker might begin a war dialing campaign to determine if there are any vulnerabilities in the organization's telecommunications system. The attacker might even try war driving, which involves driving up to the company with a laptop and a wireless card to see if there are any wireless access points (WAPs) to provide a way into the network.

Hacking Step	Description
Enumerating	During this step, the attacker will try to gain access to resources or other information, such as users, groups, and shares. The attacker can obtain this information through social engineering, network sniffing, dumpster diving, watching a user log in, or searching for credentials written down at user workstations. If the attacker can obtain a valid user name, he can begin the process of cracking the user's password.
Attacking	Attacking is the last phase of the hack, in which the hacker attempts to cause damage or a service disruption, or to steal or destroy sensitive information using various hacking tools.

Network Mappers

Network mapping tools are used to explore and gather network layout information from a network. A network map can be used to illustrate the physical connectivity of networks within an organization, and can provide detailed information on hardware, services, and traffic paths.

Ethical Hacking

Definition:

In *ethical hacking* a planned and approved attempt is made to penetrate the security defenses of a system in order to identify vulnerabilities. In an ethical hack, a friendly or designated hacker assumes the mindset of an attacker and attempts to breach security using any and all tools and techniques an attacker might employ. It may be performed by a company employee or an outside firm.

Example:

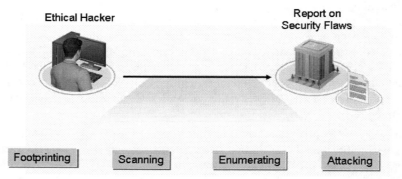

Figure 8-1: Ethical hacking.

 Performing an ethical hack is a perfect illustration of the classical adage, "Know your enemy." Understanding the hacking process and tools gives organizations a deeper and more practical appreciation of the dangers they can face through unscrupulous attackers.

Vulnerability Scanning and Penetration Testing

When a company tests a computer system or network, it is generally testing a production network that is live; security tests are rarely conducted on offline or test networks. A *vulnerability scan* passively identifies and quantifies vulnerabilities within a system, such as lacking security controls and common misconfigurations, but does not test the security features of that system. A true *penetration test* actively evaluates security by simulating an attack on a system. A penetration test will verify that a threat exists, then will actively test and bypass security controls, and finally exploit vulnerabilities on the system. Vulnerability scanning is more common than penetration testing. While the information gained from a penetration test is often more thorough, there is a risk that the system may suffer actual damage because of the security breach.

Types of Vulnerability Scans

A vulnerability scan is one of the first steps in either an attack or an ethical hack. There are two main types of vulnerability scans: scans for general vulnerabilities, such as scans for open ports, and application-specific scans, such as a password crack against a particular operating system. You will use different scanning tools depending upon the type of scan you wish to run.

> There are a variety of specialized web-based scanning services, such as ShieldsUP® from Gibson Research Corporation, available at **www.grc.com**.
>
> You can also consider registering with security event aggregators, such as **www.dshield.org** or **www.mynetwatchman.com**. They will also analyze your firewall logs and act as fully automated abuse escalation/management systems.

Box Testing Methods

When conducting a penetration test, the organization must examine the different testing methods and determine what information the tester will be given beforehand.

Test Type	Description
Black box test	This refers to a situation where the tester is given no information about the system being tested. This type of test would fall into the footprinting or scanning phase of the hacking process.
Gray box test	This refers to a situation where the tester may have knowledge of internal architectures and systems, or other preliminary information about the system being tested. This type of test would fall into the enumerating phase of the hacking process.
White box text	This refers to a situation when the tester knows about all aspects of the systems and understands the function and design of the system before the test is conducted. This type of test is sometimes conducted as follow-up to a black box test to fully evaluate flaws discovered during the black box test. This type of test would fall into the attacking phase of the hacking process.

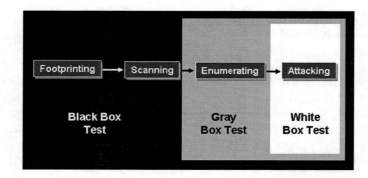

Figure 8-2: *Box testing methods.*

Security Utilities

Any security or network tool can be used for ethical or unethical purposes. To perform an ethical hack, you will need to use the same tools employed by attackers. Some tools are generally available by downloading them from the Internet, and some must be purchased from vendors. Because tools and utilities are constantly changing, it is important to continually research the available tools and their functions.

There are many different tools available for different security tasks, and some have multiple uses.

Security Utility Type	Typical Tools
Vulnerability scanning	Microsoft Baseline Security Analyzer (MBSA), Nessus®, SAINT, ISS Internet Scanner, Nmap Security Scanner, GFI LANguard™, NC4 CyberCop
Port scanning	Microsoft Port Reporter, SuperScan, ShieldsUP, Nmap Security Scanner, Netcat, pinger
Password scanning and cracking	Crack, John the Ripper, Pandora, Snadboy's Revelation, pwdump, Ophcrack, Cain & Abel
Exploits, Trojan horses, and other "stress testers"	UDPFlood, GetAdmin
Intrusion detection	NFR® BackOfficer Friendly, ISS Internet Scanner, ISS System Scanner, Snort, IDScenter, Fport, ZoneAlarm
Network and security administration	Webmin, Tripwire®, Bastille, PuTTY, HiSecWeb
Protocol analyzer, or packet sniffer	NetScout, dsniff, Wireshark, OmniPeek, Ettercap, Microsoft Network Monitor, Tcpdump, WinDump, VisualRoute

How to Scan for Vulnerabilities

Procedure Reference: Scan for Vulnerabilities

The general procedure for all types of vulnerability scans is the same:

1. Install the scanning software that is appropriate for the type of scan you want to perform.

2. Scan your system with the parameters that are appropriate for your environment.

3. If possible, scan your system from an external network as well, by using a web-based scanning tool.

4. Manually review your system audit logs as well as any logs created by the scanning program.

5. If possible, install a tool to automate the process of reviewing and analyzing audit logs.

6. If vulnerabilities are found, revisit your hardening procedures to harden your operating systems and devices.

ACTIVITY 8-3
Scanning for Port Vulnerabilities

 There is a simulated version of this activity available on the CD-ROM that shipped with this course. You can run this simulation on any Windows computer to review the activity after class, or as an alternative to performing the activity as a group in class. The activity simulation can be launched either directly from the CD-ROM by clicking the **Interactives** link and navigating to the appropriate one, or from the installed data file location by opening the C:\SPlus\Simulations\Lesson#\Activity# folder and double-clicking the executable (.exe) file.

Conditions

The services running on the Server## computer include Active Directory, DNS, Dynamic Host Configuration Protocol (DHCP), Certificate Services, and a secure website. SuperScan is available.

Scenario:

You are the security administrator for a large brokerage firm and need to make sure your new Microsoft® Windows Server® 2008 servers are secure by scanning them for open ports. The brokerage firm's IT department has had problems in the past with attackers getting access to applications on servers by getting through the firewall and accessing open ports on the servers. You have already hardened your servers and now want to check your work.

Before connecting the new Windows Server 2008 R2 servers to your network, you need to make sure not only that the base operating system is hardened, but also that no unnecessary ports are open on the servers to minimize the likelihood of attacks. You are responsible for scanning your Windows Server 2008 R2 computer.

---

1. Install SuperScan.

   a. Choose **Start→Run.**

   b. Type *C:\SPlus\Tools* and click **OK.**

   c. Double-click the **superscan4** folder, and then double-click the **SuperScan4.exe** file.

   d. In the **Open File - Security Warning** dialog box, click **Run.**

---

2. Use SuperScan to scan the default ports on your own server.

   a. On the **Scan** page, in the **IPs** section, in the **Hostname/IP** text box, type *Server##* and select the **Host and Service Discovery** tab.

   b. Verify that the **UDP port scan** and **TCP port scan** check boxes are checked, and that a default list of ports appears in each scan area. The default ports are loaded from a configuration file.

   c. Select the **Scan** tab.

   d. Click the blue triangle **Start** button to start the scan.

---

3. Examine the scan results.

    a.   When the scan is complete, click **View HTML Results.**

    b.   The report file opens in Windows Internet Explorer. Scroll down to examine the list of open ports.

    c.   The right column shows how the computer responds to a scan of each port. Close the SuperScan Report window.

    d.   Close the SuperScan 4.0 window.

    e.   Close the superscan4 window.

ACTIVITY 8-4
Scanning for Password Vulnerabilities

 There is a simulated version of this activity available on the CD-ROM that shipped with this course. You can run this simulation on any Windows computer to review the activity after class, or as an alternative to performing the activity as a group in class. The activity simulation can be launched either directly from the CD-ROM by clicking the **Interactives** link and navigating to the appropriate one, or from the installed data file location by opening the C:\SPlus\ Simulations\Lesson#\Activity# folder and double-clicking the executable (.exe) file.

 You can use Cain & Abel to perform brute force password discovery where it will attempt to determine secure passwords, meaning those that consist of alphanumeric characters, symbols and mixed casing. Unfortunately, brute force password detection can take quite a long time (such as 48 hours or more). Due to time constraints in the classroom, a dictionary attack is performed in this activity.

Conditions

The Cain & Abel application and the WinPcap packet driver are both available.

Scenario:

You are the new security administrator for an accounting firm. Your boss has asked that you verify that all client information is secure in order to ensure that no outside attempts to gather clients' confidential financial information will succeed. As part of your security audit, you want to make sure that all users, especially administrators, are using secure passwords and not common dictionary words.

---

1. Install the Cain & Abel software on your computer.

    a. Choose **Start→Run.**

    b. If necessary, type *C:\SPlus\Tools* and click **OK.**

    c. Double-click the **cain_abel** folder and then double-click the **ca_setup** file.

    d. In the **Open File - Security Warning** dialog box, click **Run.**

    e. If necessary, in the **User Account Control** message box, click **Yes.**

    f. In the Cain & Abel Installation dialog box, on the Cain & Abel page, click **Next.**

    g. On the **License Agreement** page, click **Next.**

    h. On the **Select Destination Directory** page, observe that **C:\Program Files (x86)\ Cain** is the default location and click **Next.**

    i. On the **Ready to Install** page, click **Next.**

    j. On the **Installation Completed** page, click **Finish.**

---

2. Install the packet driver software (WinPcap) on your computer.

    a.   In the **WinPcap Installation** dialog box, click **Install.**

    b.   In the **WinPcap Setup** wizard, on the **WinPcap Installer** page, click **Next.**

    c.   On the **Welcome to the WinPcap Setup Wizard** page, click **Next.**

    d.   On the **License Agreement** page, click **I Agree.**

    e.   On the **Installation options** page, click **Install.**

    f.   On the **Completing the WinPcap Setup Wizard** page, click **Finish.**

    g.   Close the cain_abel window.

---

3. Load the local SAM database.

    a.   Double-click the **Cain** desktop shortcut.

    b.   If necessary, in the **User Account Control** message box, click **Yes.**

    c.   In the **Cain** message box, click **OK.**

    d.   In the Cain window, select the **Cracker** tab.

    e.   In the left pane, select **LM & NTLM Hashes.**

    f.   On the toolbar, click the **Plus Sign (+).**

    g.   In the **Add NT Hashes from** dialog box, check the **Include Password History Hashes** check box and click **Next.**

    h.   Observe that the list of system user names appear in the right pane.

---

4. Scan for the password of the Administrator account.

    a.   Select the **Administrator** account.

    b.   Right-click and choose **Dictionary Attack→NTLM Hashes.**

    c.   In the **Dictionary Attack** dialog box, in the **Dictionary** section, right-click and choose **Add to list.**

    d.   In the **Open** dialog box, verify that Cain is the current folder and double-click the **Wordlists** folder.

    e.   Double-click the **Wordlist** text file.

    f.   Observe that the **File** column contains the full path to the Wordlist.txt file.

    g.   Click **Start.**

    h.   Observe that the password of the Administrator is not displayed on completion of the scan, which indicates that the current password is secure. Click **Exit** to close the **Dictionary Attack** dialog box.

    i.   Close the Cain window.

ACTIVITY 8-5
Scanning for General Vulnerabilities

 There is a simulated version of this activity available on the CD-ROM that shipped with this course. You can run this simulation on any Windows computer to review the activity after class, or as an alternative to performing the activity as a group in class. The activity simulation can be launched either directly from the CD-ROM by clicking the **Interactives** link and navigating to the appropriate one, or from the installed data file location by opening the C:\SPlus\ Simulations\Lesson#\Activity# folder and double-clicking the executable (.exe) file.

Setup:

MBSA 2.2 has been installed. A baseline security scan has been performed.

Scenario:

You are the security administrator for a small government agency. You have already hardened all of your servers and other computer systems, but a new regulation requires that you also perform periodic vulnerability scans to audit system security. Periodic scans will enable you to see what vulnerabilities lie in your network, and also keep track of any changes that have been made to your systems. Because you have Windows Server 2008 R2 servers installed on your network, you used MBSA as a scanning tool during the hardening process. Now that you have added various services to your server, you will also use this tool for periodic vulnerability scans.

---

1. Use MBSA to scan your system for vulnerabilities.

    a. On the desktop, double-click the **Microsoft Baseline Security Analyzer 2.2** shortcut.

    b. In the **Check computers for common security misconfigurations** section, click the **Scan a computer** link.

    c. Verify that your computer name appears in the **Computer name** text box. Uncheck the **Check for SQL administrative vulnerabilities** check box. Uncheck the **Check for security updates** check box.

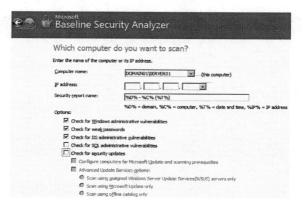

d.   Click **Start Scan.**

2.   Analyze the results of the vulnerability scan.

a.   Examine the **How to correct this** information and any **Result details** information for any issue that received a red "X" as a score.

b.   In the **Internet Information Services (IIS) Scan Results** section, under **Administrative Vulnerabilities**, notice that Parent Paths is generating an issue. Parent Paths are disabled by default in IIS 7.5, so this does not pose a security risk, however the current version of MBSA does not recognize this so an issue is generated.

c.   Click the **Back** button on the extreme left of the page title section twice.

3.   Compare the report with the baseline scan.

a.   In the left pane, click the **View security reports** link.

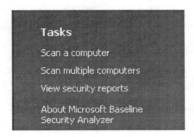

b.   On the **Choose a security scan report to view** page, next to the **Sort order** drop-down list, click the **Click here to see all security reports** link.

c.   On the **Choose a security scan report to view** page, click the earliest report in the list.

d.   On the **Report Details** page, under **Windows Scan Results,** scroll down twice to review the report.

e.   In the **Internet Information Services (IIS) Scan Results** section, in the **Administrative Vulnerabilities** section, notice that IIS common files are not installed and are generating an incomplete scan.

f.   At the bottom of the Microsoft Baseline Security Analyzer 2.2 window, click the **Previous security report** link to compare the changes.

g.   Close the Microsoft Baseline Security Analyzer 2.2 window.

TOPIC D

Mitigation and Deterrent Techniques

In the previous topic, you scanned for security threats and vulnerabilities. Scanning for threats and vulnerabilities will help you prevent most of them from materializing. In this topic, you will mitigate and deter threats and vulnerabilities.

No matter how secure a system may be, unfortunate events continue to happen. The IT security team should plan for worst-case scenarios and should have strong mitigation and deterrent techniques in place, should something go wrong.

Security Posture

Security posture is the position an organization takes on securing all aspects of its business. Strong security posture includes an initial baseline configuration for the organization, continuous security monitoring methods and remediation techniques, as well as strict mitigation and deterrent methods.

Detection vs. Prevention Controls

Detection controls are implemented to monitor a situation or activity, and react to any irregular activities by bringing the issue to the attention of administrators. *Prevention controls* are similar to detection controls, but instead of just monitoring for irregularities, they can react by blocking access completely and thereby preventing damage to a system, building, or network.

Detection vs. Prevention Based on Risk

The decision to detect or prevent attacks or unacceptable traffic is based on risk. If there is a high risk of damage to the network or organization due to a Denial of Service (DoS) attack, a prevention control that blocks the attack is most appropriate. Detection controls are best employed when experience shows that little or no threat to network security exists, and a warning of possible problems is sufficient. For example, a surveillance camera will monitor and detect when access is attempted, but it cannot prevent access. However, if a guard is placed at the access point, then if needed, he or she could not only detect, but also prevent access if it is unauthorized.

Blocking Techniques

Blocking techniques include logging the user off a system or reconfiguring the firewall to block the source.

Risk Mitigation Strategies

Risk mitigation techniques can be applied at many levels of an organization to help guard against potential risk damage.

Technique	Description
Policies and procedures	Policies and procedures can be implemented so an organization can enforce conduct rules among employees. It is crucial for an organization to distribute the appropriate policies in order to reduce the likelihood of damage to assets and to prevent data loss or theft. Policies and procedures can include: ● Privacy policy ● Acceptable use policy (AUP) ● Security policy ● Mandatory vacation procedures ● Job rotation procedures ● Audit policy ● Password policy ● Separation of duties guidelines ● Least privilege guidelines
Auditing and reviews	Perform routine audits to assess the risk of a particular operation and to verify that the current security controls in place are operating properly to secure the organization. Be sure to review existing user rights and permissions to make sure they meet your needs for confidentiality as well as accessibility of information and resources.
Security controls	Proper implementation of the appropriate technical, management, and operational controls is a powerful way to mitigate both general and specific risks.
Change management	Good change management practices can mitigate unintentional internal risks caused by inappropriate alterations to systems, tools, or the environment.
Incident management	Organizations must deal with security incidents as they arise and good management strategies can mitigate the severity of damage caused by risks.

Types of Mitigation and Deterrent Techniques

There are many different techniques used to both monitor for vulnerabilities and to mitigate issues as soon as they are detected.

Technique	Description
Performance and system monitoring	Performance and system monitoring enable you to monitor and diagnose the system and network for potential problems. In Windows systems, performance monitoring is available on the **Administrative Tools** menu. This tool can be used to quickly monitor some elements of the operation of your system. You can also gather real-time data, export data to be used in a separate program, send administrative alerts based on predefined criteria, create a performance baseline, detect network issues, and manage server performance.

Technique	Description
Monitoring system logs	Reviewing the activity recorded in log files can reveal a great deal about a suspected attack. Log files that should be monitored regularly on a set schedule are: • Event logs. • Audit logs. • Security logs. • Access logs.
Manual bypassing of electronic controls	Electronic controls are common in securing an organization's building, server rooms, and other highly secure areas. When the electronic controls have been tampered with and there is a security breach by any unauthorized individual, a manual bypass control should be implemented. This gives authorized personnel the ability to bypass the electronic control and ensure that the area is locked down and remains secure.
Hardening	General hardening procedures should be considered as a mitigation technique. In particular, the following security measures should be enforced to provide a higher level of security: • Disable all unnecessary services. • Ensure that the management interface and applications are properly protected. • Password protect all accounts. • Disable all unnecessary accounts. • Establish appropriate detection and prevention controls based on the needs of the organization.
Applying port security	Properly securing the ports on your network will prevent attackers from carrying out port scanning activities to gain information about your network. Security measures include: • Limiting and filtering Mandatory Access Control (MAC) addresses. • Configuring port authentication (802.1x). • Disabling all unused ports.
Reporting	Regular system reporting procedures should be in place to manage and enhance system capabilities. There are three reporting methods that can be utilized to support mitigation efforts made within a system: • Alarms are used to bring attention to a fault condition in the system. • Alerts are used to communicate that a condition has occurred and needs attention before it shuts down. • Trends are a snapshot of the system performance across a specified time frame.
Implementing physical security	Applying proper physical security controls and measures can be an effective deterrent technique to discourage attackers from attempting to gain access to building, grounds, systems, resources, and data. Examples might include fencing, door locks, surveillance cameras and systems, and guards.

Failsafe/Failsecure and Failopen

Failsafe, failsecure, and failopen are different ways that systems can be designed to perform when those systems cease to operate or when certain conditions are met. For example, most push lawn mowers are designed with some sort of lever that must be held in position by an operator in order for the blades to function. If that lever is released, the blades stop. This type of failsafe design is implemented to prevent harm to individuals.

A common application of this design consideration is in an organization's physical access control systems. In the event of a power failure, electric door strikes cannot be operated, so they are failsecure devices because they keep doors secured. Mechanical crashbars are failsafe devices in that they can be added to the inside of those doors to permit people to safely exit, even though the electric strike has no power. A magnetic lock is an example of a failopen device, as it leaves the door unsecured in the event of a power failure. For example, a school's exterior doors may be designed to failopen so that the fire alarm system could cut power to them to permit students and faculty to exit and emergency responders to get in, whereas the server room might be designed as failsafe/failsecure to permit staff to exit while still keeping unauthorized people out.

ACTIVITY 8-6
Monitoring for Intruders

 There is a simulated version of this activity that is available on the CD-ROM that shipped with this course. In addition to using the simulation in class, you can run it on any Windows computer to review the activity after class. The activity simulation can be launched directly from the CD-ROM by clicking the **Interactives** button and navigating to the appropriate one, or from the default installed datafile location by opening the C:\SPlus\Simulations\Lesson#\ Activity# folder and double-clicking the executable (.exe) file.

Scenario:

You are the security administrator for a large brokerage firm and need to make sure your new Windows 7 systems are secure by actively monitoring your system for intruders. The brokerage firm's IT department wants to take a proactive approach to security and catch the intruders before they do harm. You have already hardened your servers and scanned for vulnerabilities. Now, you want to be able to actively monitor for intrusions in real time, as well as to log suspicious activity for later analysis. Before connecting the new Windows 7 systems to your network, you need to make sure that the chosen intrusion detection software, Snort, is installed and configured. Once the intrusion detection software is installed and configured, you will perform periodic real-time monitoring using the IDS.

1. Monitor for intruders on a Windows 7 system.

   a. Browse to the C:\SPlus\Simulations\Lesson8\Activity6 folder.

   b. Double-click the executable file.

   c. In the **Open File - Security Warning** message box, click **Run**.

   d. Follow the on-screen steps for the simulation.

   e. Close the C:\SPlus\Simulations folder.

Lesson 8 Follow-up

In this lesson, you managed risk. When risk is identified and managed properly, the possible damage to an organization is decreased substantially. It is your responsibility to analyze risk, and properly assess and determine vulnerabilities for your organization in order to apply the most effective mitigation strategies. With these skills, you will be able to carry out a full risk analysis and apply customized security measures tailored to not only control access, but to also mitigate risk.

1. **What are the risk analysis phases you are familiar with?**

2. **What security assessment tools are you familiar with? What tools do you think you may use in the future?**

9 Managing Security Incidents

Lesson Time: 1 hour(s), 30 minutes

Lesson Objectives:

In this lesson, you will manage security incidents.

You will:

● Respond to security incidents.

● Recover from a security incident.

Introduction

This lesson will cover another phase of the network security cycle. This is the phase that you hope never arrives: your network is under attack, and you need to respond. In this lesson, you will learn to manage all aspects of a security incident.

You might hope that if you implement security well and monitor vigilantly, you will never have to live through a network attack. But attacks are inevitable. Attackers are out there every day, constantly trolling the Internet with automated tools that can uncover and penetrate susceptible systems. No matter how secure your network is, detecting an attack is a question of when, not if. The skills you will learn in this lesson will help you to respond appropriately and manage all phases of an incident.

This lesson covers all or part of the following CompTIA® Security+® (Exam SY0-301) certification objectives:

● Topic A:

■ Objective 2.3 Execute appropriate incident response procedures

● Topic B:

■ Objective 2.3 Execute appropriate incident response procedures

TOPIC A
Respond to Security Incidents

Just as you must secure an organization's infrastructure from attack, you must also plan how you would react if you were directly affected by a computer-related incident. In this topic, you will identify proper computer crime incident response processes and techniques.

The reliability of the evidence collected during an investigation is essential to the success of any future legal proceeding. The intangibility of computer crimes makes the burden of evidence all the more critical. To ensure that your evidence is reliable, you must understand how to appropriately perform investigations and collect substantial proof when incidents of computer crime arise.

Security Incident Management

Definition:

A *security incident* is a specific instance of a risk event occurring, whether or not it causes damage. Security *incident management* is the set of practices and procedures that govern how an organization will respond to an incident in progress. The goals of incident management are to contain the incident appropriately, and ultimately minimize any damage that may occur as a result of the incident. Incident management typically includes procedures to log and report on all identified incidents and the actions taken in response.

Example:

InfiniTrade Financial has created a task force specifically designed to manage all aspects of incident management within the company. The team carries out all operations using the security governance guidelines and procedures issued by management. The task force is responsible for incident analysis, incident response, incident reporting, and documentation.

Computer Crime

Definition:

A *computer crime* is a criminal act that involves using a computer as a source or target, instead of an individual. It can involve stealing restricted information by hacking into a system, compromising national security, perpetrating fraud, conducting illegal activity, or spreading malicious code. It may be committed via the Internet or a private network.

Example:

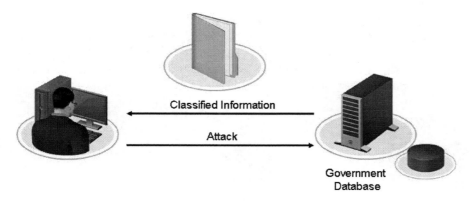

Figure 9-1: *A computer crime.*

Example: Typical Computer Crimes

Examples of typical computer crimes include unauthorized access to a computer or network, distributing illegal information via a computer network, and stealing classified information stored on a computer. Phishing and other similar social engineering attacks, if they involve illegal activity, can be categorized as computer crimes.

IRPs

Definition:

An *Incident Response Policy (IRP)* is the security policy that determines the actions that an organization will take following a confirmed or potential security breach. The IRP usually specifies:

- Who determines and declares if an actual security incident has occurred.
- What individuals or departments will be notified.
- How and when they are notified.
- Who will respond to the incident.
- And, guidelines for the appropriate response.

Example:

AFR Travel's IRP is highly detailed in some places, and highly flexible in others. For example, the list of who should respond to an incident is broken down both by job title and by equivalent job function in case a company reorganization causes job titles to change. This same flexibility is given to the department titles. However, the majority of the IRP consists of highly detailed response information that addresses how proper individuals and authorities should be notified of an incident. Since some computer attacks might still be ongoing at the time they are discovered, or since some attacks might take the communications network down entirely, AFR Travel has made sure that there are multiple lines of secure communication open during the aftermath of an incident.

Incident Response Involvement

The incident response will usually involve several departments, and, depending on the severity of the incident, may involve the media. The human resources and public relations departments of an organization generally work together in these situations to determine the extent of the information that will be made available to the public. Information is released to employees, stockholders, and the general public on a need-to-know basis.

First Responders

A *first responder* is the first experienced person or a team of trained professionals that arrive on an incident scene. In a non-IT environment, this term can be used to define the first trained person, such as a police officer or firefighter, to respond to an accident, damage site, or natural disaster. In the IT world, first responders can include security professionals, human resource personnel, or IT support professionals.

| Security Professional | Human Resources Personnel | IT Support Professional |

Figure 9-2: First responders.

Chain of Custody

The *chain of custody* is the record of evidence handling from collection through presentation in court. The evidence can be hardware components, electronic data, or telephone systems. The chain of evidence reinforces the integrity and proper custody of evidence from collection, to analysis, to storage, and finally to presentation. Every person in the chain who handles evidence must log the methods and tools they used.

Analyze and Store

Collect Evidence   Present in Court

Figure 9-3: Chain of custody.

Computer Removal

When computer crimes are reported, one of the first response activities is removing computers from the crime location. They are tagged with a chain of custody record to begin the process of making the evidence secure for future presentation in court.

Computer Forensics

Definition:

Computer forensics is the skill that deals with collecting and analyzing data from storage devices, computer systems, networks, and wireless communications and presenting this information as a form of evidence in a court of law. Primarily, forensics deals with the recovery and investigation of potential evidence. Computer forensics is a fairly new field, and so there is little standardization or consistency in practicing it across organizations and courts. Basically, computer forensics is a blend of the elements of law with computer science in analyzing evidence in a way that is permissible in the court of law.

Example:

Figure 9-4: Computer forensics.

Order of Volatility

Data is volatile and the ability to retrieve or validate data after a security incident depends on where it is stored in a location or memory layer of a computer or external device. For example, data on backup CDs or thumb drives can last for years, while data in random-access memory (RAM) may last for only nanoseconds.

The order in which you need to recover data after an incident before the data deteriorates, is erased, or is overwritten is known as the *order of volatility*. The general order of volatility for storage devices is:

- Registers, cache, and RAM.
- Network caches and virtual memory.
- Hard drives and flash drives.
- And, CD-ROMs, DVD-ROMs, and printouts.

Basic Forensic Process

There are four basic phases in a forensic process.

Basic Phase in a Forensic Process	Description
Collection phase	• Identify the attacked system and label it. • Record and acquire details from all related personnel who have access to the system, as well as the evidence material, keeping in mind the integrity of the data.

Basic Phase in a Forensic Process	Description
Examination phase	• Use automated and manual methods to forensically process collected data. • Assess and extract the evidence, keeping in mind the integrity of the data.
Analysis phase	• Analyze the results of the examination phase using methods and techniques permissible by law. • Obtain useful information that justifies the reason for the collection and examination.
Reporting phase	• Report the results of the forensic analysis including a description of the tools and methods used and why things were done that way. • Brainstorm different ways to improve existing security controls and provide recommendations for better policies, tools, procedures, and other methods in a forensic process.

Basic Forensic Response Procedures for IT

Forensic response procedures for IT help security professionals collect evidence from data in a form that is admissible in a court of law.

Forensic Response Procedure	Description
Capture system image	One of the most important steps in computer forensic evidence procedures is to capture exact duplicates of the evidence, also known as forensic images. This is accomplished by making a bit-for-bit copy of a piece of media as an image file with high accuracy.
Examine network traffic and logs	Attackers always leave behind traces; you just need to know how and where to look. Logs record everything that happens in an intrusion prevention system (IPS) or intrusion detection system (IDS), and in routers, firewalls, servers, desktops, mainframes, applications, databases, antivirus software, and virtual private networks (VPNs). With these logs, it is possible to extract the identity of hackers and provide the evidence needed.
Capture video	Video forensics is the method by which video is scrutinized for clues. Tools for computer forensics are used in reassembling video to be used as evidence in a court of law.
Record time offset	The format in which time is recorded against a file activity, such as file creation, deletion, last modified, and last accessed, has developed to incorporate a local time zone offset against GMT. This makes it easier for forensics to determine the exact time the activity took place even if the computer is moved from one time zone to another or if the time zone has deliberately been changed on a system.

Forensic Response Procedure	Description
Take hashes	Federal law enforcement agencies and federal governments maintain a list of files such as files relating to components of Microsoft® Windows® and other application software. The hash codes generated by a file or software can be compared to the list of known file hashes and hacker tools if any are flagged or marked as unknown.
Take screenshots	You should capture screenshots of each and every step of a forensic procedure, especially when you are retrieving evidence using a forensic tool. This will ensure that data present on a compromised system is not tampered with and also provides the court with proof of your use of valid computer forensic methods while extracting the evidence.
Identify witnesses	Courts generally accept evidence if it is seconded by the testimony of a witness who observed the procedure by which the evidence was acquired. A computer forensics expert witness is someone who has experience in handling computer forensics tools and is able to establish the validity of evidence.
Track man hours and expense	When the first incidents of computer crimes occurred, it would usually take less than 40 man hours to complete a forensic investigation because incidents usually involved single computers. Now, with the advances in technology and the advent of new digital media such as voice recorders, cameras, laptop computers, and mobile devices, computer forensics procedures can take up an exponentially greater amount of man hours and expenses. Also, the increase in storage device capacities and encryption affect the amount of man hours that it can take to assess any damage, and consequently increase expenses incurred in any computer forensics investigation. Capturing this expense is part of the overall damage assessment for the incident.

How to Respond to Security Incidents

Once an incident has been identified, the response team or security administrator must investigate all aspects of the security crime.

Guidelines

Some steps you might take to investigate a security crime:

● If an IRP exists, then follow the guidelines outlined to respond to the incident.

● If an IRP does not exist, then determine a primary investigator who will lead the team through the investigation process.

● Determine if the events actually occurred and to what extent a system or process was damaged.

● Document the incident.

● Assess the damage and determine the impact on affected systems.

● Determine if outside expertise is needed, such as a consultant firm.

● Notify local law enforcement, if needed.

● Secure the scene, so that the hardware is contained.

- Collect all the necessary evidence, which may be electronic data, hardware components, or telephony system components. Observe the order of volatility as you gather electronic data from various media.
- Interview personnel to collect additional information pertaining to the crime.
- Report the investigation findings to the required people.

Example:

OGC Travel has discovered that there has been an incident within the main branch computer systems. As the company's security professional, you must take the lead role in performing a full investigation.

After an initial observation of the branch computers, you determine that the security breach is with the agency's third-party client information software. You contact the consultant firm that installed the application and handles all customer service needs.

Now that you determined where the problem occurred, you can interview staff members to find out if they may have given out login information, or if a customer was left unattended at a representative's desk, giving them access to the client information program.

DISCOVERY ACTIVITY 9-1

Discussing Incident Response

Scenario:

As a security administrator for your organization, LearnMark, you have been asked to join a committee of high-level managers to develop an IRP. Before the committee's first meeting, you prepare to discuss the relevant issues.

---

1. **Based on your own professional or personal experience, what are some examples of typical computer crimes?**

---

2. **In your own words, why is it important to have an IRP?**

---

3. **What do you think are the most important components in an IRP?**

---

4. **In general, do you think it is important to notify employees of common or minor security incidents? Why or why not?**

---

5. **Why might you want to alert law enforcement officials of a security incident? Why might you want to notify the media?**

---

6. If you have Internet access, search for sample IRPs and write down the common guidelines listed in all of them.

TOPIC B

Recover from a Security Incident

Though you spend a great deal of your time ensuring that attacks do not happen, eventually you will have to react to a security incident, fix the damage, and make sure that business can get back to normal as quickly as possible. Not only will you have to accurately assess the damage to your company, but you will have to report on it as well. Communication skills are critical if you want to ensure that the incident, or one like it, will not happen again. In this topic, you will describe how to recover from a security incident and inform your organization about what happened.

Now that you have responded to a security incident, and have both collected and preserved evidence of an attack, you must help your company return to work. The faster and more efficiently you can recover from a security incident, the less financial damage is suffered, and the more likely that the company can prevent similar incidents from occurring. To fully recover from the incident, you must not only know how to fix the network, but also how to describe the problem to the key decision-makers at your company so that future incidents can be avoided.

Damage Assessment and Loss Control

During or after a security incident, a damage assessment should be done to determine the extent of damage, the origin or cause of the disaster, and the amount of expected downtime. The assessment can also determine the appropriate response strategy to employ as you move into damage control and recovery.

Damage Assessment and Loss Control at InfiniTrade Financial

Employees at InfiniTrade Financial Group discovered that its downtown branch had a physical security breach, as one of the outside doors was propped open all night. An intern discovered that her desktop computer was missing, and she immediately notified her manager, who called local law enforcement. While waiting for them to arrive, a security professional evacuated the area of the building where the attack was reported, so that employees did not inadvertently disrupt any physical evidence that might remain. They also organized a small group of people to take a quick inventory of any missing hardware; by the time the police arrived, InfiniTrade employees had learned that six computers were stolen.

Recovery Methods

After assessing the damage, you will know the extent of recovery that needs to be done. Many organizations rely on reformatting the system in case of a rootkit code attack, applying software patches, or reloading system software in case of a virus or malicious code infestations, and restoring backups in case of an intrusion or backdoor attack. Recovery methods can also involve replacing hardware in case of a physical security incident.

Recovery Methods at InfiniTrade Financial

For example, the IT team at InfiniTrade Financial Group discovered that the systems in a certain group have been affected by a virus, which is spreading to the computers of other groups. The IT team disconnects the networks that are affected and the networks that are possibly affected. The team then performs a scan of all the systems to find the virus and clean the systems using antivirus and other software. When all the affected systems are clean, they are reconnected to the network and steps are taken to install an IPS.

Incident Reports

An incident report is a report that includes a description of the events that occurred in an incident. Care should be taken to write as much detail relating to an incident as possible, such as the name of the organization, the nature of the event, names and phone numbers of contacts, the time and date of an event, and log information. However, a report should not be delayed because of problems with gathering information. Further probes can be carried out after the report has been written.

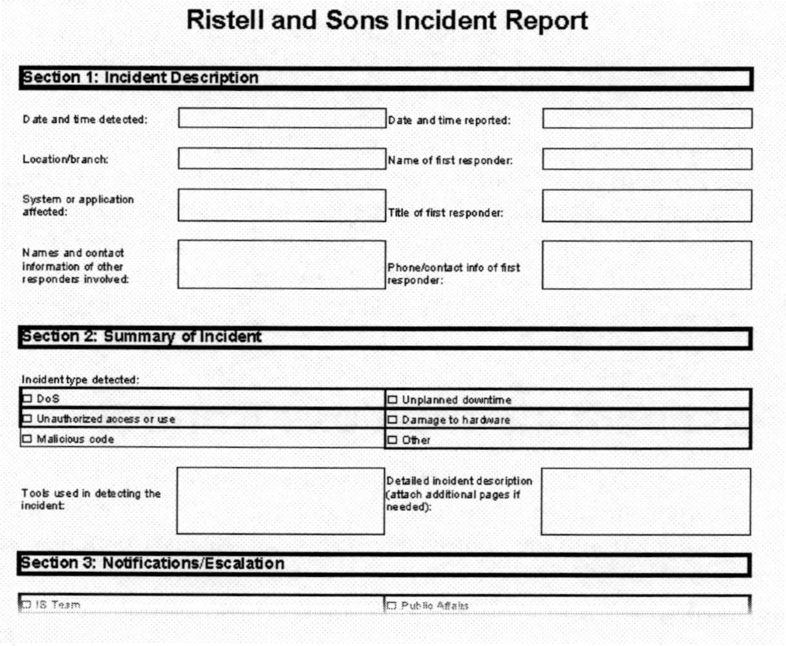

Ristell and Sons Incident Report

Section 1: Incident Description

Date and time detected:
Date and time reported:
Location/branch:
Name of first responder:
System or application affected:
Title of first responder:
Names and contact information of other responders involved:
Phone/contact info of first responder:

Section 2: Summary of Incident

Incident type detected:
☐ DoS
☐ Unplanned downtime
☐ Unauthorized access or use
☐ Damage to hardware
☐ Malicious code
☐ Other
Tools used in detecting the incident:
Detailed incident description (attach additional pages if needed):

Section 3: Notifications/Escalation

☐ IS Team
☐ Public Affairs

Figure 9-5: *An incident report.*

How to Recover from a Security Incident

Damage assessment, recovery, and reporting are important in dealing with an incident. You will can carry out these important tasks in the event of a security incident.

Guidelines

Follow these general guidelines during the recovery process.

- Some steps you might take while assessing the damage in a security incident:
    - Assess the area of damage to determine the next course of action.
    - Determine the amount of damage to the facility, hardware, systems, and networks.
    - If your company has suffered digital—rather than physical—damage, you may need to examine log files, identify which accounts have been compromised, and identify which files have been modified during the attack.
    - If your company has suffered physical—and not digital—damage, you may need to take a physical inventory to determine which devices have been stolen or damaged, which areas the intruder(s) had access to, and how many devices may have been damaged or stolen.
    - One of the most important and overlooked components of damage assessment is to determine if the attack is over; attempting to react to an attack that is still in progress could do more harm than good.
- Some steps you might take when recovering from a security incident:
    - Replace hardware and network cables in case any have been damaged or stolen.
    - Detect and delete malware and viruses from the affected systems and media.
    - Disconnect the intruded systems from the servers and shut down the server to avoid further intrusions.
    - Disable access to user accounts that have affected the network and search for all the backdoor software installed by the intruder.
    - Establish that your organization is no longer exposed to a threat by scanning the networks and systems using an IDS.
    - Reconnect the servers to the network.
    - Restore the data and network systems from the most recent backup.
    - Replace compromised data and applications or reformat the system and perform a fresh installation of the operating system.
    - Harden the networks and servers by changing passwords, installing patches, and reconfiguring firewalls and routers.
    - Inform company officials and important stakeholders of the incident, and if an insider was the source of the incident, reprimand the individual responsible according to company policies, or contact law enforcement to take action depending on the extent of the attack.
    - Write a report describing the recovery process. A summary of the report should be saved for use in future security incident responses.

- Some details you may need to capture when reporting a security incident:
  - The name of the organization.
  - The name and phone number of the person who discovered the incident.
  - The name(s) and phone number(s) of first responder(s).
  - The type of event; for instance, a physical attack, malicious code attack, or network attack.
  - The date and time of the event, including the time zone.
  - The source and destination of systems and networks, including IP addresses.
  - The operating system and antivirus software used and their versions.
  - The methods used to detect the incident; for instance, logs or IDSes.
  - The business impact of the incident.
  - The resolution steps taken.

Example: Ristell & Sons Publishing Finds a Rootkit

Ristell & Sons Publishing has discovered that a rootkit was installed on a salesman's computer, and that it has been sending customer data to an external site. The first responder is a security professional who noticed some suspicious network activity and then locked down the offending computer to prevent further activity. After investigating the incident more, he determined that the rootkit was delivered as a viral attachment sent by a client.

Since the attack concerns sensitive financial information about customers, he consults the company IRP to see who should be notified about the attack. Since this type of attack is considered theft, local law enforcement needs to be notified, as does the IT department head. The public relations department also needs to be notified via a report, as they are in charge of notifying the customers whose data has been stolen. They do not need an overly technical treatment of the incident, and so the report does not need to go into detail about the specifics of the rootkit. The security professional uses a rootkit cleaner to clean up the system and also prepares a more technical appendix to the report that is directed to the IT department; since the virus was delivered by a client and made it past the company firewall and virus protection, technical action needs to be taken. In this way, a single report on the incident can serve at least two functions in the recovery.

DISCOVERY ACTIVITY 9-2
Recovering from a Security Incident

Scenario:

You are a security professional at InfiniTrade Financial Group, a provider of financial services. Video surveillance tapes show that there was a physical security breach at the end of the work-day yesterday; an employee let an unauthorized person into the building. It is still the early stages of the investigation, and it is not clear what the attacker was doing there, nor is it clear how or when he left the building. The server rooms were not accessed, and it does not seem that any suspicious network activity occurred, but you are not yet finished going through the logs of all after-hours network activity.

1. **This was a weakness in the security of the facility. As an information security professional, why are you involved?**

2. **What is the first step you need to take in handling this incident?**

3. **What are the immediate steps you need to take to recover from any damage?**

4. Should this incident be reported to the entire company?

_____

5. Should law enforcement be notified?

_____

6. According to the company's risk assessment analysis, unauthorized trespassing was listed as high risk. In composing your report, what are some things you can do to bring that risk down to a more manageable level?

_____

Lesson 9 Follow-up

In this lesson, you dealt with the inevitable: a security attack. Try as you might, you will never achieve a network that is impervious to attack, as the methods and techniques that attackers use are constantly changing; a secure network should always be considered a moving target. Ultimately, responding to and recovering from a security incident involves both security and communication skills, since responding to a security incident is a collaborative process that many different job roles take part in.

1. **How many times have you had to consult an IRP?**

2. **What are some good approaches to writing an incident report?**

10 | Business Continuity and Disaster Recovery Planning

Lesson Time: 2 hour(s)

Lesson Objectives:

In this lesson, you will develop a BCP and DRP.

You will:

- Describe business continuity.
- Plan for disaster recovery.
- Execute DRPs and procedures.

Introduction

So far in this course, you have dealt with detecting and preventing security risks from affecting a system or network. But sometimes there are cases where the risk that occurs causes such a disruption that it threatens the existence of the business. For an organization to function uninterrupted in these situations, you will need a foolproof plan. In this lesson, you will develop a business continuity plan (BCP) and a disaster recover plan (DRP) so that you can be ready if the worst happens.

Your business depends on the availability of your IT systems, so even the slightest interruption to services can cause you to lose business. When faced with an interruption of services, what do you plan to do? Implementing a strong BCP will help mitigate the overall impact on the business, and a DRP will help you quickly recover sensitive data that has been affected or lost with a negligible loss of revenue.

This lesson covers all or part of the following CompTIA® Security+® (Exam SY0-301) certification objectives:

- Topic A:
  - Objective 2.5 Compare and contrast aspects of business continuity
- Topic B:
  - Objective 1.1 Explain the security function and purpose of network devices and technologies
  - Objective 2.5 Compare and contrast aspects of business continuity

- Topic C:
  - Objective 2.7 Execute disaster recovery plans and procedures

TOPIC A

Business Continuity

You will need to develop business continuity plans (BCPs) and disaster recover plans (DRPs) to help minimize losses at your organization. As a security professional, you need to come up with the best possible plan. In this topic, you will describe the importance of business continuity to an organization.

A security system is only as good as its ability to ward off threats and overcome disasters. Therefore, a key component of that system is to have a plan in place so that when disaster strikes, business will still continue in the interim until the issue is fixed. A BCP will help ensure continuous service to customers. As an IT security professional, you may not be responsible for overall business continuity, but you will be an important contributor to the security and IT components of the plan, so a good understanding of the plan, its components, and the process by which it is built is important.

BCPs

Definition:

A *business continuity plan (BCP)* is a policy that defines how an organization will maintain normal day-to-day business operations in the event of business disruption or crisis. The intent of the BCP is to ensure the survival of the organization by preserving key documents, establishing decision-making authority, communicating with internal and external stakeholders, protecting and recovering assets, and maintaining financial functions. The BCP should address infrastructure issues such as maintaining utilities service, utilizing high-availability or fault-tolerant systems that can withstand failure, and creating and maintaining data backups. The BCP should be reviewed and tested on a regular basis. The plan must have executive support to be considered authoritative; the authorizing executive should personally sign the plan.

Example:

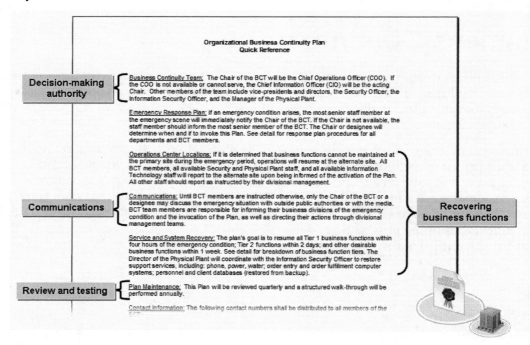

Figure 10-1: A BCP.

BIA

Definition:

A *business impact analysis (BIA)* is a preparation step in BCP development that identifies present organizational risks and determines the impact to ongoing, business-critical operations and processes if such risks actually occur. BIAs contain vulnerability assessments and evaluations to determine risks and their impact. BIAs should include all phases of the business to ensure a strong business continuation strategy.

Example:

Figure 10-2: BIA.

Example: Flood Impact

As a risk is identified, an organization determines the chance of risk occurrence and then determines the quantity of potential organizational damage. If a roadway bridge crossing a local river is washed out by a flood and employees are unable to reach a business facility for five days, estimated costs to the organization need to be assessed for lost manpower and production.

MTD

Definition:

Maximum tolerable downtime (MTD) is the longest period of time that a business outage may occur without causing irrecoverable business failure. Each business process can have its own MTD, such as a range of minutes to hours for critical functions, 24 hours for urgent functions, 7 days for normal functions, and so on. MTDs vary by company and event.

Example:

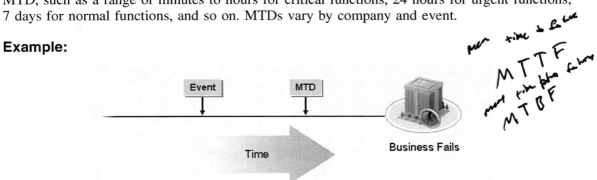

Figure 10-3: MTD.

Example: Medical Equipment Suppliers

The MTD limits the amount of recovery time that a business has to resume operations. An organization specializing in medical equipment may be able to exist without incoming manufacturing supplies for three months because it has stockpiled a sizeable inventory. After three months, the organization will not have sufficient supplies and may not be able to manufacture additional products, therefore leading to failure. In this case, the MTD is three months.

RPO

The *recovery point objective (RPO)* is the point in time, relative to a disaster, where the data recovery process begins. In IT systems, it is often the point in time when the last successful backup is performed before a disruptive event occurs.

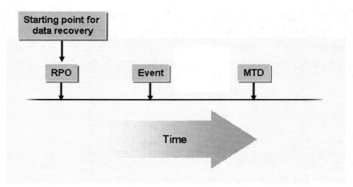

Figure 10-4: An RPO.

RPO Example

For example, if the last backup was executed Sunday afternoon and the failure occurs on the following Tuesday, then the RPO is Sunday afternoon. The latest backup is restored and processing begins to recover all activity from Sunday afternoon to the Tuesday failure point.

RTO

The *recovery time objective (RTO)* is the length of time within which normal business operations and activities can be restored following a disturbance. It includes the necessary recovery time to return to the RPO and reinstate the system and resume processing from its current status. The RTO must be achieved before the MTD. *Mean time to recovery (MTTR)* is the average time taken for a business to recover from an incident or failure and is an offset of the RTO. If MTTR exceeds the given RTO, then business operations need to switch to the alternate site.

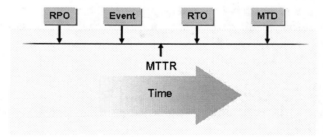

Figure 10-5: An RTO.

Continuity of Operations Plan

A *continuity of operations plan* is the component of the BCP that provides best practices to mitigate risks, and best measures to recover from the impact of an incident. An effective continuity of operations plan can include:

● Auditing of resources, staff, and operational management.

● Auditing storage facilities, data centers, operating systems, and software and applications.

● Auditing networks such as the local area network (LAN) and the wireless area network (WAN), including remote access and authentication systems.

● Analyzing comprehensive risk and vulnerability.

● Creating data backups, recovery methods, and emergency response procedures.

● And, establishing a process on how to manage operations during a disaster.

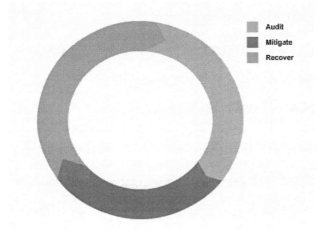

Figure 10-6: Important steps in a continuity of operations plan.

Alternate Sites

Definition:

As part of a BCP, an organization can maintain various types of alternate sites that can be used to restore system functions. A *hot site* is a fully configured alternate network that can be online quickly after a disaster. A *warm site* is a location that is dormant or performs non-critical functions under normal conditions, but which can be rapidly converted to a key operations site if needed. A *cold site* is a predetermined alternate location where a network can be rebuilt after a disaster.

Example:

Primary Site

Business Functions
Transfer to Alternate
Site

Figure 10-7: Alternate site.

Example: Alternate Site Scenarios

An example of a hot site would be a secondary operations center that is fully staffed and in constant network contact with the primary center under normal conditions. A warm site might be a customer service center that could be converted quickly to use as a network-maintenance facility, if needed. And a cold site might be nothing more than a rented warehouse with available power and network hookups, where key equipment could be moved and installed in the event of disaster.

IT Contingency Planning

Definition:

An *IT contingency plan* is a component of the BCP that specifies alternate IT contingency procedures that you can switch over to when you are faced with an attack or disruption of service leading to a disaster for an organization. Interim measures can include operating out of an alternate site, using alternate equipment or systems, and relocating the main systems. The effectiveness of an IT contingency plan depends upon:

- Key personnel understanding the components of the IT contingency plan and when and how it should be initiated when the organization is facing an attack or disruption of service.

- Reviewing a checklist from time to time to see that all the aspects of an IT contingency plan are in place, such as recovery strategies including alternate sites.

- And, providing adequate training to employees and management to exercise the contingency plan, and maintaining the plan and reexamining it from time to time.

Example:

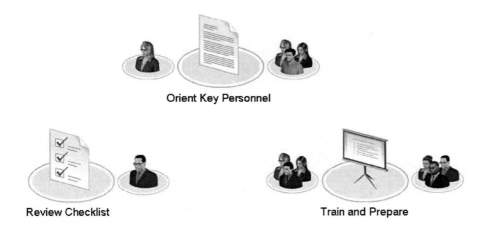

Orient Key Personnel

Review Checklist

Train and Prepare

Figure 10-8: IT contingency planning.

Succession Planning

Definition:

A *succession plan* ensures that all key business personnel have one or more designated back-ups who can perform critical functions when needed. A succession plan identifies the individuals, who they can replace, which functions they can perform, and how they need to be trained.

Example:

Chief Information Officer

IT Director

Senior IT Administrator

Figure 10-9: Succession planning.

Business Continuity Testing Methods

You can employ various methods to test a BCP, as well as familiarize staff with their duties and responsibilities.

BCP Testing Method	Description
Paper testing methods	*Reviewing plan contents.* Because they are familiar with the BCP construction, plan developers review the BCP's contents. However, because of their involvement as developers, they often have a limited view of corporate needs that can cause biased opinions.
	Analyzing the solution. Senior management and division and department heads perform an additional analysis to ensure that the business continuity solution fulfills organizational recovery requirements. Because these individuals view the process from a corporate standpoint, they help to confirm that the BCP properly meets expectations.
	Using checklists. Checklists confirm whether the BCP meets predetermined, documented business needs.
Performing walkthroughs	Walkthroughs specifically focus on each BCP phase. Planners and testers walk through the individual steps to validate the logical flow of the sequence of events as a group.
Parallel testing	This test is used to ensure that systems perform adequately at any alternate offsite facility, without taking the main site offline.
	Simulations effectively test the validity and compliance of the BCP. In a simulation, each part of the plan is executed, with the exception of replicating and causing an outage. Although calls are made and specific actions are taken, the real event response is simulated.
	Simulations are instrumental in verifying design flaws, recovery requirements, and implementation errors. By identifying these solution discrepancies, process improvements can be applied that help ensure high-level plan maintenance.
Cutover	This test mimics an actual business disruption by shutting down the original site to test transfer and migration procedures to the alternate site and to test operations in the presence of an emergency.

ACTIVITY 10-1
Discussing Business Continuity Planning

Scenario:

In this activity, you will discuss the development schemes, contingency requirements, and other components involved in business continuity planning.

1. **As the security administrator, you are responsible for ensuring that your BCP coincides with the organization's needs. What are your goals while establishing a BCP? (Select all that apply.)**

   a) Preserve important documents.

   b) Establish decision-making authority.

   c) Analyze fault tolerance.

   d) Maintain financial functions.

2. **Your organization is located in an area where there is a threat of hurricanes. As a member of the BCP team, you need to determine what effect there would be if a hurricane halted business activities at your organization. Which BCP component is this an example of?**

   a) Continuity of operations

   b) BIA

   c) IT contingency planning

   d) Succession planning

3. **Which part of the plan specifies interim sites and systems you can switch to following a disaster?**

   a) RPO

   b) BIA

   c) IT contingency plan

   d) Succession plan

4. **You recommend the company pay a small monthly rental fee for a warehouse with phone and power hookups to use as a:**

   a) Hot site

   b) Cold site

   c) Warm site

5. **Match each BCP testing method with its description.**

___ Parallel testing

    a. A testing method that mimics an actual business disruption by shutting down the original site to test transfer and migration procedures to the alternate site.

___ Paper testing

    b. A testing method in which a group reviews and focuses on each BCP process component.

___ Performing walkthroughs

    c. A testing method where each part of the plan is executed, with the exception of replicating and causing an outage.

___ Cutover

    d. A testing method that confirms whether the BCP meets predetermined, documented business needs.

6. **You and your colleague have just performed a walkthrough of the plan that would be put into effect in the event of a denial of service (DoS) attack to your company website. The two of you think that you need to perform more rigorous tests to ensure the effectiveness of the BCP. What are some other testing methods you might want to recommend?**

TOPIC B
Plan for Disaster Recovery

You learned that your organization needs to have a plan for overall business continuity so that business operations can continue with little or no interruption in a disaster. As part of that plan, as an IT security professional, you need to ask specific technical questions such as "what about the sensitive data that has been lost or damaged in the attack?" In this topic, you will develop a plan for disaster recovery.

Disaster recovery planning is crucial for the security of large business systems. In order for organizations to ensure the safety of information systems, they must be proactive and develop an effective DRP to make sure that if there were ever a major system attack or environmental event, sensitive information can be protected or, at the worst, recovered.

DRPs

Definition:

A *disaster recovery plan (DRP)* is a plan that prepares an organization to react appropriately if the worst were to happen, be it a natural or a man-made disaster, and provides the means to recover from such disaster. DRPs help organizations to recover from an incident without the loss of much time and money. The plan's most important concern, however, is the safety of personnel. A DRP can include:

● A list and contact information of individuals responsible for recovery.

● An inventory of hardware and software.

● A record of important business and customer information that you would require to continue business.

● A record of procedure manuals and other critical information such as the BCP and IT contingency plans.

● And, specification for alternate sites.

 The contents of a BCP and DRP overlap, and the terms are sometimes used interchangeably.

Example:

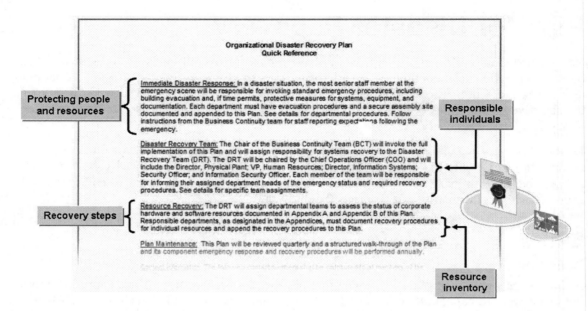

Figure 10-10: A DRP.

Fault Tolerance

Fault tolerance is the ability of a network or system to withstand a foreseeable component failure and continue to provide an acceptable level of service. There are several categories of fault tolerance measures, including those that protect power sources, disks and data storage, and network components. Fault tolerant systems often employ some kind of duplication or redundancy of resources to maintain functionality if one component is damaged or fails.

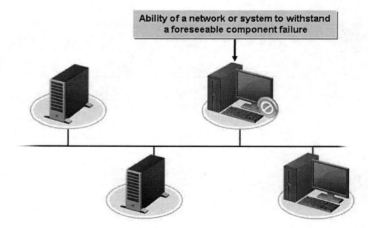

Figure 10-11: Fault tolerance.

Redundancy Measures

Each possible failure point has its appropriate redundancy measures.

 There are various resources you can consult for more information on RAID and RAID levels including the websites of various RAID solution vendors.

Failure Point	Redundancy Measure
Disks	The *Redundant Array of Independent Disks (RAID)* standards are a set of vendor-independent specifications mostly for fault tolerant configurations on multiple-disk systems. If one or more of the disks fail, data can be recovered from the remaining disks. RAID can be implemented through operating system software, but hardware-based RAID implementations are more efficient and are more widely deployed. There are several RAID levels, each of which provides a different combination of features and efficiencies. RAID levels are identified by number; RAID 0, RAID 1, and RAID 5 are the most common. All RAID forms except for RAID 0 reduce the threat of loss due to disk failures and provide protection.
Circuits	To reduce the damage caused by the loss of a communications circuit in a data network, a backup circuit should be made available and installed to serve as a redundant connection. The backup circuit may be used on either an on-demand basis or all the time. If the primary circuit is interrupted, the network continues to operate on the second, or backup, circuit on a limited performance basis.
Servers	Server clustering allows servers to work together to provide access, ensuring minimal data loss from a server failure. Should one of the servers in the cluster fail, the remaining servers, or server, will assume the responsibilities, but with the possibility of decreased performance. When the failed server is restored, it will integrate back into the cluster and reinstate with a minimal noticeable shift in performance.
Routers	*Router redundancy* is the technique of deploying multiple routers in teams to limit the risk of routing failure should a router malfunction. The routers in a redundant environment share common configurations and act as one to route and control information. They communicate with each other to determine if everything is functioning well. If a redundant router fails, the remaining routers assume the load and sustain the routing process.
General hardware	Keeping used or spare parts on hand for emergencies is good practice. You should be aware that there could be some security or backwards-compatibility issues with some of the spare parts (such as wireless routers, decommissioned laptops, slower central processing units [CPUs], or old switches). Periodically add spare parts to your network to test them; in the event of an emergency, they can be the difference between shutting down business, or operating at a reduced—but acceptable—level.
Power supplies	A recent feature of power supplies is to include two or more units built into one system with capabilities for each to supply power to the entire system. If one of the units fails, then by means of a hot swap built into the server, the other unit supplies power.
Network adapters	Systems can also be supplied with built-in redundant network adapters that automatically hot-swap if one fails.

MTBF

Mean time between failures (MTBF) is the rating on a device or devices that predicts the expected time between failures. Based on the MTBF of a system, you must consider and plan for the necessary redundancy measures.

High Availability

Definition:

High availability is a rating that expresses how closely systems approach the goal of providing data availability 100 percent of the time while maintaining a high level of system performance. High-availability systems are usually rated as a percentage that shows the proportion of expected uptime to total time. Some of the methods used in achieving this include clustering, load balancing, and redundancy measures.

Example:

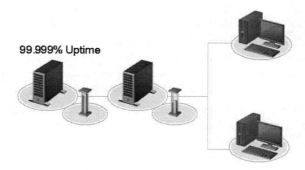

99.999% Uptime

Figure 10-12: High availability.

Five Nines

An uptime rating of 99.999% or "five nines" is a very high level of availability, resulting in less than six minutes of downtime per year. "Six nines," or 99.9999% uptime, results in around 30 seconds of downtime per year, but comes with an associated proportional increase in cost.

Disaster Recovery Testing and Maintenance

Every DRP should be tested periodically as part of its implementation, and your DRP development process should include an evaluation phase to ensure its effectiveness. You can use the testing methods and evaluation techniques similar to those used to evaluate a BCP, such as paper testing, performing walkthroughs, parallel testing, and cutover. After the plan has been completed, you should review it at least yearly and make any maintenance-level changes required based on the results of the review as well as the results of periodic testing.

How to Plan for Disaster Recovery

To plan for disaster recovery, you must properly assess your organization's current state of readiness, and you must know when and how to improve any limitations of the current strategy.

Guidelines

To plan for disaster recovery, keep the following guidelines in mind:

● If your organization has not tested the BCP recently, do so. Conduct several offline scenarios that only utilize backup resources.

● If you are creating or improving the BCP and/or DRP, research any available templates that might help guide you. Websites such as **www.disasterrecoveryforum.com** or **www.disasterrecoveryworld.com** are good places to begin.

● Ensure that there are redundancy measures in place for servers, power supplies, and your ISP.

● Verify that the company has access to spare hardware and peripherals for emergency use, and that the devices are secure enough to conduct business with.

● Review any service level agreements (SLAs) that are in place so that you have an idea of what constitutes acceptable downtime.

● Create a line of communication that does not make use of company resources, so it does not break should the company lose power after hours. Do the same in the event that the city or regional power is down.

● Identify and document all single points of failure, as well as any up-to-date redundancy measures.

● Make sure that the company's redundant storage is secure.

● Be sure that your DRP includes provisions for regular tests of the plan. You might want to schedule a "fire drill," where one day, all managers are moved to an offsite location, unannounced. This helps to simulate a disaster or emergency, which does not always provide ample warning.

● Employees must receive training to understand the importance of the DRP.

Example:

vLearners, Inc. is a large e-learning company with a growing international client base. The company offers a variety of learning and technological solutions to their clients. Every 12 to 18 months, the IT department revisits the preparedness of the organization to withstand a disaster. They begin with an analytical look at both the BCP and the DRP as they currently exist, and then they modify them as necessary; this only comes after a careful assessment of the organization's recent security history, as well as an assessment of the landscape of security in the general business world.

While it is not always financially feasible for the company to have an unannounced offsite fire drill, the IT department does regularly test the viability of the company's backup servers for the intranet, the secure servers that contain clients' billing and financial information, and those servers that actually host the e-learning courses. After conducting these tests, the IT department members determine how many backup resources they need to maintain uptime, how many spare peripherals they need to save in case of an emergency, and how many options they have should their ISP lose service for an extended period of time.

The IT department also revisits the emergency contact information for all those employees identified in the BCP and DRP who will have a hand in disaster recovery. Those employees are then tested on how quickly they can get the backup networks operational, and how quickly they can use spare hardware and peripherals to function as secure, temporary network devices. Consistent and systematic planning saves time and money in the long run should something unforeseeable happen to a company's network resources.

DISCOVERY ACTIVITY 10-2
Creating a DRP

Scenario:

You are a security professional at Ristell & Sons Publishing, a small but rapidly growing publishing company. With a growing roster of employees, a larger network infrastructure, and more remote network access by traveling employees, the company has decided that it has outgrown its original security policies. You have been asked to create the company's first DRP.

1. **Which are common components that should be in Ristell & Sons' DRP? (Select all that apply)**

   a) A list of employees' personal items.

   b) Contact information for key individuals.

   c) An inventory of important hardware and software.

   d) Plans to reconstruct the network.

2. **Ristell & Sons Publishing is willing to set aside some capital to install a fault tolerance system. What can you suggest?**

3. **Assume that Ristell & Sons Publishing is located in a climate and location identical to the company you work for now. What are some unique geographical or weather-related conditions you might need to account for, but that might not be a consideration for other companies?**

4. **Assume that a high-level manager has expressed some dissatisfaction with the notion of a "fire drill" to test the company's preparedness for a disaster; it seems he is leery of so much paid time being used in an unproductive way, and he wonders if you cannot just write a detailed plan instead. What are some things you can mention to help persuade him that such an unannounced drill is necessary?**

5. Once you have the DRP and other components in place, what do you do to make sure it works smoothly?

TOPIC C

Execute DRPs and Procedures

Even though you know how important it is to create and test a DRP, the true test of a plan is putting it into effect in a true disaster situation. In this topic, you will execute a DRP and its procedures.

What is the use of a good DRP if it is not well executed? Knowing who to contact and knowing how to execute a DRP in the best way possible will help get business back up and running in no time and avoid all unnecessary losses to the organization.

The Disaster Recovery Process

The disaster recovery process includes several steps to properly resume business operations after a disruptive event.

Disaster Recovery Step	Description
Notify stakeholders	Stakeholders should be informed of a business-critical disaster. They may consist of senior management, board members, investors, clients, suppliers, employees, and the public. Different categories of stakeholders are notified at different times and the level of detail follows the notification procedures in your policy.
Begin emergency operations	The DRP should contain detailed steps regarding specific emergency services. An incident manager should be appointed to assume control of the situation and ensure the safety of personnel.
Assess the damage	A damage assessment should be conducted to determine the extent of incurred facility damages, to identify the cause of the disaster if it is unclear, and to estimate the amount of expected downtime. This assessment can also determine the appropriate response strategy. For instance, a full recovery to a remote site may not be warranted if damage is limited to parts of the business that do not threaten operational functions.
Assess the facility	It is necessary to assess the current facility's ability to continue being the primary location of operation. If the facility has been adversely affected and has suffered significant losses, relocating to an alternate site may be the best option.
Begin recovery process	Once you have notified stakeholders, performed the initial emergency operations, and assessed the damage and the facility's ability to function, then it is time to start the recovery process.

The Recovery Team

Definition:

The *recovery team* is a group of designated individuals who implement recovery procedures and control recovery operations in the event of an internal or external disruption to critical business processes. The recovery team immediately responds in an emergency and restores critical business processes to their normal operating capacity, at the remote or recovery site, once key services and information systems are back online. Team members might include systems managers, systems administrators, security administrators, facilities specialists, communications specialists, human resources staff, and legal representatives.

Example:

Figure 10-13: *The recovery team provides immediate response.*

Secure Recovery

The BCP or DRP must include provisions for securely recovering data, systems, and other sensitive resources. This might mean designating a trusted administrator to supervise the recovery, as well as documenting the steps and information needed to restore the processes, systems, and data needed to recover from the disaster, and instructions for continuing operations either at the primary site or an alternate site. The secure recovery process should be reviewed and tested on a regular basis.

Figure 10-14: *Secure recovery.*

Backup Types and Recovery Plans

The process of recovering data from a backup varies depending on the backup types that were included in the original backup plan. There are three main types of backups.

Microsoft 10-tip method

Backup Type	Description
Full backup	All selected files, regardless of the state of the archived bit, are backed up. The *archive bit* is a file property that essentially indicates whether the file has been modified since it was last backed up. A full backup then clears the archive bit.
Differential backup	All selected files that have changed since the last full backup are backed up. A differential backup does not clear the archive bit. When differential backups are used, you must restore the last full backup plus the most recent differential backup.
Incremental backup	All selected files that have changed since the last full or differential backup are backed up. It clears the archive bit. An incremental backup typically takes less time to perform than a differential backup because it includes less data. When incremental backups are used, you must restore the last full backup plus all subsequent incremental backups.

Backout Contingency Plans

A *backout contingency plan* is a documented plan that includes specific procedures and processes that are applied in the event that a change or modification made to a system must be undone. The plan may include key individuals, a list of systems, backout time frames, and the specific steps needed to fully undo a change. Part of the plan may also include a backup plan which may be deployed as part of the backout processes and procedures.

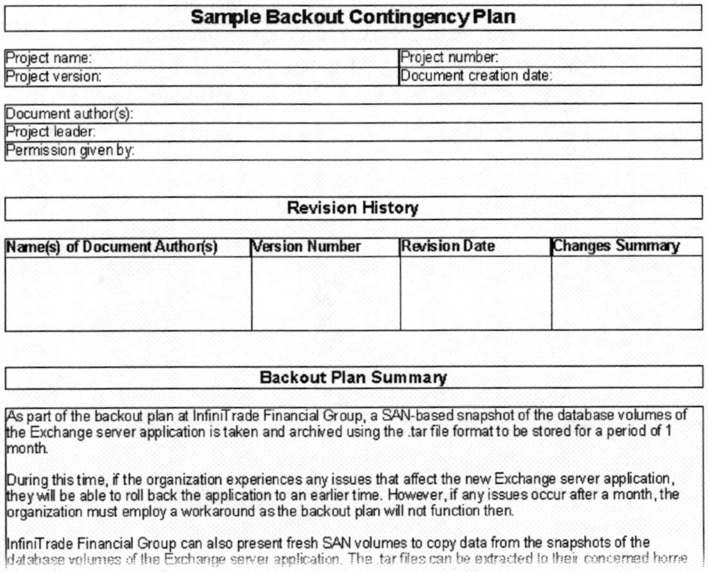

Figure 10-15: A backout contingency plan.

Secure Backups

Backing up sensitive or important data is only part of the solution, as that backup also needs to be secure. Storing copies of sensitive or critical information is a sensible security practice, and should not simply be limited to a secondary hard disk, a Compact Disc-Recordable (CD-R), or a tape archive. A backup can be considered most secure if it is offline and offsite, and stored in an environment that is physically locked and protected from environmental intrusions such as fire or water.

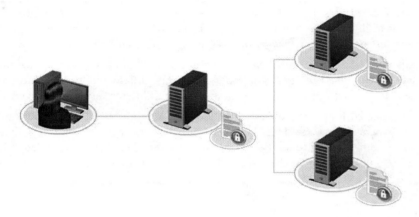

Figure 10-16: Secure backups.

Backup Storage Locations

The magnetic tapes or other physical media used to create data backups must be stored securely, but must remain accessible in case the data is needed. Many organizations employ both onsite and offsite backup storage. The onsite storage location is for the most recent set of backups, so that they can be accessed quickly if a data restoration is needed during normal operations. The offsite location is a secure, disaster-resistant storage facility where the organization keeps either a duplicate or an older backup set to protect it against any damage caused by disaster conditions at the primary site.

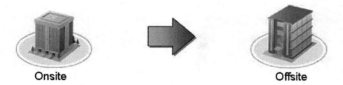

Onsite   Offsite

Figure 10-17: Backup storage locations.

How to Execute DRPs and Procedures

To execute DRPs and procedures, you need to ensure that the DRPs are in place and can be readily implemented in the event of the disaster.

Guidelines

To execute DRPs and procedures, keep the following guidelines in mind:

- The organization needs to identify the team that will handle the disaster situation, including the incident manager.

- Each disaster recovery team member must have clearly laid out roles and responsibilities and must be easily accessible to the other employees.

- Employees must be aware of the members of the disaster recovery team and must know who they need to contact in the event of a disaster.

- The disaster recovery team must work out a backup plan for the incident that will ensure that the continuity of the business is not affected as an aftermath of the disaster.

- Inform stakeholders as specified in your DRP.

- Roll out emergency services, such as an alternate site, under the control of the incident manager.

- The damage to the main site should be assessed and the recovery team should be brought in to repair any physical damage and assess the extent to which the main site can be restored.

- A restoration of the backup should be done of all files that have been compromised or deleted.

- Decisions should be made to purchase or replace missing system elements.

- Once the recovery process is completed, document the steps taken and save a report to be used in case of another recovery process.

Example:

vLearners, Inc. is faced with a situation where a fire destroyed many data cables, a few systems, and one of the servers. Mary, the chief information security officer, has to execute a recovery process to get the business up and running in the shortest possible time, as the company is experiencing a high volume of customers using their courses and recently they have received a lot of complaints about inaccessibility.

Mary calls in the disaster recovery team that has been put together to face this type of situation. She has a list of the roles each person in her team has to play. She gives them a list of names that correspond to a list of duties and asks them to contact each other in case they need support. The team will plan a specific disaster recovery strategy for the situation based on the order of importance of items on the DRP list.

Then, Mary informs the director of the organization about the plan, who then informs the stakeholders. Meanwhile, operations are transferred to an alternate site and the recovery team is supervised by Mary to assess and repair the damage to the systems. A backup restore for all the files is performed, and Mary documents all the steps taken during the recovery process and presents a report to the organization once the disaster is contained.

DISCOVERY ACTIVITY 10-3
Executing DRPs and Procedures

Scenario:

You are the chief information security officer at your organization and you need to execute the best possible DRP and procedures to get your company's systems back up and running in least amount of time as possible.

1. **What should you keep in mind while choosing a good recovery team?**

   a) Include individuals who can do an analysis of the damage that the crisis has caused to the organization.

   b) Include individuals who can implement the proper procedures in response to the disruption to critical business processes.

   c) Include individuals who can record the history of the evidence of a computer crime from collection, to presentation in court, to return or disposal.

   d) Include individuals who determine how much money and effort will go into a recovery plan.

2. **Match each disaster recovery step with its description.**

___	Begin emergency operations	a.	If a facility has been adversely affected and has suffered significant losses, relocating to an alternate site may be the best option.
___	Assess the damage	b.	An incident manager should be appointed to assume control of the situation and ensure personnel safety.
___	Notify stakeholders	c.	These consist of senior management, board members, investors, clients, suppliers, and employees.
___	Assess the facility	d.	This is a check to determine the extent of incurred facility expenses, the cause of the disaster, and the expected down time.

3. **You have been assigned to perform a secure recovery; what does your task include?**

4. You have to decide on the kind of backup source you will use to recover data and restore function to the business in the least possible time. What type of backup could you choose?

_____

5. What types of backup storage locations can you suggest to store data for your company?

_____

Lesson 10 Follow-up

In this lesson, you developed a BCP and a DRP so that your organization's processes will be uninterrupted and continuous without fail.

1. **What risks are prevalent in your field of expertise and how do you prevent them?**

2. **What kind of alternate site does your organization maintain? Why?**

Follow-up

In this course, you learned the skills and information you will need to implement and monitor security on networks, applications, and operating systems, and respond to security breaches. You also covered the learning objectives that you will need to prepare for the CompTIA Security+ (Exam SY0-301) Certification examination. If you combine this class experience with review, private study, and hands-on experience, you will be well prepared to demonstrate your security expertise both through professional certification and with solid technical competence on the job.

What's Next?

Your next step after completing this course will probably be to prepare for and obtain your CompTIA® Security+® Certification. In addition, there are a number of advanced security courses and certifications that you might want to pursue following the CompTIA Security+ (Exam SY0-301) course, including Certified Information Security Manager (CISM®) Certification and Information Certified Information Services Security Professional (CISSP®). You might also wish to pursue further technology-specific training in operating system or network design, implementation and support, or in application development and implementation.

A | Mapping Course Content to the CompTIA® Security+® (Exam SY0-301) Objectives

Exam Objective	Security+ Certification Lesson and Topic Reference
Domain 1.0 Network Security	
1.1 Explain the security function and purpose of network devices and technologies	
• Firewalls	Lesson 3, Topic A
	Lesson 4, Topic A
	Lesson 8, Topic A
• Routers	Lesson 3, Topics A and D
	Lesson 10, Topic B
• Switches	Lesson 2, Topic C
	Lesson 3, Topic A
• Load Balancers	Lesson 3, Topic A
• Proxies	Lesson 3, Topic A
	Lesson 4, Topic B
• Web security gateways	Lesson 3, Topic A
• VPN concentrators	Lesson 3, Topic A
• NIDS and NIPS (Behavior based, signature based, anomaly based, heuristic)	Lesson 3, Topic A
• Protocol analyzers	Lesson 3, Topic A
	Lesson 8, Topics A and B
• Sniffers	Lesson 3, Topic A
	Lesson 8, Topics A and B
• Spam filter, all-in-one security appliances	Lesson 8, Topics A and B
	Lesson 4, Topic A

Exam Objective	Security+ Certification Lesson and Topic Reference
Domain 1.0 Network Security	
1.1 Explain the security function and purpose of network devices and technologies	
• Web application firewall vs. network firewall	Lesson 3, Topic A
• URL filtering, content inspection, malware inspection	Lesson 3, Topic A

Exam Objective	Security+ Certification Lesson and Topic Reference
1.2 Apply and implement secure network administration principles	
• Rule-based management	Lesson 3, Topic D
• Firewall rules	Lesson 4, Topic A
• VLAN management	Lesson 3, Topic D
• Secure router configuration	Lesson 3, Topic D Lesson 4, Topic D
• Access control lists	Lesson 1, Topic B
• Port Security	Lesson 3, Topic D Lesson 8, Topic D
• 802.1x	Lesson 3, Topic E
• Flood guards	Lesson 3, Topic D
• Loop protection	Lesson 3, Topic D
• Implicit deny	Lesson 1, Topics B and E Lesson 3, Topic D
• Prevent network bridging by network separation	Lesson 3, Topic D
• Log analysis	Lesson 3, Topic D

Exam Objective	Security+ Certification Lesson and Topic Reference
1.3 Distinguish and differentiate network design elements and compounds	
• DMZ	Lesson 3, Topic C
• Subnetting	Lesson 3, Topic B
• VLAN	Lesson 3, Topic B
• NAT	Lesson 3, Topic B Lesson 4, Topic A

Exam Objective	Security+ Certification Lesson and Topic Reference
1.3 Distinguish and differentiate network design elements and compounds	
● Remote Access	Lesson 3, Topic B
	Lesson 5, Topic A
● Telephony	Lesson 3, Topic B
● NAC	Lesson 3, Topic B
● Virtualization	Lesson 3, Topic B
	Lesson 4, Topic A
● Cloud Computing	Lesson 3, Topic B
■ Platform as a Service	Lesson 3, Topic B
■ Software as a Service	Lesson 3, Topic B
■ Infrastructure as a Service	Lesson 3, Topic B

Exam Objective	Security+ Certification Lesson and Topic Reference
1.4 Implement and use common protocols	
● IPSec	Lesson 3, Topic C
● SNMP	Lesson 3, Topic C
● SSH	Lesson 3, Topic C
● DNS	Lesson 2, Topic C
	Lesson 3, Topic C
● SSL	Lesson 3, Topic C
	Lesson 6, Topic B
● TCP/IP	Lesson 2, Topic C
	Lesson 3, Topic C
● FTPS	Lesson 3, Topic C
● HTTPS	Lesson 3, Topic C
● SFTP	Lesson 3, Topic C
● SCP	Lesson 3, Topic C
● ICMP	Lesson 2, Topic C
	Lesson 3, Topic C
● IPv4 vs. IPv6	Lesson 3, Topic C

Exam Objective	Security+ Certification Lesson and Topic Reference
1.5 Identify commonly used default network ports	
• FTP	Lesson 2, Topic C
	Lesson 3, Topic C
• SFTP	Lesson 3, Topic C
• FTPS	Lesson 3, Topic C
• TFTP	Lesson 3, Topic C
• TELNET	Lesson 3, Topic C
• HTTP	Lesson 2, Topic E
	Lesson 3, Topic C
• HTTPS	Lesson 3, Topic C
• SCP	Lesson 3, Topic C
• SSH	Lesson 3, Topic C
• NetBIOS	Lesson 2, Topic C
	Lesson 3, Topic C

Exam Objective	Security+ Certification Lesson and Topic Reference
1.6 Implement wireless network in a secure manner	
• WPA	Lesson 3, Topic E
• WPA2	Lesson 3, Topic E
• WEP	Lesson 3, Topic E
• EAP	Lesson 3, Topic E
• PEAP	Lesson 3, Topic E
• LEAP	Lesson 3, Topic E
• MAC filter	Lesson 1, Topic B
	Lesson 2, Topic C
• SSID broadcast	Lesson 3, Topic E
• TKIP	Lesson 3, Topic E
• CCMP	Lesson 3, Topic E
• Antenna Placement	Lesson 3, Topic E
• Power level controls	Lesson 3, Topic E

Exam Objective	Security+ Certification Lesson and Topic Reference
2.0 Compliance and Operational Security	
2.1 Explain risk related concepts	
● Control types	Lesson 8, Topic A
■ Technical	Lesson 8, Topic A
■ Management	Lesson 8, Topic A
■ Operational	Lesson 8, Topic A
● False positives	Lesson 8, Topic A
● Importance of policies in reducing risk	Lesson 8, Topic A
■ Privacy policy	Lesson 8, Topic A
■ Acceptable use	Lesson 1, Topic E
■ Security policy	Lesson 1, Topic E Lesson 7 Topic C Lesson 8, Topic D
■ Mandatory vacations	Lesson 1, Topics B and E Lesson 8, Topic D
■ Job rotation	Lesson 1, Topics B and E Lesson 8, Topic D
■ Separation of duties	Lesson 1, Topics B and E Lesson 8, Topic D
■ Least privilege	Lesson 1, Topics B and E Lesson 5, Topic B Lesson 8, Topic D
● Risk calculation	Lesson 8, Topic A
■ Likelihood	Lesson 8, Topic A
■ ALE	Lesson 8, Topic A
■ Impact	Lesson 8, Topic A
● Quantitative vs. qualitative	Lesson 8, Topic A
● Risk-avoidance, transference, acceptance, mitigation, deterrence	Lesson 8, Topics A and D
● Risks associated to Cloud Computing and Virtualization	Lesson 8, Topic A

Exam Objective	Security+ Certification Lesson and Topic Reference
2.2 Carry out appropriate risk mitigation strategies	
● Implement security controls based on risk	Lesson 8, Topic D
● Change management	Lesson 1, Topic E
	Lesson 8, Topic A
● Incident management	Lesson 8, Topic D
● User rights and permissions reviews	Lesson 8, Topic D
● Perform routine audits	Lesson 8, Topic D
● Implement policies and procedures to prevent data loss or theft	Lesson 8, Topic D

Exam Objective	Security+ Certification Lesson and Topic Reference
2.3 Execute appropriate incident response procedures	
● Basic forensic procedures	Lesson 7, Topic B
	Lesson 9, Topic A
■ Order of volatility	Lesson 9, Topic A
■ Capture system image	Lesson 9, Topic A
■ Network traffic and logs	Lesson 9, Topic A
■ Capture video	Lesson 9, Topic A
■ Record time offset	Lesson 9, Topic A
■ Take hashes	Lesson 9, Topic A
■ Screenshots	Lesson 9, Topic A
■ Witnesses	Lesson 9, Topic A
■ Track man hours and expense	Lesson 9, Topic A
● Damage and loss control	Lesson 9, Topic B
● Chain of custody	Lesson 7, Topic B
	Lesson 9, Topic A
● Incident response: first responder	Lesson 9, Topic A

Exam Objective	Security+ Certification Lesson and Topic Reference
2.4 Explain the importance of security related awareness and training	
● Security policy training and procedures	Lesson 7, Topic B
	Lesson 8, Topic B
● Personally identifiable information	Lesson 5, Topic B
● Information classification: Sensitivity of data (hard or soft)	Lesson 5, Topic B
● Data labeling, handling and disposal	Lesson 7, Topic C
● Compliance with laws, best practices and standards	Lesson 7, Topic B
● User habits	Lesson 7, Topic A
■ Password behaviors	Lesson 7, Topic C
■ Data handling	Lesson 7, Topic C
■ Clean desk policies	Lesson 7, Topic C
■ Prevent tailgating	Lesson 7, Topic C
■ Personally owned devices	Lesson 7, Topic C
● Threat awareness	Lesson 7, Topic C
■ New viruses	Lesson 7, Topic C
■ Phishing attacks	Lesson 7, Topic C
■ Zero days exploits	Lesson 7, Topic C
● Use of social networking and P2	Lesson 7, Topic C

Exam Objective	Security+ Certification Lesson and Topic Reference
2.5 Compare and contrast aspects of business continuity	
● Business impact analysis	Lesson 10, Topic A
● Removing single points of failure	Lesson 10, Topic B
● Business continuity planning and testing	Lesson 10, Topic A
● Continuity of operations	Lesson 10, Topic A
● Disaster recovery	Lesson 10, Topic B
● IT contingency planning	Lesson 10, Topic A
● Succession planning	Lesson 10, Topic A

Exam Objective	Security+ Certification Lesson and Topic Reference
2.6 Explain the impact and proper use of environmental controls	
● HVAC	Lesson 7, Topic A
● Fire suppression	Lesson 7, Topic A
● EMI shielding	Lesson 7, Topic A
● Hot and cold aisles	Lesson 7, Topic A
● Environmental monitoring	Lesson 7, Topic A
● Temperature and humidity controls	Lesson 7, Topic A
● Video monitoring	Lesson 7, Topic A

Exam Objective	Security+ Certification Lesson and Topic Reference
2.7 Execute disaster recovery plans and procedures	
● Backup / backout contingency plans or policies	Lesson 10, Topic C
● Backups, execution and frequency	Lesson 10, Topic C
● Redundancy and fault tolerance	Lesson 10, Topic B
■ Hardware	Lesson 10, Topic B
■ RAID	Lesson 10, Topic B
■ Clustering	Lesson 10, Topic B
■ Load balancing	Lesson 3, Topic A
■ Servers	Lesson 10, Topic B
● High availability	Lesson 10, Topic B
● Cold site, hot site, warm site	Lesson 10, Topic B
● Mean time to restore, mean time between failures, recovery time objectives and recovery point objectives	Lesson 10, Topic A

Exam Objective	Security+ Certification Lesson and Topic Reference
2.8 Exemplify the concepts of confidentiality, integrity and availability (CIA)	Lesson 1, Topic B

Exam Objective	Security+ Certification Lesson and Topic Reference
3.0 Threats and Vulnerabilities	
3.1 Analyze and differentiate among types of malware	
● Adware	Lesson 2, Topic E
● Virus	Lesson 2, Topic E
● Worms	Lesson 2, Topic E
● Spyware	Lesson 2, Topic E
● Trojan	Lesson 2, Topic E
● Rootkits	Lesson 2, Topic E
● Backdoors	Lesson 2, Topic E
● Logic bomb	Lesson 2, Topic E
● Botnets	Lesson 2, Topic E

Exam Objective	Security+ Certification Lesson and Topic Reference
3.2 Analyze and differentiate among types of attacks	
● Man-in-the-middle	Lesson 2, Topics C and D
● DDoS	Lesson 2, Topic C
● DoS	Lesson 2, Topic C
● Replay	Lesson 2, Topic C
● Smurf attack	Lesson 2, Topic C
● Spoofing	Lesson 2, Topic C
● Spam	Lesson 2, Topics A and C
● Phishing	Lesson 2, Topic A
● Spim	Lesson 2, Topic A
● Vishing	Lesson 2, Topic A
● Spear phishing	Lesson 2, Topic A
● Xmas attack	Lesson 2, Topic C
● Pharming	Lesson 2, Topic A
● Privilege escalation	Lesson 1, Topic B Lesson 5, Topic B
● Malicious insider threat	Lesson 1, Topic A
● DNS poisoning and ARP poisoning	Lesson 1, Topics A and C
● Transitive access	Lesson 2, Topic C

Exam Objective	Security+ Certification Lesson and Topic Reference
3.2 Analyze and differentiate among types of attacks	
● Client-side attacks	Lesson 1, Topics C and E

Exam Objective	Security+ Certification Lesson and Topic Reference
3.3 Analyze and differentiate among types of social engineering attacks	
● Shoulder surfing	Lesson 1, Topic A
● Dumpster diving	Lesson 1, Topic A
● Tailgating	Lesson 1, Topic A
● Impersonation	Lesson 1, Topic A
● Hoaxes	Lesson 1, Topic A
● Whaling	Lesson 1, Topic A
● Vishing	Lesson 1, Topic A

Exam Objective	Security+ Certification Lesson and Topic Reference
3.4 Analyze and differentiate among types of wireless attacks	
● Rogue access points	Lesson 2, Topic D
● Interference	Lesson 2, Topic D
● Evil twin	Lesson 2, Topic D
● War driving	Lesson 2, Topic D
● Bluejacking	Lesson 2, Topic D
● Bluesnarfing	Lesson 2, Topic D
● War chalking	Lesson 2, Topic D
● IV attack	Lesson 2, Topic D
● Packet sniffing	Lesson 2, Topic D

Exam Objective	Security+ Certification Lesson and Topic Reference
3.5 Analyze and differentiate among types of application attacks	
● Cross-site scripting	Lesson 2, Topic E
● SQL injection	Lesson 2, Topic E

Exam Objective	Security+ Certification Lesson and Topic Reference
3.5 Analyze and differentiate among types of application attacks	
● LDAP injection	Lesson 2, Topic E
● XML injection	Lesson 2, Topic E
● Directory traversal/command injection	Lesson 2, Topic E
● Buffer overflow	Lesson 2, Topic E
● Zero day	Lesson 2, Topic E
● Cookies and attachments	Lesson 2, Topic E
● Malicious add-ons	Lesson 2, Topic E
● Session hijacking	Lesson 2, Topic C
● Header manipulation	Lesson 2, Topic E

Exam Objective	Security+ Certification Lesson and Topic Reference
3.6 Analyze and differentiate among types of mitigation and deterrent techniques	
● Manual bypassing of electronic controls	Lesson 8, Topic D
■ Failsafe/secure vs. failopen	Lesson 8, Topic D
● Monitoring system logs	Lesson 8, Topic D
■ Event logs	Lesson 8, Topic D
■ Audit logs	Lesson 8, Topic D
■ Security logs	Lesson 8, Topic D
■ Access logs	Lesson 8, Topic D
● Physical security	Lesson 7, Topic A
■ Hardware locks	Lesson 7, Topic A
■ Mantraps	Lesson 7, Topic A
■ Video surveillance	Lesson 7, Topic A
■ Fencing	Lesson 7, Topic A
■ Proximity readers	Lesson 7, Topic A
■ Access list	Lesson 7, Topic A
● Hardening	Lesson 8, Topic D
■ Disabling unnecessary services	Lesson 8, Topic D
■ Protecting management interfaces and applications	Lesson 8, Topic D
■ Password protection	Lesson 8, Topic D

Exam Objective	Security+ Certification Lesson and Topic Reference
3.6 Analyze and differentiate among types of mitigation and deterrent techniques	
▪ Disabling unnecessary accounts	Lesson 8, Topic D
● Port security	Lesson 8, Topic D
▪ MAC limiting and filtering	Lesson 8, Topic D
▪ 802.1x	Lesson 8, Topic D
▪ Disabling unused ports	Lesson 8, Topic D
● Security posture	Lesson 8, Topic D
▪ Initial baseline configuration	Lesson 8, Topic D
▪ Continuous security monitoring	Lesson 8, Topic D
▪ Remediation	Lesson 8, Topic D
● Reporting	Lesson 8, Topic D
▪ Alarms	Lesson 8, Topic D
▪ Alerts	Lesson 8, Topic D
▪ Trends	Lesson 8, Topic D
● Detection controls vs. prevention controls	Lesson 8, Topic D
▪ IDS vs. IPS	Lesson 3, Topic A
▪ Camera vs. guard	Lesson 8, Topic D

Exam Objective	Security+ Certification Lesson and Topic Reference
3.7 Implement assessment tools and techniques to discover security threats and vulnerabilities	
● Vulnerability scanning and interpret results	Lesson 8, Topics B and C
● Tools	Lesson 8, Topics B and C
▪ Protocol analyzer	Lesson 8, Topics B and C
▪ Sniffer	Lesson 8, Topics B and C
▪ Vulnerability scanner	Lesson 8, Topics B and C
▪ Honeypots	Lesson 8, Topic B
▪ Honeynets	Lesson 8, Topic B
▪ Port scanner	Lesson 8, Topics B and C
● Risk calculations	Lesson 8, Topic A
▪ Threat vs. likelihood	Lesson 8, Topic A

Exam Objective	Security+ Certification Lesson and Topic Reference
3.7 Implement assessment tools and techniques to discover security threats and vulnerabilities	
● Assessment types	Lesson 8, Topic B
■ Baseline reporting	Lesson 8, Topic B
■ Code review	Lesson 8, Topic B
■ Determine attack surface	Lesson 8, Topic B
■ Architecture	Lesson 8, Topic B
■ Design reviews	Lesson 8, Topic B

Exam Objective	Security+ Certification Lesson and Topic Reference
3.8 Within the realm of vulnerability assessments, explain the proper use of penetration testing versus vulnerability scanning	
● Penetration testing	Lesson 8, Topic C
■ Verify a threat exists	Lesson 8, Topic C
■ Bypass security controls	Lesson 8, Topic C
■ Actively test security controls	Lesson 8, Topic C
■ Exploiting vulnerabilities	Lesson 8, Topic C
● Vulnerability scanning	Lesson 8, Topic C
■ Passively testing security controls	Lesson 8, Topic C
■ Identify vulnerability	Lesson 8, Topic C
■ Identify lack of security controls	Lesson 8, Topic C
■ Identify common misconfiguration	Lesson 8, Topic C
● Black box	Lesson 8, Topic C
● White box	Lesson 8, Topic C
● Gray box	Lesson 8, Topic C

Exam Objective	Security+ Certification Lesson and Topic Reference
4.0 Application, Data and Host Security	
4.1 Explain the importance of application security	
● Fuzzing	Lesson 4, Topic B
● Secure coding concepts	Lesson 4, Topic B

Exam Objective	Security+ Certification Lesson and Topic Reference
4.0 Application, Data and Host Security	
4.1 Explain the importance of application security	
■ Error and exception handling	Lesson 4, Topic B
■ Input validation	Lesson 4, Topic B
● Cross-site scripting prevention	Lesson 4, Topic B
● Cross-site Request Forgery (XSRF) prevention	Lesson 4, Topic B
● Application configuration baseline (proper settings)	Lesson 4, Topic B
● Application hardening	Lesson 4, Topic B
● Application patch management	Lesson 4, Topic B

Exam Objective	Security+ Certification Lesson and Topic Reference
4.2 Carry out appropriate procedures to establish host security	
● Operating system security and settings	Lesson 4, Topic B
● Anti-malware	Lesson 4, Topic B
■ Anti-virus	Lesson 4, Topic B
■ Anti-spam	Lesson 4, Topic B
■ Anti-spyware	Lesson 4, Topic B
■ Pop-up blockers	Lesson 4, Topic B
■ Host-based firewalls	Lesson 4, Topic B
● Patch management	Lesson 4, Topic B
● Hardware security	Lesson 4, Topic B
■ Cable locks	Lesson 4, Topic B
■ Safe	Lesson 4, Topic B
■ Locking cabinets	Lesson 4, Topic B
● Host software baselining	Lesson 4, Topic B
● Mobile devices	Lesson 4, Topic D
■ Screen lock	Lesson 4, Topic D
■ Strong password	Lesson 4, Topic D
■ Device encryption	Lesson 4, Topic D
■ Remote wipe/sanitation	Lesson 4, Topic D
■ Voice encryption	Lesson 4, Topic D

Exam Objective	Security+ Certification Lesson and Topic Reference
4.2 Carry out appropriate procedures to establish host security	
■ GPS tracking	Lesson 4, Topic D
● Virtualization	Lesson 3, Topic B
	Lesson 4, Topic D

Exam Objective	Security+ Certification Lesson and Topic Reference
4.3 Explain the importance of data security	
● Data Loss Prevention (DLP)	Lesson 4, Topic C
● Data encryption	Lesson 4, Topic C
■ Full disk	Lesson 4, Topic C
■ Database	Lesson 4, Topic C
■ Individual files	Lesson 4, Topic C
■ Removable media	Lesson 4, Topic C
■ Mobile devices	Lesson 4, Topic C
● Hardware based encryption devices	Lesson 4, Topic C
■ TPM	Lesson 4, Topic C
■ HSM	Lesson 4, Topic C
■ USB encryption	Lesson 4, Topic C
■ Hard drive	Lesson 4, Topic C
● Cloud computing	Lesson 3, Topic B

Exam Objective	Security+ Certification Lesson and Topic Reference
5.0 Access Control and Identity Management	
5.1 Explain the function and purpose of authentication services	
● RADIUS	Lesson 5, Topic A
● TACACS	Lesson 5, Topic A
● TACACS+	Lesson 5, Topic A
● Kerberos	Lesson 5, Topic A
● LDAP	Lesson 5, Topic A
● XTACACS	Lesson 5, Topic A

Exam Objective	Security+ Certification Lesson and Topic Reference
5.2 Explain the fundamental concepts and best practices related to authentication, authorization and access control	
● Identification vs. authentication	Lesson 1, Topic B
● Authentication (single factor) and authorization	Lesson 1, Topic B
● Multifactor authentication	Lesson 1, Topic C
● Biometrics	Lesson 1, Topic C
● Tokens	Lesson 1, Topic C
● Common access card	Lesson 1, Topic C
● Personal identification verification card	Lesson 1, Topic C
● Smart card	Lesson 1, Topic C
● Least privilege	Lesson 1, Topics B and E Lesson 4, Topic A
● Separation of duties	Lesson 1, Topics B and C
● Single sign on	Lesson 1, Topic B
● ACLs	Lesson 1, Topic B
● Access control	Lesson 1, Topic B Lesson 5, Topic A
● Mandatory access control	Lesson 1, Topic B
● Discretionary access control	Lesson 1, Topic B
● Role/rule-based access control	Lesson 1, Topic B
● Implicit deny	Lesson 1, Topics B and E Lesson 4, Topic A
● Time of day restrictions	Lesson 1, Topic B
● Trusted OS	Lesson 4, Topic A
● Mandatory vacations	Lesson 1, Topics B and E
● Job rotation	Lesson 1, Topics B and E

Exam Objective	Security+ Certification Lesson and Topic Reference
5.3 Implement appropriate security controls when performing account management	
● Mitigates issues associated with users with multiple account/roles	Lesson 5, Topic B
● Account policy enforcement	Lesson 5, Topic B

Exam Objective	Security+ Certification Lesson and Topic Reference
5.3 Implement appropriate security controls when performing account management	
■ Password complexity	Lesson 4, Topic A
■ Expiration	Lesson 5, Topic B
■ Recovery	Lesson 5, Topic B
■ Length	Lesson 5, Topic B
■ Disablement	Lesson 5, Topic B
■ Lockout	Lesson 5, Topic B
● Group based privilege	Lesson 5, Topic B
● User assigned privileges	Lesson 5, Topic B

Exam Objective	Security+ Certification Lesson and Topic Reference
6.0 Cryptography	
6.1 Summarize general cryptography concepts	
● Symmetric vs. asymmetric	Lesson 1, Topic D
● Fundamental differences and encryption methods	Lesson 1, Topic D
■ Block vs. stream	Lesson 1, Topic D
● Transport encryption	Lesson 3, Topic C
● Non-repudiation	Lesson 1, Topics B and D Lesson 3, Topic C
● Hashing	Lesson 1, Topic D
● Key escrow	Lesson 6, Topic F
● Steganography	Lesson 1, Topic D
● Digital signatures	Lesson 1, Topic D Lesson 6, Topic A
● Use of proven technologies	Lesson 1, Topic D
● Elliptic curve and quantum cryptography	Lesson 1, Topic D

Exam Objective	Security+ Certification Lesson and Topic Reference
6.2 Use and apply appropriate cryptographic tools and products	
● WEP vs. WPA/WPA2 and preshared key	Lesson 3, Topic E
● MD5	Lesson 1, Topic D

Exam Objective	Security+ Certification Lesson and Topic Reference
6.2 Use and apply appropriate cryptographic tools and products	
● SHA	Lesson 1, Topic D
● RIPEMD	Lesson 1, Topic D
● AES	Lesson 1, Topic D
● DES	Lesson 1, Topic D
● 3DES	Lesson 1, Topic D
● HMAC	Lesson 1, Topic D
● RSA	Lesson 1, Topic D
● RC4	Lesson 1, Topic D
● One-time-pads	Lesson 1, Topic D
● CHAP	Lesson 5, Topic A
● PAP	Lesson 5, Topic A
● NTLM	Lesson 1, Topic D
● NTLMv2	Lesson 1, Topic D
● Blowfish	Lesson 1, Topic D
● PGP/GPG	Lesson 5, Topic A
● Whole disk encryption	Lesson 4, Topic C
● TwoFish	Lesson 1, Topic D
● Comparative strengths of algorithms	Lesson 1, Topic D
● Use of algorithms with transport encryption	Lesson 3, Topic C
■ SSL	Lesson 3, Topic C Lesson 6, Topic C
■ TLS	Lesson 3, Topic C
■ IPSec	Lesson 3, Topic C
■ SSH	Lesson 3, Topic C
■ HTTPS	Lesson 3, Topic C

Exam Objective	Security+ Certification Lesson and Topic Reference
6.3 Explain the core concepts of public key infrastructure	
● Certificate authorities and digital certificates	Lesson 6, Topic A
■ CAs	Lesson 6, Topics A, B and C
■ CRLs	Lesson 6, Topic E

Exam Objective	Security+ Certification Lesson and Topic Reference
6.3 Explain the core concepts of public key infrastructure	
● PKI	Lesson 6, Topic A
● Recovery agent	Lesson 6, Topic E
● Public key	Lesson 6, Topic A
● Private key	Lesson 6, Topics A, B and C
● Registration	Lesson 6, Topic A
● Key escrow	Lesson 6, Topic F
● Trust models	Lesson 6, Topic A

Exam Objective	Security+ Certification Lesson and Topic Reference
6.4 Implement PKI, certificate management and associated components	
● Certificate authorities and digital certificates	Lesson 6, Topic A
■ CAs	Lesson 6, Topic A
■ CRLs	Lesson 6, Topic E
● PKI	Lesson 6, Topic A
● Recovery agent	Lesson 6, Topic E
● Public key	Lesson 6, Topics A and F
● Private key	Lesson 6, Topic F
● Registration	Lesson 6, Topics D and E
● Key escrow	Lesson 6, Topic F
● Trust models	Lesson 6, Topic A

Lesson Labs

Lesson labs are provided as an additional learning resource for this course. The labs may or may not be performed as part of the classroom activities. Your instructor will consider setup issues, classroom timing issues, and instructional needs to determine which labs are appropriate for you to perform, and at what point during the class. If you do not perform the labs in class, your instructor can tell you if you can perform them independently as self-study, and if there are any special setup requirements.

Lesson 2 Lab 1

Classifying Attacks

Activity Time: 15 minutes

Scenario:

Your IT department wants to know when they are being attacked and what type of attacks are occurring. As the new security administrator for your organization, you plan to take a look at some sample attacks that have occurred in your organization and classify them into the appropriate categories.

1. A help desk representative in your organization sniffs the network for user accounts and passwords. She then changes the passwords and this leaves a user unable to connect to the system to access any service. What type of attack(s) did the attacker use?

2. The help desk receives a call from someone claiming to be a support person asking for the fully qualified domain name (FQDN) and IP address of the web server in your organization. A short while later, no one on the Internet can get to your web server because the performance has suddenly dropped. What type of attack(s) did the attacker use?

3. The HR manager, Susan Brown, requests IT support to fix an issue on her system. The IT support person fixes the issue and also installs a key logger application on the system without Susan's knowledge. Later, he uses the information from the logger to remotely access Susan's system and gathers her personal details. He uses these details to create an account impersonating Susan on a social network site. What type of attack(s) did the attacker use?

4. A user forwards an email with attachments to other users in the organization. The email states that a person is in dire need of help and to please forward the email to others immediately. It causes a virus to spread within the organization. What type of attack(s) did the attacker use?

5. **An attacker scans your network and finds Port 21 open. She then retrieves a user name and password for your server. After logging on, she creates an account with administrative privileges. Later, she logs on with this account and steals data. What type of attack(s) did the attacker use?**

Lesson 3 Lab 1
Securing Network Traffic

Activity Time: 45 minutes

 You can find a suggested solution for this activity (Lesson 3 Lab Solution.htm) in the Solutions folder in the student data files location.

 The lab setup instructions are available on the CD-ROM and in the Lab Setup folder in the student data files location.

Setup:
You have two Microsoft® Windows Server® 2008 R2 computers available, named BankServer1 and BankServer2. Both are members of the same domain.

Scenario:
You are a network administrator of a newly started bank. With new branches of the bank coming up in major cities, you are asked to implement several simple network protocols to enable multi-level communications within the organization. Also, you are asked to secure the network traffic between computers in the network.

1. Verify network connectivity between the two computers, and verify that you can access resources between the two systems.

2. On both BankServer1 and BankServer2, create a custom Microsoft Management Console (MMC) console containing **IP Security Policy Management** and **IP Security Monitor.**

3. Modify the appropriate IP Security (IPSec) policy for your computer to use a pre-shared key of *!NewKey!*

4. Assign the policy to your domain.

5. Start the IPSec service and test the connection between the servers.

Lesson 4 Lab 1
Implementing Firewall Rules Using a Host Firewall

Activity Time: 45 minutes

 You can find a suggested solution for this activity (Lesson 4 Lab 1 Solution.htm) in the Solutions folder in the student data files location.

 The lab setup instructions are available on the CD-ROM and in the Lab Setup folder in the student data files location.

Setup:
You have two Microsoft® Windows Server® 2008 R2 computers available. Both are members of the same domain.

Scenario:
You are the security administrator of a regional bank. While monitoring the server logs, you noticed that there are attempts to connect to the server using common networking tools. Because you find this to be a potential threat that can reveal server details, you decide to block those connectivity attempts on the server.

1. On the system designated as the client, check network connectivity to the server using the **ping** command.

2. On the system designated as the server, create a custom inbound rule to block the Internet Control Message Protocol (ICMP) version 4 (ICMPv4) service.

3. On the system designated as the client, recheck the network connectivity to the server using the **ping** command.

Lesson 4 Lab 2

Configuring the Mozilla® Firefox® Web Browser

Activity Time: 20 minutes

 You can find a suggested solution for this activity (Lesson 4 Lab 2 Solution.htm) in the Solutions folder in the student data files location.

Data Files:

FirefoxSecurity.rtf

Setup:

To set up for this lab, download and install Mozilla® Firefox® on any Windows-based system.

Scenario:

You are the security administrator for AFR Travel, and you have secured your new Microsoft® Windows Server® 2008 R2 computers and the systems have been operational for the past week. As per the company standard, you have installed Mozilla® Firefox®. You need to configure Mozilla Firefox to ensure that the likelihood of attack is kept to the minimum.

The IT department has designed a security deployment plan for Mozilla Firefox users. The new policy is documented as FirefoxSecurity.rtf. This configuration needs to be set up manually on a test system to verify that clients will still have the appropriate level of web access after security is deployed.

1. Allow cookies only from specific sites.

2. Set the master password.

3. Enable warning messages.

4. Enable the Online Certificate Status Protocol (OCSP) server connection validation.

Lesson 5 Lab 1
Managing Accounts

Activity Time: 45 minutes

 You can find a suggested solution for this activity (Lesson 5 Lab Solution.htm) in the Solutions folder in the student data files location.

 The lab setup instructions are available on the CD-ROM and in the LessonLabSetup folder in the student data files location.

Scenario:

Following a security breach in one of the bank branches, the security administration team has decided to tighten up security in account settings. You have been asked to create a group policy to enforce account management principles.

1.   Create a new group policy by the name **BankPolicy** and link it to the domain.

2.   Enforce strong password rules such as:
   ● Password history
   ● Password length
   ● Password age
   ● Password complexity

3.   Set the account lockout duration to 10 minutes.

4.   Set the account lockout threshold to three invalid logon attempts.

5.   Update the policy.

6.   Create a user account and verify whether the policy has taken effect.

Lesson 6 Lab 1

Managing and Using Certificates

Activity Time: 60 minutes

 You can find a suggested solution for this activity (Lesson 6 Lab Solution.htm) in the Solutions folder in the student data files location.

 The lab setup instructions are available on the CD-ROM and in the LessonLabSetup folder in the student data files location.

Scenario:

You are the security administrator for a bank. The bank is preparing to implement a plan to use certificates to secure its email communications, especially for its remote laptop users. So far, you have installed the standalone root Certificate Authority (CA) called for in the bank's Public Key Infrastructure (PKI) migration plan. Now, you need to test user certificate enrollment before the email administrators begin relying on certificates for email security. You also need to verify that users can back up their individual private keys and that the backup procedure is successful. Once you are done testing and verifying, you can revoke your test certificate and publish the Certificate Revocation List (CRL). The planning document calls for daily updates to the CRL.

1. Install the standalone root CA on BankServer1.

2. Configure Active Directory so that authenticated users have permissions to enroll certificates using the **User** template.

3. Create a file-based request for a new web server certificate from your CA and submit the request.

4. Issue the requested server certificate.

5. Bind the secure protocol to the default website.

6. Enable secure communication for the certificate server website.

7. Request an email certificate for your user account.

8. Issue the pending request.

9. Install the new certificate.

10. Revoke the certificate, change the CRL publishing interval, and publish the CRL.

Lesson 7 Lab 1

Implementing a Physical Security Policy for an Organization

Activity Time: 20 minutes

Data Files:

InfiniTradeSecurityPolicy.rtf

Scenario:

As the security administrator for your organization, which is located in London, you have been assigned the task of implementing a security policy. You are basing your policy, InfiniTradeSecurityPolicy.rtf, on a sample template. Currently, the top priority at your organization is physical security, as someone recently broke into company headquarters and stole hardware and data. You need to protect over £100,000 worth of new equipment that is now centrally stored in your computing center. At the minimum, you will be implementing the following security measures in the computing center:

1. Locks will be placed on computer room doors.

2. Blinds will be installed on windows.

3. No computers will be placed by windows.

4. Locks will be placed on windows.

5. Motion-detection and perimeter intruder alarms will be installed.

6. All contractors will be escorted in and out of the facility.

You need to determine what other security recommendations in the InfiniTradeSecurityPolicy.rtf document your organization should adopt and you need to enforce the policy once it is finalized.

1. **Which security level does your organization fall under? Why?**

2. Besides using blinds and locks on the windows, what else could you recommend using to secure the windows from unauthorized access?

3. Once the motion-detection alarms are installed, what procedure will you need to follow to verify they are working properly?

4. Given the security requirements of this company and the category of risk the computing center falls into, what other physical security recommendations could you make, based on this document?

Lesson 8 Lab 1
Researching Internet Security Resources

Activity Time: 30 minutes

To complete this activity, you will need a computer with a web browser and a connection to the Internet.

Scenario:

You have recently been hired to assist the security administrator at a large university. To bring yourself up to speed on the issues, tools, and information you will need in your new job role, you plan to spend some time researching current security information and resources that are available on the Internet.

1. Open your web browser and connect to the Internet search site of your choice.

2. Search for articles and information related to risk analysis and assessment tools and techniques. Explore the content on some of the sites you find.

3. Search for articles, utilities, and information related to vulnerability assessment tools and techniques. Explore the content on some of the sites you find.

4. Search for articles, utilities, and information related to vulnerability scanning. Explore the content on some of the sites you find.

5. Search for articles, utilities, and information related to vulnerability and risk mitigation. Explore the content on some of the sites you find.

6. Search for any other security-related topics that interest you, or scan recent news items on websites such as **www.zone-h.org** or **www.securityfocus.com**.

Lesson 9 Lab 1
Researching Security Incidents

Activity Time: 30 minutes

Scenario:

In this activity, you will research real-world security incidents and compare them to possible incidents within your own company or organization.

1. Open your web browser and connect to the Internet search site of your choice.

2. Search for **database hacked.** Explore the content on some of the sites you find. Compare the types of data stolen to the types of data that your company stores that involves information on its employees, clients, or partners.

3. Search for **credit card numbers stolen.** Explore the content on some of the sites you find. Compare some of the information you find to the financial risk at your company.

4. Search for **server hacked.** Explore the content on some of the sites you find. Compare the methods of attack that characterize each of the incidents, particularly the complexity of the hack.

5. Search for **Windows vulnerabilities.** Explore the content on some of the sites you find. Are the vulnerabilities that you found unique to a certain kind of server, such as a file server, or a database server?

6. Search for **Unix vulnerabilities.** Explore the content on some of the sites you find. Are the vulnerabilities that you found unique to a certain kind of server, such as a file server, or a database server?

7. Search for **IT disaster.** Explore the content on some of the sites you find. Compare some of the fallout from natural disasters to the types of disasters that are likely in your company's region.

8. Search for **downtime damage.** Explore the content on some of the sites you find. What kind of business would be halted or hindered if your company had a comparable amount of downtime?

9. What are some other specific search terms you can think of that will provide information on IT security incidents? Feel free to research those terms and determine if the resulting information will have relevance to the security requirements in your organization.

Lesson 10 Lab 1

Researching Business Continuity and Disaster Recovery

Activity Time: 30 minutes

Scenario:

You are the information security officer and your organization needs your help in reviewing and implementing business continuity and disaster recovery. You will research business continuity plans (BCPs) and a disaster recover plans (DRPs) and compare them to the existing plans within your own company or organization so that you can improve the plans already in place.

1. Open your web browser and connect to the Internet search site of your choice.

2. Search for **business continuity plans** and **business continuity testing methods.** Explore the content on some of the sites you find. Compare these findings to the plans in place in your organizations, if you are familiar with them, or to the needs your organization might have.

3. Search for **business impact analysis.** Explore the content on some of the sites you find. Compare these findings to the business impact analysis (BIA) procedures in place in your organization, if you are aware of them. Suggest ways to improve them, or suggest how BIA should be approached in your organization.

4. Search for **continuity of operations plans.** Explore the content on some of the sites you find. Compare these findings to the continuity of operations plan in place in your organization, if you have one, and suggest ways to improve the plan. Or, consider what your organization's plan should include.

5. Search for **disaster recovery plans** and **disaster recovery plan testing.** Explore the content on some of the sites you find. Compare these findings to your organization's plan and suggest what your organization's plan should include.

6. Search for **IT contingency plans** and **succession planning.** Explore the content on some of the sites you find. Compare these findings to the plans in place in your organization, if you are aware of them. Suggest ways to improve your organization's plans or ways IT contingency or succession planning should be approached.

7. Search for **fault tolerance** and **redundancy measures.** Explore the content on some of the sites you find. Compare these findings to the fault tolerance systems and redundancy measures already in place in your organization, if you are aware of them. Suggest ways to improve fault tolerance and redundancy measures or ways these measures should be approached.

8. Search for **alternate sites.** Explore the content on some of the sites you find. What kind of site would best suit your organization? A cold site, warm site, or hot site? Are there different functions within your organization with different needs?

9. What are some other specific search terms you can think of that will provide assistance with implementing BCPs and DRPs? Feel free to research those terms and determine if the resulting information will have relevance to the planning requirements in your organization.

Solutions

Lesson 1

Activity 1-1

1. **As an information security officer, what are the information security goals that you need to keep in mind while defining the protection you will need? (Select all that apply.)**

   ✓ a) Prevention

      b) Auditing

   ✓ c) Recovery

   ✓ d) Detection

2. **What are applicable forms of vulnerabilities? (Select all that apply.)**

   ✓ a) Improperly configured software

   ✓ b) Misuse of communication protocols

   ✓ c) Damage to hardware

      d) Lengthy passwords with a mix of characters

3. **Match each fundamental security concept with its corresponding description.**

d	Vulnerability	a.	Exposure to the chance of damage or loss.
e	Threat	b.	An event where an attacker has access to your computer system without authorization.
a	Risk	c.	A countermeasure that you need to put in place to avoid, mitigate, or counteract a security risks due to a threat or attack.
c	Control	d.	A condition that leaves a system open to attack.
b	Intrusion	e.	An event or action that could potentially result in the violation of a security requirement.

4. **Match each security description(s) to its security management process.**

_b_	Select the appropriate method to protect systems.	a.	Implementation
_a_	Install the selected control mechanism.	b.	Identification
_c_	Analyze important steps that improve the performance of controls.	c.	Monitoring

5. **Detail the differences between a threat, vulnerability, and risk.**

   Answers will vary, but may include: A threat is any potential violation of security policies or procedures. A vulnerability is any condition that leaves a system open to attack. A risk is an exposure to the chance of damage or loss, and signifies the likelihood of a hazard or dangerous threat.

Activity 1-2

1. **The three most fundamental goals of computer security are: (Select all that apply.)**

   ✓ a) Confidentiality

   b) Auditing

   ✓ c) Integrity

   d) Privilege management

   ✓ e) Availability

2. **A biometric handprint scanner is used as part of a system for granting access to a facility. Once an identity is verified, the system checks and confirms that the user is allowed to leave the lobby and enter the facility, and the electronic door lock is released. This is an example of which of the Four As? (Select all that apply.)**

   ✓ a) Authentication

   ✓ b) Authorization

   ✓ c) Access control

   d) Auditing

3. **Katie's handprint is matched against a record in the system that indicates that she has been assigned clearance to view the contents of secret documents. Later, at her desk, she tries to connect to a folder that is marked Top Secret, and access is denied. This is an example of:**

   ✓ a) MAC.

   b) DAC.

   c) RBAC.

   d) Rule-based access control.

4. **At the end of the day, security personnel can view electronic log files that record the identities of everyone who entered and exited the building along with the time of day. This is an example of:**

    a) Authentication.

    b) Authorization.

    c) Access control.

  ✓ d) Auditing.

5. **An administrator of a large multinational company has the ability to assign object access rights and track users' resource access from a central administrative console. Users throughout the organization can gain access to any system after providing a single user name and password. This is an example of:**

    a) Auditing.

    b) Security labels.

  ✓ c) Privilege management.

    d) Confidentiality.

6. **Match the access control principle to its definition.**

b	Implicit deny	a.	No one person should have too much power or responsibility.
c	Least privilege	b.	Everything that is not explicitly allowed is denied.
a	Separation of duties	c.	Users and software should only have the minimal level of access that is necessary for them to perform the duties required of them.
d	Job rotation	d.	No one person stays in a vital job role for too long a time period.

7. **Match each security control with its description.**

a	Authentication	a.	Validating an individual's credentials.
c	Authorization	b.	Tracking system events.
d	Access control	c.	Determining rights and privileges for an individual.
b	Auditing	d.	Assigning rights and privileges on objects.

Activity 1-3

1. **Brian works at a bank. To access his laptop, he inserts his employee ID card into a special card reader. This is an example of:**

    a) User name/password authentication.

    b) Biometrics.

  ✓ c) Token-based authentication.

    d) Mutual authentication.

2. **To access the server room, Brian places his index finger on a fingerprint reader. This is an example of:**

   a) Password authentication.

   b) Token-based authentication.

   ✓ c) Biometric authentication.

   d) Multi-factor authentication.

3. **To withdraw money from an automatic teller machine, Nancy inserts a card and types a four-digit PIN. This incorporates what types of authentication? (Select all that apply.)**

   ✓ a) Token-based

   ✓ b) Password

   c) Biometrics

   ✓ d) Multi-factor

   e) Mutual

4. **What is the best example of token-based authentication?**

   a) It relies on typing a code.

   b) It relies on a card and a PIN.

   c) It relies on a user's physical characteristics.

   ✓ d) It relies on a card being inserted into a card reader.

5. **True or False? Mutual authentication protects clients from submitting confidential information to an insecure server.**

   ✓ True

   ___ False

6. **Match each authentication method with its description.**

_b_	Mutual authentication	a.	A security mechanism where a user's credentials are compared against credentials stored on a database.
_a_	User name/password authentication	b.	A security mechanism that requires that each party in a communication verify its identity.
_d_	Biometric authentication	c.	An object that stores authentication information.
_c_	Token	d.	Authentication based on physical characteristics.

7. **How does multi-factor authentication enhance security?**

   Because the attacker must obtain at least two authentication factors, not just one, in order to breach the system. This can be particularly difficult with biometrics, or "who you are" authentication, where at least one of the factors is a unique physical characteristic of an individual.

Activity 1-4

1. **Match each symmetric encryption algorithm with the correct description.**

_c_	DES	a.	A symmetric encryption algorithm that encrypts data by processing each block of data three times using a different key each time.
_a_	3DES	b.	A series of algorithms all containing variable key lengths.
_f_	AES	c.	A block-cipher symmetric encryption algorithm that encrypts data in 64-bit blocks using a 56-bit key with 8 bits used for parity.
_b_	RC 4, 5, and 6	d.	A freely available 64-bit block cipher algorithm that uses a variable key length.
_e_	Twofish	e.	A symmetric key block cipher that uses a pre-computed encrypted algorithm called an S-box.
_d_	Blowfish	f.	A symmetric 128-, 192-, or 256-bit block cipher developed by Belgian cryptographers Joan Daemen and Vincent Rijmen and adopted by the U.S. government as its encryption standard to replace DES.

2. Which algorithm is a hashing encryption algorithm?

✓ a) SHA

   b) AES

   c) RSA

   d) 3DES

3. Which of the following is a specific set of actions used to encrypt data?

   a) Steganography

   b) Key

✓ c) Cipher

   d) Digital signature

4. Match each asymmetric encryption algorithm with the correct description.

_c_	RSA	a.	A cryptographic protocol that provides for secure key exchange and formed the basis for most later public key implementations.
_a_	Diffie-Hellman	b.	A public key encryption algorithm named for its developer that is based on Diffie-Hellman.
_b_	Elgamal	c.	The first successful algorithm for asymmetric encryption. It has a variable key length and block size and is still widely used.
_d_	Elliptic curve cryptography	d.	A public key encryption technique that leverages the algebraic structures of elliptic curves over finite fields.

5. **True or False? A digital signature is an application of hashing encryption, because the signature is never transformed back to cleartext.**

   ✓ True

   ___ False

6. **What are the distinctions between an encryption algorithm and a key?**

   The encryption algorithm is the general rule or instruction set applied to the data to transform it to ciphertext. The key is the actual value used by the algorithm. A different key value results in different ciphertext, although the basic encryption process is the same.

7. **What is a potential drawback of symmetric encryption?**

   The need to share the key between the two parties creates the potential for key compromise or loss.

8. **What makes public key encryption potentially so secure?**

   The keys are not shared between the parties.

9. **Considering that hashing encryption is one-way and the hash is never decrypted, what makes hashing encryption a useful security technique?**

   Because two parties can hash the same data and compare hashes to see if they match, hashing can be used for data verification in a variety of situations, including password authentication. Hashes of passwords can be sent between the two parties rather than the passwords themselves. A hash of a file or a hash code in an electronic message can be verified by both parties after information transfer.

Activity 1-5

1. **Open and review the policy file. What type of policy document is this?**

   a) Acceptable use policy

   b) Audit policy

   c) Extranet policy

   ✓ d) Password policy

   e) Wireless standards policy

2. **Which standard policy components are included in this policy? (Select all that apply.)**

   ✓ a) Policy statement

   ✓ b) Standards

   ✓ c) Guidelines

   d) Procedures

3. **How often must system-level administrators change their passwords to conform to this policy?**

   The password policy states that administrator passwords should be changed monthly to remain secure.

4. **To conform to this policy, how often must regular system users change their passwords?**

   The password policy states that regular system users should change their passwords every three months to stay secure.

5. **According to this policy, what is the minimum character length for a password and how should it be constructed?**

   Eight characters is the minimum length for security purposes and you should try and include numbers and special characters to make it more secure.

6. **Why is "password1" not a good choice for a password?**

   It contains a common usage word that is also found in dictionaries.

Lesson 2

Activity 2-1

1. **Social engineering attempt or false alarm? A supposed customer calls the help desk and states that she cannot connect to the e-commerce website to check her order status. She would also like a user name and password. The user gives a valid customer company name, but is not listed as a contact in the customer database. The user does not know the correct company code or customer ID.**

   ✓ Social engineering attempt

   ___ False alarm

2. **Social engineering attempt or false alarm? The VP of sales is in the middle of a presentation to a group of key customers and accidentally logs off. She urgently needs to continue with the presentation, but forgets her password. You recognize her voice on the line, but she is supposed to have her boss make the request according to the company password security policy.**

   ___ Social engineering attempt

   ✓ False alarm

3. **Social engineering attempt or false alarm? A new accountant was hired and would like to know if he can have the installation source files for the accounting software package, so that he can install it on his computer himself and start work immediately. Last year, someone internal compromised company accounting records, so distribution of the accounting application is tightly controlled. You have received all the proper documentation for the request from his supervisor and there is an available license for the software. However, general IT policies state that the IT department must perform all software installations and upgrades.**

   ___ Social engineering attempt

   ✓ False alarm

4. **Social engineering attempt or false alarm? Christine receives an instant message asking for her account name and password. The person sending the message says that the request is from the IT department, because they need to do a backup of Christine's local hard drive.**

   ✓ Social engineering attempt

   __ False alarm

5. **Social engineering attempt or false alarm? Rachel gets an email with an attachment that is named NewVirusDefinitions.vbs. The name in the email is the same as the IT software manager, but the email address is from an account outside the company.**

   ✓ Social engineering attempt

   __ False alarm

6. **Social engineering attempt or false alarm? A user calls the help desk stating that he is a phone technician needing the password to configure the phone and voice-mail system.**

   ✓ Social engineering attempt

   __ False alarm

7. **Social engineering attempt or false alarm? A vendor team requests access to the building to fix an urgent problem with a piece of equipment. Although the team has no work order and the security guard was not notified of the visit, the team members are wearing shirts and hats from the preferred vendor.**

   ✓ Social engineering attempt

   __ False alarm

8. **Social engineering attempt or false alarm? The CEO of the organization needs to get access to market research data immediately. You definitely recognize her voice, but a proper request form has not been filled out to modify the permissions. She states that normally she would fill out the form and should not be an exception, but she urgently needs the data.**

   __ Social engineering attempt

   ✓ False alarm

9. **Social engineering attempt or false alarm? A purchasing manager is browsing a list of products on a vendor's website when a window opens claiming that software has detected several thousand files on his computer that are infected with viruses. Instructions in the official-looking window indicate the user should click a link to install software that will remove these infections.**

   ✓ Social engineering attempt

   __ False alarm

Activity 2-2

1. **A disgruntled employee removes the UPS on a critical server system and then cuts power to the system, causing costly downtime. This physical threat is a(n): (Select all that apply.)**

    ✓ a) Internal threat.

    b) External threat.

    ✓ c) Man-made threat.

    d) False alarm.

2. **A power failure has occurred due to a tree branch falling on a power line outside your facility, and there is no UPS, or a generator. This physical threat is a(n):**

    a) Internal threat.

    ✓ b) External threat.

    c) Man-made threat.

    d) False alarm.

3. **A backhoe operator on a nearby construction site has accidently dug up fiber optic cables, thus disabling remote network access. This physical threat is a(n): (Select all that apply.)**

    a) Internal threat.

    ✓ b) External threat.

    ✓ c) Man-made threat.

    d) False alarm.

4. **While entering the building through the rear security door, an employee realizes he has left his car keys in his car door lock. He has already swiped his badge to open the door, so he props it open with his briefcase while he returns to his car to retrieve his keys. He has the door in view at all times and no one else enters while the door is propped open. He locks the door behind him once he is in the building. This is a(n):**

    a) Internal attack.

    b) External attack.

    c) Man-made attack.

    ✓ d) False alarm.

Activity 2-3

1. **While you are connected to another host on your network, the connection is suddenly dropped. When you review the logs at the other host, it appears as if the connection is still active. This could be a(n):**

    a) IP spoofing attack.

    b) Replay attack.

    c) Man-in-the-middle attack.

    ✓ d) Session hijacking attack.

2. **Your e-commerce web server is getting extremely slow. Customers are calling stating that it is taking a long time to place an order on your site. This could be a(n):**

   a) DNS poisoning attack.

   ✓ b) DoS attack.

   c) Backdoor attack.

   d) ARP poisoning attack.

3. **Tina, the network analysis guru in your organization, analyzes a network trace capture file and discovers that packets have been intercepted and retransmitted to both a sender and a receiver during an active session. This could be a(n):**

   a) IP spoofing attack.

   b) Session hijacking attack.

   c) Replay attack.

   ✓ d) Man-in-the-middle attack.

4. **Your intranet webmaster, Tim, has noticed an entry in a log file from an IP address that is within the range of addresses used on your network. But, Tim does not recognize the computer name as valid. Your network administrator, Deb, checks the DHCP server and finds out that the IP address is not similar to any in their list of IP addresses in that particular domain. This could be a(n):**

   ✓ a) IP spoofing attack.

   b) Replay attack.

   c) Man-in-the-middle attack.

   d) Session hijacking attack.

5. **Match the network-based attack with the corresponding description.**

_e_	Social network attack	a.	An attack that is launched by malware propagating through peer-to-peer networks.
_a_	P2P attack	b.	A network attack where an attacker inserts himself between two hosts to gain access to their data transmissions.
_c_	Eavesdropping attack	c.	An attack that uses special monitoring software to gain access to private network communications to steal the content of the communication.
_b_	Man-in-the-middle attack	d.	A network attack where an attacker captures network traffic and stores it for retransmitting at a later time.
_d_	Replay attack	e.	An attack that is targeted towards popular websites and services like Facebook, Twitter, and MySpace.

6. **True or False? A DNS poisoning attack can be used to cause a DoS condition.**

   ✓ True

   ___ False

Activity 2-4

1. **John is given a laptop for official use and is on a business trip. When he arrives at his hotel, he turns on his laptop and finds a wireless access point with the name of the hotel, which he connects to for sending official communications. He may become a victim of which wireless threat?**

    a) Interference

    b) War driving

    c) Bluesnarfing

    ✓ d) Rogue access point

2. **A new administrator in your company is in the process of installing a new wireless device. He is called away to attend an urgent meeting before he can secure the wireless network, and without realizing it, he forgot to switch the device off. A person with a mobile device who is passing the building takes advantage of the open network and hacks the network. Your company may become vulnerable to which type of wireless threat?**

    a) Interference

    ✓ b) War driving

    c) Bluesnarfing

    d) Rogue access point

3. **Every time Margaret decided to work at home, she would get frustrated with the poor wireless connection. But when she gets to her office, the wireless connection seems normal. What might have been one of the factors affecting Margaret's wireless connection when she worked at home?**

    a) Bluesnarfing

    ✓ b) Interference

    c) IV attack

    d) Evil twins attack

4. **Chuck, a sales executive, is attending meetings at a professional conference that is also being attended by representatives of other companies in his field. At the conference, he uses his smartphone with a Bluetooth headset to stay in touch with clients. A few days after the conference, he finds that competitors' sales representatives are getting in touch with his key contacts and influencing them by revealing what he thought was private information from his email and calendar. Chuck is a victim of which wireless threat?**

    a) Packet sniffing

    b) Bluejacking

    ✓ c) Bluesnarfing

    d) Rogue access point

5. **Match the wireless threat with its description.**

_e_	Interference	a.	A threat where a rogue access point in a public access location has been configured so that it appears to be genuine.
_a_	Evil twins	b.	A threat where the attacker sends out unwanted signals from a mobile device with unsolicited content.
_d_	War chalking	c.	A threat where an attacker captures data and registers data flows to analyze what data is contained in a packet.
_c_	Packet sniffing	d.	A threat where symbols are used to mark off a sidewalk or wall to indicate that there is an open wireless network which may be offering Internet access.
_b_	Bluejacking	e.	A threat where the wireless signal is jammed due to other wireless signals operating in the area.

Activity 2-5

1. **Kim, a help desk staffer, gets a phone call from Alex in human resources stating that he cannot log on. Kim looks up the account information for Alex and sees that the account is locked. This is the third time the account has locked this week. Alex insists that he was typing in his password correctly. Kim notices that the account was locked at 6 A.M.; Alex says he was in a meeting at a client's site until 10 A.M. today. This could be a(n):**

   ✓ a) Password attack.

   b) Backdoor attack.

   c) Malicious code attack.

   d) Application attack.

2. **Which of the following is the best example of a malicious code attack?**

   a) Your password has been changed without your knowledge.

   ✓ b) Your antivirus software has detected the Stuxnet worm.

   c) Your software keeps coming up with errors every time you click the Menu button.

   d) In a system audit, you notice a foreign system accessing your files on a daily basis without proper permissions.

3. **Which are the traits of a backdoor attack? (Select all that apply.)**

   ✓ a) It can be the first step in a takeover attack which completely controls a system.

   b) It typically generates unsolicited pop-up advertisements, counterfeit virus scans, or software update notifications.

   ✓ c) A backdoor attack is typically delivered through the use of a Trojan horse or other malware.

   ✓ d) It is a mechanism for gaining access to a computer that bypasses or subverts the normal methods of authentication.

4. **Match the following malicious code types with their descriptions.**

_b_	Virus	a.	A piece of code that spreads from one computer to another on its own, not by attaching itself to another file.
_a_	Worm	b.	A sample of code that spreads from one computer to another by attaching itself to other files.
_d_	Logic bomb	c.	Software that is intended to take full or partial control of a system at the lowest levels.
_c_	Rootkit	d.	A piece of code that sits dormant on a target computer until it is triggered by the occurrence of specific conditions, such as a specific date and time.

5. **Match the following application attacks to their descriptions.**

_d_	Cross-site scripting	a.	An attack where the attacker manipulates the information that is passed between web servers and clients in HTTP requests.
_c_	LDAP injection	b.	An attack that submits invalid query data to a database server by accessing the client side of the application.
_b_	SQL injection	c.	An attack that targets web-based applications by fabricating directory service statements that depend on user input.
_a_	Header manipulation	d.	An attack that is directed towards sites with dynamic content by introducing malicious scripts or by taking over the session before the user session cookies expire.

Lesson 2 Follow-up

Lesson 2 Lab 1

1. **A help desk representative in your organization sniffs the network for user accounts and passwords. She then changes the passwords and this leaves a user unable to connect to the system to access any service. What type of attack(s) did the attacker use?**

   Eavesdropping and Denial of Service (DoS) attacks.

2. **The help desk receives a call from someone claiming to be a support person asking for the fully qualified domain name (FQDN) and IP address of the web server in your organization. A short while later, no one on the Internet can get to your web server because the performance has suddenly dropped. What type of attack(s) did the attacker use?**

   Social engineering and Denial of Service (DoS) or Distributed Denial of Service (DDoS) attacks.

3. The HR manager, Susan Brown, requests IT support to fix an issue on her system. The IT support person fixes the issue and also installs a key logger application on the system without Susan's knowledge. Later, he uses the information from the logger to remotely access Susan's system and gathers her personal details. He uses these details to create an account impersonating Susan on a social network site. What type of attack(s) did the attacker use?

Social network attack and a possible backdoor attack.

4. A user forwards an email with attachments to other users in the organization. The email states that a person is in dire need of help and to please forward the email to others immediately. It causes a virus to spread within the organization. What type of attack(s) did the attacker use?

Malicious code and social engineering attacks.

5. An attacker scans your network and finds Port 21 open. She then retrieves a user name and password for your server. After logging on, she creates an account with administrative privileges. Later, she logs on with this account and steals data. What type of attack(s) did the attacker use?

Port scanning, eavesdropping, and backdoor attacks.

Lesson 3

Activity 3-1

1. What is the correct description for each network technology?

f	Router	a.	Has multiple network ports and combines multiple physical network segments into a single logical network.
a	Switch	b.	Protects a system or network by blocking unwanted network traffic.
c	Proxy server	c.	Can isolate internal networks from the Internet by downloading and storing Internet files on behalf of internal clients.
b	Firewall	d.	Spreads out the work among the devices in a network.
d	Load balancer	e.	Contains firewall, intrusion prevention, load balancing, filtering, and reporting functionalities.
e	All-in-one security appliance	f.	Connects multiple networks that use the same protocol.

2. Which technology is only used for monitoring and capturing the content of data communications on a network?

a) IDS

b) NIPS

c) Spam filter

✓ d) Sniffer

3. **What is the difference between a host-based, network-based, and web application-based firewall?**

   Host-based firewalls are used to protect a single computer, while network-based firewalls are installed to protect all the computers on a network. Web application-based firewalls are implemented to secure a single application.

4. **Your organization is in the process of implementing security controls throughout the corporate network. A security device is needed to actively scan and monitor network activity and then alert and block any access that is suspicious. What device is the best option in this scenario?**

   a) IDS

   ✓ b) NIPS

   c) Sniffer

   d) Spam filter

Activity 3-2

1. **What is the role of NAT on a network?**

   You use network address translation (NAT) to conceal your internal network's IP addressing scheme from the public Internet. To do so, you configure a router with a single public IP address on its interface that connects to the Internet. Then, you configure the router's second interface with a private, non-routable IP address. NAT then translates between the public and private IP addressing schemes.

2. **Which telephony technology allows telephone, email, fax, web, and computer actions to be integrated to work together?**

   a) PBX

   b) VoIP

   ✓ c) CTI

   d) NAT

3. **What is the correct cloud computing service type for each description?**

b	Software	a. An organization uses the cloud to provide Microsoft® Windows® 7 access to all their employees.
a	Platform	b. An organization uses the cloud to provide photo editing applications to their employees.
c	Infrastructure	c. An organization uses the cloud to provide access to data center functionalities.

4. **Your organization is in the testing phase of a new accounting application and needs to verify its functionality on various operating systems before deploying it to customers, but is dealing with hardware availability issues. What network design component would you suggest in this scenario?**

   Answers may vary, but should include virtualization technology. This option allows you to install a number of operating system versions on the same computer.

Lesson 4

Activity 4-2

6. **According to general system hardening guidelines, what additional software should you install to combat malware on all systems?**

   a) Security Configuration Wizard

   ✓ b) Antivirus software

   c) A firewall

   d) Database software

Activity 4-5

1. **Why should organizations invest in data security?**

   Implementing proper data security throughout an organization will not only protect the organization's sensitive data from being stolen, but will protect an employee's personal information from unauthorized access. Data cannot be bought back.

2. **What is the correct description for each hardware-based encryption device?**

_c_	TPM	a.	Cryptoprocessor device that can be attached to servers and computers to provide digital key security.
_a_	HSM	b.	Encryption that can be implemented specifically to provide additional security for removable data storage.
_b_	USB	c.	A specification that includes the use of cryptoprocessors to create a secure computing environment.
_d_	Hard drive	d.	Encryption that is applied to protect every bit of data stored in the disk.

3. **What data encryption method should you implement when you need to send data for the company's annual earnings report as an attachment in an email from your mobile device to the board of directors of your organization?**

   a) Database encryption

   ✓ b) Email encryption

   c) Mobile device encryption

   d) Full disk encryption

4. **How can data leakage affect your organization, and how could it be prevented?**

   Data leakage occurs unintentionally through normal user activities without the users knowing they are compromising the security of data. Because of this, it is crucial for organizations to ensure that users are aware of what data leakage is, and how they can better prevent it from happening.

Activity 4-6

1. **What are some of the security concerns you have about the common mobile devices you use or support?**

   Concerns will vary, but may include mobile devices that are lost or stolen are at greater risk to be used in a malicious way to gain unauthorized access; the use of personal mobile devices when accessing and sending company email, servers, or services; some mobile devices may not be equipped with the right level of security features or encryption functionality needed to ensure the right level of security.

2. **Your organization requires that you ensure your BlackBerry is secured from unauthorized access in case it is lost or stolen. To prevent someone from accessing data on the device immediately after it has been turned on, what security control should be used?**

   a) GPS tracking

   b) Device encryption

   ✓ c) Screen lock

   d) Sanitization

3. **How can the use of mobile devices by employees affect the security of an organization?**

   Mobile devices can function much like a regular computer, therefore, when they are used to send and receive corporate emails, and to access systems and data within the corporate network, they are a vulnerability. If lost or stolen, the devices can be used to access sensitive data or launch attacks. Mobile devices should be secured just as any other system on the corporate network.

Lesson 6

Activity 6-4

5. **Why did the connection fail?**

   ✓ a) Because the server now requires secure communications

   b) Because you typed an invalid URL

   c) Because you did not log on

   d) Because the certificate has expired

6. **How can you connect successfully?**

   a) By using the SFTP protocol.

   ✓ b) By using the HTTPS protocol.

   c) By using a certificate to authenticate the user.

   d) By logging on as a different user.

Activity 6-7

2. **When will clients know that the certificate has been revoked?**
    - a) When the certificate expires
    - b) When they connect to the website
    - ✓ c) When the CRL is published
    - d) When the client requests a new certificate

3. **If an attacker maliciously revokes certificates, how could they be recovered?**
    - a) By renewing the CA certificates
    - b) By republishing the CRL
    - c) By reissuing the certificates
    - ✓ d) By restoring the CA from a backup

Activity 6-9

7. **What should you do with the removable backup media?**
    - a) Store it in the server room with the CA.
    - ✓ b) Store it in a separate secure location.
    - c) Leave it in the drive for convenient access.

Lesson 7

Activity 7-1

1. **What types of physical security controls would you suggest for the main server room?**

    Answers will vary, but should be focused on access controls surrounding the room such as door locks with identification systems, surveillance systems, and possibly an alarm system.

2. **What are some common environmental exposures that InfiniTrade may consider when evaluating the overall security of its new building?**

    Answers will vary depending on the specific environment a building is in, but common exposures could include water damage and flooding, power failures and flooding, and fires.

3. **What type of environmental controls should InfiniTrade Financial consider as part of their relocation?**

    Answers will vary, but should include proper fire prevention, detection, and suppression controls. These systems will most likely be standard and will be implemented according to the fire code guidelines set forth by the local fire department, but other special fire suppression systems may be needed to appropriately secure the organization's most sensitive assets, such as any server room and data centers.

Activity 7-2

1. **An employee unintentionally opens an attachment that causes a virus to spread within the organization. Does the policy call for legal action?**

   According to section 4.3, there is no call for legal action against the employee in this situation because the employee was unaware of the virus. However, disciplinary action may be taken to be sure the user understands the "extreme caution" provision in section 4.2. The only legal action that may be considered is against the individual who actually sent the virus.

2. **An employee emails a copy of a new type of encryption software program to a user in a foreign country for testing. Does the policy call for legal action?**

   According to section 4.3, depending on your locality and the destination country, this may be a legal violation of export control laws and legal action might be taken.

3. **An employee scans your network for open ports. Does the policy call for legal action?**

   According to section 4.3, there is no call for legal action in this situation. However, disciplinary action may be taken.

4. **An employee forwards an email that appears to be a Ponzi or Pyramid scheme. Does the policy call for legal action?**

   According to section 4.3, the policy does not call for legal action in this situation. However, disciplinary action may be taken.

5. **Two employees have an argument at lunchtime. During the afternoon, one user sends a threatening email to the other. The second employee is afraid to leave the building unescorted that evening. Does the policy call for legal action?**

   According to section 4.3, hostile or threatening messages could be considered a form of harassment, which could be subject to legal action.

Activity 7-3

1. **A virus has spread throughout your organization, causing expensive system downtime and corrupted data. You find that the virus sent to many users was an email attachment that was forwarded by an employee. The employee that received the original email was fooled into believing the link it contained was a legitimate marketing survey. You quickly determine that this is a well-known email hoax that had already been posted on several hoax-related websites. When questioned, the employee said that he thought it sounded as if it could be legitimate, and he could not see any harm in "just trying it." How could better user training and awareness have helped this situation?**

   If the employees had been aware of the dangers of opening email attachments, and had been more knowledgeable about how to identify email hoaxes, it is unlikely that the virus would have spread as far. If the initial employee, in particular, had been better informed, you might have been able to keep the virus out of your organization altogether.

2. **What specific training steps do you recommend taking in response to this incident?**

   Because this was a widespread incident, your response must include better security awareness for all users. You could distribute or prominently post a notice regarding the incident, or review proper guidelines for opening email attachments and for identifying email hoaxes. You could distribute links to common hoax-debunking websites to make it easy for employees to research possible hoaxes. You could also review your new-hire training procedures to be sure they include information on email security.

3. **You come in on a Monday morning to find laptops have been stolen from several employees' desks over the weekend. After reviewing videotapes from the security cameras, you find that as an employee exited the building through the secure rear door on Friday night, she held the door open to admit another individual. You suspect this individual was the thief. When you question the employee, she states that the individual told her that he was a new employee who had not yet received his employee badge, that he only needed to be in the building for a few minutes, and that it would save him some time if she could let him in the back door rather than having to walk around to the receptionist entrance. Your security policy states that no one without identification should be admitted through the security doors at any time, but the employee says she was unaware of this policy. You ask her to locate the security policy documents on the network, and she is unable to do so. How could better user education have helped this situation?**

   Regardless of the specific policy, if the employee had been informed and been made more aware of some common-sense security guidelines, she might have not admitted the stranger without question.

4. **What user training steps do you recommend taking in response to this incident?**

   This seems to be an isolated incident, so you should be sure to address it with the employee in question and the employee's manager, by reviewing all security policies with her and emphasizing the possible consequences of her actions. You should probably also post all security policies and best practices in an easily accessible location on the network and send out a company-wide reminder about them. However, because this employee never even attempted to refer to the policy, the inaccessibility of the policy documents was not a contributing factor in this incident. Finally, you should review your new-hire security training procedures from time to time to be sure they include common-sense tips and guidelines on building security.

5. **One of your competitors has somehow obtained confidential data about your organization. There have been no obvious security breaches or physical break-ins, and you are puzzled as to the source of the leak. You begin to ask questions about any suspicious or unusual employee activity, and you begin to hear stories about a sales representative from out of town who did not have a desk in the office and was sitting down in open cubes and plugging her laptop in to the corporate network. You suspect that the sales representative was really an industrial spy for your competitor. When you ask other employees why they did not ask the sales representative for identification or report the incident to security, the other employees said that, giving their understanding of company policies, they did not see anything unusual or problematic in the situation. You review your security policy documents and, in fact, none of them refer to a situation like this one. How could better user education have helped this situation?**

   In this case, it is not apparent that there were any problems in the education process. Users were aware of the presence of policy documents, but the documents themselves were inadequate because they did not deal with the dangers of this type of situation.

6. **What user training steps do you recommend taking in response to this incident?**

You need to update your network acceptable use policy to make it clear what kind of authorization an individual needs in order to access the corporate network from within the building. You also need to disseminate this new information to all employees. You might want to follow this up in a few weeks or months with a "staged" attack of a similar nature, to see how employees respond.

Lesson 7 Follow-up

Lesson 7 Lab 1

1. **Which security level does your organization fall under? Why?**

According to section 3.2.4 of the policy, the organization is in security level 4, due to the monetary value of the equipment you need to protect in a single location.

2. **Besides using blinds and locks on the windows, what else could you recommend using to secure the windows from unauthorized access?**

According to section 3.3 of the policy, you could install obscurity filming or even metal bars.

3. **Once the motion-detection alarms are installed, what procedure will you need to follow to verify they are working properly?**

According to section 3.3 of the policy, you will need to perform a walktest to verify that the alarms have been installed correctly.

4. **Given the security requirements of this company and the category of risk the computing center falls into, what other physical security recommendations could you make, based on this document?**

Answers may vary; for example, the escorted contractors should give 48 hours of notice on what they will be doing. Computers could be placed at least 5 feet from external windows.

Lesson 8

Activity 8-1

1. **What are some obvious vulnerabilities surrounding the InfiniTrade Financial computer room and what others would you investigate?**

Answers will vary, but the obvious vulnerability is the room's close proximity to the main lobby. Other vulnerabilities you might notice are the type of walls installed around the room. You can verify that they extend from floor to ceiling and that they do not contain large vents that could be used as access points. You might check to see if there are other doors to the room and if they are secured.

2. **Based on the known vulnerabilities for the computer room, what potential threats exist?**

   While there may be many specific risks, the main concern here is that visitors coming and going could easily view the type of physical access control used to get into the computer room. Another potential threat is that visitors could be in a position to see the access code being entered and could use it to gain access themselves.

3. **What do you think the potential impact would be if an unauthorized access attempt was successful?**

   The impact would be large in this case, due to what is stored inside the computer room. Unauthorized users could gain access to the sensitive data stored in the servers and use this against the organization and therefore demolish the organization's credibility.

4. **What risk mitigation strategies would you use in this situation to reduce the risks surrounding the physical access of the computer room?**

   Answers will vary, but may include implementing better security controls, such as operational controls including a computer room security guard.

Lesson 9

Activity 9-1

1. **Based on your own professional or personal experience, what are some examples of typical computer crimes?**

   Unauthorized access to a computer or network

   Distributing illegal information via a computer network

   Stealing classified information stored on a computer

   Social engineering attacks that involve illegal activity

2. **In your own words, why is it important to have an IRP?**

   Answers will vary, but generally, an IRP is important because it will help reduce confusion during a security incident by detailing who should respond to an incident and in what fashion, and it will minimize the impact such an incident will have on an organization.

3. **What do you think are the most important components in an IRP?**

   Answers will vary, but may include the definition of an incident, the classification of the incident's urgency level, and the process flow of the incident response (reporting the incident, determining how to investigate it, and reviewing the effectiveness of the response).

4. **In general, do you think it is important to notify employees of common or minor security incidents? Why or why not?**

   Answers will vary. You should notify the employees when an incident affects safety, workflows, or job responsibilities. It is not recommended or appropriate to advertise or publicize problems outside of need-to-know requirements.

5. Why might you want to alert law enforcement officials of a security incident? Why might you want to notify the media?

Answers will vary, but generally, you would want to notify law enforcement if the incident was serious enough to have a financial impact or other consequence that might warrant a criminal investigation. You might notify the media to warn other companies to protect against a specific type of attack or if the incident had any effects on the organization that might be important to stockholders.

6. If you have Internet access, search for sample IRPs and write down the common guidelines listed in all of them.

Answers will vary, but an IRP will specify who determines and declares if an actual incident has occurred, who should be notified about an incident and when, who will respond to an incident, and guidelines for appropriate response procedures that have been tested.

Activity 9-2

1. This was a weakness in the security of the facility. As an information security professional, why are you involved?

Answers will vary, but some companies make no distinction between the physical infrastructure and IT, especially since the actual security used to maintain a secure building requires implementing and maintaining a network infrastructure. For example, the video surveillance camera that caught images of the trespasser needs a network to send its images to be monitored or stored. Another reason is that the physical network infrastructure or its devices are fairly vulnerable in this case, even if it is not clear what the attacker was doing there, or if the attack happened off-camera. Any recommendations for how the company can recover from this type of attack will likely involve increased technological security or surveillance, both of which will fall into the job duties of an IT security professional.

2. What is the first step you need to take in handling this incident?

The first step would be for you to assess the extent of damage caused. Check if any critical systems were damaged or if network cables were unplugged. If no external damage is visible, then you need to scan the systems to see if any files were deleted or if malware or backdoor programs were installed. After finding any possible damage, you need to calculate the time it will take to repair the damage caused.

3. What are the immediate steps you need to take to recover from any damage?

Answers will vary, but you need to replace hardware if it was damaged or stolen and delete malware that has been injected into systems. Disconnect the affected systems if they are capable of spreading viruses and inform officials of your plans to recover from the incident. When you know that your systems are no longer exposed to any threats, then you can reconnect them back to the servers and restore the necessary back up to continue operations.

4. Should this incident be reported to the entire company?

The company security policy most likely prohibits allowing unauthorized visitors into the building. If this is the case, then this highlights a serious vulnerability, and reviewing the acceptable use policy (AUP) and end user policy with the entire company might be in order. Even if the security policy makes no mention of allowing visitors into the building, it would be a good time to review the security policy and best practices with the entire staff. On the other hand, there is a potential downside to this, as alerting employees of this incident might alarm them unnecessarily.

5. **Should law enforcement be notified?**

   Yes. While the types of crimes that require legal intervention might be different in your region, this type of attack does constitute trespassing, which is illegal.

6. **According to the company's risk assessment analysis, unauthorized trespassing was listed as high risk. In composing your report, what are some things you can do to bring that risk down to a more manageable level?**

   Answers will vary, but may include recommendations such as mantraps, keypads, or smart cards required at all access points, and more explicit guidelines in the security policy for unauthorized personnel.

Lesson 10

Activity 10-1

1. **As the security administrator, you are responsible for ensuring that your BCP coincides with the organization's needs. What are your goals while establishing a BCP? (Select all that apply.)**

   ✓ a) Preserve important documents.

   ✓ b) Establish decision-making authority.

       c) Analyze fault tolerance.

   ✓ d) Maintain financial functions.

2. **Your organization is located in an area where there is a threat of hurricanes. As a member of the BCP team, you need to determine what effect there would be if a hurricane halted business activities at your organization. Which BCP component is this an example of?**

       a) Continuity of operations

   ✓ b) BIA

       c) IT contingency planning

       d) Succession planning

3. **Which part of the plan specifies interim sites and systems you can switch to following a disaster?**

       a) RPO

       b) BIA

   ✓ c) IT contingency plan

       d) Succession plan

4. **You recommend the company pay a small monthly rental fee for a warehouse with phone and power hookups to use as a:**

       a) Hot site

   ✓ b) Cold site

       c) Warm site

5. **Match each BCP testing method with its description.**

    c   Parallel testing

    a. A testing method that mimics an actual business disruption by shutting down the original site to test transfer and migration procedures to the alternate site.

    d   Paper testing

    b. A testing method in which a group reviews and focuses on each BCP process component.

    b   Performing walkthroughs

    c. A testing method where each part of the plan is executed, with the exception of replicating and causing an outage.

    a   Cutover

    d. A testing method that confirms whether the BCP meets predetermined, documented business needs.

6. **You and your colleague have just performed a walkthrough of the plan that would be put into effect in the event of a denial of service (DoS) attack to your company website. The two of you think that you need to perform more rigorous tests to ensure the effectiveness of the BCP. What are some other testing methods you might want to recommend?**

Parallel testing and cutover testing.

Activity 10-2

1. **Which are common components that should be in Ristell & Sons' DRP? (Select all that apply)**

    a) A list of employees' personal items.

    ✓ b) Contact information for key individuals.

    ✓ c) An inventory of important hardware and software.

    ✓ d) Plans to reconstruct the network.

2. **Ristell & Sons Publishing is willing to set aside some capital to install a fault tolerance system. What can you suggest?**

Answers may vary, but you can suggest implementing a better RAID standard, backup circuits, server clustering, spare hardware, and a redundant power supply.

3. **Assume that Ristell & Sons Publishing is located in a climate and location identical to the company you work for now. What are some unique geographical or weather-related conditions you might need to account for, but that might not be a consideration for other companies?**

Answers will vary, but you some locales might particularly be concerned with natural disasters such as hurricanes, tornados, river flooding, ice storms, heavy snowfall, and so on.

4. **Assume that a high-level manager has expressed some dissatisfaction with the notion of a "fire drill" to test the company's preparedness for a disaster; it seems he is leery of so much paid time being used in an unproductive way, and he wonders if you cannot just write a detailed plan instead. What are some things you can mention to help persuade him that such an unannounced drill is necessary?**

Answers will vary, but should contain some reference to the cost of being unprepared. If a company were to never test their DRP or BCP, then how does one really know if they will work? A company might be spending a lot of money on non-billable projects during a "fire drill," but such a drill could ensure that business is actually able to continue if disaster struck the company. You can also mention the legal ramifications or liability exposure of being unprepared for a disaster situation.

5. **Once you have the DRP and other components in place, what do you do to make sure it works smoothly?**

Answers may vary, but you can perform a walkthrough or parallel testing, and when you are sure it all works well, you can even perform a cutover. Also make sure there is a system in place to review the plan annually and make any maintenance-level changes.

Activity 10-3

1. **What should you keep in mind while choosing a good recovery team?**

   a) Include individuals who can do an analysis of the damage that the crisis has caused to the organization.

   ✓ b) Include individuals who can implement the proper procedures in response to the disruption to critical business processes.

   c) Include individuals who can record the history of the evidence of a computer crime from collection, to presentation in court, to return or disposal.

   d) Include individuals who determine how much money and effort will go into a recovery plan.

2. **Match each disaster recovery step with its description.**

_b_	Begin emergency operations	a.	If a facility has been adversely affected and has suffered significant losses, relocating to an alternate site may be the best option.
_d_	Assess the damage	b.	An incident manager should be appointed to assume control of the situation and ensure personnel safety.
_c_	Notify stakeholders	c.	These consist of senior management, board members, investors, clients, suppliers, and employees.
_a_	Assess the facility	d.	This is a check to determine the extent of incurred facility expenses, the cause of the disaster, and the expected down time.

3. **You have been assigned to perform a secure recovery; what does your task include?**

   As a designated and trusted officer, you need to supervise the recovery, making sure to document each step taken, noting the information needed to restore the processes and system. You might also note the data that is needed to recover from the disaster and important instructions to maintain the continuity of operations.

4. **You have to decide on the kind of backup source you will use to recover data and restore function to the business in the least possible time. What type of backup could you choose?**

It depends on what your best backup source is. Usually you want the backup source that is most current and accessible. Rebuilding data directly from a RAID array is preferred; if that is not possible, use a local backup, then an offsite backup.

5. **What types of backup storage locations can you suggest to store data for your company?**

Answers may vary, but can include an onsite storage location where the most recent set of backups are stored so they can be accessed quickly for use in normal day-to-day operations. You may also choose a disaster-resistant offsite location to securely store a duplicate backup of all data present and past.

Glossary

3DES
(Triple DES) A symmetric encryption algorithm that encrypts data by processing each block of data three times using a different DES key each time.

802.11
A family of specifications developed by the IEEE for wireless LAN technology.

802.11a
A fast, secure, but relatively expensive protocol for wireless communication. The 802.11a protocol supports speeds up to 54 Mbps in the 5 GHz frequency.

802.11b
Also called Wi-Fi, short for "wired fidelity," 802.11b is probably the most common and certainly the least expensive wireless network protocol used to transfer data among computers with wireless network cards or between a wireless computer or device and a wired LAN. The 802.11b protocol provides for an 11 Mbps transfer rate in the 2.4 GHz frequency.

802.11g
A specification for wireless data throughput at the rate of up to 54 Mbps in the 2.4 GHz band that is a potential replacement for 802.11b.

802.11i
A standard that adds AES security to the 802.11 standard.

802.11n
A wireless standard for home and business implementations that adds QoS features and multimedia support to 802.11a and 802.11b.

802.1x
An IEEE standard used to provide a port-based authentication mechanism for wireless communications using the 802.11a and 802.11b protocols.

Access Control List
See ACL.

access control
In security terms, the process of determining and assigning privileges to various resources, objects, and data.

account management
A common term used to refer to the processes, functions, and policies used to effectively manage user accounts within an organization.

account phishing
In social networking, an attack where an attacker creates an account and gets to be on the friends list of an individual just to try to obtain information about the individual and his circle of friends or colleagues.

account policy
A document that includes an organization's user account management guidelines.

account privileges

Permissions granted to users that allow them to perform various actions such as creating, deleting, and editing files, and also accessing systems and services on the network.

accountability

In security terms, the process of determining who to hold responsible for a particular activity or event.

accounting

See auditing.

ACL

(Access Control List) In a DAC access control scheme, this is the list that is associated with each object, specifying the subjects that can access the object and their levels of access.

Active Directory

The standards-based directory service from Microsoft that runs on Microsoft Windows Servers.

Address Resolution Protocol

See ARP.

Advanced Encryption Standard

See AES.

adware

Software that automatically displays or downloads advertisements when it is used.

AES

(Advanced Encryption Standard) A symmetric 128-, 192-, or 256-bit block cipher based on the Rijndael algorithm developed by Belgian cryptographers Joan Daemen and Vincent Rijmen and adopted by the U.S. government as its encryption standard to replace DES.

ALE

(annual loss expectancy) The total cost of a risk to an organization on an annual basis.

algorithm

In encryption, the rule, system, or mechanism used to encrypt the data.

all-in-one security appliance

A single network device that is used to perform a number of security functions to secure a network.

annual loss expectancy

See ALE.

anomaly-based monitoring

A monitoring system that uses a database of unacceptable traffic patterns identified by analyzing traffic flows.

anti-malware software

A category of software programs that scan a computer or network for known viruses, Trojans, worms, and other malicious software.

anti-spam

A program that will detect specific words that are commonly used in spam messages.

anti-spyware

Software that is specifically designed to protect systems against spyware attacks.

antivirus software

An application that scans files for executable code that matches specific patterns that are known to be common to viruses.

application attacks

Attacks that are targeted at web-based and other client-server applications.

archive bit

A file property that essentially indicates whether the file has been modified since the last back up.

ARP poisoning

A method in which an attacker with access to the target network redirects an IP address to the MAC address of a computer that is not the intended recipient.

ARP

(Address Resolution Protocol) The mechanism by which individual hardware MAC addresses are matched to an IP address on a network.

asymmetric encryption

A two-way encryption scheme that uses paired private and public keys.

attachment attack

An attack where the attacker can merge malicious software or code into a downloadable file or attachment on an application server so that users download and execute it on client systems.

attack surface

The portion of a system or application that is exposed and available to attackers.

attack

Any technique that is used to exploit a vulnerability in any application on a computer system without the authorization to do so.

attacker

A term for a user who gains unauthorized access to computers and networks for malicious purposes.

auditing

In security terms, the process of tracking and recording system activities and resource access. Also known as accounting.

authentication

In security terms, the process of uniquely identifying a particular individual or entity.

authorization

In security terms, the process of determining what rights and privileges a particular entity has.

availability

The fundamental security goal of ensuring that systems operate continuously and that authorized persons can access data that they need.

backdoor attack

A type of attack where the attacker creates a software mechanism to gain access to a system and its resources. This can involve software or a bogus user account.

backdoor

A mechanism for gaining access to a computer that bypasses or subverts the normal method of authentication.

backout contingency plan

A documented plan that includes specific procedures and processes that are applied in the event that a change or modification made to a system must be undone.

baseline report

A collection of security and configuration settings that are to be applied to a particular system or network in the organization.

BCP

(business continuity plan) A policy that defines how normal day-to-day business will be maintained in the event of a business disruption or crisis.

behavior-based monitoring

A monitoring system that detects changes in normal operating data sequences and identifies abnormal sequences.

BIA

(business impact analysis) A BCP preparatory step that identifies present organizational risks and determines the impact to ongoing, business-critical operations if such risks actualize.

biometrics

Authentication schemes based on individuals' physical characteristics.

birthday attack

A type of password attack that exploits weaknesses in the mathematical algorithms used to encrypt passwords, in order to take advantage of the probability of different password inputs producing the same encrypted output.

black box test

A test in which the tester is given no information about the system being tested.

black hat

A hacker who exposes vulnerabilities for financial gain or for some malicious purpose.

block cipher

A type of symmetric encryption that encrypts data one block at a time, often in 64-bit blocks. It is usually more secure, but is also slower, than stream ciphers.

Blowfish
A freely available 64-bit block cipher algorithm that uses a variable key length.

bluejacking
A method used by attackers to send out unwanted Bluetooth signals from PDAs, mobile phones, and laptops to other Bluetooth-enabled devices.

bluesnarfing
A process in which attackers gain access to unauthorized information on a wireless device using a Bluetooth connection.

Bluetooth
A short-range wireless radio network transmission medium usually used between two personal devices, such as between a mobile phone and wireless headset.

botnet
A set of computers that has been infected by a control program called a bot that enables attackers to exploit them to mount attacks.

brute force attack
A type of password attack where an attacker uses an application to exhaustively try every possible alphanumeric combination to try cracking encrypted passwords.

buffer overflow attack
A type of DoS attack that exploits fixed data buffer sizes in a target piece of software by sending data that is too large for the buffer.

business continuity plan
See BCP.

business impact analysis
See BIA.

CA hierarchy
A single CA or group of CAs that work together to issue digital certificates.

CA
(Certificate Authority) A server that can issue digital certificates and the associated public/private key pairs.

CAC
(Common Access Card) See smart card.

CAST-128
A symmetric encryption algorithm with a 128-bit key, named for its developers, Carlisle Adams and Stafford Tavares.

CBC encryption
(Cipher Block Chaining encryption) A block encryption model where before a block is encrypted, information from the preceding block is added to the block. In this way, you can be sure that repeated data is encrypted differently each time it is encountered.

CCMP
(Counter Mode with Cipher Block Chaining Message Authentication Code Protocol) An AES cipher-based encryption protocol used in WPA2.

Certificate Authority
See CA.

certificate management system
A system that provides the software tools to perform the day-to-day functions of a PKI.

certificate repository
A database containing digital certificates.

Certificate Revocation List
See CRL.

CFB encryption
(Cipher Feedback mode encryption) A block encryption model that allows encryption of partial blocks rather than requiring full blocks for encryption.

chain of custody
The record of evidence history from collection, to presentation in court, to disposal.

Challenge Handshake Authentication Protocol
See CHAP.

change management
A systematic way of approving and executing change in order to assure maximum security, stability, and availability of information technology services.

CHAP

(Challenge Handshake Authentication Protocol) An encrypted remote access authentication method that enables connections from any authentication method requested by the server, except for PAP and SPAP unencrypted authentication.

CIA triad

(confidentiality, integrity, availability) The three principles of security control and management: confidentiality, integrity, and availability. Also known as the information security triad or triple.

Cipher Block Chaining encryption

See CBC encryption.

Cipher Feedback mode encryption

See CFB encryption.

cipher

A method for concealing the meaning of text.

ciphertext

Data that has been encoded with a cipher and is unreadable.

cleartext

The unencrypted form of data. Also known as plaintext.

clickjacking

An attack that forces a user to unintentionally click a link. An attacker uses opaque layers or multiple transparent layers to trick a user.

cloud computing

A method of computing that relies on the Internet to provide the resources, software, data, and media needs of a user, business, or organization.

code reviews

An evaluation used in identifying potential weaknesses in an application.

cold site

A predetermined alternate location where a network can be rebuilt after a disaster.

computer crime

A criminal act that involves the use of a computer as a source or target, instead of an individual.

computer forensics

A skill that deals with collecting and analyzing data from storage devices, computer systems, networks, and wireless communications and presenting this information as a form of evidence in the court of law.

confidentiality

The fundamental security goal of keeping information and communications private and protecting them from unauthorized access.

continuity of operations plan

A plan that includes best practices to mitigate risks and attacks and the best measures to recover from an incident.

controls

The countermeasures that you need to put in place to avoid, mitigate, or counteract security risks due to threats or attacks.

cookie manipulation

An attack where an attacker injects a meta tag in an HTTP header making it possible to modify a cookie stored in a browser.

cookie

A small piece of text saved on a computer by a web browser that consists of one or more name-value pairs holding bits of information useful in remembering user preferences.

correction control

A control that helps to mitigate a consequence of a threat or attack from hazardously affecting the computer system.

Counter mode encryption

See CTR encryption.

Counter Mode with Cipher Block Chaining Message Authentication Code Protocol

See CCMP.

cracker

A user who breaks encryption codes, defeats software copy protections, or specializes in breaking into systems.

CRL

(Certificate Revocation List) A list of certificates that are no longer valid.

cross-site scripting

An attack that is directed towards sites with dynamic content by introducing malicious scripts or by taking over the session before the user session cookies expire.

cryptography

The science of hiding information.

cryptoprocessor

A microprocessor that provides cryptographic functions.

CTR encryption

(counter mode encryption) A block encryption model that is similar to OFB and uses a counter as input.

DAC

(Discretionary Access Control) In DAC, access is controlled based on a user's identity. Objects are configured with a list of users who are allowed access to them. An administrator has the discretion to place the user on the list or not. If a user is on the list, the user is granted access; if the user is not on the list, access is denied.

Data Encryption Standard

See DES.

data sanitation

The method used to repeatedly delete and overwrite any traces or bits of sensitive data that may remain on a device after data wiping has been done.

data security

The security controls and measures taken in order to keep an organization's data safe and accessible and to prevent unauthorized access.

data wiping

A method used to remove any sensitive data from a mobile device and permanently delete it.

data

A general term for the information assets of a person or organization. In a computer system, data is generally stored in files.

DDoS attack

(Distributed Denial of Service attack) A network attack in which an attacker hijacks or manipulates multiple computers (through the use of zombies or drones) on disparate networks to carry out a DoS attack.

deciphering

The process of reversing a cipher.

demilitarized zone

See DMZ.

Denial of Service attack

See DoS attack.

DES

(Data Encryption Standard) A symmetric encryption algorithm that encrypts data in 64-bit blocks using a 56-bit key with 8 bits used for parity.

detection control

A control that helps to discover if a threat or vulnerability has entered into the computer system.

detection controls

Controls that are implemented to monitor a situation or activity, and react to any irregular activities by bringing the issue to the attention of administrators.

detection

The act of determining if a user has tried to access unauthorized data, or scanning the data and networks for any traces left by an intruder in any attack against the system.

device

A piece of hardware such as a computer, server, printer, or smartphone.

DHCP

(Dynamic Host Control Protocol) A protocol used to automatically assign IP addressing information to IP network computers.

Diameter

An authentication protocol that allows for a variety of connection types, such as wireless.

dictionary attack

A type of password attack that automates password guessing by comparing encrypted passwords against a predetermined list of possible password values.

differential backup

A backup that backs up all files in a selected storage location that have changed since the last full backup.

Diffie-Hellman

A cryptographic protocol that provides for secure key exchange.

digital certificate

An electronic document that associates credentials with a public key.

digital signature

An encrypted hash value that is appended to a message to identify the sender and the message.

directory service

A network service that stores identity information about all the objects in a particular network, including users, groups, servers, client computers, and printers.

directory traversal

An attack that allows access to commands, files, and directories that may or may not be connected to the web document root directory.

disaster recovery plan

See DRP.

Discretionary Access Control

See DAC.

Distributed Denial of Service attack

See DDoS attack.

DMZ

(demilitarized zone) A small section of a private network that is located between two firewalls and made available for public access.

DNS hijacking

An attack in which an attacker sets up a rogue DNS server. This rogue DNS server responds to legitimate requests with IP addresses for malicious or non-existent websites.

DNS poisoning

An attack in which an attacker exploits the traditionally open nature of the DNS system to redirect a domain name to an IP address of the attacker's choosing.

DNS

(Domain Name System) The service that maps names to IP addresses on most TCP/IP networks, including the Internet.

Domain Name Server

A server that is part of the DNS system. DNS servers respond to requests for a domain name with the appropriate IP address.

Domain Name System

See DNS.

DoS attack

(Denial of Service attack) A network attack in which an attacker disables systems that provide network services by consuming a network link's available bandwidth, consuming a single system's available resources, or exploiting programming flaws in an application or operating system.

drive-by download

A program that is automatically installed on a computer when you access a malicious site, even without clicking on a link or giving consent.

drone

Unauthorized software introduced on multiple computers to manipulate the computers into mounting a DDoS attack. Also called a zombie.

DRP

(disaster recovery plan) A plan that prepares the organization to react appropriately in a natural or a man-made disaster and provides the means to recover from a disaster.

dumpster diving

A human-based attack where the goal is to reclaim important information by inspecting the contents of trash containers.

Dynamic Host Control Protocol

See DHCP.

EAP

(Extensible Authentication Protocol) An authentication protocol that enables systems to use hardware-based identifiers, such as fingerprint scanners or smart card readers, for authentication.

eavesdropping attack

A network attack that uses special monitoring software to gain access to private communications on the network wire or across a wireless network. Also known as a sniffing attack.

ECB encryption

(Electronic Code Block encryption) A block encryption model where each block is encrypted by itself. Each occurrence of a particular word is encrypted exactly the same.

ECC

(elliptic curve cryptography) An asymmetric encryption technique that leverages the algebraic structures of elliptic curves over finite fields.

electromagnetic interference

See EMI.

Electronic Code Block

See ECB encryption.

Elgamal

A public key encryption algorithm developed by Taher Elgamal.

elliptic curve cryptography

See ECC.

EMI

(electromagnetic interference) A disruption of electrical current that occurs when a magnetic field around one electrical circuit interferes with the signal being carried on an adjacent circuit.

enciphering

The process of applying a cipher.

encryption

A security technique that converts data from plain, or cleartext form, into coded, or ciphertext form so that only authorized parties with the necessary decryption information can decode and read the data.

enumerating

The stage of the hacking process in which the attacker will try to gain access to users and groups, network resources, shares, applications, or valid user names and passwords.

environmental controls

A system or device that is implemented to prevent or control environmental exposures or threats.

ethical hacking

Planned attempts to penetrate the security defenses of a system in order to identify vulnerabilities.

evil twin attack

In social networking, an attack where an attacker creates a social network account to impersonate a genuine user, becoming friends with others and joining groups, and thus getting access to various types of personal and professional information. In wireless networking, a type of rogue access point at a public site that is configured to look like a legitimate access point in order to tempt a user to choose to connect to it.

Extensible Authentication Protocol

See EAP.

eXtensible Markup Language

See XML.

fault tolerance
The ability of a network or system to withstand a foreseeable component failure and continue to provide an acceptable level of service.

File Transfer Protocol Secure
See FTPS.

File Transfer Protocol
See FTP.

firewall
A software or hardware device that protects a system or network by blocking unwanted network traffic.

first responder
The first person or team to respond to an accident, damage site, or natural disaster in an IT company.

flood guard
A tool used by network administrators and security professionals to protect resources from flooding attacks, such as DDoS attacks.

footprinting
The stage of the hacking process in which the attacker chooses a target organization or network and begins to gather information that is publicly available. Also called profiling.

FTP-SSL
See FTPS.

FTP
(File Transfer Protocol) A communications protocol that enables the transfer of files between a user's workstation and a remote host.

FTPS
(File Transfer Protocol Secure) A protocol that combines the use of FTP with additional support for TLS and SSL.

full backup
A backup that backs up all selected files regardless of the state of the archived bit.

fuzzing
A testing method used to identify vulnerabilities and weaknesses in applications, by sending the application a range of random or unusual input data and noting failures and crashes.

GNU Privacy Guard
See GPG.

GPG
(GNU Privacy Guard) A free open-source version of PGP that provides the equivalent encryption and authentication services.

gray box test
A test in which the tester may have knowledge of internal architectures and systems, or other preliminary information about the system being tested.

group based privileges
Privileges that are assigned to an entire group of users within an organization.

group policy
A centralized configuration management feature available for Active Directory on Windows Server systems.

guessing
A human-based attack where the goal is to guess a password or PIN through brute force means or by using deduction.

guideline
A suggestion for meeting a policy standard or best practices.

hacker
A user who excels at programming or managing and configuring computer systems, and has the skills to gain access to computer systems through unauthorized or unapproved means.

hardening
A security technique in which the default configuration of a system is altered to protect the system against attacks.

hardware attack
An attack that targets a computer's physical components and peripherals, including its hard disk, motherboard, keyboard, network cabling, or smart card reader.

Hardware Security Module
See HSM.

hardware-based encryption devices
A device or mechanism that provides encryption, decryption, and access control.

hash value
See hash.

hash
The value that results from hashing encryption. Also known as hash value or message digest.

hashing encryption
One-way encryption that transforms cleartext into a coded form that is never decrypted.

header manipulation
An attack where the attacker manipulates the header information that is passed between web servers and clients in HTTP requests.

heating, ventilation, and air conditioning
See HVAC system.

heuristic monitoring
A monitoring system that uses known best practices and characteristics in order to identify and fix issues within the network.

high availability
A rating that expresses how closely systems approach the goal of providing data availability 100 percent of the time while maintaining a high level of system performance.

HMAC
(Hash-based Message Authentication Code) A method used to verify both the integrity and authenticity of a message by combining cryptographic hash functions, such as MD5, or SHA-1 with a secret key.

hoax
An email-based or web-based attack that tricks the user into performing undesired actions, such as deleting important system files in an attempt to remove a virus, or sending money or important information via email or online forms.

honeynet
An entire dummy network used to lure attackers.

honeypot
A security tool used to lure attackers away from the actual network components. Also called a decoy or sacrificial lamb.

host-based firewall
Software that is installed on a single system to specifically guard against networking attacks.

host/personal firewall
A firewall installed on a single or home computer.

hot and cold aisles
A method used within data centers and server rooms as a temperature and humidity control method.

hot site
A fully configured alternate network that can be online quickly after a disaster.

hotfix
A patch that is often issued on an emergency basis to address a specific security flaw.

HSM
(Hardware Security Module) A cryptographic module that can generate cryptographic keys.

HTTP
(Hypertext Transfer Protocol) A protocol that defines the interaction between a web server and a browser.

HTTPS
(Hypertext Transfer Protocol Secure) A secure version of HTTP that supports e-commerce by providing a secure connection between a web browser and a server.

HVAC system

(heating, ventilation, and air conditioning) A system that controls the air quality and flow inside a building.

hybrid password attack

An attack that utilizes multiple attack methods including dictionary, rainbow table, and brute force attacks when trying to crack a password.

Hypertext Transfer Protocol Secure

See HTTPS.

Hypertext Transfer Protocol

See HTTP.

IaaS

(Infrastructure as a Service) A method that uses the cloud to provide any or all infrastructure needs.

ICMP flood attack

A type of DoS attack that exploits weaknesses in ICMP. Specific attacks include Smurf attacks and ping floods.

ICMP

(Internet Control Message Protocol) An IP network service that reports on connections between two hosts.

identification

In security terms, the process of attaching a human element to an authentication.

identity management

An area of information security that is used to identify individuals within a computer system or network.

identity theft

A crime that occurs when an individual's personal information or data is stolen and used by someone other than the authorized user.

IDS

(intrusion detection system) A software and/or hardware system that scans, audits, and monitors the security infrastructure for signs of attacks in progress.

IM

(instant messaging) A type of communication service which involves a private dialogue between two persons via instant-text-based messages over the Internet.

impersonation

A type of spoofing in which an attacker pretends to be someone they are not, typically an average user in distress, or a help desk representative.

implicit deny

The principle that establishes that everything that is not explicitly allowed is denied.

incident management

Practices and procedures that govern how an organization will respond to an incident in progress.

Incident Response Policy

See IRP.

incremental backup

A back up that backs up all files in a selected storage location that have changed since the last full or differential backup.

information security triad

See CIA triad.

information security

The protection of available information or information resources from unauthorized access, attacks, thefts, or wipeouts.

Infrastructure as a Service

See IaaS.

initialization vector

See IV.

input validation

Any technique used to ensure that the data entered into a field or variable in an application is within acceptable bounds for the object that will receive the data.

instant messaging

See IM.

integrity
The fundamental security goal of ensuring that electronic data is not altered or tampered with.

interference
Within wireless networking, the phenomenon by which radio waves from other devices interfere with the 802.11 wireless signals.

Internet Control Message Protocol
See ICMP.

Internet Protocol Security
See IPSec.

intrusion detection system
See IDS.

intrusion prevention system
See IPS.

intrusion
An instance of an attacker accessing your computer system without the authorization to do so.

IP version 4
See IPv4.

IP version 6
See IPv6.

IPS
(intrusion prevention system) An inline security device that monitors suspicious network and/or system traffic and reacts in real time to block it.

IPSec
(Internet Protocol Security) A set of open, non-proprietary standards that you can use to secure data as it travels across the network or the Internet through data authentication and encryption.

IPv4
(IP version 4) An Internet standard that uses a 32-bit number assigned to a computer on a TCP/IP network.

IPv6
(IP version 6) An Internet standard that increases the available pool of IP addresses by implementing a 128-bit binary address space.

IRP
(Incident Response Policy) The security policy that determines the actions that an organization will take following a confirmed or potential security breach.

IT contingency plan
An alternate plan that you can switch over to when faced with an attack or disruption of service.

IV attack
An attack where the attacker is able to predict or control the IV of an encryption process, thus giving the attacker access to view the encrypted data that is supposed to be hidden from everyone else except the user or network.

IV
(initialization vector) A technique used in cryptography to generate random numbers to be used along with a secret key to provide data encryption.

job rotation
The principle that establishes that no one person stays in a vital job role for too long a time period.

Kerberos
An authentication system in which authentication is based on a time-sensitive ticket-granting system. It uses a SSO method where the user enters access credentials that are then passed to the authentication server, which contains the allowed access credentials.

key escrow agent
A third party that maintains a backup copy of private keys.

key escrow
A method for backing up private keys to protect them while allowing trusted third parties to access the keys under certain conditions.

key generation

An asymmetric encryption process of generating a public and private key pair using a specific application.

key

In cryptography, a specific piece of information that is used in conjunction with an algorithm to perform encryption and decryption.

L2TP

(Layer Two Tunneling Protocol) The de facto standard VPN protocol for tunneling PPP sessions across a variety of network protocols such as IP, frame relay, or ATM.

Layer Two Tunneling Protocol

See L2TP.

LDAP injection

An attack that targets web-based applications by fabricating LDAP statements that typically are created by user input.

LDAP

(Lightweight Directory Access Protocol) A simple network protocol used to access network directory databases, which store information about authorized users and their privileges as well as other organizational information.

LEAP

(Lightweight Extensible Authentication Protocol) Cisco Systems' proprietary EAP implementation.

least privilege

The principle that establishes that users and software should only have the minimal level of access that is necessary for them to perform the duties required of them.

Lightweight Directory Access Protocol

See LDAP.

Lightweight Extensible Authentication Protocol

See LEAP.

load balancer

A network device that performs load balancing as its primary function.

load balancing

The practice of spreading out the work among the devices in a network.

log

A record of significant events. In computing, it is using an operating system or application to record data about activity on a computer.

logging

The act of creating a log.

logic bomb

A piece of code that sits dormant on a target computer until it is triggered by the occurrence of specific conditions, such as a specific date and time. Once the code is triggered, the logic bomb "detonates," performing whatever action it was programmed to do.

M of N scheme

A mathematical control that takes into account the total number of key recovery agents (N) along with the number of agents required to perform a key recovery (M).

MAC address

(Media Access Control address) A unique physical address assigned to each network adapter board at the time of manufacture.

MAC

(Mandatory Access Control) A system in which objects (files and other resources) are assigned security labels of varying levels, depending on the object's sensitivity. Users are assigned a security level or clearance, and when they try to access an object, their clearance is compared to the object's security label. If there is a match, the user can access the object; if there is no match, the user is denied access.

malicious add-on

An add-on that is meant to look like a normal add-on, except that when a user installs it, malicious content will be injected to target the security loopholes that are present in a web browser.

malicious code attack

A type of software attack where an attacker inserts malicious software into a user's system.

malicious insider threat

A threat originating from an employee in an organization who performs malicious acts, such as deleting critical information or by sharing this critical information with outsiders, which may result in certain amount of losses to the organization.

malware

Malicious code, such as viruses, Trojans, or worms, which is designed to gain unauthorized access to, make unauthorized use of, or damage computer systems and networks.

man-in-the-middle attack

A form of eavesdropping where the attacker makes an independent connection between two victims and steals information to use fraudulently.

management controls

Procedures implemented to monitor the adherence to organizational security policies.

Mandatory Access Control

See MAC.

mantrap

A physical security control system that has a door at each end of a secure chamber.

maximum tolerable downtime

See MTD.

MD4

(Message Digest 4) This hash algorithm, based on RFC 1320, produces a 128-bit hash value and is used in message integrity checks for data authentication.

MD5

(Message Digest 5) This hash algorithm, based on RFC 1321, produces a 128-bit hash value and is used in IPSec policies for data authentication.

mean time between failures

See MTBF.

mean time to recovery

See MTTR.

Media Access Control address

See MAC address.

media

A method that connects devices to the network and carries data between devices.

Message Digest 4

See MD4.

Message Digest 5

See MD5.

message digest

See hash.

MTBF

(mean time between failures) The rating on a device or devices that predicts the expected time between failures.

MTD

(maximum tolerable downtime) The longest period of time a business can be inoperable without causing the business to fail irrecoverably.

MTTR

(mean time to recovery) The average time taken for a business to recover from an incident or failure.

multi-factor authentication

Any authentication scheme that requires validation of at least two of the possible authentication factors.

multifunction network device

Any piece of network hardware that is meant to perform more than one networking task without having to be reconfigured.

mutual authentication

A security mechanism that requires that each party in a communication verifies its identity.

NAC

(Network Access Control) The collection of protocols, policies, and hardware that govern access on devices to and from a network.

NAS

(Network Access Server) A RADIUS server configuration that uses a centralized server and clients.

NAT

(Network Address Translation) A simple form of Internet security that conceals internal addressing schemes from the public Internet by translating between a single public address on the external side of a router and private, non-routable addresses internally.

NetBIOS

A simple, broadcast-based naming service.

Network Access Control

See NAC.

Network Access Server

See NAS.

network adapter

Hardware that translates the data between the network and a device.

Network Address Translation

See NAT.

network intrusion detection system

See NIDS.

network intrusion prevention system

See NIPS.

network operating system

Software that controls network traffic and access to network resources.

network-based firewall

A hardware/software combination that protects all the computers on a network behind the firewall.

NIDS

(network intrusion detection system) A systems that uses passive hardware sensors to monitor traffic on a specific segment of the network.

NIPS

(network intrusion prevention system) An active, inline security device that monitors suspicious network and/or system traffic and reacts in real time to block it.

non-repudiation

The security goal of ensuring that the party that sent a transmission or created data remains associated with that data.

NT LAN Manager

See NTLM.

NTLM

(NT LAN Manager) An authentication protocol created by Microsoft for use in its products.

OFB encryption

(Output Feedback mode encryption) A block encryption model that converts a block cipher into a stream cipher which is fed back as input of a block cipher.

Open Directory

The directory service that ships as part of Mac OS X Server.

operational controls

Security measures implemented to safeguard all aspects of day-to-day operations, functions, and activities.

order of volatility

The order in which volatile data should be recovered from various storage locations and devices following a security incident.

orphaned account

A user account that remains active even after the employee has left the organization.

Output Feedback mode encryption

See OFB encryption.

P2P attack

An attack that is launched by malware propagating within a P2P architecture to launch DoS attacks.

P2P

(peer-to-peer) A network that has a broadcast application architecture that distributes tasks between peer systems who have equal privileges, and in which resource sharing, processing, and communications controls are decentralized.

PaaS

(Platform as a Service) A method that uses the cloud to provide any platform type services.

packet sniffing

An attack on wireless networks where an attacker captures data and registers data flows in order to analyze what data is contained in a packet.

Paillier cryptosystem

An asymmetric encryption algorithm developed by Pascal Paillier.

PAP

(Password Authentication Protocol) A remote access authentication service that sends user IDs and passwords as cleartext.

password attack

Any type of attack in which the attacker attempts to obtain and make use of passwords illegitimately.

Password Authentication Protocol

See PAP.

password stealer

A type of software that can capture all passwords and user names entered into the IM application or social network site that it was designed for.

patch management

The practice of monitoring for, evaluating, testing, and installing software patches and updates.

patch

A small unit of supplemental code meant to address either a security problem or a functionality flaw in a software package or operating system.

PCBC encryption

(Propagating or Plaintext Cipher Block Chaining encryption) A block encryption model that causes minimal changes in the ciphertext while encrypting or decrypting.

PEAP

(Protected Extensible Authentication Protocol) Similar to EAP-TLS, PEAP is an open standard developed by a coalition made up of Cisco Systems, Microsoft, and RSA Security.

peer-to-peer

See P2P.

penetration test

A method of evaluating security by simulating an attack on a system.

Personally Identifying Information

See PII.

PGP

(Pretty Good Privacy) A method of securing emails created to prevent attackers from intercepting and manipulating email and attachments by encrypting and digitally signing the contents of the email using public key cryptography.

pharming

An attack in which a request for a website, typically an e-commerce site, is redirected to a similar-looking, but fake, website.

phishing

A type of email-based social engineering attack, in which the attacker sends email from a spoofed source, such as a bank, to try to elicit private information from the victim.

physical security controls

Implemented security measures that restrict, detect, and monitor access to specific physical areas or assets.

physical security

The implementation and practice of various control mechanisms that are intended to restrict physical access to facilities.

PII

(Personally Identifying Information) The pieces of information that a company uses or prefers to use to identify or contact an employee.

ping flood attack

A common name for ICMP flood attack. It is a type of DoS attack in which the attacker attempts to overwhelm the target system with ICMP Echo Request (ping) packets.

ping sweep

A scan of a range of IP addresses to locate active hosts within the range.

PKCS #10—Certification Request Syntax Standard

A PKCS that describes the syntax used to request certification of a public key and other information.

PKCS #7—Cryptographic Message Syntax Standard

A PKCS that describes the general syntax used for cryptographic data such as digital signatures.

PKCS

(Public Key Cryptography Standards) A set of protocol standards developed by a consortium of vendors to send information over the Internet in a secure manner using a PKI.

PKI

(Public Key Infrastructure) A system that is composed of a CA, certificates, software, services, and other cryptographic components, for the purpose of enabling authenticity and validation of data and/or entities.

plaintext

Un-encoded data. Also known as cleartext.

Platform as a Service

See PaaS.

PMI

(Privilege Management Infrastructure) An implementation of a particular set of privilege management technologies.

Point-to-Point Protocol

See PPP.

Point-to-Point Tunneling Protocol

See PPTP.

policy statement

An outline of the plan for an individual security component.

pop-up blockers

Software that prevents pop-ups from sites that are unknown or untrusted and prevents the transfer of unwanted code to the local system.

pop-up

A window or frame that loads and appears automatically when a user connects to a particular web page.

port scanning attack

An attack where an attacker scans your systems to see which ports are listening in an attempt to find a way to gain unauthorized access.

port

The endpoint of a logical connection that client computers use to connect to specific server programs.

PPP

(Point-to-Point Protocol) The VPN protocol that is an Internet standard for sending IP datagram packets over serial point-to-point links.

PPTP

(Point-to-Point Tunneling Protocol) A VPN protocol that is an extension of the PPP remote access protocol.

Pretty Good Privacy

See PGP.

prevention control

A control that helps to prevent a threat or attack from exposing a vulnerability in the computer system.

prevention controls

Controls that can react to anomalies by blocking access completely and thereby preventing damage to a system, building, or network.

prevention

The security approach of blocking unauthorized access or attacks before they occur.

private key

The component of asymmetric encryption that is kept secret by one party during two-way encryption.

private root CA

A root CA that is created by a company for use primarily within the company itself.

privilege bracketing

The task of giving privileges to a user only when needed and revoking them as soon as the task is done.

Privilege Management Infrastructure

See PMI.

privilege management

The use of authentication and authorization mechanisms to provide an administrator with centralized or decentralized control of user and group role-based privilege management.

procedure

Instructions that detail specifically how to implement a policy.

profiling

The same as footprinting.

Propagating or Plaintext Cipher Block Chaining encryption

See PCBC encryption.

Protected Extensible Authentication Protocol

See PEAP.

protocol analyzer

This type of diagnostic software can examine and display data packets that are being transmitted over a network.

protocol

Software that controls network communications using a set of rules.

proxy server

A system that isolates internal networks from the Internet by downloading and storing Internet files on behalf of internal clients.

Public Key Cryptography Standards

See PKCS.

Public Key Infrastructure

See PKI.

public key

The component of asymmetric encryption that can be accessed by anyone.

public root CA

A root CA that is created by a vendor for general access by the public.

quantum cryptography

A type of encryption based on quantum communication and quantum computation.

qubit

In quantum cryptography, a unit of a unit of data that is encrypted by entangling data with a sub-atomic particle such as a photon or electron that has a particular spin cycle. A qubit is the equivalent of a bit in computing technology.

RA

(Registration Authority) An authority in a PKI that processes requests for digital certificates from users.

RACE Integrity Primitives Evaluation Message Digest

See RIPEMD.

RADIUS

(Remote Authentication Dial-in User Service) A standard protocol for providing centralized authentication and authorization services for remote users.

RAID

(Redundant Array of Independent Disks) A set of vendor-independent specifications for fault tolerant configurations on multiple-disk systems.

rainbow tables
Sets of related plaintext passwords and their hashes.

RBAC
(Role-Based Access Control) A system in which access is controlled based on a user's role. Users are assigned to roles, and network objects are configured to allow access only to specific roles. Roles are created independently of user accounts.

RC algorithms
(Rivest Cipher algorithms) A series of variable key-length symmetric encryption algorithms developed by Ronald Rivest.

Recovery Point Objective
See RPO.

recovery team
A group of designated individuals who implement recovery procedures and control the recovery operations in the event of an internal or external disruption to critical business processes.

recovery time objective
See RTO.

recovery
The act of recovering vital data present in files or folders from a crashed system or data storage devices when data has been compromised or damaged.

Redundant Array of Independent Disks
See RAID.

reflected attack
An attack where the attacker poses as a legitimate user and sends information to a web server in the form of a page request or form submission.

reflected DoS attack
A type of DoS attack that uses a forged source IP address when sending requests to a large number of computers. This causes those systems to send a reply to the target system, causing a DoS condition.

Registration Authority
See RA.

remote access
The ability to connect to systems and services from an offsite or remote location using a remote access method.

Remote Authentication Dial-In User Service
See RADIUS.

replay attack
A type of network attack where an attacker captures network traffic and stores it for retransmission at a later time to gain unauthorized access to a network.

reputation
The public's opinion of a particular company based on certain standards.

resource
Any virtual or physical components of a system that have limited availability. A physical resource can be any device connected directly to a computer system. A virtual resource refers to any type of file, memory location, or network connection.

RIPEMD
(RACE Integrity Primitives Evaluation Message Digest) A message digest algorithm that is based on the design principles used in MD4.

risk analysis
The security management process for addressing any risk or economic damages that affect an organization.

risk management
The practice of managing risks from the initial identification to mitigation of those risks.

risk
An information security concept that indicates exposure to the chance of damage or loss, and signifies the likelihood of a hazard or dangerous threat.

Rivest Cipher
See RC algorithms.

Rivest Shamir Adelman
See RSA.

rogue access point
An unauthorized wireless access point on a corporate or private network, which allows unauthorized individuals to connect to the network.

Role-Based Access Control
See RBAC.

rollup
A collection of previously issued patches and hotfixes, usually meant to be applied to one component of a system, such as the web browser or a particular service.

root CA
The top-most CA in the hierarchy and consequently, the most trusted authority in the hierarchy.

rootkit
Software that is intended to take full or partial control of a system at the lowest levels.

router redundancy
A technique for employing multiple routers in teams to limit the risk of routing failure should a router malfunction.

router
A device that connects multiple networks that use the same protocol.

RPO
(Recovery Point Objective) The point in time, relative to a disaster, where the data recovery process begins.

RSA
The first successful algorithm to be designed for public key encryption. It is named for its designers, Rivest, Shamir, and Adelman.

RTO
(recovery time objective) The length of time within which normal business operations and activities must be restored following a disturbance.

rule-based access control
A non-discretionary access control technique that is based on a set of operational rules or restrictions.

rule-based management
The use of operational rules or restrictions to govern the security of an organization's infrastructure.

S-box
A relatively complex key algorithm that when given the key, provides a substitution key in its place.

SaaS
(Software as a Service) A method that uses the cloud to provide application services to users.

scanning
The phase of the hacking process in which the attacker uses specific tools to determine an organization's infrastructure and discover vulnerabilities.

schema
A set of rules in a directory service for how objects are created and what their characteristics can be.

SCP
(Secure Copy Protocol) A protocol that is used to securely transfer computer files between a local and a remote host, or between two remote hosts, using SSH.

Secure Copy Protocol
See SCP.

Secure Hash Algorithm
See SHA.

Secure Socket Tunneling Protocol
See SSTP.

Secure Sockets Layer
See SSL.

security architecture review
An evaluation of an organization's current security infrastructure model and security measures.

security auditing
Performing an organized technical assessment of the security strengths and weaknesses of a system.

security baseline
A collection of security configuration settings that are to be applied to a particular host in the enterprise.

security incident
A specific instance of a risk event occurring, whether or not it causes damage.

security policy
A formalized statement that defines how security will be implemented within a particular organization.

security posture
The position an organization takes on securing all aspects of its business.

separation of duties
The principle that establishes that no one person should have too much power or responsibility.

Service Pack
A collection of system updates that can include functionality enhancements, new features, and typically all patches, updates, and hotfixes issued up to the point of the release of the Service Pack.

session hijacking attack
An attack where the attacker exploits a legitimate computer session to obtain unauthorized access to an organization's network or services.

SFTP
(Simple File Transfer Protocol) An early unsecured file transfer protocol that has since been declared obsolete.

SHA
(Secure Hash Algorithm) A hash algorithm modeled after MD5 and considered the stronger of the two because it produces a 160-bit hash value.

shoulder surfing
A human-based attack where the goal is to look over the shoulder of an individual as he or she enters password information or a PIN.

signature-based monitoring
A monitoring system that uses a predefined set of rules provided by a software vendor to identify traffic that is unacceptable.

Simple File Transfer Protocol
See SFTP.

Simple Network Management Protocol
See SNMP.

single sign-on
See SSO.

Skipjack
A block cipher algorithm designed by the U.S. National Security Agency (NSA) for use in tamper-proof hardware in conjunction with the Clipper Chip.

smart card
A device similar to a credit card that can store authentication information, such as a user's private key, on an embedded microchip.

Smurf attack
A common name for ICMP flood attack. It is a type of DoS attack in which a ping message is broadcast to an entire network on behalf of a victim computer, flooding the victim computer with responses.

sniffer
A device or program that monitors network communications on the network wire or across a wireless network and captures data.

sniffing attack
A network attack that uses special monitoring software to gain access to private communications on the network wire or across a wireless network. Also known as an eavesdropping attack.

SNMP

(Simple Network Management Protocol) An application-layer service used to exchange information between network devices.

social engineering attack

A type of attack where the goal is to obtain sensitive data, including user names and passwords, from network users through deception and trickery.

Software as a Service

See SaaS.

software attack

Any attack that targets software resources including operating systems, applications, protocols, and files.

source code

Software code that is generated by programming languages, which is then compiled into machine code to be executed by a computer. Access to source code enables a programmer to change how a piece of software functions.

spam filter

A program used to read and reject incoming messages that contain target words and phrases used in known spam messages.

spam

An email-based threat that floods the user's inbox with emails that typically carry unsolicited advertising material for products or other spurious content, and which sometimes deliver viruses. It can also be utilized within social networking sites such as Facebook and Twitter.

spear phishing

An email-based or web-based form of phishing which targets particularly wealthy individuals. Also known as whaling.

spim

An IM-based attack just like spam but which is propagated through instant messaging instead of through email.

spoofing

A human-based or software-based attack where the goal is to pretend to be someone else for the purpose of identity concealment. Spoofing can occur in IP addresses, MAC addresses, and email.

spyware

Surreptitiously installed malicious software that is intended to track and report the usage of a target system or collect other data the author wishes to obtain.

SQL injection

An attack that injects an SQL query into the input data directed at a server by accessing the client side of the application.

SQL

(Structured Query Language) A programming and query language common to many large-scale database systems.

SSH

(Secure Shell) A protocol for secure remote logon and secure transfer of data.

SSL

(Secure Sockets Layer) A security protocol that uses certificates for authentication and encryption to protect web communication.

SSO

(single sign-on) An aspect of privilege management that provides users with one-time authentication to multiple resources, servers, or sites.

SSTP

(Secure Socket Tunneling Protocol) A protocol that uses the HTTP over SSL protocol and encapsulates an IP packet with a PPP header and then with an SSTP header.

standard

A definition of how adherence to a policy will be measured.

steganography

The practice of attempting to obscure the fact that information is present.

stored attack
An attack where an attacker injects malicious code or links into a website's forums, databases, or other data.

stream cipher
A relatively fast type of encryption that encrypts data one bit at a time.

strong password
A password that meets the complexity requirements that are set by a system administrator and documented in a password policy.

Structured Query Language
See SQL.

subnetting
The division of a large network into smaller logical networks.

subordinate CA
Any CAs below the root in the hierarchy.

succession plan
A plan that ensures that all key business personnel have one or more designated backups who can perform critical functions when needed.

switch
A device that has multiple network ports and combines multiple physical network segments into a single logical network.

symmetric encryption
A two-way encryption scheme in which encryption and decryption are both performed by the same key. Also known as shared-key encryption.

SYN flood attack
A type of DoS attack in which the attacker sends multiple SYN messages initializing TCP connections with a target host.

TACACS
(Terminal Access Controller Access Control System) Provides centralized authentication and authorization services for remote users.

TACACS+
Cisco's extension to the TACAC protocol that provides multi-factor authentication.

tailgating
A human-based attack where the attacker will slip in through a secure area following a legitimate employee.

takeover attack
A type of software attack where an attacker gains access to a remote host and takes control of the system.

TCB
(Trusted Computing Base) The hardware, firmware, and software components of a computer system that implement the security policy of a system.

TCP/IP
(Transmission Control Protocol/Internet Protocol) A non-proprietary, routable network protocol suite that enables computers to communicate over all types of networks.

technical controls
Hardware or software installations that are implemented to monitor and prevent threats and attacks to computer systems and services.

telephony
Technology that provides voice communications through devices over a distance.

Temporal Key Integrity Protocol
See TKIP.

Terminal Access Controller Access Control System
See TACACS.

threat
Any potential violation of security policies or procedures.

time of day restriction
A security control that allows the user to access the system only for a certain time period which can be set using a group policy.

TKIP
(Temporal Key Integrity Protocol) A security protocol created by the IEEE 802.11i task group to replace WEP.

TLS

(Transport Layer Security) A security protocol that uses certificates and public key cryptography for mutual authentication and data encryption over a TCP/IP connection.

token

A physical or virtual object that stores authentication information.

TOS

(Trusted Operating System) The operating system component of the TCB that protects the resources from applications.

TPM

(Trusted Platform Module) A specification that includes the use of cryptoprocessors to create a secure computing environment.

transitive access attack

An attack that takes advantage of the transitive access given in order to steal or destroy data on a system.

transitive access

Access given to certain members in an organization to use data on a system without the need for authenticating themselves.

Transmission Control Protocol/Internet Protocol

See TCP/IP.

Transport Layer Security

See TLS.

Triple DES

See 3DES.

Trojan horse

An insidious type of malware that is itself a software attack and can pave the way for a number of other types of attacks.

trust model

A CA hierarchy.

Trusted Computing Base

See TCB.

Trusted Operating System

See TOS.

Trusted Platform Module

See TPM.

tunneling

A data-transport technique in which a data packet is encrypted and encapsulated in another data packet in order to conceal the information of the packet inside.

Twofish

A symmetric key block cipher, similar to Blowfish, consisting a block size of 128 bits and key sizes up to 256 bits.

UDP flood

A type of DoS attack in which the attacker attempts to overwhelm the target system with UDP ping requests. Often the source IP address is spoofed, creating a DoS condition for the spoofed IP.

URL filtering

The inspection of files and packets to block restricted websites or content.

URL shortening service

An Internet service that makes it easier to share links on social networking sites by abbreviating URLs.

user assigned privileges

Privileges that are assigned to a system user and can be configured to meet the needs of a specific job function or task.

virtual local area network

See VLAN.

virtual private network

See VPN.

virtualization

A class of technology that separates computing software from the hardware it runs on via an additional software layer, allowing multiple operating systems to run on one computer simultaneously.

virus

A sample of code that spreads from one computer to another by attaching itself to other files.

vishing

Voice phishing, a human-based attack where the attacker extracts information while speaking over the phone or leveraging IP-based voice messaging services (VoIP).

VLAN

(virtual local area network) A point-to-point physical network that is created by grouping selected hosts together, regardless of their physical location.

Voice over IP

See VoIP.

VoIP

(Voice over IP) A term used for a technology that enables you to deliver telephony communications over a network by using the IP protocol.

VPN concentrator

A single device that incorporates advanced encryption and authentication methods in order to handle a large number of VPN tunnels.

VPN protocol

A protocol that provides VPN functionality.

VPN

(virtual private network) A private network that is configured within a public network, such as the Internet.

vulnerability scan

An assessment that identifies and quantifies weaknesses within a system, but does not test the security features of that system.

vulnerability

Any condition that leaves a system open to attack.

WAP

(Wireless Application Protocol) A protocol designed to transmit data such as web pages, email, and newsgroup postings to and from wireless devices such as mobile phones, PDAs, and handheld computers over very long distances, and display the data on small screens in a web-like interface.

war chalking

Using symbols to mark off a sidewalk or wall to indicate that there is an open wireless network which may be offering Internet access.

war driving

The act of searching for instances of wireless LAN networks while in motion, using wireless tracking devices like PDAs, mobile phones, or laptops.

warm site

A location that is dormant or performs non-critical functions under normal conditions, but which can be rapidly converted to a key operations site if needed.

web application-based firewall

A firewall that is deployed to secure an organization's web-based applications and transactions from attackers.

web security gateway

A software program used primarily to block Internet access to a predefined list of websites or category of websites within an organization or business.

WEP

(Wired Equivalency Protocol) A protocol that provides 64-bit, 128-bit, and 256-bit encryption using the RC4 algorithm for wireless communication that uses the 802.11a and 802.11b protocols.

whaling

An email-based or web-based form of phishing which targets particularly wealthy individuals. Also known as spear phishing.

white box test

A test in which the tester knows about all aspects of the systems and understands the function and design of the system before the test is conducted.

white hat

A hacker who exposes security flaws in applications and operating systems so manufacturers can fix them before they become widespread problems.

Windows security policies
Configuration settings within the Windows operating systems that control the overall security behavior of the system.

Wired Equivalency Protocol
See WEP.

Wireless Application Protocol
See WAP.

wireless security
Any method of securing your wireless LAN network to prevent unauthorized network access and network data theft while ensuring that authorized users can connect to the network.

Wireless Transport Layer Security
See WTLS.

worm
A piece of code that spreads from one computer to another on its own, not by attaching itself to another file.

WTLS
(Wireless Transport Layer Security) The security layer of a WAP and the wireless equivalent of TLS in wired networks.

XML injection
An attack that injects corrupted XML query data so that an attacker can gain access to the XML data structure and input malicious code or read private data.

XML
(eXtensible Markup Language) A widely adopted markup language used in many documents, websites, and web applications.

XTACACS
An extension to the original TACACS protocol.

zero day exploit
A hacking attack that occurs immediately after a vulnerability is identified, when the security level is at its lowest.

zombie
Unauthorized software introduced on multiple computers to manipulate the computers into mounting a DDoS attack. Also called a drone.

Index

3DES, 35
802.11, 149
  protocol standards, 149
802.11a, 149
802.11b, 149
802.11g, 149
802.11i, 150
802.11n, 149
802.1x, 150

A

acceptable use, 43
acceptable use policy, 44
  Also See: AUP
acceptance, 307
access control, 14
  methods, 14
Access Control List
  See: ACL
access point
  rogue, 80
account access restrictions, 218
account management, 217
  guidelines, 218
  security controls, 218
account phishing, 69
account policy, 217
account privileges, 217
accountability, 14
accounting
  See: auditing
accounts
  multiple, 218
ACK, 65

acknowledgement
  See: ACK
ACL, 14
Active Directory, 200
  backing up, 201
  group policy, 219
Address Resolution Protocol
  See: ARP
Advanced Encryption Standard
  See: AES
advanced security, 183
adware, 86
AES, 35
alarms, 285
  control panel, 287
ALE, 306
algorithm, 31
  simple encryption, 31
all-in-one security appliance, 97
alternate sites, 357
  scenarios, 358
annual loss expectancy
  See: ALE
anomaly-based monitoring, 101
anti-malware software, 164
  types, 164
anti-spam, 164
anti-spyware, 164
antivirus software, 164
APIPA, 116
application attack, 89
  types, 89
application hardening, 179
Application layer, 65

T

TACACS, 211
TACACS+, 211
tailgating, 55
take hashes, 338
takeover attack, 89
TCB, 160
TCP, 65
TCP/IP, 65, 115
  and HTTP, 117
  layers, 65
  services, 116
technical controls, 308
telephony, 111
temperature, extreme, 62
Temporal Key Integrity Protocol
    See: TKIP
Terminal Access Controller Access Control System
    See: TACACS
the cloud, 112
threat, 5, 303
  vulnerability-assessed, 305
threat assessment, 305
threats and vulnerabilities
  environmental, 62
  physical, 60
  wireless, 80
three-factor authentication
    See: multi-factor authentication
time of day restrictions, 18
TKIP, 150
TLS, 119, 123
    Also See: FTPS
  and SSL, 119
token, 24
tornado, 62
TOS, 160
TPM, 190
tracking, 338
Trade Secret classification, 216
transference, 307
transitive access, 75
  attack, 75
Transmission Control Protocol
    See: TCP
Transmission Control Protocol/Internet Protocol
    See: TCP/IP

Transport layer, 65
Transport Layer Security
    See: TLS
Triple DES
    See: 3DES
Trojan horse, 86, 318
trust model, 232
Trusted Computing Base
    See: TCB
Trusted Operating System
    See: TOS
Trusted Platform Module
    See: TPM
tunneling, 204
two-factor authentication
    See: multi-factor authentication
Twofish, 35

U

UDP, 65
  flood, 72
Uniform Resource Locator
    See: URL
URL, 103, 180
  filtering, 103
  shortening service, 69
USB, 190
user assigned privilege, 217
User Datagram Protocol
    See: UDP
user ID requirements, 218
user name authentication, 23
user security
  responsibilities, 296

V

video surveillance, 285
virtual local area network
    See: VLAN
virtual private network
    See: VPN
virtualization, 111
  security techniques, 166
virus, 85, 86
vishing, 54
VLAN, 108
  management, 139
  vulnerabilities, 109